D0546258

ORIGINS

CANADIAN HISTORY TO CONFEDERATION

R. DOUGLAS FRANCIS/RICHARD JONES/DONALD B. SMITH

Holt, Rinehart and Winston of Canada, Limited
Toronto

Copyright © 1988
Holt, Rinehart and Winston of Canada, Limited
All rights reserved

It is illegal to reproduce any portion of this book except by special arrangement with the publishers. Reproduction of this material without authorization by any duplication process whatsoever is a violation of copyright.

Every effort has been made to determine and locate copyright owners. In the case of any omissions, the publisher will be pleased to make suitable acknowledgements in future editions.

Canadian Cataloguing in Publication Data

Francis, R.D. (R. Douglas), 1944-
   Origins: Canadian history to Confederation

Companion volume to: Destinies: Canadian history
since Confederation.
Bibliography: p.
Includes index.
ISBN 0-03-921705-1

1. Canada – History – To 1763 (New France).
2. Canada – History – 1763-1867.   I. Jones,
Richard, 1943-   .   II. Smith, Donald B.,
1946-   .   III. Title.

FC161.F73 1988   971   C87-094454-1
F1026.F73 1988

Cover: "Nicholas Vallard's Atlas": map of northeast coast of North America 1547 HM 29 (9) Reproduced by permission of The Huntington Library, San Marino, California.

Publisher: Susan Lilholt
Editor: Tessa McWatt
Publishing Services Manager: Karen Eakin
Editorial Co-ordinator: Edie Franks
Copy Editor: Wendy Jacobs
Cover and Interior Design: John Zehethofer
Typesetting and Assembly: Q Composition Inc.
Printing and Binding: Metropole Litho Inc.

Printed in Canada
   2 3 4 5   92 91 90 89 88

Preface

Origins and *Destinies* sketch the history of Canada from the beginning of human occupation to the present. The purpose of both volumes is to outline how this immense country (the second largest in the world) came to be, to explain how its regions developed, and to relate the common history of its diverse population. Throughout our two volumes we have paid attention to Canada's various regions while keeping the country as a whole the central focal point of the study.

This project began in 1983, when we, as professors of Canadian history, felt the need to synthesize and supplement the older texts conceived and written in the 1940s and 1950s, many of them still in use. We wanted a full and up-to-date introduction for first year university and college students, one which incorporated the new historical findings of the last quarter century—the social as well as the political and economic accounts of our past.

Origins, our first volume, tells the history of pre Confederation Canada— the native people, the coming of the Norse, the Portuguese, the Spanish, the Basques, and particularly the French and the British, who eventually established permanent European settlements. Anyone seeking to understand our diversity today must look at the pre-Confederation era when our present regional personalities were first formed in Atlantic Canada, the St. Lawrence River valley, the Great Lakes, the Red River, and on the Pacific Coast.

Destinies, our second volume, takes the story of the British North American colonies from 1867 to the present day. We show how Canada came to take the transcontinental form it did, and how the various groups within its boundaries came together to form one country. We have pointed out the various regional, ethnic, and social tensions in our nation's history, as well as the means by which these differences have been resolved in the past.

The text is designed with the student of introductory Canadian history in mind. Each chapter treats a major topic, theme, or period, and includes subsections to aid students in organizing the material. Through the use of fully documented quotations from works by Canadian historians and up-to-date annotated bibliographical references at the conclusion of each chapter, we identify the major historical writings on the events covered. As well, we have provided a "Related Readings" section at the end of each chapter. This section indicates useful articles in the second edition of R. Douglas Francis and Donald B. Smith, eds., *Readings in Canadian History*, Volume I: *Pre-Confederation*, and Volume II: *Post-Confederation*.

The map on the cover depicts the coast of Newfoundland and the Saint Lawrence River, with North at the bottom of the page and East at the left. The geography will be more familiar if you turn the map upside down.

No one knows if Vallard was the artist or the owner of the atlas containing this map. Also open to debate is the identity of the black-bearded leader of the European colonists. The scene is believed to be Jacques Cartier landing at Stadacona. However, the presence of the richly-dressed ladies and gentlemen suggests this may be the Sieur de Roberval at France-Roy.

iv

Publisher's Note to Instructors and Students

This text book is a key component of your course. If you are the instructor of this course, you undoubtedly considered a number of texts carefully before choosing this as the one that will work best for your students and you. The authors and publishers of this book spent considerable time and money to ensure its high quality, and we appreciate your recognition of this effort and accomplishment.

If you are a student, we are confident that this text will help you to meet the objectives of your course. You will also find it helpful after the course is finished, as a valuable addition to your personal library. So hold on to it.

As well, please don't forget that photocopying copyright work means the authors lose royalties that are rightfully theirs. This loss will discourage them from writing another edition of this text or other books, because doing so will simply not be worth their time and effort. If this happens, we all lose—students, instuctors, authors, and publishers.

And since we want to hear what you think about this book, please be sure to send us the stamped reply card at the end of the text. This will help us to continue publishing high-quality books for your courses.

Acknowledgements

In the preparation of *Origins* we have benefited enormously from the advice and suggestions of many Canadian historians. We would like to thank Gratien Allaire of the Faculté Saint-Jean, University of Alberta; Phillip Buckner of the University of New Brunswick; Jean Daigle of the Université de Moncton; Olive Dickason of the University of Alberta; John Dickinson of the Université de Montréal; Robin Fisher of Simon Fraser University; Gerald Friesen of the University of Manitoba; James Hiller of Memorial University of Newfoundland; Douglas Leighton of the University of Western Ontario; Ken Munro of the University of Alberta; Colin Read of the University of Western Ontario; and Phyllis Senese of the University of Victoria; who each read and provided us with criticisms of individual chapters within their respective research areas. On several specific issues we benefited from the comments of: Michel Granger of Brooks, Alberta (on the Acadians); James Helmer of the University of Calgary (on recent archaeological findings); Ingeborg Marshall of Portugal Cove, Newfoundland (on the Beothuk); Bea Medicine of the University of Calgary (on the native peoples' view of their origins); Dale Miquelon of the University of Saskatchewan (on recent historical writing on the economic impact of the conquest of New France); Keith Regular of Elkford, B.C. (on Newfoundland); Daniel Richter of Dickinson College, Carlisle, Pennsylvania (on the Iroquois Confederacy).

For *Destinies*, we would like to thank the following people, who read chapters of the manuscript and offered valuable criticism and advice: Douglas Baldwin of Acadia University; Gail Cuthbert-Brandt of Glendon College, York University; John English of the University of Waterloo; Gerald Friesen of the University of Manitoba; Jim Miller of the University of Saskatchewan; William Morrison of Brandon University; Howard Palmer of the University of Calgary; Margaret Prang of the University of British Columbia; John Thompson of McGill University; Keith Walden of Trent University; and William Westfall of York University.

The following historians read the entire manuscript for Holt, Rinehart and Winston. Although they did not always agree with our approach and interpretation, they offered very valuable suggestions for improving the final manuscript.

For *Origins*, we wish to thank Joseph Cherwinski of Memorial University of Newfoundland, Douglas Leighton of the University of Western Ontario, Olive Dickason of the University of Alberta, and Phyllis Senese of the University of Victoria.

For *Destinies*, we thank William Acheson of the University of New Brunswick, Thomas Socknat of the University of Toronto, Donald Swainson of Queen's University, and Eric Sager of the University of Victoria.

All errors and omissions, of course, remain our responsibility.

For making these volumes possible we warmly thank Tony Luengo, formerly of Holt, Rinehart and Winston, who first accepted the proposal, and to Tessa McWatt for seeing it to completion. We are also indebted to Edie Franks, Editorial Co-ordinator, and to Wendy Jacobs, our copy-editor, as well as all the others at Holt, Rinehart and Winston involved in the production of *Origins* and *Destinies*.

The office staff of the Department of History at the University of Calgary performed the heroic task of typing up many of the numerous drafts of the manuscript. Our thanks to Liesbeth von Wolzogen, Olga Leskiw, Marjory McLean, Jodi Steeves, and Joyce Woods, and to Barbara Nair for preparing the index for *Origins*.

Douglas Francis wishes to thank Pat Kates and her staff in Secretarial Services at York University for typing drafts of his chapters of the manuscripts during his sabbatical year, and the staff at McLaughlin College, York University, for providing him with office space and a pleasant atmosphere during that year.

To our wives, Barbara, Lilianne, and Nancy, for their support during this project, we owe debts too enormous to describe.

For our children:

Marc, Myla, and Michael Francis
Marie-Noëlle, Stéphanie, Serge-André, and Charles-Denis Jones
David and Peter Smith

A small part of Canada's future

List of Maps

Contents

CONTENTS

x

CONTENTS

xii

xiii

CHAPTER ONE

The First Canadians

The first and fundamental question of Canadian history still remains un-   *1*
answered. Despite centuries of debate we do not know for certain the
place of origin of the first Canadians. Indian elders argue that their people
emerged from this continent. In contrast, most archaeologists contend that
early man migrated here from Siberia, although the archaeologists themselves dispute when the migration first occurred. All experts do agree,
however, that the original inhabitants of North America were living on
this continent at least ten thousand years before the Europeans' arrival.

Origin of Man in North America

Many Canadian Indian elders accept as a spiritual truth—one revealed in
sacred myths, dreams, and visions—that their ancestors originated in North
America. They believe that their origin myths are as valid as are the origin
stories of the Christians. Young Blackfoot-speaking children in present-
day southern Alberta, for example, learn many stories about Napi or "Old
Man," the creator of the world as they know it today. Other Canadian
tribes have their own explanations of the earth's beginning, but the Blackfoot's is one of the most descriptive and complete.

In the beginning, water covered the entire world. One day, though, the
curious Napi decided to find out what lay below. He sent first a duck,
then an otter and a badger. But all dived in vain. Then Napi asked a
muskrat to plunge into the depths. He was gone so long that Napi feared
that he had drowned. At last the muskrat surfaced holding a ball of mud.
The Old Man took this small lump and blew upon it. It magically began
to grow until it became the whole earth. Napi then piled up rocks to make
mountains, dug out river and lake beds, filled them with water, and
covered the plains with grass. He made all the birds and animals, and

finally people. Patiently he taught the men and women how to hunt and how to live. His work completed, the Old Man climbed a high mountain and disappeared. Some say Napi's home lay in the Rocky Mountains at the headwaters of the Alberta river that bears his name, The Oldman.[1]

This spiritual view is vitally important, for it offers the key to understanding the first Canadians, their cultures, and their rights to the land. To them, Canada is their homeland, a place where they have always lived.

Modern scientists, unlike native spiritual persons, restrict themselves to observable data and limit themselves to the testing of information observed in the natural world. Their discussion of the origin of man eliminates the spiritual universe entirely—the Old Testament's Book of Genesis as well as the Blackfoot's story of Napi—introducing and interpreting only the data at hand. From archaeological and geological evidence scientists have advanced theses arguing that man did not evolve independently in the Americas. Many of them believe that the remote ancestors of today's Amerindians migrated to the Americas from Siberia.[2] Recently, a number of archaeologists have argued that other migrations possibly occurred by sea, principally to South America, from across the Pacific.

Archaeologists believe that *Homo habilis*, the first direct ancestor of man, first appeared nearly two million years ago in Africa. A more advanced form, *Homo erectus*, followed approximately one and a half million years ago in Asia, Africa, and Europe. About one hundred thousand years ago *Homo sapiens neanderthalensis*, or the *Neanderthal*, emerged in Asia, Africa, and Europe. Our direct ancestor, fully modern man, can be identified an estimated thirty-five to forty thousand years ago. Physical evidence (that is early hominid bones found in Africa, Asia, and Europe but not the Americas) leads most archaeologists to conclude that the human species originated outside of the Americas.

It is widely agreed among archaeologists that the early inhabitants of North America crossed over from Siberia during the last Ice Age. With so much of the earth's water locked in ice, sea levels dropped and the continental shelf emerged from the sea. One area thus affected was the shallow region of the Bering Strait. From the strait a broad level plain, Beringia, emerged. This land bridge, which at times was more than thirteen hundred kilometres wide, existed for much of the period from fourteen thousand to seventy thousand years ago. Then the cold climate was so dry that glaciers could not form.

Beringia is believed to have been a rich steppe-tundra with many species of large, cold-adapted grazing animals. This land bridge served as a highway for animals passing back and forth between Asia and the Americas. Many archaeologists believe that an ice-free corridor at times existed along the eastern slope of the Rockies, providing the animals with a pathway southward, or that perhaps an ice-free coastal corridor also existed. Across the Beringia land bridge and down the ice-free corridor humans followed the animals, gradually advancing into the heart of the continent. They spread throughout North, Central, and South America, conquering the longest frontier ever traversed, the more than fifteen thousand kilometres from Alaska to Patagonia, the tip of South America.

Three Archaeological Hypotheses

Scientists are far from agreeing when this migration occurred. The three main schools of thought about this migration may be labelled the radical, the liberal, and the conservative. The supporters of the radical theory contend that humans have lived in the Americas for at least one hundred thousand years. Yet the radical theory's critics reply that there is no firm evidence of humans in northeastern Asia before approximately thirty thousand or so years ago. More modest in their claims, the liberals argue that the first humans probably migrated into North America beginning about 30 000 B.C. The liberals support their hypotheses by referring to sites without human skeletal remains but which have good evidence of early human occupation, such as the Monte Verde site in Chile, South America. At its lowest level of occupation Monte Verde has evidence of a simple stone technology, with tools only slightly modified, possibly as early as thirty-three-thousand years ago.

3

The conservatives, however, reject both the radical and liberal views. They accept as evidence only those artifacts found in sealed deposits with organic matter that can be radiocarbon-dated. In addition, they limit themselves to distinctively styled artifacts—objects that have been worked upon much more than those cited by the radicals and liberals. The earliest known distinctive weapon or fluted point the conservatives accept comes from Fort Rock cave in eastern Oregon and is radiocarbon-dated at approximately 11 000 B.C.

The discovery in 1927 of a fluted point between the ribs of an extinct bison excavated near the town of Folsom in northeastern New Mexico also provided concrete archaeological proof that humans had reached the Americas while the animals of the last Ice Age still lived. The Folsom style dates to about 8500 B.C. A fluted-point site in central Nova Scotia, Debert, is contemporary with Folsom, as are two other Canadian sites—Sibbald Creek, west of Calgary, Alberta; and Charlie Lake Cave, north of Fort St. John, British Columbia. These three sites in present-day Canada all confirm man's presence at least ten thousand years ago.

About 8000 B.C. a drastic change in climate became evident in the northern hemisphere. For reasons still not completely understood, the great ice sheets (more than three kilometres thick) still covering much of present-day Canada and the northern United States began to melt. The runoff so raised the sea level that thousands of kilometres of coastline were flooded. The land bridge ceased to exist and the Bering Strait was created.

The melting ice then progressively freed for human occupation present-day northern United States and Canada. For hundreds of generations the frontier moved northward.

The ecology changed as well. The absence of ice sheets in formerly glaciated territories meant that wind and rainfall patterns shifted. Forests replaced grasslands, and deserts developed. As habitats changed, some animals became extinct, especially such large grazing animals as mammoths, American camels, and a very large race of bison that foraged on the grasslands. Thus, although the warmer climate opened up the northern half of the continent for settlement, it also contributed to the extinction of many valuable game species.

Civilizations of the Americas

4

About five thousand years ago the ice receded to approximately its present northern position. Bering Strait attained its present width of approximately eighty kilometres, and land animals could no longer cross between Siberia and Alaska. People still made that journey, but no longer did they come from Asia's inland centres; they were sea-mammal hunters and fishermen who traded across the strait. The native American nations now grew through natural population increase and not through migration.

In the millenium to follow, the Amerindians of present-day Canada stood on the perimeter of the major economic and social developments. The peak of technological and social complexity in the Americas was reached in present-day Mexico, Central America, and the Andes of Peru, where population densities were the highest on the two continents. Agriculture and, in other areas, rich sea resources, formed the basis of these civilizations, since a permanent food supply (based for the agriculturalists on corn, beans, and squash) made a settled life possible. During the period from approximately 1500 B.C. to the year 1 the first urban communities appeared. In the centuries to follow these became large centres with temples and other large structures such as: plazas, chiefs' houses, and highways, all constructed with carved and painted stone.

The New World civilizations developed without the aid of Europe's domesticated animals—horses, oxen, and donkeys. Although the principle of the wheel was known (wheeled toys have been found in various parts of Mexico), the idea remained undeveloped, since without animals for transport (other than the dog and in the Andes, the llama) these civilizations had little use for it. The New World also lacked ample supplies of usable copper and tin, which would have allowed for the replacement of stone tools with more efficient ones. The Peruvians did make a few bronze tools from metal washed down in the streams, but Mexico and the Yucatan had none.

Despite the absence of the wheel and iron tools, the Indians made remarkable advances and achievements. The Maya in Central America, for example, developed a sophisticated system of mathematics and used a symbol for zero five hundred years before the Hindus did. The Maya were also skilled in astronomy, enough to work out a year of 365 days and the cycle of the planet Venus. They could calculate eclipses and recorded the calculations in a writing system that was both pictographic and phonetic. In the Andes region, irrigation was highly developed, as was the building of bridges and roads. The Incas erected stone walls using enormous rocks cut to fit so tightly that a knife blade could not be pushed between two blocks. They also did metalwork of the highest quality, in gold and silver.

THE MOUNDBUILDERS

The ancient Indian agriculturalists carried corn from its place of origin, (probably southern Mexico) and adapted it to varied climates. About two thousand years ago farming—and with it settled life—replaced gathering and hunting in certain sections of the present-day United States. One of the most impressive groups touched by the agricultural revolution were the so-called moundbuilders of the Ohio River valley, who constructed gigantic sculptured earthworks in geometric designs, sometimes in the shape of humans, birds, or serpents. Some of these constructions were nearly twenty-five metres high. Their culture evolved slowly and by roughly two thousand years ago had developed considerable complexity.

Archaeologists have located thousands of mounds used as burial sites and have excavated several earthen-walled enclosures, including one enormous fortification with a circumference of over five kilometres, enclosing the equivalent of fifty modern city blocks. The moundbuilders participated in an extensive trading network. In the mounds of the Ohio peoples have been found large ceremonial blades chipped from obsidian, obtained from deposits in what is now Yellowstone National Park in Montana; embossed breastplates, ornaments, and weapons made from copper nuggets from the Great Lakes; decorative objects cut from mica sheets from the southern Appalachians; as well as ornaments made from shark and alligator teeth, and shells from the Gulf of Mexico.

The moundbuilder's culture declined about 500 A.D., due perhaps to the attacks of other tribes or perhaps severe changes in climate that undermined agriculture. Another similar culture farther to the west replaced it, one based on intensive agriculture. Centred on present-day St. Louis, it extended over most of the Mississippi watershed, from Wisconsin to Louisiana, and from Oklahoma to Tennessee. From 700 A.D. to 1000 A.D.

the influence of this Mississippian culture was felt farther to the east, among the less technologically advanced woodland Indian tribes, and transformed their societies. The Iroquoian-speaking tribes of the Lower Great Lakes and the St. Lawrence valley adopted the agricultural traditions of the moundbuilders and the Mississippians.

POPULATION GROWTH

The development of agriculture contributed to a much greater population growth, as the cultivation of as little as one percent of the land greatly increased the food supply. Recent estimates for the aboriginal population of the Americas in the mid-fifteenth century run as high as one hundred million people, or approximately one-sixth of the human race at that time. It is now believed that the population north of Mexico may have reached ten million before European contact. Indian groups achieved such densities because they lived in a relatively disease-free zone, and many tribes, including the Iroquoians living in present-day southern Ontario and southwestern Quebec, had domesticated high-yield cereals and tubers, allowing them to feed a large population.

In coming to the Americas the Europeans entered two continents which in some areas had populations as high as that of their homelands. Europeans reduced these American populations drastically, however, by unintentionally bringing with them diseases that the Indians in the Americas had never before experienced; the Indians had travelled through an Arctic environment, in which many of the diseases found in temperate and tropical climates did not survive. Moreover, the migrating Indian groups were biologically too small to sustain those diseases. Subsequently, the Indians lacked any defence against contagious diseases like smallpox and measles. Alfred Crosby, a biological historian, writes that, "In theory, the initial appearance of these diseases is as certain to have set off deadly epidemics as dropping lighted matches into tinder is certain to cause fires."[3] The resulting death rates after European contact in some areas of the Americas reached 90–95 percent. By the early twentieth century the number of Indians and Inuit in Canada and the United States was less than one million.

Classifying Canada's Amerindian Population

When classifying Canada's Amerindian population three distinct methods have frequently been employed: linguistic, tribal, and cultural. Each (particularly the first two) are less than fully satisfactory. A division according

7

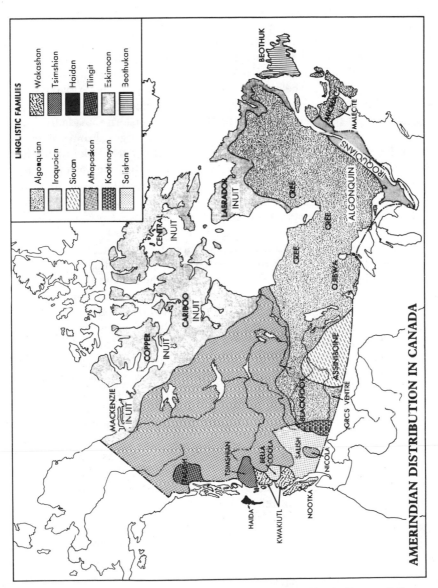

LINGUISTIC FAMILIES

Wakashan
Tsimshian
Haidan
Tlingit
Eskimoan
Beothukan

Algonquian
Iroquoian
Siouan
Athapaskan
Kootenayan
Salishan

BEOTHUK

MICMAC
MALECITE

IROQUOIANS

CREE
ALGONQUIN

LABRADOR
INUIT

CENTRAL
INUIT

CREE

CREE

OJIBWA

CARIBOO
INUIT

COPPER
INUIT

ASSINIBOINE

MACKENZIE
INUIT

BLACKFOOT

GROS VENTRE

SALISH

NICOLA

NOOTKA

HAIDA

KWAKIUTL

AMERINDIAN DISTRIBUTION IN CANADA

P.G. Cornell, J. Hamelin, F. Ouellet, and M. Trudel, *Canada, Unity in Diversity* (Toronto, 1967), p. 14.

to linguistics reveals that Canada today contains eleven separate indigenous language families; one of these is Eskimo-Aleut, which includes the tongue spoken by the Inuit. There are ten Indian language families. A language from one family differs as much from that of another as English does from Chinese; within families, languages are related to each other as say, English is to Dutch.

Michael Foster, an ethnologist in the Canadian Ethnology Service of the National Museum of Man in Ottawa, has classified Canada's first languages.[4] Seven of the ten Indian language families (Salishan, Tsimshian, Wakashan, as well as the Haida, Tlingit, Kootenayan, and Athapaskan) are found in British Columbia. The Siouan-speaking group is found only on the prairies and the foothills of the Rockies. In eastern Canada live the Iroquoians. The Algonquian (or Algonkian), the largest group, extend from the Atlantic coast to the Rockies. Throughout the Yukon and the Northwest Territories and the northern sections of the four western provinces live the Athapaskans, the second-largest native linguistic family in Canada. As nearly as can be determined, fifty-three distinct languages are today spoken in Canada and, no doubt, once there were probably more.

This linguistic classification of the Amerindians unfortunately leads to the linking together of widely separated tribes that differed in every way but in language, and to separate them from neighbouring groups that differed only in speech. The Micmac Indians of the present-day Maritime provinces and the Blackfoot of the prairies, for instance, although separated by four thousand kilometres, are joined together in the Algonquian linguistic family; in reality, they lived entirely different lives, in total unawareness of the other's existence. Conversely, the Haida Indians of the Queen Charlotte Islands resembled their mainland neighbours, the Tsimshians, in everything except language, which was totally unrelated.

The division of Canada's original inhabitants by political divisions also poses problems. Tribes, that is, groups of people bound together by a common culture and language and acting as a unit in relations with their neighbours, certainly existed. Among some groups, though, the ties between the various bands were not strong. Remoter bands diverged considerably in dialect and, in some cases, had so readily assimilated the customs of alien peoples around them that they lost all feeling of political unity with their far-distant relatives.

NATIVE CULTURE AREAS

Rather than the linguistic and political divisions, the anthropologists' concept of culture areas provides the best description of Indian groups in present-day Canada recognizing, as it does, how climate and regional

CANADA'S NATIVE CULTURE AREAS

Arctic
Subarctic
Northeast
Great Plains
Plateau
Northwest Coast

9

The National Atlas of Canada, 5th edition, **Canada, Indian and Inuit Communities and Languages**.
Produced by the Surveys and Mapping Branch, Department of Energy, Mines and Resources, Ottawa,
Canada. Printed 1980.

resources influence the development of societies and technologies. Native
North American societies can thus be classified into six such areas: North
Pacific, Plateau, Plains, Subarctic, Arctic, and Eastern Woodlands. An
examination of each culture area broadens our understanding of Canada's
original inhabitants before European contact.

North Pacific

The North Pacific Coastal area is rich in marine resources. The Coast
Range in British Columbia and Cascade Mountains in the states of Washington and Oregon cut off the maritime peoples of the coastal regions
from the inland hunters and fishermen—except where low-lying regions,
such as the Columbia River valley, allowed for contact. The Indians fished
for herring, smelt, eulachon (candle-fish), halibut, and several species
popularly called cod. In addition, sea mammals were numerous: whales,
seals, sea lions, porpoises, and the sea otter. Of all these foods however,
salmon became the basic staple of the coastal people. The Indians speared,

netted, and trapped it in huge quantities, and then sun-dried or smoked it for year-round use.

The abundant rainfall and warm temperatures produced a lush vegetation. The North Pacific peoples used the cedars and firs of the coastal rain forest for houses, dugout canoes, and for woodworking crafts (carved boxes, bowls, dishes, ladles). This availability of supplies and food made the North Pacific coast the most densely populated area in Canada.

The Pacific Coast peoples lived the year round in villages located usually in sheltered island coves or on channels near the mouth of rivers. Each village was generally independent of others, but on occasion (particularly at times of war), several might join together. Their communal activities included the potlatch or large ceremonial feast. At a potlatch the host gave away gifts to gain his community's approval of his new title, along with his right to the myths he could tell and the songs he could sing.

In contrast to the other culture areas in Canada, a hierarchical social structure evolved on the Northwest Coast. At the bottom stood the slaves taken in war and then above them, everyone else in a very precise social ranking.

Archaeologists judge that the native peoples of the Northwest Coast have, for the most part, been resident in the same territories in which the Europeans first found them for at least the previous two thousand years. The linguistic complexity of the region—with its nineteen distinct languages—suggests that, linguistically, it is an "old area" and the most likely starting point for migrations of successive groups to the east and to the south. The North Pacific Coast culture area extended from northern California to the Alaskan panhandle.

Plateau

The Plateau culture area, the smallest of the six, takes in the high plateau between the British Columbia coastal mountains and the Rockies. It extends southward through western Montana, Idaho, and eastern Washington and Oregon. The Canadian portion of the Plateau area is essentially the same as that locally described as "the interior" of British Columbia. Hot, dry summers and cold winters are common throughout the Plateau. In Canada the Plateau societies include the Kootenay in the east, the Interior Salish societies in the west, and the Athapaskan-speaking groups to the north. The Plateau Indians depended on salmon, and thus their populations were largest downriver, where the fish were most abundant. In dress, customs, and religion, these transitional Plateau people resembled far more the Plains' tribes than they did the North Pacific Coast groups. They were semi-migratory, non-agricultural, and small in population, in contrast with the Pacific bands.

Plains

East of the Plateau region lies the Plains culture area, in the broad central region of North America west of the Mississippi and Red River valleys and east of the Rockies. It is an area in which open grasslands predominate, with tall grass in the east and short grass in the west. Like the North Pacific and Plateau areas, the Plains extend north–south, reaching from northern Alberta and Saskatchewan and western Manitoba through to Texas. The region has a continental climate—hot, dry summers and cold winters. In the eighteenth century, tribes belonging to three linguistic families lived on the Canadian Plains: the Algonquian, Athapaskan, and the Siouan.

THE BUFFALO

11

The buffalo, which fed on the grasslands, was the foundation of the Plains Indians' culture. Its flesh furnished the Indians with lodge covers, warm overcoats, bedding, and moccasins. The Indians made shields from the thick hide of the buffalo's neck, carved spoons and drinking cups from its horns, and created thread and bow string from sinew. The Blackfoot termed the buffalo's flesh "real meat," implying that all other meat was inferior. An estimated sixty million buffalo lived on the Great Plains in the early nineteenth century.

Indians hunted the buffalo on foot in small nomadic bands, usually 50–100 persons, since this number could most effectively handle a drive. These drives required excellent organization, particularly in the foothills, where the buffalo were stampeded over the edge of cliffs. Archaeologists have found some of the earliest evidence of a human presence in North America on the Great Plains, at sites associated with buffalo hunting that are nearly ten thousand years old. One such location is Head-Smashed-In Buffalo Jump, a World Heritage Site in the Old Man River valley near Fort Macleod in southwestern Alberta.

THE HORSE

The horse had originally existed in the Americas and then disappeared. Its reintroduction to Mexico by the Spaniards in the sixteenth century soon transformed Plains Indian culture. Until the return of the horse, the North American Indians' only domesticated animal capable of being used to transport goods was the dog. The horse reached the Canadian Plains by the 1730s through intertribal trade and raiding. By giving the Indians a new means of transportation, the horse made buffalo hunting much more efficient, since the Plains Indians no longer had to follow the herds on foot. With the horse, mounted warriors could simply surround a buffalo herd without having to drive it into an enclosure or over a cliff.

The Plains Indians adapted the dog *travois* (a device made of two trailing tepee poles on which was attached a platform or net for holding a load) for use with the horse. With a horse-drawn *travois* a warrior could carry a load of 150 kg, in contrast to that of about 35 kg pulled by a dog. The horse could also travel twenty kilometres, or twice as far in a day. Now the Indians could carry more than the basic necessities. They could keep extra suits of clothing, additional buffalo robes for winter, and carry more dried provisions.

12 Subarctic

To the north lies the Subarctic culture area, which is much less densely populated than the Plains. It reaches across the Canadian Shield from the Labrador coast, to the mouth of the Yukon River. Except where it touches the Rocky Mountains, the land is low-lying and covered with coniferous trees. The northern boundary is near the tree line, since the Indians lacked the means to live beyond the tree line in the winter months. Although the winters are long and harsh, the forests provide shelter. Members of two linguistic families lived in the Subarctic: in the west the Athapaskan-speaking groups, or "Dene" (pronounced "de-ne" or "de-nay"), which is their word for "the people"; and in the east, the Subarctic Algonquians.

The Subarctic peoples lived in summer encampments of several hunting bands, with perhaps a hundred Indians situated at good fishing sites. In the autumn they broke up into bands that scattered in search of food. They lived in isolation in their hunting territories from early autumn until the following spring. Approximately 25–30 people, closely related either by family ties or by marriage, constituted a hunting band. A senior respected male directed the group, and in consultation with the other men he decided where and when they would hunt and camp. Many of the Dene and Algonquians relied heavily on the moose, whose importance to them was comparable to that of the buffalo to the Plains Indian. Because of the thin distribution of game animals over vast areas of the boreal forest, Subarctic human population densities were among the lowest in the world.

Arctic

Immediately to the north of the Subarctic, beyond the tree line, lies the Arctic. For about eight months of the year, most of the Arctic is snow-covered and extensive portions of its seas frozen. The broad area of the Arctic generally includes most of Alaska, Canada north of the tree line, and Greenland. The human inhabitants of this area are the Inuit, commonly called Eskimo, who, generally speaking, live on the northern tundra.

Today, all of the people known as Inuit speak languages related to one another, which suggests these languages derived from a single ancestral tongue. Their languages are distantly related to those of the Chukchi, Koryak, and Kamehadal peoples of northeastern Siberia and unrelated to those of any Amerindian tribe; this supports the theory that the Inuit originated relatively recently in Asia. Racially as well, the Inuit are more closely related to Siberian peoples than to the Indian populations to the south.

Apparently, the Inuit's distant ancestors developed the ability to survive during winters on the treeless tundra. Surprisingly, the Arctic can provide hunters and fishermen with a basic subsistence. Although the farther one travels from the equator towards the poles the fewer species of animals, the populations of these same few species are relatively large. In certain localities, migration and the availability of food lead to dense seasonal concentrations of many species, such as the caribou, walrus, and seals.

Over the centuries the Arctic peoples, known to archaeologists as Paleoeskimos, developed hunting techniques to allow for a more efficient exploitation of their environment. As early as four thousand years ago they had become the primary inhabitants of Arctic Canada. The people of what archaeologists have termed the Dorset culture, developed new objects—the soapstone lamp, snow houses, and dog sleds. The Dorset Paleoeskimo culture emerged about twenty-five hundred years ago.

By 1000 A.D. an Alaskan people, the Thule, the direct ancestors of the modern Inuit, entered the central Arctic. They appear to have caused the disappearance of the Dorset people, either through warfare or perhaps by absorbing them into their own communities. The Thule immigrants introduced a sophisticated sea-hunting culture to the area from Alaska. They brought whale-hunting techniques to the east. By about 1400 A.D. a sparse Thule population occupied most of Arctic Canada north of the tree line. All modern Canadian and Greenlandic Inuit are descended from them.

13

Eastern Woodlands

The Eastern Woodlands cultural area extended roughly from the Atlantic region westward to the Upper Great Lakes, south to Ohio and Virginia, and north to the southern boundary of the eastern Subarctic. Climate and soil conditions south of the Canadian Shield allowed some tribes to grow corn, beans, and squash. Within the Canadian Eastern Woodlands lived Indians belonging to two linguistic families: the Algonquians, a migratory people primarily dependent on hunting and fishing; and the Iroquoians, semi-sedentary and horticultural. The many tribes of the Algonquian family occupied the northern part of the region, and the Iroquoians much of present-day southern Ontario and neighbouring New York State.

THE ALGONQUIANS

The Algonquian-speaking tribes on the eve of European contact were numerous. In the Atlantic region resided the Micmac (in the Maritimes) and the closely related Malecite (in present-day western New Brunswick). North of the St. Lawrence and east of the St. Maurice River were the Montagnais. The Algonquins (Algonkins), the tribe that gave its name to the entire Algonquian linguistic family, lived in the Ottawa valley. (Note that the tribal name ends in "quin" and that of the linguistic family in "quian.") Still farther west were the Nipissings on Lake Nipissing, the Ottawas (Odawa) on Manitoulin Island in Lake Huron, and the Ojibwas (Chippewas) around Lake Superior. On Newfoundland resided the Beothuk. Now extinct, the Beothuk might also have been Algonquian-speaking, or perhaps (the available evidence is inadequate for firm conclusions) they belonged to a separate linguistic family.

Although many Algonquian groups practised some horticulture, hunting and fishing provided the principal source of food of those north of the Great Lakes. During the winter they broke up into family groups and went in search of deer, elk, bear, beaver, and other game animals. In the spring they met at maple groves to gather and boil the tree sap. The women undertook some agricultural work in the summer, at which time the men fished. During the fall they gathered wild rice and in the more southern areas they harvested corn. Then they returned to the hunting territories.

Several winter hunting groups apparently joined together for summer fishing. Each fishing band had a name, its own hunting territory, and its own leader, although this leader had relatively little power or authority. The warriors of these male-centred hunting groups usually obtained wives from neighbouring bands, thus maintaining friendly ties. Adjacent bands sharing a common language and customs generally were known as a tribe— but their unity really was more cultural than political, since the band was the only clearly defined political unit. The Algonquians, unlike the Iroquoians on the eve of European contact, had no central governing authority.

THE IROQUOIANS

Initially, the Woodlands people were primarily hunters and gatherers, but gradually many in the area south of the Canadian Shield adapted to agriculture. Crops of Mexican and Central American origin played an important role in the development of Iroquoian culture. About 500 A.D. corn appears to have spread northward from the Ohio and Illinois areas, adapting to the shorter growing season and the more rigorous climate. Some form of tobacco probably entered eastern Canada as early as 2500 years ago, corn about 1500 years ago, and beans around 1000 years ago. With the addition of beans, which are high in protein, rapid population growth occurred, since the combination of corn and beans partially freed the Indians from the necessity of supplementing their corn diet with animal protein.

Initially, the Iroquoians' horticulture supplemented their traditional hunting and fishing, but later this role became reversed; hunting and fishing came to supplement farming. The Iroquoians in the vicinity of the lower Great Lakes came to depend on their crops for up to four-fifths of the food they consumed. As Iroquoian society was transformed from hunting to farming, women assumed the roles of planting, cultivating, and harvesting the crops. Women, by taking over the major responsibilities of farming, freed the men for hunting, fishing, trading, and warfare.

15

The only societies that could afford the luxury of war were those which either controlled their environment to a significant degree (as did the Iroquoian farmers) or which enjoyed an ample food supply (as on the North Pacific coast or on the Plains, after the arrival of the horse). In southern Ontario, evidence of hostilities between the farming communities, from as early as 800 A.D. has been discovered. Palisaded villages have been found which date back to this time. From the end of the fourteenth century A.D. the Iroquoians maintained villages about one hectare in extent, heavily fortified with as many as three log palisades, and equipped with platforms from which stone throwers and archers could defend the townsite.

The Iroquoian peoples farmed in villages of up to fifteen hundred inhabitants and, in some exceptional cases, even larger. Several families belonging to the same clan lived together in dwellings called "longhouses" consisting of a framework of saplings, often arched in a barrel shape, and covered with sheets of bark. Stretching more than half a football field in length, some large structures reportedly housed up to thirty families, although smaller structures usually accommodated about ten each. The Iroquoians divided the longhouses into apartments that were usually occupied by closely related families. A corridor ran down the middle of the house, and families on each side shared fireplaces.

Each of the families in the longhouse usually would be related through the female line (ideally, sisters and their families). The core of any household consisted of a number of females descended from a common ancestress. When a man married he moved to his wife's home, where authority was invested in an elderly woman. In Iroquoian society the older women had real social and political power. The matrons of the appropriate families elected the chiefs, who were males, and these head women could also vote out of office any chief who displeased them.

Aboriginal Canada on the Eve of European Contact

On the eve of the European arrival in northeastern North America in the sixteenth century, it is clear that the Iroquoian cultures had changed rapidly over the preceding centuries. Larger settlements had appeared, tribes and possibly confederacies had evolved, and in some cases warfare was being waged on an expanded scale.

The two most prominent groups among the Iroquoians in the sixteenth century were the Hurons, located south of Georgian Bay, and the Iroquois or the Five Nations Confederacy, who occupied the territory south of the St. Lawrence and Lake Ontario, from the Richelieu River in the east to Lake Erie in the west. In the St. Lawrence Valley lived another group of Iroquoians, neither Huron nor Iroquois, and now called the Laurentian Iroquois.

16

Five hundred years ago the Indians alone inhabited Canada. The way in which each group lived was largely decided by the nature and the abundance of the resources of the country they occupied. The division of the groups into culture areas parallels almost exactly the country's geographical areas: the west coast, the interior of British Columbia, the prairies, the northern Canadian Shield, the eastern woodlands, and the Arctic. In addition to cultural differences, linguistic diversity existed as well. The native peoples of the six culture areas belonged to eleven linguistic families (one Inuit, and ten Indian), split into over fifty languages.

Five centuries ago there was no single Canadian Indian people, or single Indian language, but many different peoples with different cultures and languages. From Newfoundland to Vancouver Island, from the Great Lakes to the Arctic Ocean, the native peoples were as different from each other as are Spaniards, Scots, and Slovaks—and, in many cases, even more so.

NOTES

[1] This paraphrasing of the origin story is based on the account presented in John Ewers, *The Blackfeet* (Norman, 1958), pp. 3–4.
[2] Alice Kehoe includes a very important discussion on the "Conflict of Opinion on the Origin of Native American Population," in *North American Indians: A Comprehensive Account* (Englewood Cliffs, N.J., 1981), pp. 1–4.
[3] Alfred W. Crosby, "Virgin Soil Epidemics as a Factor in the Aboriginal Depopulation in America," *William and Mary Quarterly*, 3rd series, 33 (1976): 290.
[4] Michael K. Foster, "Canada's First Languages," *Language and Society*, 7 (Winter/Spring 1982): 7–16.

Related Readings

Two essays in R. Douglas Francis and Donald B. Smith, *Readings in Canadian History: Pre-Confederation*, 2d ed. (Toronto, 1986) are particularly useful for this chapter: see Jacques Rousseau and George W. Brown, "The Indians of Northeastern North America," pp. 3–15; and Chief John Snow's text, "The Oral History of the Stoneys," pp. 45–56.

BIBLIOGRAPHY

Two valuable overviews by anthropologists are Alice B. Kehoe's *North* 17 *American Indians: A Comprehensive Account* (Englewood Cliffs, N.J., 1981), and R. Bruce Morrison and C. Roderick Wilson, eds., *Native Peoples: The Canadian Experience* (Toronto, 1986). Also helpful is Diamond Jenness' older study, *The Indians of Canada* (Ottawa, 1932).

J.V. Wright's *Six Chapters of Canada's Prehistory* (Ottawa, 1976) reviews the archaeological record. The most up-to-date summary is Alan Lyle Bryan's "The Prehistory of the Canadian Indians," in *Native Peoples*, edited by Morrison and Wilson, pp. 22–44; and his study, *New Evidence for the Pleistocene Peopling of the Americas* (Orono, Maine, 1986). A popular summary is Thomas Y. Canby's "The Search for the First Americans," *National Geographic*, 156, 3 (September 1979): 330–63. Henry F. Dobyns, *Native American Historical Demography: A Critical Bibliography* (Bloomington, Ind., 1976) provides useful demographic information. For details on the impact of disease, consult Alfred W. Crosby, "Virgin Soil Epidemics as a Factor in the Aboriginal Depopulation in America," *William and Mary Quarterly*, 3rd series, 33 (1976): 289–99.

A series of six booklets by Edward S. Rogers—*The Indians of Canada: A Survey, Indians of the North Pacific Coast, Indians of the Subarctic, Indians of the Plains, Iroquoians of the Eastern Woodlands, Algonquians of the Eastern Woodlands* (Toronto, 1970) describes the culture areas, as do the short summaries in *The Canadian Encyclopedia*, vol. 2 (Edmonton, 1985), pp. 1201–11. Surveys also appear in *Native Peoples*, edited by Morrison and Wilson, and in Kehoe, *North American Indians*. Two of the volumes in the series *Handbook of North American Indians* are invaluable: June Helm, ed., *Subarctic*, vol. 6, (Washington, 1981); and Bruce G. Trigger, ed., *Northeast*, vol. 15 (Washington, 1978). Also see Robert McGhee, *Canadian Arctic Prehistory* (Toronto, 1978) for the Arctic culture area. Another useful study on native languages is Michael K. Foster's "Canada's First Languages," *Language and Society*, 7 (Winter–Spring 1982): 7–16.

The early maps in the *Historical Atlas of Canada*, vol. 1 (From the beginning to 1800), edited by R. Cole Harris (Toronto, 1987), are based on the most recent archaeological discoveries, and contain a wealth of new information about the first Canadians.

18

CHAPTER TWO

The Europeans' Arrival

The strange boat carrying the tall leafless tree spread with a gigantic white blanket must have amazed the hunters along the Labrador and Newfoundland coast. They believed that the land ended somewhere beyond the horizon of their island, and never before in their long history had anyone seen such a sight emerging from the edge of the world. Upon the small sea monster's back rode beings with hair on their faces and with skin like the underbelly of a fish. The year was about 1000 A.D., and the aliens were the Norse, who for a brief period explored the coasts of the West Atlantic from their base in Greenland. After an interlude of nearly five centuries other Europeans followed in quick succession: the English, the Portuguese, the French, the Spaniards, and the Basques. But, before beginning to narrate the Europeans' arrival in present-day Canada a word of caution must be given.

The lack of abundant source materials makes the writing of any account of the Europeans' initial arrival a formidable task. We have only a few oral traditions from the Norse and a small number of European explorers' journals before the seventeenth century. Unfortunately, we have no direct accounts written by the original Canadians and few narratives composed by the tens of thousands of early European mariners, fishermen, and fur traders. Morris Bishop, a modern biographer of Samuel de Champlain, who was the founder of Quebec in 1608, put it best when he wrote: "In reading history one must always be impressed by the fact that our knowledge is only a collection of scraps and fragments that we put together into a pleasing design, and often the discovery of one new fragment would cause us to alter utterly the whole design."[1] With that caution in mind, a sketch of the Europeans' arrival in present-day Canada can be drawn.

Arrival of the Norse

If we are to believe popular history and oral traditions, other national groups crossed the Atlantic before the Norse. Fifteen hundred years earlier, the Greeks wrote about Atlantis, a lost continent in the west. In the early Middle Ages other tales circulated about the celebrated Irish saint, Brendan, said to have found new lands by sailing west in the sixth century A.D. But none of the earlier accounts can be proven, except that of the Norse.

From the ninth to the twelfth century Scandinavia was the leading European sea power, with a commercial empire extending from Russia in the east to Sicily in the south, and to Normandy, Ireland, and Greenland in the west. The Norse were the western world's most expert navigators. Their occupation of parts of modern Greenland was but a continuation of their voyages from the mainland of Europe: before 800 A.D., to the Faeroe islands, roughly 300 km north of Scotland, to Iceland by 870 A.D., and to Greenland by 985 A.D. Without compasses (they were only introduced in the twelfth century) the Norse estimated their position on the high seas by constantly measuring, with a very crude device, the location of the North Star. On their way home from Iceland to Norway, they occasionally landed in Ireland or Scotland.

Eric the Red (Eirikr Thorvaldsson), the founder of the Norse settlements on Greenland in 985 A.D., sailed westward, driven by more than a Viking's sense of adventure. Outlawed from his native Norway for murder, he escaped to Iceland, only to become again involved in a feud. Banished for more killings he fled farther west, towards a land which had reportedly been sighted by storm-driven sailors. After he sailed about 800 km to the west he found a vast uninhabited subcontinent; on its west coast this land had green, reasonably level pastures, impressive fjords, and headlands, all of which reminded him of his native Norway. Rich in game animals, with a sea full of fish and large mammals such as seals and walrus, the land could support many Icelanders. Eric named the inviting, unoccupied country "Greenland," which was an accurate description of what he had seen on the west coast. Returning to Iceland he encouraged others to migrate with him to this promising land. Accompanied by fourteen or fifteen shiploads of Icelanders, the Norse adventurer founded two settlements. The Icelanders persevered, raising cows, horses, sheep, pigs, and goats. Recent excavations of the remains of Eric's own farm have uncovered a surprisingly large and comfortable establishment, built with thick walls of stone and turf to protect against the chilling winds.

The Norse made another important discovery in 986 A.D. In the second year of Eric's settlement, Bjarni Herjölfsson, owner of a ship trading between Norway and Iceland, went to join Eric in Greenland. En route he and his crew met with stormy and cloudy weather and were driven off course for several days. When the weather cleared they sighted a flat land covered with woods. As this country did not fit the account he had heard of Greenland, he sailed north until he reached the country that answered his description of the new land. Bjarni was thus the first known European to sight eastern North America (probably Labrador, roughly four days' sailing from Eric's Greenlandic settlements), although he never landed there.

Eric's second son, Leifr (or Leif) Eiriksson, grew up hearing the tales about Bjarni and the forested land to the south. Timber was a precious commodity on Greenland, which had no trees. In the year 1001, at the age of twenty-one, he bought Bjarni's ship and assembled a crew of thirty-five to explore the lands southwest of Greenland.

Experts now agree that Leif's expedition sailed by Baffin Island, which he called "Helluland" (Flat Stone Land). Farther south he landed in a forested area—probably the coast of central Labrador—and named it "Markland" (Wood Land). Continuing on, he reached his final destination, which scholars have placed anywhere between Labrador and Florida. This attractive wintering place he called "Vinland" (Wineland), after its plentiful grapes. After wintering there and doing more exploring, Leif and his crew took in a cargo of timber and grapes (or "wineberries"; probably these were wild red currants, gooseberries, or the mountain cranberry), then set sail for Greenland. On this voyage they did not meet any other human beings.

In the opening decade of the eleventh century, the Norse sponsored several expeditions from Greenland to the western lands. Leif's brother, Thorvaldr, led the next voyage to Vinland, again in Bjarni's ship. With his crew of thirty he reached the Vinland houses and settled in there for the winter, catching fish to supplement their provisions brought from Greenland. During the summer months Thorvaldr explored the coast to the south, meeting no one.

CONFLICT BETWEEN THE NORSE AND THE NATIVE PEOPLES

Violence and brutality characterized the first recorded contact between Europeans and Canada's native peoples. Apparently, Thorvaldr and his men the second summer followed the coast northward, where they encountered on shore nine *skraelings*, or "barbarians," as the Norse called them, sleeping under three skin boats. Immediately the Norse murdered eight of the nine. The one *skraeling* who escaped later returned with others in a fleet of "skin boats"—because of this reference in the Vinland Sagas some experts believe these *skraelings* were not Indians but Inuit using kayaks. In the skirmish that ensued, a *skraeling* arrow hit Thorvaldr,

21

mortally wounding him and forcing the crew to return to Vinland and to Greenland the following spring. A few brief, usually hostile encounters followed on subsequent expeditions. The development of hostile relations with the natives prevented the establishment of a permanent colony.

After one final attempt to colonize Vinland, led by Freydis, Eric the Red's daughter, the Norse gave up the effort. From the eleventh to fourteenth centuries the Greenlandic Norse returned to buy wood from the *skraelings*, but they never returned to colonize the area.

For nearly five hundred years the native peoples were undisturbed by European colonists. The original Canadians had prevented European settlement, thanks to their larger populations, the Norse's tenuous supply lines, the natives' knowledge of their own homeland, and the Europeans' lack of a clear superiority in weaponry. Five centuries later, however, with the development of firearms, the Europeans would have a growing military advantage.

22

THE SAGAS' HISTORICAL VALUE

Many questions about the Norse remain unresolved. It is important to indicate the limitations of the source materials. We know of Eric the Red, Bjarni, Leif Eiriksson, and the later Viking explorers not from journals and accounts of first-hand witnesses but from sagas or stories passed on orally from generation to generation—for two, perhaps three hundred years, before they were written down. These sagas, told by expert storytellers, were designed to hold an audience spellbound; no doubt, in the telling many of the original facts were embellished and then re-embellished. Within the tales, legend and fiction are intermingled with real events and geographical places. Yet they undoubtedly have a factual basis as well. In the late 1950s researchers who used these sagas as clues actually located a Norse settlement on the northern coast of Newfoundland—proof that they visited Canada.

In 1960 the first and only widely accepted Norse site in North America was discovered by Helge Ingstad and excavated by his archaeologist wife, Anne Stine Ingstad. At l'Anse-aux-Meadows in northern Newfoundland (see page 320), archaeological crews unearthed the remains of eight sod-walled structures similar to those constructed by the Norse in Iceland and Greenland. Radiocarbon-dating of Norse artifacts found at the site indicated a date of occupancy in the vicinity of 1000 A.D.—the date of the Vinland expeditions. Among the artifacts were two small objects of great importance: one was a bronze pin, used by the Norse to fasten their cloaks on the right shoulder, to leave their arms free to wield a sword; the other was a spindle whorl used by the Norse women to make yarn from wool (indicating that perhaps there were women in the first Norse settlement in North America). The absence of a midden (or refuse heap) containing bones and other debris, as well as the fact that none of the houses was rebuilt or had major repairs, hints that the occupancy lasted for only a few years at the most.

THE NORSE IN GREENLAND

Archaeologists have also found evidence of Norse activity in Canada's Arctic archipelago. The Norse voyaged northward to trade along the Greenlandic coast and westward to Baffin and Ellesmere Islands, as late as the fourteenth century. Excavations of a team of archaeologists have produced more Norse specimens on the east coast of Ellesmere Island than in any other area of North America. Among the Thule people's winter house ruins, dating between 1250 A.D. and 1350 A.D., archaeologists have found such Norse-derived materials as ship rivets, chainmail pieces, two pieces of woven woolen cloth, oak pieces, barrel-bottom fragments, and many copper and iron pieces.

23

Increasingly colder and drier conditions led the Thule, or pre-Inuit peoples, southward from Ellesmere Island after 1200, to follow their food supply—the seals. When in 1200–1300 the climate in the area became colder, Greenland agriculture was threatened. In contrast, the Thule made a successful adjustment to the Arctic environment, with their warm clothing, summer tents, and winter houses. In terms of efficiency, the skin boats in which they hunted seals were better suited to Arctic waters than the small Norse wooden boats.

The Greenland settlements vanished by the early fifteenth century, certainly by 1425 or 1450. At the height of Greenland's prosperity an estimated 2000–4000 people, and perhaps as many as 6000 lived there. Their prosperity, precariously built on the walrus-ivory trade, was doomed when the Portuguese began importing African elephant ivory. Moreover, the Black Death epidemic of 1349 struck Norway and Iceland severely, killing one out of three—a loss that cost the Norse their command of the seas. In these years the annual ship from Norway bringing vital supplies no longer appeared.

Entry of the Portuguese and the Spanish

The Portuguese had replaced the Scandinavians as the leading European sea power by the fifteenth century. Portugal's proximity to the Arab world had allowed the small kingdom to acquire valuable new navigational ideas.

At a time when most western European countries were experiencing civil strife, Portugal enjoyed political unity. Prince Henry the Navigator promoted maritime exploration by initiating, organizing, and sending expeditions across the Atlantic. He built a fortress at Cape Saint Vincent on the southwestern tip of Portugal. This site became Europe's leading centre for cartography, navigation, and shipbuilding. His experiments in shipbuilding resulted in a new, fast, sea-going vessel—the caravel. These longer and narrower ships with two masts became the discoverers' standard ship; Christopher Columbus's three vessels were all of caravel design.

The Portuguese advances came quickly. Like the Norse, they island-hopped across the Atlantic. By 1420 they had reached Madeira and by 1427 the Azores, which lie a third of the way across the Atlantic. But then their voyages across the Atlantic ceased, for they were setting out into the western ocean at seasons and in latitudes where strong westerly winds make navigation for sailing vessels dangerous. Checked in the mid-Atlantic, they focussed their attention instead on discovering a sea route around Africa to India. In 1488 the Portuguese expedition of Bartholomeu Dias rounded the Cape of Good Hope, and within ten years the Portuguese reached India.

EUROPE'S INTEREST IN EXPANSION

At least three impulses led the Portuguese—and later the Spaniards, the French, the English, and the Dutch—to expand beyond Western Europe, an expansion that led directly to the conquest of the Americas. The first was curiosity, the desire to find a better land than that in which they lived. Second, from the thirteenth century onward, they sought a route to "the Indies," as China, Japan, Indonesia, and India were then collectively called. For want of refrigeration, the preservation of meats required spices, which commanded very high prices. Finally, the Europeans voyaged overseas to convert the "heathen" to Christianity.

Why did the Europeans become the great discoverers at the end of the fifteenth century? Why not the Chinese or the Arabs? Both of the latter groups had extensive maritime experience. Arabs living on the western and northwestern borders of the Indian Ocean were at least as far advanced in the sciences required for seafaring (astronomy, geography, mathematics, and the art of navigation) as their European contemporaries.

Long before Prince Henry the Navigator began sponsoring voyages along the west coast of Africa, the Arabs had explored the east coast of Africa to the Mozambique channel opposite the island of Madagascar, which is about fifteen hundred kilometres north of the Cape of Good Hope. But the Arabs felt no need to go farther, since their territories included the rich variety of tropical plants and animals, as well as minerals, that Europe sought. The Arabs in the Indian Ocean were "already there."

Similarly, well over a thousand years before the extensive voyages of Prince Henry's ships, the Chinese had evolved a strong maritime tradition. In the early fifteenth century, in fact, the Chinese had built a remarkable navy with which for at least five hundred years they traded with the Islamic world. The Chinese had introduced the compass to Europe roughly two to three centuries earlier, and they had developed elaborate navigational charts showing detailed compass bearings. But the motivation of the Chinese was different. They went to other lands not as traders or conquerors but to broadcast the greatness and the wealth of China, the Central Kingdom. The expeditions sent out by the Chinese emperor in the early fifteenth century were the most vast until then seen; one, in fact, consisted of nearly forty thousand crew members and a flotilla of more than three hundred ships.

Had the Chinese admirals been followed by a procession of Chinese Columbuses, Magellans, and Cabots, the history of the world might have been quite different. But a great withdrawal began in the mid-1430s, when the Chinese emperor ordered officials to suppress all seafaring. Just as the Europeans began to set on their great explorations, landbound China sealed its borders. The Central Kingdom, which considered itself the centre of the world, no longer ventured abroad.

The Europeans instead of the Arabs or the Chinese led the way to the Americas. Europe, which in the Middle Ages borrowed almost everything from abroad, and whose influence and power was dwarfed by that of Islam and China, now became the continent of colonizers. Europe was motivated not only by the excitement of exploration but also by commercial incentives: cargo of Oriental silks or spices from the East Indies yielded profits tenfold or more for the importer.

25

THE VOYAGE OF COLUMBUS, 1492

In ancient times it was believed in Europe that Asia could be reached by sailing west from the Atlantic coast. Aristotle, the Greek philosopher, for example, said that it was possible to cross from Spain to the Indies. Two thousand years later, many Europeans held the same view, including Christopher Columbus. When the Italian mariner proposed his expedition to the king and queen of Spain essentially he did so in these terms: Let the Portuguese take the long eastward route around Africa to the Indies; I will find the direct route across the Atlantic.

At the age of forty-one, Columbus already had extensive seafaring experience behind him: under the Portuguese flag he had sailed from above the Arctic Circle nearly to the equator, and from the Aegean Sea westward to the outer Azores. In 1492 he sailed southward to the Canary Islands, avoiding the strong westerly winds of the North Atlantic, and then westward, reaching land that Europeans had not found before. Columbus returned convinced that he had reached the Indies—in 1492 no one dreamed of the existence of what would be called the "New World." He named the original inhabitants of the Americas "Indians," believing until his death in 1506 that he had sailed to India.

THE EUROPEANS' INITIAL PERCEPTIONS OF THE INDIANS

26   The Europeans initially perceived the Indians as a threatening people who had to be controlled and whose culture had to be transformed according to Christian principles. The French later called them "*salvages*" or "*sauvages,*" people both rude and fierce living in a manner closer to that of wild animals than to that of humans. The Wild Man of the Woods, an ancient European folk figure in Europe, greatly influenced the Europeans' image of the Indian.

Columbus' voyage led to a fierce maritime rivalry between Spain and Portugal. In 1493 the king and queen of Spain approached Pope Alexander VI and asked him for the right to evangelize in the territories they had recently "discovered." The Pope drew a line of demarcation through the mid-Atlantic, from the north pole to the south. By the Treaty of Tordesillas in 1494 both Spain and Portugal agreed to move the Pope's line of division one hundred leagues farther west. Everything to the west of the line belonged to Spain, while the land to the east belonged to Portugal. (This division later brought a substantial part of Brazil, and Newfoundland into Portugal's sphere).

The English and the French Join the Spaniards and the Portuguese

Other European nations refused to accept the treaty decision, which would have prevented them from travelling to Asia. As soon as news of Columbus's first two Atlantic voyages to "Asia" reached England, King Henry VII sponsored his own expedition, selecting John Cabot (Giovanni Caboto), an Italian mariner like Columbus, to lead it. The merchants of the English port of Bristol, anxious to secure direct access to the spices of the east, bore all costs.

Very little is known of Cabot, largely because of his son, Sebastian, who himself became a "famous" sailor by later claiming that he—not his father—had made the discoveries. From the fragments of information that survive and came to light a century ago, we know that Cabot was roughly Columbus' age; possibly they grew up together in Genoa. An experienced mariner, he had been to Mecca for the spice trade. Once he learned of Columbus' journey to islands off the coast of "Asia," Cabot resolved to reach the Indies by a shorter northern route. He first sought support in Seville and Lisbon. When that attempt failed he tried England, where in 1496 Henry VII granted him letters patent to sail, making the Italian navigator his agent over any new-found lands.

Cabot set sail from Bristol, the westernmost port of England, on May 20, 1497, in the *Matthew*, a fast and able craft. Unlike the Norsemen the Italian navigator had the benefit of compass, quadrant, and traverse table. On June 24 he sighted land, probably Newfoundland. Here, claiming the land for Henry VII, he planted the flags of England and of Venice. Strangely, he explored no farther, perhaps because he had only a small crew and wished to avoid conflict with hostile natives. Instead, he fished off what he believed was the coast of Asia. The seas so swarmed with fish that the sailors caught them simply by letting down and drawing up baskets weighted with stones. He found the great continental shelf of Newfoundland, the shallow areas called banks, which were favourite breeding places of the cod. Cabot also discovered to the south a large passage (the Gulf of St. Lawrence) that he believed was a direct route to China and India.

Encouraged by this information, the English king sponsored a second voyage the following year. In May 1498 Cabot sailed again from Bristol with five ships. Shortly out of port, one vessel turned back in distress to Ireland, and Bristol never heard of the fate of the other four. With Cabot's disappearance, followed shortly by the death of Henry VII, English interest in the search for a Northwest Passage temporarily lapsed. Nevertheless, John Cabot's first voyage announced England's arrival in the Americas. The voyage also brought the Grand Banks fishery to the attention of the fishing fleets of England, France, Spain, Portugal, and the Basque country, on the frontier of Spain and Portugal. Canada's first great business—fishing—was thus born.

THE PORTUGUESE IN THE NORTH ATLANTIC

Soon after Cabot came the Portuguese. For the most part, Portugal focussed its attention on the sea route to Africa and on Brazil, which it claimed in 1500. Yet, at least in the Azores, interest still existed in the discovery of the Northwest Passage to Cathay. The Azoreans believed that the "new lands" discovered by Cabot lay to the east of the line of demarcation, hence in Portugal's sphere.

A *lavrador* (small land proprietor), João Fernandes, received letters patent from the Portuguese king in 1499 to search for and discover islands in the Portuguese half of the world. Although of no significant geographic interest, his voyage led to the naming of a large section of Canada's Atlantic coastline. In 1500 Fernandes reached Greenland. When the Azorean farmer first sighted the huge land mass the Portuguese humorously called it "Tierra del Lavrador," Land of the Farmer. A century later, when mapmakers learned of the old Norse name "Greenland," they revived it and shifted the name Labrador to the south.

In 1500 the Portuguese sent another expedition under Gaspar Corte-Real, who sailed to a land he termed Tierra Verde. This undoubtedly was Newfoundland. The Azorean sea captain knew how rich west Africa had been as a source of slaves for Portugal, and he sought to make Tierra Verde a second. When he returned again in 1501, he kidnapped fifty-seven Indians and sent them back to Europe with his brother Miguel. But Gaspar Corte-Real and his crew never returned. Like Cabot and his four ships he was lost with all hands, as was Miguel when he came back to search for his lost brother.

Despite the dangers of navigating the uncharted North Atlantic, the Portuguese fishermen annually fished the Grand Banks and the coastal waters of Newfoundland. They sailed extensively along the outer Newfoundland coast. Several place names, now corrupted in English or French versions, testify to their travels: Cape Race (from *raso*, shaved), at the southeastern corner of Newfoundland; Fermeuse Harbour (from *fremoso*, beautiful), about halfway from the cape to St. John's harbour; Cape Spear (from the Portuguese *de espera*, hope), just south of St. John's harbour.

Since the Corte-Reals's expeditions did not produce any riches, the Portuguese lost interest for two decades in North Atlantic exploration. But around 1520 they scored a victory in this international competition. In 1520, if not earlier, João Alvares Fagundes made a voyage along the south coast of Newfoundland and into the Gulf of St. Lawrence. Upon his return the Portuguese shipowner asked the Portuguese king for the same rights granted to the Corte-Real brothers. The king complied, giving him complete property rights, jurisdiction, and privileges over this region. Fagundes then obtained colonists from Portugal and the Azores and established the first European colony in northeastern North America since the Norse.

The Portuguese probably settled on Cape Breton Island, but after a year or so, difficulties arose with the local Indians. Jean Alfonce, a French navigator, recorded the colony's fate several years later: "Formerly the Portuguese sought to settle the land...but the natives of the country put an end to the attempt and killed all those who came there."

28

FRENCH INTEREST IN THE NORTH ATLANTIC

In 1513 a historic event occurred in Central America: the Spaniard Vasco Núñez de Balboa crossed the mountainous Isthmus of Panama and found another ocean—the Pacific. This astonishing discovery of a second ocean of undetermined size strongly suggested that the Americas were separate continents, not outcroppings of Asia. The Spanish-sponsored Magellan expedition (which circled the world between 1519 and 1522), confirmed the existence of a New World.

French mariners then entered the competition. Of all the European powers in the early sixteenth century, France was perhaps the best situated to dominate northeastern North America. After Fagundes' failure, Portugal had little interest—apart from the cod fisheries—in this supposedly poor region of the New World. France, however, had twice the population of Portugal and Spain together, and six times that of England. It also had more ocean-facing territory and as many (or more) seaports as England, and far greater wealth. Yet it was not until 1524 that the French king, François I, became involved in North Atlantic exploration. He acted in response to the return of the Magellan expedition in 1522, which brought back a cargo of precious spices from the east. 29

Asia remained France's objective. Two areas in the North Atlantic remained to be explored: that between Florida and Newfoundland (the most promising), and that between Labrador and Greenland. The French selected an Italian mariner, Giovanni da Verrazzano, as commander of the privately financed French expedition, which enjoyed the patronage of François I. The survival of Verrazzano's journal marks the beginning of a much fuller documentation on the history of North Atlantic exploration.

Verrazzano searched the North American coast from the Carolinas to Gaspé. At one point the Italian navigator believed he had found a route to Asia. Just north of what is now North Carolina, beyond a narrow strip of coastline, he thought that he saw the sea. Since it was commonly believed that the Atlantic joined the Pacific somewhere near Florida, the explorer hastily concluded that he had sighted a new and narrower Panama-type isthmus. The error had a long life. For many years afterwards, cartographers placed the Pacific Ocean just north of Florida, almost reaching the Atlantic. Gradually, as more became known about the continent, the mapmakers placed the Pacific farther away from the shores of the Atlantic. But as late as the mid-eighteenth century, one European map still showed the Pacific covering much of present-day western Canada, as far as Manitoba. (See page 341).

Despite Verrazzano's failure to find a passage leading from the Atlantic to Asia, he had completed a quick and significant reconnaissance of the Atlantic seaboard from Florida to Cape Breton. France now had a relatively clear and full picture of the eastern North American coastline. Verrazzano's discoveries were not immediately followed up, however, as France went to war against the Hapsburgs (the rulers of Austria, the Low Countries, and Spain). These conflicts prevented the sponsorship of a second voyage.

Only a few months after Verrazzano's voyage the Spanish-sponsored expedition of Esteban Gómez in 1524–25 re-surveyed the Atlantic coast from Florida to the Grand Banks. Not wishing to return empty handed, the sea captain kidnapped a large number of Indians on the New England or Nova Scotia coast and took them back to Spain to sell as slaves. Later, the Spanish king freed the fifty-eight Indians who reached Spain alive, but their subsequent fate is unknown. (The fate of Gómez is known: in 1538 Indians ambushed and killed him and the members of his gold- and silver-seeking expedition on the banks of the Paraguay River in South America.)

30   Jacques Cartier's Three Voyages

Verrazzano's successor was Jacques Cartier, a mariner from the wealthy port of Saint-Malo in Brittany, northwestern France. Fishermen from Saint-Malo and other northern French ports had already sailed to the Grand Banks and inshore Newfoundland. Cartier probably gained his first maritime experience on these runs. Comments in his reports also imply that he had already been to Brazil. The French Crown expected the expedition of 1534 to find a passage to Asia and to reveal lands rich in gold and other precious commodities. Cartier left Saint-Malo in late April 1534, with two ships and sixty-one men; they reached the Strait of Belle-Isle between Labrador and Newfoundland in late May. Unimpressed with the area, Cartier called it "the land God gave Cain."

After skirting the shores of Newfoundland and surveying the coastline, Cartier entered the Gulf of St. Lawrence. He passed by the Magdalen Islands and Prince Edward Island to land at Chaleur Bay, which today divides Quebec from New Brunswick. Here the French met the Micmac Indians, members of the Algonquian linguistic family. Cartier's reference in his journal is the first written record (and the first reference since the Vinland Sagas) to a trading exchange between Indians and Europeans—one initiated by the Indians themselves, who from shore, "set up a great clamour and made frequent signs to us to come on shore, holding up to us some furs on sticks." Before Cartier's arrival, European fishermen had no doubt previously traded with these Indians, who brought furs to exchange for the newcomers' iron knives, kettles, and hatchets.

When the French moved northward to Gaspé they encountered another large group of Indians who had come from the interior to fish. These Iroquoian Indians differed greatly from the Micmacs. Inexperienced in trading with Europeans, they brought no furs with them. The French gave the Indians "knives, glass beads, combs, and other trinkets of small value" to win their friendship. To serve as guides for their next voyage and to gain information about the country the French also kidnapped two sons of the chief, Donnacona, and took them back to France for the winter to learn French.

CARTIER'S YEAR IN THE ST. LAWRENCE VALLEY 1535/36

Cartier accomplished much in one summer, locating and charting an inland sea. The next year (1535) he returned with three ships. Taignoagny and Domagaya, the chief's sons, proved much luckier than many of their fellow Indians kidnapped in the sixteenth century and shipped to Europe. They survived their stay in France to return with Cartier and his 110 men, guiding them to their village of Stadacona (present-day Quebec). Later, Cartier recorded in a short list that he kept on the journey a word that his two guides used constantly to refer to their home: "They call a town, *Canada.*"[2] En route, Cartier gave the name St. Lawrence to a cove that he stopped at, after the Christian martyr whose feast day it was (August 10). From this cove the entire gulf and the great river later obtained their names.

The Iroquoians at Stadacona saw the French as powerful and valuable trading partners. When Cartier, though, mentioned to Chief Donnacona that he intended to travel inland, the old chief strongly objected—a natural reaction. The Stadaconans understandably wanted to monopolize the inland trade and barter the interior groups' furs for more of the precious European iron tools. Cartier paid Donnacona no heed and went westward in early October.

By Cartier's estimate more than a thousand natives greeted him by the edge of the river at Hochelaga, a palisaded town of fifty longhouses— much more impressive than Stadacona. Much better suited for agriculture than Stadacona, Hochelaga could support a larger population. That afternoon Cartier climbed the summit of the hill he called Mont Royal, which eventually became pronounced "Montréal." From this vantage point he had a magnificent view of the well-cultivated cornfields and the longhouses below him. To the north lay the Laurentians and the Green Mountains. The Adirondacks were to the south, and the St. Lawrence flowed from west to east. But to his dismay he noticed the Lachine rapids to the west, which no boat larger than a canoe could pass. The French stayed just one day, then returned downriver. It being too late to depart safely for France, he and his men prepared to winter over at Stadacona.

The story of that winter at Stadacona is one of mounting tensions. Certain patterns of behaviour were established which would continue long

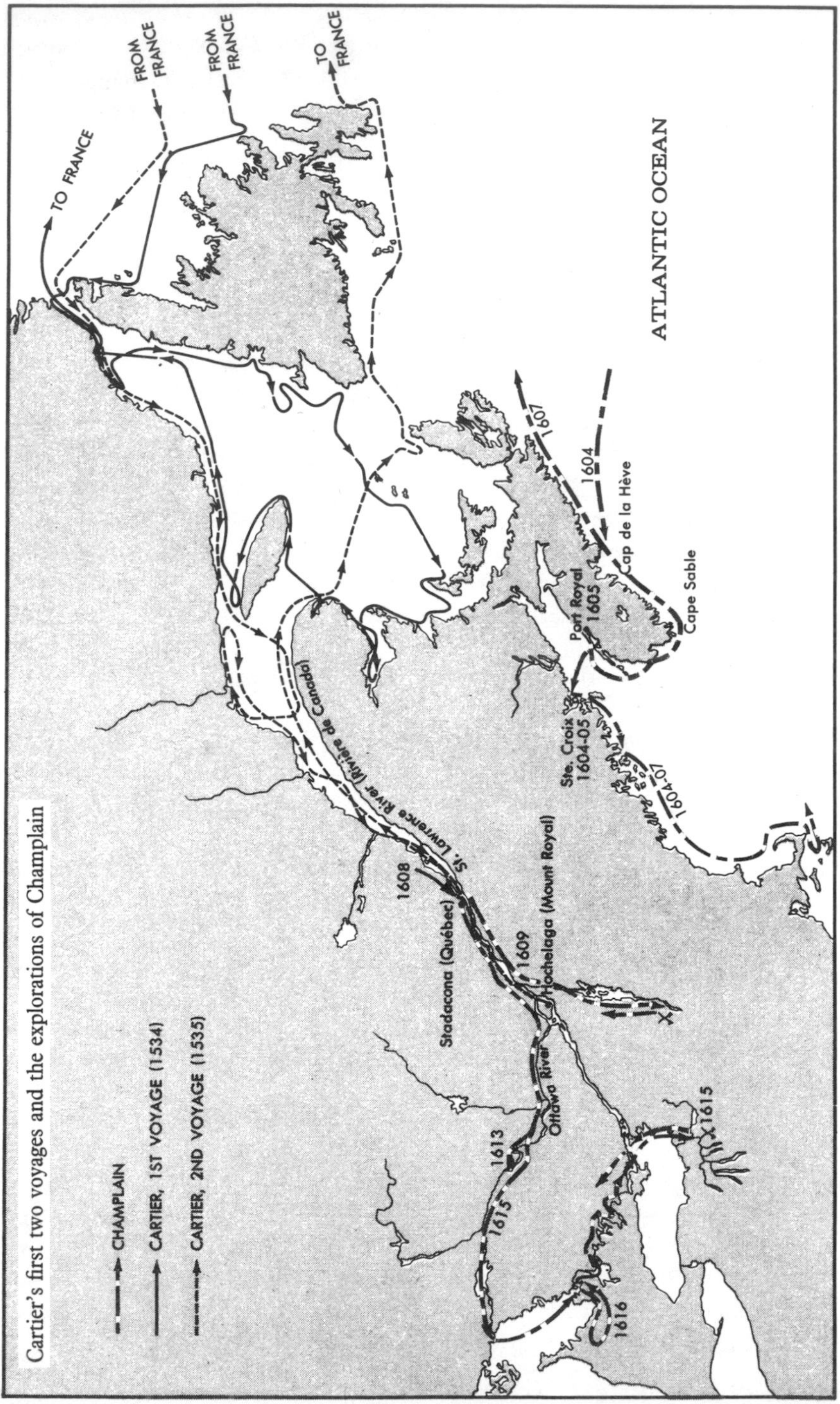

32

ATLANTIC OCEAN

Cartier's first two voyages and the explorations of Champlain

→ CHAMPLAIN
→ CARTIER, 1ST VOYAGE (1534)
→ CARTIER, 2ND VOYAGE (1535)

TO FRANCE
FROM FRANCE
FROM FRANCE
TO FRANCE

Cap de la Hève
Cape Sable
Port Royal 1605
Ste. Croix 1604-05
1604
1604-07
607

St. Lawrence River (Rivière de Canada)

1608
Stadacona (Québec)
1609
Hochelaga (Mount Royal)
Ottawa River
1613
1615
1615
1616

Cornell, Hamelin, Ouellet, Trudel, *Canada, Unity in Diversity*, p. 22.

after Cartier. Like other western Europeans after him, Cartier believed in the superiority of Christian civilization. He did not recognize that the Indians, as non-Christians, had any land rights. By travelling upriver without first obtaining Donnacona's permission, Cartier had intruded on their trading rights. The French who were left behind also built a small fort during Cartier's absence—an act that infringed on the Indians' land rights. Domagaya and Taignoagny contributed to the unrest by telling the Stadaconans that the French cheated them and that they should obtain better value for their fresh meat and fish.

The winter, much longer and colder in Canada than in France, proved a nightmare to the French. By January and February ice nearly four metres thick locked in the ships, and on land the snow lay over a metre deep. To add to the sailors' problems scurvy broke out. Twenty-five (one-quarter of Cartier's men) died before the French learned from Domagaya the Indians' cure: boiling the bark and leaves of the annedda (the white cedar) to make a brew having a high content of ascorbic acid (vitamin C).

33

Despite the Indians' help, Cartier remained antagonistic to Donnacona and his people. Anxious to obtain more information about the lands to the west, particularly the rich "kingdom of the Saguenay" which the Indians had spoken of, the French mariner kidnapped Donnacona, his two sons, and three of his principal supporters. The French understood this fabulous land to be rich in gold and silver, a second Mexico. (In reality, stories of the "Saguenay" probably referred to the native copper deposits around Lake Superior.) After promising to return his hostages the following year, Cartier left in the spring of 1536 with his prisoners, as well as with four children presented to him by Donnacona and by the chief of a neighbouring village. The Indians never saw "Canada" again.

Cartier entered the port of Saint-Malo in mid-July 1536, after an absence of fourteen months. On this journey he had made important contributions: he proved that Newfoundland was an island, charted much of the Gulf of St. Lawrence, and discovered a great river, the St. Lawrence, which later was France's entry-point into the interior. His geographical exploration was not to be surpassed by any other French explorer until Champlain in the early 1600s.

THE CARTIER/ROBERVAL EXPEDITIONS, 1541/42

Cartier's third voyage in 1541 had colonization as its objective, as well as exploration for the famed "kingdom of the Saguenay" and the Northwest Passage. The expedition split into two groups, with Cartier wintering at Cap Rouge, about fifteen kilometres upriver from Stadacona. His superior, Jean-François de La Roque de Roberval followed the next year. At Cap

Rouge Cartier unloaded cattle and supplies and planted crops, making it quite clear that he and the 150 French colonists had come to stay. Very little information has survived regarding the settlement that winter, but a later report stated that the Indians killed thirty-five Europeans.

By the spring Cartier had had enough. With a cargo of minerals that he thought were gold and diamonds he sailed for France. En route he met Roberval in Newfoundland, but disobeying his superior's orders, he went back to France to offer his precious minerals to the king. An old French proverb still used in Brittany and Normandy owes its origin to Cartier's third voyage: *"Faux comme un diamant du Canada"* (fake as a Canadian diamond). The gold turned out to be iron pyrites and the alleged diamonds, quartz.

Roberval had with him some two hundred settlers. They had a terrible winter at the site of Cartier's settlement, which they rebuilt. Fifty colonists, ignorant of the cure, died from scurvy. The next summer Roberval returned to France. An inscription on a French map of 1550 best explains the reasons for the colony's failure: "It was impossible to trade with the people of that country because of their austerity, the intemperate climate of said country, and the slight profit." The royal treasury, which had paid most of the expenses of the Cartier-Roberval expedition, lost all it had invested.

France, still at war with Spain, and soon to be torn by a civil war between Roman Catholics and Protestants, left Canada to its native inhabitants. French fishermen, whalers, and traders continued to come in great numbers, but there was no formal colonization attempted for another half-century.

The harsh climate, poor relations with the Indians, the failure to find gold, and the inability of the fur trade to support a colony, defeated the first colonization attempts. In the late 1550s France directed its colonization efforts instead towards Brazil and, in the early 1560s, to the present-day southeastern United States, until the Portuguese and Spanish respectively destroyed these French colonies.

After Cartier and Roberval

European fishermen maintained contact with northeastern North America in the mid-sixteenth century. The Newfoundland fishery became a major international attraction. Between March and October of each year, large fishing fleets—Portuguese, Basque, French, and English—gathered. They supplied the markets of western Europe and the Mediterranean with the "beef of the sea" (dried cod). The estimated number of men and ships travelling to the Newfoundland fishery was perhaps twice as great as those sailing to ports in the Gulf of Mexico and the Caribbean. By the 1570s an estimated 8 000–10 000 fishermen annually crossed the Atlantic to fish the Grand Banks.

The fishermen employed two methods of preserving the fish. In the "green" or "wet" fishery the fishermen salted the catch directly onboard ship. In the "dry" or "shore" fishery they took the catch ashore and dried it on specially built stagings, or "flakes" (see chapter 17). The "dry" fishermen became the first Europeans to establish summer settlements along the Atlantic coast of what is now Canada. Some "dry" fishermen obtained furs from the Indians as souvenirs, and for their own use.

THE BASQUES' WHALE FISHERY

Among the most active nationalities on the Atlantic seacoast were the Basques, who came for cod and for whales. By the early 1540s the Spanish Basques had established a type of whale fishery in the Strait of Belle Isle; it flourished for a half-century. Sixteenth-century Europeans treasured whale oil as a prime source of light, an all-purpose lubricant, an additive to drugs, and as a major ingredient of scores of products such as soap and pitch. Each season the fishery employed about two thousand men who remained in Newfoundland-Labrador waters for six months, until mid-January. At the Basque shore stations, Inuit and Indian groups could obtain European materials on an annual basis from fixed geographical locations in southern Labrador, perhaps on the Gaspé coast as well. Marc Lescarbot, the early French chronicler, noted that the natives trading along the Gaspé shore during the first decade of the seventeenth century spoke a trade language that was half Basque.

ENGLISH ACTIVITY IN THE NORTH ATLANTIC AND THE ARCTIC

The English established fishing posts in the eastern part of the Avalon Peninsula in southeastern Newfoundland while the French visited along the southern and western shores of Newfoundland. In August 1583 Sir Humphrey Gilbert repeated Cabot's act of taking formal possession of Newfoundland for England. His colonizing expedition, however, proved unsuccessful. It was destroyed by a mutiny ashore and storms at sea—events all recorded by the expedition's chronicler, Stephen Parmenius, a Hungarian scholar who left Oxford University to join Gilbert.

England sponsored a number of expeditions north of Newfoundland in the late sixteenth and early seventeenth centuries. In the 1570s, Spain seemed likely to conquer the Netherlands and control England's ports of entry to the continent. Anxious to expand trade, England revived its interest in the Northwest Passage. In 1576, only a few months before Sir Francis Drake left to plunder Spanish shipping in the Pacific, Martin Frobisher sailed on a more peaceful mission—opening a passage to India and China by way of the Northwest.

The English ships sailed for the storm- and fog-laden sea between Labrador and Greenland. Frobisher, thirty-seven years old, a mariner of great reputation, left with three ships and fifty men. Off Baffin Island he encountered Inuit who came to trade meat and furs for iron objects and clothing. The Inuit showed they were no strangers to European ships (no doubt, vessels of the Newfoundland fishing fleet) by doing gymnastic exercises in the ship's rigging. Frobisher, however, failed to find a strait either on this first journey or on two subsequent voyages in 1577 and 1578. Ten years later the expert seaman and navigator, John Davis, in three successive summers (1585–87) followed up Frobisher's work, but without success. The reason is that the technology for the penetration of the Arctic Archipelago did not exist in the late sixteenth century. It was as impossible a goal for that age as a landing on the moon would have been in 1900.

Native Perceptions of the Europeans

Unfortunately, almost no contemporary information has survived about how the North American Indians and Inuit perceived the first Europeans— the Norse, Portuguese, French, Basque, and English. Evidence from French missionaries' records of the sixteenth and seventeenth centuries shows the Indians' amazement at the white man's material objects and their abundant supply, however. The Iroquoians of the Great Lakes termed the Europeans "iron-men."

The Europeans' metal tools and weapons were worth many animal skins to the Indians. The newcomers' steel axes lightened the labour of gathering firewood. Their copper cooking pots were not fragile like the Indians' pottery vessels or perishable like their wooden boxes and birch-bark kettles. For cutting meat and wood, durable steel knives performed much better than those of stone. Steel awls and needles made sewing and the working of hides and leather much easier.

European trade goods immediately entered the extensive Indian trading networks, and interior groups obtained them long before they ever saw a European. Archaeology has confirmed, for example, the presence of European trade goods among the Seneca south of Lake Ontario, an Iroquoian tribe located hundreds of kilometres from the Atlantic, by the early sixteenth century. Steel had already come into general use by the end of the sixteenth

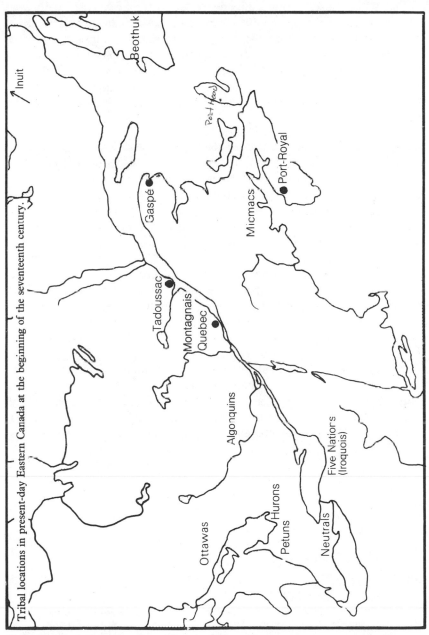

Tribal locations in present-day Eastern Canada at the beginning of the seventeenth century.

37

M. Trudel, *Introduction to New France* (Toronto, 1968), p. 24.

century; it was used in place of stone by the Senecas to cut axe blades. They also cut their arrowheads from brass.

Yet, if the native peoples initially regarded the newcomers with awe (interpreting their possession of metal objects as evidence of some great supernatural power), the amazement quickly passed. The Europeans proved ill at ease in the interior and lacked the Amerindians' endurance in forest travel. Missionary reports in the early seventeenth century reveal that the Indians noted the French's slowness in learning how to use canoes, snowshoes, and everything else which to the Indians seemed commonplace.

The original Canadians in present-day Atlantic and Arctic Canada witnessed the arrival of the first Europeans—the Norse—around 1000 A.D., and of the English, Portuguese, French, Spanish, and the Basques, five centuries later. The early European navigators crossed the North Atlantic at great personal risk. They sailed in tiny ships into the unknown, encountering as a matter of course enormous waves, very strong gales, and immense seas. John Cabot, the Corte-Real brothers, and Sir Humphrey Gilbert, all lost their lives in their explorations. In the words of Samuel Eliot Morison, the American Maritime historian: "North America became a graveyard for European ships and sailors."[3] Yet, the Europeans persisted in crossing the North Atlantic. Some came in search of a Northwest Passage to China and the Indies. Others—the vast majority—were lured on by the promise of economic gain, first in the cod and the whale fisheries, and later in the fur trade.

As late as 1600 no permanent European settlement existed in present-day Canada. But Samuel de Champlain would successfully found the first only eight years later. Quebec would serve as France's advance trading post. With the founding of the French colony the European penetration of the original Canadians' homeland began, and our documentary sources become more abundant.

NOTES

[1] Morris Bishop, *Champlain: The Life of Fortitude* (Toronto, 1963; first published 1948), p. 26.
[2] H.P. Biggar, ed., *The Voyages of Jacques Cartier, published from the original with translations, notes, and appendices* (Ottawa, 1924), p. 245. For an important discussion of other possible origins of the word "Canada," see Olive P. Dickason, "Appendix 1: Origin of the Name 'Canada'," in *The Myth of the Savage and the Beginnings of French Colonialism in the Americas* (Edmonton, 1984), pp. 279–80.
[3] Samuel Eliot Morison, *The European Discovery of America. The Northern Voyages. 500–1600* (New York, 1971), p. xi.

Related Readings

R. Douglas Francis and Donald B. Smith, *Readings in Canadian History: Pre-Confederation*, 2d ed. (Toronto, 1986) contains the following essays of value to this topic: Robert McGhee's "Possible Norse-Eskimo Contacts in the Eastern Arctic," pp. 58–66; and Selma Barkham's "The Basques: Filling a Gap in Our History between Jacques Cartier and Champlain," pp. 66–75. Arthur J. Ray's "Fur Trade History as an Aspect of Native History," pp. 162–73, discusses whether the fur traders exploited the native peoples.

BIBLIOGRAPHY

Two delightfully written summaries of the early European explorers' accounts are available: Samuel Eliot Morison's *The European Discovery of America: The Northern Voyages A.D. 500–1600* (New York, 1971) and Daniel J. Boorstin's *The Discoverers: A History of Man's Search to Know His World and Himself* (New York, 1983). Less colourful in its presentation but very informative is David B. Quinn's *North America from Earliest Discovery to First Settlements: The Norse Voyages to 1612* (New York, 1977). Economic aspects are briefly reviewed by Michael Bliss in *Northern Enterprise: Five Centuries of Canadian Business* (Toronto, 1987). Marcel Trudel's "In Search of Asia," *Horizon Canada*, number 2 (1984): 25–31, provides a good short review of the first European visitors to present-day Canada. *The Dictionary of Canadian Biography*, vol. 1: 1000–1700 (Toronto, 1966), contains many useful biographical portraits.

For the Norse experience in Greenland and North America, see Kate Gordon (with an essay by Robert McGhee), *The Vikings and their Predecessors* (Ottawa, 1981), and Robert McGhee's "Contact between Native North Americans and the Medieval Norse: A Review of the Evidence," *American Antiquity*, 49, 1 (1984): 4–26. Helge Ingstad tells the story of the discovery of the Anse aux Meadows site in his *Westward to Vinland: The Discovery of Pre-Columbian Norse House-sites* (London, 1969). Peter Schledermann's "Inuit Prehistory and Archaeology," in *A Century of Canada's Arctic Islands*, edited by Morris Zaslow (Ottawa, 1981), pp. 245–56, reviews the recent finds of Norse objects on Ellesmere Island.

Bruce Trigger's *The Children of Aataentsic: A History of the Huron People to 1660*, vol.1 (Montreal, 1976) provides background information on the reaction of the St. Lawrence valley Indians to Cartier and Roberval. For an understanding of the Cartier-Roberval expeditions, consult these two surveys: Olive Patricia Dickason, *The Myth of the Savage and the Beginnings of French Colonialism in the Americas* (Edmonton, 1984), and Marcel Trudel, *The Beginnings of New France, 1524–1663* (Toronto, 1973). Cornelius Jaenen reviews the cultural interaction between the French and the Indians in *Friend and Foe* (Toronto, 1976).

On Basque activity in northeastern North America, see Selma Barkham, "A Note on the Strait of Belle Isle during the period of Basque contact with Indians and Inuit," *Etudes/Inuit/Studies* 4 (1980): 51-58; and "The Basque Whaling Establishments in Labrador, 1536–1632: A Summary," *Arctic* 37 (1984): 515–19. A well-illustrated series of articles (including contributions by James A. Tuck and Robert Grenier) entitled "Discovery in Labrador: A 16th-Century Basque Whaling Port and its Sunken Fleet," appeared in the *National Geographic*, 168, 1 (July 1985): 40–71. Laurier Turgeon reviews European fishermen's activities in the area in "Pour redécouvrir notre 16e siècle: Les pêches à Terre-Neuve d'après les archives notariales de Bordeaux," *Revue d'histoire de l'Amérique française*, 39 (1985–86): 523–49.

A survey of the Frobisher and Davis expeditions in Arctic waters appears in L.H. Neatby, *In Quest of the North West Passage* (Toronto, 1958). William W. Fitzhugh's essay, "Early Contacts North of Newfoundland before A.D. 1600," in *Culture in Contact: The European Impact on Native Cultural Institutions in Eastern North America A.D. 1000–1800*, edited by William W. Fitzhugh (Washington, 1985), pp. 23–43, reviews the period between the Norse expeditions and that of Davis and Frobisher.

For excellent maps on early European exploration, see the *Historical Atlas of Canada*, vol. 1, edited by R. Cole Harris (Toronto, 1987).

CHAPTER THREE

The Beginnings of New France

A small fur-bearing animal, the beaver, was the real founder of New France. In the late sixteenth century furs commanded a high price in Europe. No fabric then available rivalled the warmth, wearability, and beauty of furs, which were in great demand for both men's and women's clothing. Persons of importance wore them to display their rank and wealth. Fur coats, muffs, wraps, gloves, fur-trimmed garments and, most important, wide brimmed beaver hats, all came into fashion.

As the beaver already had become almost extinct in Europe, merchants eagerly sought cast-off Indian beaver robes. When worn or slept in, the long guard hairs on the robes loosened and fell out, leaving only the fine, soft underfur. Hat makers could then process it into a smooth surface unequalled by any type of woven cloth. By the end of the sixteenth century hundreds of French traders sailed to Tadoussac, at the mouth of the Saguenay River in Quebec, to bargain for pelts.

Jacques Cartier's three voyages established a French claim to the Gulf of St. Lawrence but international recognition came only with successful occupation. The development of the fur trade brought the French back permanently. The volume of trade convinced France to establish a monopoly to bring it under control. To obtain the monopoly the Crown insisted on two provisions being met: the private fur-trading company had first to promote colonization and, second, to send Roman Catholic missionaries to Christianize the Indians.

One generation after Champlain founded Quebec in 1608 the French colony in "Canada," as the St. Lawrence valley became known, had grown to three small settlements. A fragile French community existed in the St. Lawrence valley by the late 1640s. The fur traders, together with a large clerical contingent who had come to convert and serve the Indians, maintained the colony.

Rise of the Fur Trade

In the Gulf of St. Lawrence and along the Atlantic coastline the fur trade had begun as a by-product of the fishing industry in the mid-sixteenth century. By coming back each year to the same locality, the French established good trading relationships with the local Indians. As the demand for furs increased in Europe, several French merchants began in the 1580s to send out ships commissioned solely to trade.

Fur was an ideal product for the European traders: it could not be produced at home, it was light in weight, easily packaged and transported and, in the early years, highly profitable. The Indians, already skilled traders, wanted to barter for the Europeans' metal goods. They brought in "coat beaver" or pelts that had been worn before being traded. They also brought "parchment pelts," which were dried immediately after skinning.

Initially, the Indians perceived that the exchange posed no danger to their independence. Yet there was a danger, for by the early seventeenth century the Algonquians on the Atlantic coast had lost much of their former self-sufficiency and become reliant on the Europeans.

The fur trade led to revolutionary changes in the Indians' way of life. It gradually transformed the coastal groups from hunters and fishermen into trappers. Prior to European contact the Micmac spent more than half the year living on the coast, since the sea supplied as much as ninety percent of their diet. Their desire for trade goods, however, now led them to spend longer periods each year hunting inland, searching for fur-bearing animals. This change in their traditional activities affected their winter diet. They no longer accumulated their usual summer food stores and relied partly on the dried foods they received in trade.

Tadoussac became the Europeans' principal centre for trade on the Gulf of St. Lawrence. Pre-existing trading networks led from there to Hudson Bay in the north and to New England in the south. Jacques Noël, a nephew of Jacques Cartier, went to Tadoussac and much farther west in the mid-1580s. He saw the ruins of his uncle's forts at Stadacona, viewed the Lachine rapids, and climbed Mont Royal. In those years as many as twenty vessels could be seen at one time in the summer at Tadoussac.

Trade reached such a volume by the 1590s that the French Crown established a monopoly to control it. The monopolists' colonization schemes proved expensive, however. Early attempts all failed as French colonists suffered a disastrous winter at Tadoussac in 1600–01, when only five of the sixteen men survived the winter. The Marquis de La Roche-Mesgouez, a French nobleman, had in 1598 established an outpost on Sable Island (about two hundred kilometres off present-day Nova Scotia, close to the fishing grounds) but it also failed. In 1603 La Roche repatriated to France the eleven survivors.

In 1603 a distinguished French official, Aymar de Chaste, Vice-Admiral

42

of France, obtained the monopoly. He in turn appointed as his representative in America François Gravé Du Pont, an eprienced captain who had already made fishing voyages to the St. Lawrence. On Gravé's ship in 1603, as a sort of observer-chronicler, sailed Samuel de Champlain, a young seaman in his twenties. The two men remained partners for nearly thirty years and together helped to establish the first permanent French settlement in the Americas.

Samuel de Champlain

Considering Champlain's important role in the founding of New France, it is surprising how little is known about his family background and youth. He was probably born about 1580 and not necessarily 1570, as was formerly believed. Most likely he came from Brouage, a port north of Bordeaux in western France and one of the principal sources of salt for the fishing fleet. At an early age he went to sea and became a competent ship's captain and an authority on navigation. The earliest references to him document his service in the royal army. As a soldier in his mid-teens young Samuel knew war and the sight of death. His body and spirit were toughened by service in a Renaissance European army, whose soldiers' actions, in the words of E. Pocquet, a French historian, could be summarized by five phrases: to steal possessions, to carry off cattle, to burn homes, to kill men, and to rape women.[1]

43

After his army service Champlain undertook a voyage to the West Indies that kept him away from France for two and a half years. He returned to France in 1601 and at court enjoyed a pension from the king. At the court the young man came to know Aymar de Chaste, who had invited him to sail with Gravé.

Much had changed among the native population of the St. Lawrence valley since the journeys of Cartier and Roberval. Champlain saw large numbers of Algonquians at Tadoussac and at several encampments along the St. Lawrence, but no Iroquoians, who had mysteriously left.

How did this displacement come about? Unfortunately, we have no complete accounts of the St. Lawrence valley from the time of Cartier and Roberval to that of Champlain, only hypotheses. Harold Innis, a Canadian economic historian, believed that the Laurentian Iroquoians were driven out of the St. Lawrence valley and from along the Gulf coast by eastern Algonquian tribes. They had obtained iron weapons before the Laurentian Iroquoians, which gave them a technological advantage in warfare.

Recently, Bruce Trigger, an anthropologist who has done extensive research on the ethnohistory of northeastern North America, has advanced another theory. Trigger speculates that raids by the Iroquois living in present-day New York State led to the expulsion of the St. Lawrence

Iroquoians. He proposes that the landlocked New York Iroquois became anxious for European trade goods but found them difficult to obtain from either the Saint Lawrence Iroquoians or from the Algonquians. The Mohawk, the most easterly tribe of the Iroquois Confederacy, in desperation attacked the natives of the St. Lawrence valley. In their ensuing raids they dispersed the Laurentian Iroquoians, some of whom possibly journeyed westward to join the Huron on the Georgian Bay on Lake Huron. Archaeologists, he adds, have established that European goods had reached all of the New York Iroquois tribes by 1600. These, Trigger surmises, must have been largely obtained as booty from the Laurentian Iroquoians. Although both explanations for the disappearance of the St. Lawrence Iroquoians are helpful, the data is lacking to reach any definite conclusions.

Following Cartier's route as far as Montreal, Gravé and Champlain made a careful examination of the St. Lawrence valley that summer. They learned much about the *pays d'en haut*, the country north and west of the St. Lawrence valley. They also learned for the first time of a nation called the "good Iroquois" (the Huron) who lived by a great lake to the northeast (Lake Huron). The natives also told them about the geography of the interior—Lakes Ontario and Erie, and the extraordinary Niagara Falls. These Algonquians had a good working knowledge of the lower Great Lakes and had travelled on them. Their trading network reached 2500 km into the interior from the Atlantic.

With the end of summer approaching and, with it, the end of fur trading for the season, Gravé and Champlain returned to France. De Chaste had died during their absence, and Pierre Du Gua de Monts, was granted the monopoly.

The First French Settlements in Acadia

Today we take for granted that Quebec was the natural site for France's first permanent settlement in present-day Canada. In reality, however, the French initially rejected Quebec. From 1604 to 1607 de Monts, accompanied by Gravé and by Champlain, who served as the cartographer, searched elsewhere for the ideal place to establish a colony. To escape the competition from traders who refused to respect the monopoly of the St. Lawrence fur trade, they sailed southward to the present-day Maritime provinces, a region with a climate milder than the St. Lawrence and one potentially rich in mineral resources. They also chose a more southerly location for the colony in the hope that the coastline might reveal a shortcut to Asia. In 1604 many Europeans still believed that the inlet of the great western sea, reported by Verrazzano nearly a century earlier, existed not far to the west of the Atlantic coast.

44

Armed with vice-regal powers and a ten-year trading monopoly, de Monts and his colonists reached the south coast of Nova Scotia. They sailed up the Bay of Fundy and entered the Annapolis Basin, named Port-Royal by Champlain (see page 32). The party crossed to the New Brunswick shore, passed a large river that they named the St. John, and wintered on a small island near the mouth of the St. Croix river, which is now part of the border between Maine and New Brunswick. Roughly one-half of the seventy-nine men died of scurvy before spring, and many more were close to death. The losses suffered in all of these early European attempts to found colonies in the New World proved incredibly high; starvation and scurvy took many lives.

After a summer exploring the coastline the French stayed the next winter at Port-Royal. The colony formed there became the first agricultural settlement of Europeans on soil that is now Canadian. The French again explored the coastline the following summer and then wintered at Port-Royal.

45

After two years of considerable expenditures in Acadia, unsuccessfully searching for mineral resources and the Northwest Passage, de Monts realized the limitations of the area. Along the winding and indented coasts of the Maritimes he simply could not enforce his fur-trade monopoly. An entrepreneur needed only a ship, a crew, and a supply of trade goods to sail to the Maritimes to make his fortune. Annually, eighty ships poached on de Monts' domain, and his profits were insufficient to cover the cost of Port-Royal.

Champlain stayed at Port-Royal for his third and final winter in Acadia in 1606–07. For really the first time in their history in northeastern North America the French had a successful winter and, in fact, enjoyed themselves, largely thanks to the Order of Good Cheer founded by Champlain. The order, the first social club in Canada, required that every gentleman at Port-Royal become, in turn, chief steward and caterer for a day. Ceremoniously wearing the chain of office, each steward prepared meals and made out the next day's menus. In friendly rivalry each man vied with the others to serve game and fish in abundance, in addition to the ever-present bread and salt cod. They sang favourite old songs and composed new ones on the spot. In 1606 Marc Lescarbot, a poet and a playwright in the party, presented *Théâtre de Neptune*, the first theatrical production in Canadian history. And yet, despite the festivities of that third long Acadian winter, de Monts could no longer afford to sponsor Port-Royal.

Ironically, at the very moment that the French temporarily abandoned their colony in Acadia, the English settled permanently in North America. In 1607 the Virginia Company established Jamestown. As an arena of future European colonization, northeastern North America now belonged to the French and the English, the Portuguese having long abandoned their interest in the area.

Founding of Quebec

In 1608 Champlain and Gravé led an expedition back to Quebec, where they could control access to the interior and prevent competition from other traders. Champlain, as de Monts' agent, constructed a *habitation*, a collection of wooden buildings built in the form of a quadrangle and surrounded by a stockade and moats. The *habitation* stood in the shadow of a towering cliff above it, at the very point where the St. Lawrence suddenly narrows before widening out once more. (*Kebek* is the Algonquian word for "strait" or "narrow passage.") Champlain's post became the heart of the first permanent French settlement in present-day Canada.

In hindsight, one might ask why was there not any opposition by the native people to the French occupation of Quebec. Like the Spanish, Portuguese, English, and Dutch, the French believed that, as a Christian nation, they could simply claim all non-Christian lands. Yet while most Europeans believed themselves to be the representatives of the world's superior civilization, with the right to occupy others' territory, the Indians in northeastern North America regarded the land as theirs. Each Montagnais band around Tadoussac and Quebec, for example, occupied a specific territory; the boundaries were well known and usually well marked by recognizable geographical features. But the French were fortunate to have entered a war zone. The Montagnais welcomed the French traders armed with muskets, since they provided the Montagnais with security against future Iroquois raids. Their trading post at Quebec also ensured that the Montagnais could always obtain badly needed iron goods.

Gravé left Quebec with a load of furs in mid-September, leaving Champlain and twenty-seven others at the new post. Once again, the French were ill prepared for a severe Canadian winter. Twenty of the twenty-eight died, two-thirds from scurvy and one-third from dysentery. Seemingly indestructible, Champlain was himself smitten with scurvy but survived. The following summer he set out to strengthen his relationship with the Algonquian Indians—the Montagnais around Quebec and the Algonquians, the Algonquian-speaking Indians of the Ottawa valley.

Early French-Indian Policy

The French had no sooner established Quebec than the Algonquians, their Indian trading partners, wanted Champlain to join their war parties. Since he depended on them for furs, Champlain obliged. In 1609 he joined the Algonquians and several Hurons in an attack on the Iroquois to the southwest. The arquebuses, French guns used by Champlain and two of his men, frightened the Iroquois, who lost the battle of Lake Champlain. The next summer Champlain and his Indian allies again defeated a Mohawk war party near the mouth of the Richelieu River, forcing them to withdraw. Another important reason helps to account for the departure of the Iroquois: no longer were they cut off from European trade goods once Dutch traders navigated the Hudson River in present-day New York State.

The Franco-Algonquian alliance proved invaluable to the French. From the Algonquians the French learned much in the early years of the colony. They adapted themselves to the Indians' means of transport, since apart from a few footpaths around Quebec, one could only travel by boat, particularly in the birchbark canoes used by the natives. When the rivers froze in the winter, the French had to use Indian snowshoes and toboggans. When they used snowshoes the French wore moccasins. They also relied on the native food supply. As late as 1643 Quebec was almost entirely dependent on Indian hunting for its fresh meat supply. The Algonquians taught the French how to grow maize or Indian corn, beans, pumpkins, and squash on the clearings left behind by the departed Iroquoians. From the Indians they learned how to make maple sugar and to gather wild berries, particularly the blueberry. The Algonquians also trained the first Frenchmen how to survive in the interior.

In Brazil the French had begun the practice of sending young men to live with the Brazilians to learn their languages and way of life. Champlain also wanted cultural go-betweens, or as they would become known in Canada coureurs de bois [literally "runners of the woods"] men who would cement France's economic and political alliance with the Algonquians and their allies, the Hurons.

In 1610 Champlain arranged to have a young eighteen-year-old Frenchman who had already lived in Quebec for two winters (probably Etienne Brûlé) to go with the Hurons, with whom the French wanted to open direct trade. Brûlé no doubt was the first European to visit the Huron country and to see Lakes Huron, Ontario, Superior, and Erie.

In return, Champlain, on the natives' insistence, took Savignon, brother of a Huron headman and roughly the same age as Brûlé, into his custody. From Savignon the French learned about the Huron Confederacy, an alliance of several tribes with a population of thirty thousand.

Quebec's founder spent the following year in France lobbying for his colony's survival. Truly, without Champlain at this stage there would have been no New France. In late 1612 Henri de Bourbon, Prince de Condé, a cousin of the king, obtained the fur trade monopoly and the title Viceroy of New France. Condé confirmed Champlain office as his lieutenant in the colony; this in effect (but not in title) made Champlain the governor of New France. The faithful de Monts, still loyal to Canada, became a stockholder in Condé's new company, the Rouen and St. Malo Company. At last, Champlain brought some sort of order to the fur trade and had kept the tiny trading post at Quebec alive.

Champlain made his last wilderness journey in the summer of 1615, one to strengthen the Franco-Huron alliance. As traffic increased on the

Ottawa River the Iroquois raids had reached a new intensity, and the Algonquins now badly needed allies. In return for their assistance, the Algonquins now permitted the Hurons to travel down-river to trade directly with the French. In 1615 the Algonquins also allowed the French passage along the Ottawa, a privilege denied them but four years earlier.

While in Huronia, Champlain concluded treaties of friendship with individual Huron headmen, affirming French support in their wars provided that the Hurons traded with them. By joining a large war party of Hurons and Algonquins against the Iroquois, he convinced the Hurons of his concern for their well-being. After being wounded in the attack, Champlain wintered in the Hurons' country and won their trust. Henceforth, Frenchmen could live securely among their Huron allies. Although they still had to pay tolls to the Algonquins for using the Ottawa River, the Huron took their furs to New France. By the 1620s the Hurons supplied from one-half to two-thirds of all the furs obtained by the French.

Slow Growth of New France

The colony, which only really existed to collect furs, grew slowly. During the winter of 1620–21 sixty people lived at Quebec. The private trading companies, whose interest lay in profits, not colonization, failed to meet the requirement of their monopoly grant that they bring out settlers to New France. But, in their defence, it must be said that settlement posed a real problem. Thanks to the co-operation of the Indians, the fur trade required few Europeans, and there was no incentive for Europeans to settle in the northern colony. To whom could the would-be farmers sell their produce? No market existed.

New France was still pathetically small when compared to the other European colonies in the New World located in areas of greater agricultural potential. The English colony of Virginia—whose economy was based on tobacco, a crop that attracted a great deal of capital and required many immigrants—developed rapidly. By 1627 Virginia alone had two thousand inhabitants, or twenty times New France's population. New France simply did not have the economic attraction of Virginia or even of the newly-established Dutch colony of New Netherlands in the Hudson River valley, which had two hundred settlers by 1625. By allying the French with the Hurons in the interior, however, Champlain had built up the necessary network for the fur trade.

The Hurons' country was the focal point of the St. Lawrence–Great Lakes trading system and made New France possible. Each year the Hurons traded their large surpluses of corn for the northern Algonquians' furs. With the development of the fur trade the northern hunting peoples spent more time trading or trapping beavers and less time hunting and fishing. Huronia became, more than ever before, the granary for the northern Algonquians.

Regional trade, largely built upon pre-European contact trading patterns, thus grew rapidly to meet the demands of the French fur traders. The Indians, however, had the upper hand in the exchange. From the very beginning the French traders had to learn the Hurons' language, since few Hurons acquired any French.

The Company of One Hundred Associates

In 1627 the French government, after observing the English and Dutch successes in America, wanted to end the colony's total dependency on one industry. A period of disorder afflicted France from 1610 (the year of the assassination of King Henry IV) until peace was restored in 1624. In that year Louis XIII handed the government over completely to the capable Cardinal Richelieu, who for eighteen years (1624–42) was the master of France. The cardinal worked to unify France under the Crown and to make France the leading nation in Europe, with strong colonies overseas.

49

Richelieu intended to extend French overseas commerce and authority by organizing several monopolistic trading companies. Mercantilism, the dominant economic philosophy of Europe, held that colonies existed to enrich the mother country by exporting raw materials and by importing finished manufactured products from the mother country. Like every other European government of the day, the French looked upon overseas colonies as areas to be exploited. Only French ships could carry the goods to and from the colony. From its overseas colonies Richelieu believed that France could draw strength and riches to increase its stature in Europe.

The Cardinal sponsored a new company, the "Hundred Associates" (barred to Protestants), to develop and exploit New France's resources and to encourage missionary activity. The Hundred Associates had the active support of the French government and obtained working capital from one hundred investors. This meant that nearly two-fifths of the shareholders were government office-holders, one-fifth merchants, and the remainder nobles and clergy. The company became the seigneur (discussed in chapter five) of all the lands claimed by France in North America; it had a monopoly on all commerce, including the fur trade, and the right to cede land to settlers in seigneurial tenure. In return for its privileges the company promised to populate New France by bringing out four thousand settlers, all French and Roman Catholic, within fifteen years. The charter also stipulated that all baptized Indians would enjoy the same rights of citizenship as did the colonists from France. Never before had a French company been given so much.

Unfortunately for New France, the project began at the worst possible time—war had just broken out with England. In 1627 the Kirke brothers, English privateers, seized Tadoussac and captured off Gaspé the French ships bringing four hundred settlers to New France. Returning in 1629 they attacked Quebec. Cut off from France, his provisions long exhausted, Champlain and his starving garrison surrendered in July 1629. Champlain and the ailing Gravé left Quebec in the general French evacuation.

Still New France's greatest lobbyist and champion, Champlain urged the French ambassador in England to begin negotiations for the return of Quebec. For three years the St. Lawrence remained closed to the French, which meant heavy losses for the Hundred Associates. The Anglo-French discussions dragged on and on. Charles I, who had married Louis XIII's sister, refused to hand back the captured territories until his French brother-in-law paid his sister's full dowry. Finally, when Louis XIII agreed to hand over all sums outstanding, the English left the St. Lawrence and Port-Royal in Acadia. In 1632 the Hundred Associates could finally resume the program established in 1627. Returning to New France in 1633, Champlain made one last major initiative. He founded a post above Quebec in 1634 at Trois-Rivières.

Champlain deserves full credit for establishing New France, the Laurentian colony in northeastern North America. With the founder's death on Christmas Day, 1635, the effective leadership in the fur-trading colony passed into the hands of the religious orders, in particular, the Jesuits.

Contribution of the French Religious Orders

French religious orders came to the colony to convert the Indians to Christianity and to assimilate them into French life. The first French missionaries assigned the task were the Récollets, who were a branch of the Franciscan Friars, a community without a rich financial base. Three Récollet priests and a lay brother arrived at Quebec in 1615. Five years later they opened a monastery at Notre-Dame des Anges, several kilometres from Quebec. The Récollets initially hoped that their seminary would train a native clergy for the colony, but they found the Indians had no desire to be made into Frenchmen. The seminary soon closed for lack of students and funds.

In an attempt to solve their financial problems the Récollets sought to collaborate with the Society of Jesus, a wealthy and powerful order founded by Ignatius Loyola a century earlier. From 1625 to 1629 the Jesuits assisted the Récollets in establishing missions in New France. This highly disciplined order, renowned for its ability to attract able and often well-born candidates, was also known for its willingness to take on the most dangerous tasks. Jesuits had already served in the front lines of the Roman Catholic church's campaign to reclaim Protestant Europe. These highly educated men would write some of the best contemporary descriptions of New France in their *Relations,* or reports back to France.

After the English occupation of New France, Cardinal Richelieu gave the Jesuits a monopoly of the Canadian mission field. Their work now began in earnest. Yet when they began a school for Indian children, they encountered the same problems as the Récollets.

Simply enlisting native students was difficult. Parents refused to let their children go, and finally the priests had to give presents to the parents in order to gain students for the seminary. Of these, many ran away and others became ill and died. The deaths increased the parents' resistance to their children's schooling, as did the French custom of physically punishing children; this practice was foreign to the Indians' methods of childrearing.

When Ursuline nuns arrived in the colony in 1639 they came with the specific purpose of instructing Indian girls. Over the next thirty years the nuns succeeded in teaching a few girls to read and write. It was difficult work. In 1668 Marie de l'Incarnation, foundress of the Ursuline Order in New France, wrote: "We have observed that of a hundred that have passed through our hands we have scarcely civilized one. We find docility and intelligence in these girls but, when we are least expecting it, they clamber over our wall and go off to run with their kinsmen in the woods, finding more to please them there than in all the amenities of our French house."

51

THE JESUITS' WORK WITH THE ALGONQUIANS

The Jesuits learned the Indian languages, introduced schools, and provided medical care to the Indians. To help fight the strange new diseases like smallpox and measles, the Indians eventually accepted the nuns' invitation to care for the sick. The Indians left the aged and the infirm at what they called the "house of death" (since the mortality rate was so high) and thus avoided killing or abandoning to die those who could not travel to the hunting territories. The nuns admired the charity with which the natives cared for each other and their patience when ill.

Like the Récollets before them, the Jesuits supported the idea of encouraging the Algonquians to settle down. They believed a nomadic life to be contrary to the laws of the church and incompatible with Christian life. The Jesuits also felt that the Algonquians would accept the new religion more easily if they would live in the French manner, in settled agricultural communities.

To accomplish their goal the Jesuits hired workmen to help the Montagnais clear farmland and build a small village at the foot of the cliff of Cap aux Diamants (where Jacques Cartier's men had mined for diamonds

52

National Archives of Canada / C5855.

Jesuit preaching to the Algonquian Indians of the Great Lakes. These Indians called the French Wa-mit-ig-oshe, men who wave a piece of wood over their heads. The drawing is by C.W. Jefferys (1869-1951), a Canadian artist who is well-known for his visual reconstructions of Canadian history.

a century earlier), about seven kilometres above Quebec. Upon receiving the fortune of the Noël Brulart de Sillery, formerly a minister and ambassador of the king, the Jesuits gave the name St. Joseph de Sillery to the reserve of approximately thirty-five hundred hectares.

By 1641 the Sillery reserve contained some thirty families and more than 150 baptized converts. A few Montagnais lived in completed one-room houses and the others in bark wigwams. Some Algonquians from Trois-Rivières joined them in clearing land and planting crops. But the constant threat of Iroquois attacks checked the development of the community. Throughout the 1640s the village men frequently left for long periods on war parties, at which time those left behind abandoned the village for the safety of Quebec. Sillery then became a ghost town. Disease also struck, carrying away a number of the important converts. The village itself was divided into a Christian faction and a somewhat larger non-Christian faction. An Iroquois raid in 1655 and a fire in 1656 that destroyed the mission residence, the church, and most of the small houses finished off the Indian village of Sillery. It never recovered. By 1663 French farmers occupied most of the Sillery land.

The Jesuits promoted their work in their annual reports or *Relations*, publications that helped the order to hold the interest of Roman Catholic supporters in France. In 1635 the Jesuits established a college for Amerindian boys at Quebec, and classes began that year. This school was the first institution of higher learning north of Mexico, having been established a year before Harvard University was founded in Massachusetts. Four years later, in 1639, the Jesuits encouraged the Ursulines and the *Soeurs Hospitalières* (the Hospital nuns of Dieppe) to begin a school for girls and a hospital at Quebec.

53

Originally, these institutions were also established for the Indians. The church, in effect, became the second industry of the colony. The Jesuits, Ursulines, and the Hospital nuns came in number to serve the Indians and in turn brought out *engagés*, or indentured workers on three-year contracts, to help them. These newcomers created a market for agricultural produce in the colony. Upon being discharged some *engagés* stayed and began to farm.

THE FOUNDING OF MONTREAL

The church supported the colony and helped to expand settlement. The Jesuits worked with the Société de Notre-Dame de Montréal, an association of priests and laymen, founded in 1639 in Paris. The Société initially raised a considerable amount of money and obtained a grant for the island of Montreal.

Paul de Chomedey de Maisonneuve, a thirty-three-year-old career soldier, stepped forward to command the first settlers sent out to establish the colony of Ville-Marie. At Quebec the citizens did their best to discourage Maisonneuve and his band of forty colonists from continuing up the St. Lawrence, now beset by Iroquois attacks. The zealot replied that if every tree on the island be changed into an Iroquois his honour would still oblige him to found the new religious colony on the island of Montreal.

The Société de Notre-Dame believed that a mission settlement remote and independent from the main settlement at Quebec would attract Indians to settle permanently around it, once it was endowed with a church, a school, and a hospital. Then the Indians could be converted to Christianity. The organizers chose the former site of Hochelaga, located at the confluence of the Ottawa and the St. Lawrence rivers, and one easy of access for the Algonquian-speaking tribes.

In 1642 the settlers reached their destination and established farms on the fields cleared by the Hochelegans. Despite an initial burst of enthusiasm, Ville-Marie grew slowly. The only sizeable influx of new settlers, one hundred in all, arrived in 1653. Two factors prevented the expansion of the remote colony of Montreal: the Société's quick loss of enthusiasm for its missionary enterprise and raids by the Iroquois. Since the colony was situated above the Mohawk invasion route—the Richelieu River, it was threatened in the early 1640s with the possibility of becoming totally isolated. The Société de Notre-Dame de Montréal's objective of evangelizing and teaching the Algonquians how to farm could not be achieved at this time and was abandoned.

54

The Habitants' Company

The Company of One Hundred Associates never overcame the effects of the English occupation of Quebec between 1629 and 1632. By the early 1640s it stood on the verge of bankruptcy, heavily in debt and unable to supply the funds needed to maintain and to defend the colony. The leading settlers in 1645—really a small group of businessmen, fifteen at most—took matters into their own hands and formed the Habitants' Company. While reserving its rights of ownership over all of New France, the Company of One Hundred Associates ceded to the habitants the fur monopoly. Henceforth, however, the Habitants' Company had to pay the costs of Canada's administration. This included payments to the governor and the military officers for the maintenance of forts and garrisons, the upkeep of the clergy, and the responsibility of bringing twenty male and female settlers to the colony each year.

New France in the Mid-1640s

In 1645—a decade after Champlain's death—the French colony in the valley of the St. Lawrence contained six hundred residents and a few hundred *engagés*. Clerical intervention in the 1630s had greatly increased the population, but it still remained smaller than that of a single large Iroquoian village. This slow growth is puzzling when one considers the advantages of emigrating from France. Landless peasants or workers settling in Canada could obtain all the land they wished; moreover, they could enjoy privileges denied their class in France and avoid paying royal taxes.

Nevertheless, emigration from France to New France was unpopular. No doubt France's domestic problems—the civil war and religious strife of the 1630s and 1640s—had prevented some from leaving. Certainly, the state provided little encouragement. Protestants had little incentive to establish themselves in the colony, since after 1627 neither Protestant worship nor teaching was permitted in Canada by the terms of the Hundred Associates' charter.

The obvious discomfort of emigrating also discouraged many. First, the would-be colonists faced the dangers of crossing the North Atlantic, a voyage that took anywhere from three weeks to more than three months. On these voyages food supplies sometimes ran out, if headwinds continued too long; then scurvy took its toll. (If fewer than ten percent of the ship's company died during a crossing the captain considered the voyage most successful).

The peasants and artisans who arrived safely faced the challenge of clearing the virgin forest. At best, a man could clear one hectare in a year. Much of this difficult work had to be performed in the summer months, when the black flies and mosquitos made life intolerable. On top of the hardships of crossing the north Atlantic and the difficulties of clearing land, the new arrivals faced the danger of Iroquois raids, which resumed in earnest in the 1640s. Every male capable of bearing arms—and many women—had to be ready at all times to fight for their lives.

All this having been said, emigrants did leave France in the 1630s and 1640s in the hundreds. They left for the French Antilles, for the islands of Martinique and Guadaloupe in particular, where, despite warfare with the local Carib Indians, employment could be had. Unlike the northern fur trade, tobacco and cotton required a great deal of unskilled labour. Within a decade the total white population of the French Antilles was estimated at seven thousand. Emigrants from France saw little economic opportunity in New France in the mid-1640s, and this is the real reason for its small population.

The fur trade had made the colony. New France depended upon the thousands of Algonquians and Hurons who hunted, trapped, prepared the beaver pelts, and carried them hundreds of kilometres to Quebec. Within a generation France had advanced a thousand kilometres into the interior, establishing a firm trading alliance with the Hurons. But in early 1649 it was doubtful whether New France, with a resident population of barely one thousand, could survive in the face of determined Iroquois attacks.

NOTE

[1] E. Pocquet, *Histoire de Bretagne*, vol. 5 p. 320; cited in Morris Bishop, *Champlain: The Life of Fortitude* (Toronto, 1963; first published 1948), p. 8.

BIBLIOGRAPHY

Marcel Trudel provides an overview of the period in his *The Beginnings of New France, 1524–1663* (Toronto, 1973). A shorter summary appears in W.J. Eccles' *The Canadian Frontier, 1534–1760* (New York, 1969). His later work, *France in America* (New York, 1972), also contains information on the early French colonies in the Caribbean, as well as in New France and Acadia. Allen W. Trelease reviews the Dutch colony along the Hudson River, in *Indian Affairs in Colonial New York: The Seventeenth Century* (Port Washington, N.Y., 1971; first published 1960). Contemporary maps and illustrations appear in André Vachon, in collaboration with Victorin Chabot and André Desrosiers, *Dreams of Empire: Canada Before 1700* (Ottawa, 1982).

56 For Indian affairs, Bruce Trigger's *The Children of Aataentsic: A History of the Huron People to 1660*, vol. 1 (Montreal, 1976) is invaluable; a shorter summary appears in his Canadian Historical Association Booklet (no. 30), *The Indians and the Heroic Age of New France* (1977). An older study, A.G. Bailey's *The Conflict of European and Eastern Algonkian Cultures, 1504–1700* (Toronto, 1969; first published 1937), is still valuable, particularly for the information on the Micmac and Montagnais. Ruth Holmes Whitehead and Harold McGee's *The Micmac: How Their Ancestors Lived Five Hundred Years Ago* (Halifax, 1983) provides a good popular review of the Micmac; see also Virginia Miller's "The Micmac: A Maritime Woodland Group," in *Native Peoples: The Canadian Experience*, edited by R. Bruce Morrison and C. Roderick Wilson (Toronto 1986), pp. 324–352. Carolyn Gilman's *Where Two Worlds Meet: The Great Lakes Fur Trade* (St. Paul, Minn., 1982) covers the economic aspects of early Indian-European contact. An excellent article written for the Italian Canadian Studies Association is John A. Dickinson's "Les Amérindiens et les débuts de la Nouvelle-France," *Canada ieri e oggi* (Bari, Italy, 1986), vol. 3, pp. 87-108.

Two well-written biographies of Champlain are available: Morris Bishop, *Champlain: The Life of Fortitude* (Toronto, 1963 first published 1948); and *Samuel de Champlain: Father of New France* (Boston, 1972). Marcel Trudel has also contributed the entry on Champlain in the *Dictionary of Canadian Biography*, vol. 1: 1000–1700 (Toronto, 1966), pp. 186–99. For an understanding of Champlain's Indian policy one must, however, supplement these three studies with Trigger's *Children of Aataentsic*. Champlain's "real" birth date (most likely around 1580, not 1570 or 1567) is analyzed by Jean Liebel, in "On a vieilli Champlain," *Revue d'histoire de l'Amérique française*, 32,2 (septembre 1978): 229–37.

Valuable sources on the subject of the Algonquians in the St. Lawrence valley include James P. Ronda's "The Sillery Experiment: A Jesuit-Indian Village in New France, 1637–1663," *American Indian Culture and Research Journal*, 3, 1(1979): 1–18; and Cornelius J. Jaenen, "Problems of Assimilation in New France, 1603–1645," *French Historical Studies*, 4, 3 (1966):

265–89, themes that he has elaborated upon in *Friend and Foe: Aspects of French-Amerindian Cultural Contact in the Sixteenth and Seventeenth Centuries* (Toronto, 1976). Olive Dickason's *The Myth of the Savage and the Beginnings of French Colonialism in the Americas* (Edmonton, 1984) and John Webster Grant's *Moon of Wintertime: Missionaries and the Indians of Canada in Encounter since 1534* (Toronto, 1984) are both very useful for their review of missionary activities in New France. Biographical articles appear in *Dictionary of Canadian Biography*, vol. 1, see in particular the sketches of Jacques Noël, p. 520; François Gravé du Pont, pp. 345–346; Pierre Du Gua de Monts, pp. 291–295; Etienne Brûlé, pp. 130–133; Marie Guyart, dite Marie de l'Incarnation, pp. 351–359; and Paul de Chomedey de Maisonneuve, pp. 212–222.

Extremely valuable maps of early Acadia and of New France are contained in vol. 1 of the *Historical Atlas of Canada*, edited by R. Cole Harris (Toronto, 1987).

57

CHAPTER FOUR

The Resistance of the Iroquois

58   Although both the Huron and the Iroquois confederacies belonged to the same linguistic family and shared the same culture, the early chroniclers of New France praised the former and condemned the latter. In any discussion of the Iroquois and Hurons' struggle, therefore, one must keep in mind the highly biased nature of the written source materials. It is unfortunate that we have no contemporary accounts written by the Iroquois. Yet we do have a story, handed down by word of mouth from generation to generation, of the Iroquois' perception of their enemies. The account, in several variations, relates the founding of the League of the Five Nations or Iroquois Confederacy, which became the Six Nations after the Tuscaroras joined them in the 1720s. It provides a rich source of information about the values of the "People of the Longhouse," as the Iroquois called themselves.

Formation of the League of the Iroquois

The founders of the Five Nations Confederacy conceived it as the nucleus of a much larger union. Historians such as Paul A.W. Wallace now generally agree that it was established by the late fifteenth century. Wallace has carefully studied various versions of the myth and consulted with members of the Six Nations to write *The White Roots of Peace*, about how Dekanahwideh, the culture hero of the Iroquois, brought the Great Peace to Iroquoia.[1]

The core of the narrative begins with Dekanahwideh's arrival in the country of the Iroquois. The Iroquoian nations at this time constantly raided each other's villages and also suffered attacks by the powerful Algonquians. All order and public safety had broken down, and Dekanahwideh found his way blocked by a notorious cannibal. Immediately the peacemaker went to the cannibal's house and, finding it empty, climbed onto the bark roof and waited. Lying prone on the roof he peered straight down through the the smoke hole to create his own reflection on the surface of the kettle full of water below.

When the cannibal returned he placed his victim's body in his cooking pot. But while bending over the kettle he saw Dekanahwideh's face reflected from the water's surface. Thinking the image of wisdom and strength was his own he became greatly disturbed, because he had never dreamed that he possessed such noble qualities. He stepped back and began to think about the brutal life he had been leading. In revulsion the cannibal emptied the kettle of its human contents and resolved henceforth to stop his killing. Just then Dekanahwideh came down from the roof and explained the Great Spirit's Message of Peace and Power. When the cannibal accepted it, Dekanahwideh gave him the name, Hiawatha, which meant, "He Who Combs," for he would comb the twists out of peoples' perverted minds.

59

The lawgiver and his spokesman then visited the Five Nations and, with varying degrees of difficulty, persuaded them to come under the Tree of Peace and form a union called the Kanonsionni, the Longhouse. Dekanahwideh then planted the Tree of Peace, a great white pine with white healthy roots extending to the four corners of the earth, so that all nations of good will could follow the roots to their source and take shelter with the others under the great tree. On top he placed an eagle to warn of danger. Then he put antlers on the heads of the fifty chiefs representing the Five Nations and gave them the Words of the Law.

A new political structure was thus erected to maintain peace among the Iroquois and gradually to draw the surrounding tribes into the League. In Iroquois eyes, the fact that the Huron refused the tree of peace proved that they were an evil, hostile people.

Knowledge of the teaching credited to Dekanahwideh helps to explain the Iroquois' feelings of superiority to their neighbours: it was among the Iroquois that the tree of peace had first been planted. The Five Nations stood at the centre of the universe. In the late 1640s this knowledge gave them great self-confidence and sense of purpose.

The Missionaries' Arrival in Huronia

At the moment of French–Indian contact in the seventeenth century the Hurons and the Iroquois were at war. A desire for war honours and prestige no doubt contributed to their hostility. Participation in a war party, if successful, raised a man's standing in his clan and village. It increased his chances of an advantageous marriage and his hopes of one day becoming a village leader. Moreover, the necessity of avenging the dead led to more warfare, since the Iroquois and the Hurons believed the souls of the dead could not rest in peace until revenge had been secured. This led to an escalation of the feuding between the two hostile Iroquoian groups.

With the arrival of the Europeans, economic motives joined those of prestige and the blood feud as causes of Indian warfare. Both the Iroquois and the Hurons needed a steady supply of furs in order to buy the European trade goods they now badly wanted for a better life.

The struggle between the Iroquois and the Hurons was of immense importance to New France. By the 1620s the Huron had become the French's principal economic partners, exchanging corn and European goods with the neighbouring Algonquians for furs. These Indians in turn traded as far north as James Bay and with the Great Lakes Algonquians who traded along the shores of Lakes Michigan and Superior.

The goods the Huron obtained from trade stimulated the development of a richer culture. As elsewhere on the continent, the fur trade led to a greater development of their culture. The Hurons decorated their pottery with more complicated patterns and used iron knives to produce more intricate bone carving. Their rituals became more elaborate.

60

THE JESUITS AND THE HURONS

Shortly after the French established an economic alliance with the Hurons, they secured the right to send Roman Catholic ministers to Huronia. Champlain despatched Récollet missionaries in 1615, and then the Jesuit fathers who entered Huronia in 1627. As a necessary pre-condition for the Franco-Huron alliances' renewal the French insisted after the English occupation of Quebec that the Hurons allow French Jesuits to live in Huronia. Reluctantly, the Hurons agreed. In 1634 Jean de Brébeuf and two companions reopened the Huron mission. The order spared none of its resources in its effort to build up the mission. In addition to priests, they used French lay workers (*donnés*) whose contracts assured them of lifetime support but no wages.

Once the Jesuits thoroughly mastered the Huron language they were able to communicate their ideas to the would-be converts. They also used non-verbal methods: pictures of holy subjects or of the sufferings of lost souls; religious statues; coloured beads as prizes for successful memorization; ceremonies, chants, and processions on holy days or on such occasions as baptisms, marriages, and funerals. They decorated the churches with crosses, bells, and candles, creating a colourful visual display. Yet, in this initial period their efforts to welcome Hurons to the church led to few conversions. The Jesuits made some progress, but the gulf between the two societies remained very great.

Essentially the problem was that, for the Indian, the meaning of existence was to maintain harmony with nature. Their sacred stories explained
the fundamental relationships of the universe: the relations between man
and earth, between man and animals, between the sun and the moon,
between sickness and health. Christianity differed from the Hurons' religion in viewing the world as provisional, one preparatory to the new
order of God's kingdom. John Webster Grant, the Canadian religious
historian, wrote that if the Indians' religious symbol was the circle, the
Christian's "might well be an arrow running from the creation of the world
through God's redeeming acts in history to the final apocalypse."[2] The
two world views thus clashed.

To gain a Huron audience, the Jesuits emphasized the similarities between the Hurons' faith and their own. They pointed out that both believed
in a supernatural power that influenced their lives, one which the Hurons
located in the sun or sky and the Jesuits in heaven. Both Huron shamans
and Roman Catholic priests encouraged personal contact with the supernatural. Every Huron—especially a young man at puberty—was expected,
through fasting and a vision quest, to find his own guardian spirit. The
Jesuits similarly encouraged spiritual quests and valued fasts and vigils.
The common reliance on prayer revealed a shared conviction that divine
power controlled warfare, caused rain or drought, and gave health or
disease. Finally, both Jesuits and Hurons accepted the idea of an afterlife;
for Indians it was a pleasant place where life continued essentially as on
earth, and for Christians it was heaven.

61

These common elements aside, the differences between the two religions
were enormous. The chief difference lay in the Christian insistence that
only one deity ruled the universe, in contrast to the Hurons' belief that
many supernatural beings existed. The Jesuits, even when they had mastered the language, found it difficult to translate many terms, particularly
their theological ideas, such as that of the Trinity and the Incarnation.

Marriage was definitely a controversial matter. The Jesuits found the
Hurons' sexual behaviour aberrant. Among the Hurons divorce was easy
and frequent, in contrast with the Jesuits' ideal of the indissolubility of
marriage. Since Huron children by custom belonged to the mother, divorce
did not endanger family stability—the Hurons did not see how lifetime
marriage was superior to their custom. Moreover, they could not understand the Jesuits' practice of sexual self-denial.

Human sinfulness and the need for salvation were also important areas
where the Jesuits found no common ground with the Huron. Of course,
the Indians distinguished between good and evil conduct, but they had
no concept similar to the missionaries' idea of universal guilt, of a fundamental inadequacy in human nature. Like most native North Americans, the Hurons believed that almost all people would experience the
same pleasant afterlife, regardless of how they had lived on earth. For the
Jesuits, heaven and hell existed. The only way to escape hell was through

Christianity. This concept of a place of torment proved very difficult to convey.

The Jesuits tried to convince the Hurons that biblical standards were worth accepting. They argued for some changes in the Huron culture: the curtailment of easy divorce; the observance of marriages binding for life; and an end to frequent feasts and an undue reliance on dreams. The Hurons perceptively saw, though, that the missionaries threatened to subvert their value structure and way of life, since the Jesuits would stop the rituals they regarded as essential to successful hunting, good health, and survival. As a Huron chief complained to Brébeuf: "You are talking of overthrowing the country."

62 NEW EPIDEMICS STRIKE HURONIA

The French brought more than European trade goods and a Christian missionary message with them. They unknowingly brought to Huronia diseases of European origin that devastated the Hurons and their neighbours. Although the nature of the first three epidemics in the mid-1630s is unknown, that of 1639 was smallpox. The epidemics killed more than half the Huron population, reducing it to ten thousand. The Hurons lived in communities that were half empty. Since old people and children had died in the greatest number, this meant that the Hurons lost much of their traditional religious lore, which tended to be a prerogative of the elderly. The death of so many children foretold a serious shortage of warriors in the next decade.

In the late 1630s the Jesuits suffered from the Hurons' belief that they were sorcerers who brought disease. The Hurons recognized three major sources of illness: natural causes, unfulfilled desires of a person's soul (alleviated by a form of dream-fulfillment), and witchcraft. It was not surprising that the Hurons blamed the disease on their visitors, which the last and most serious epidemic had not touched. The Jesuits' celibacy suggested that the "white shamans" were nurturing great supernatural power for the purposes of witchcraft. They seemed to be causing death by their incomprehensible rituals, since after they touched sick babies with drops of water, many died.

As the epidemics became more severe the Hurons' fear of the Jesuits increased. Longhouses and even whole villages refused entrance to them. The Hurons harassed and threatened the Jesuits and their workmen. On at least two occasions, in 1637 and 1640, general Huron councils discussed the death penalty for the missionaries or at least the possibility of forcing the sorcerers to return to the St. Lawrence valley. Yet they pursued neither course of action. Many of the leading chiefs realized that the Hurons had no other source of European goods than those from the French, and by the late 1630s they believed that they could not live without these goods. Since trading relations with the French had to be maintained, they tolerated the missionaries.

HURON CHRISTIAN CONVERTS

During the epidemics of the mid-1630s the missionaries under Jean de Brébeuf's direction worked in selected Huron villages, spending most of their time mingling with the villagers. Jérôme Lalemant, the new superior of the Huron mission, changed this policy in 1638. He constructed a permanent mission headquarters of stone and timber buildings. Begun in 1639, Sainte-Marie included residences, chapels, workshops, and a hospital within its fortified walls. Adjacent to Sainte-Marie the Jesuits cleared fields and planted crops.

63

Inspired by accounts of the Jesuits' missions in Paraguay in South America, Lalemant hoped that the Huron converts might be led to settle at Sainte-Marie and to adopt French customs. When they refused to leave their villages and abandon their clans, he established permanent Jesuit residences in the major Huron towns. The priests visited other villages on assigned circuits.

In the early 1640s conversions in number began. Several factors contributed to the increase in conversions. No doubt the Jesuits' continued explanations of the two faiths' common themes helped. The Jesuits' own unquestioned bravery during the Iroquois attacks influenced others to convert. Simple economics also influenced many Huron traders. As anthropologist Bruce Trigger has pointed out, French traders and government officials accorded the Christian Indians far greater honour and gave them additional presents at Quebec and Trois-Rivières. Another incentive to convert came from the French policy of selling guns only to those Indians who were baptized. In 1648, when only 15 percent of the Huron population had been baptized, more than half the traders who came to Trois-Rivières were already Christians or were receiving instruction.

Thanks to the dedicated efforts of the Jesuits, their stressing of the common bridges between the two faiths, and the obvious economic advantages of conversion, by 1646 the Huron Christian community numbered five hundred and was growing.

The development of a Christian faction in Huronia, however, seriously divided the community. The priests forbade converts to participate in public Huron feasts and celebrations, and they had to abandon all their traditional religious practices. To avoid involvement in native rituals, Christian warriors often refused to fight alongside traditionalists. Conversion on occasion also resulted in divorce and in the Christian warriors' expulsion from their wives' or mothers' longhouses.

The Final Struggle Between the Hurons and the Iroquois

At the very moment that disease weakened them and their internal cohesion was reduced by the growth of a Christian faction, the Hurons faced their greatest military threat from the Iroquois. The invitation issued to the Hurons to join the Five Nations had been refused. In the 1640s, with an increasing shortage of beaver pelts in their own territory, the Iroquois needed an increased supply to purchase European goods. The Huron country was adjacent to the fur-rich areas around the Upper Great Lakes that the western Iroquois wanted to exploit.

64

THE ESCALATION OF HOSTILITIES

The possession of guns made the Iroquois a much more formidable foe. Beginning about 1639 they began to obtain firearms from English traders in the Connecticut Valley and then directly from Dutch traders on the upper Hudson River. Much more readily than before, they could raid the tribes living to the north. The longer and heavier Dutch guns were superior to those sold by the French to Christian converts.

By the late 1640s the Iroquois had superiority in firearms. Bruce Trigger estimates that in 1648 the Huron probably had no more than 120 guns, while the Iroquois had more than 500. These early guns were clumsy to handle and in many ways were not that much superior to the bow and arrow, but their thunderous noise and ability to inflict mortal wounds made them a source of terror. They also increased the self-confidence of those who owned them.

The successful Iroquois attacks of the early 1640s contributed to the growth of a faction of Huron traditionalists prepared to end the Huron Confederacy's trading alliance with the French. These Hurons believed peace with their enemies—with whom they at least were closely allied in customs and speech—was preferable to cultural extinction by the Jesuits. In the end, however, the majority of the traditionalists mistrusted the Iroquois more than the French; they sided with the Christian Hurons in opposing the termination of the French alliance. The defeat of the anti-Jesuit Hurons ended organized resistance to the missionaries. Opposition to the Jesuits declined, and many of their former opponents listened to their message. By 1649 about one Huron in two had been baptized.

In mid-March 1649 the Iroquois brought the Jesuit experiment to an abrupt halt. Without warning, a large Iroquois army struck a small Huron village, killing or capturing all but ten of the four hundred people living there. They used the village as a base camp to destroy other settlements. Hurons who had been earlier captured and adopted by the Iroquois played a leading role in the attacks. The Hurons, together with the Iroquois, tortured the French priests they captured, regarding them as sorcerers responsible for the destruction of their country. Familiar with the frequent baptizing of dying children, the Hurons repeatedly baptized Father Jean de Brébeuf and Gabriel Lalemant (the nephew of Jérôme Lalemant, now the superior of all the Jesuits in Canada) with boiling water, then further tortured and finally executed them.

Over the course of the campaign seven hundred Hurons died or were captured. The attacks threw the surviving settlements into chaos. The Huron, seeing their position as untenable, burned their villages and within two weeks deserted them. Hunger and contagious diseases claimed many Huron refugees who spent the winter on Christian Island, just offshore from Huronia. A small number of survivors eventually accompanied the Jesuits to Quebec, where the order established a fortified mission for them on Ile d'Orléans, just east of the town. Others joined the Algonquians to the north. In the next few years a number of Hurons voluntarily joined the Iroquois, many of them becoming fully integrated members of the tribes into which they were adopted.

65

ADOPTION OF CAPTIVES

After the defeat of the Hurons the Iroquois attacked and dispersed other Iroquoian peoples: first the Petuns, then the Neutrals, and then the Eries. The Five Nations adopted large numbers of the captives, just as they had previously taken in many Hurons. On account of a serious depletion in their own numbers (through disease and frequent warfare) the Iroquois needed to find replacements. As the neighbouring Iroquoians had the same mixed economies of agriculture, hunting and fishing, and shared related languages and similar religious beliefs, they were ideal candidates for adoption by the Five Nations.

The Fall of Huronia

The fall of Huronia greatly disrupted the fur trade on which the colony's economy depended. Yet, as Bruce Trigger notes: "The situation would have been far worse for the French if the Huron traditionalists had been able to conclude an alliance with the Iroquois."[3] The diversion of furs to

66

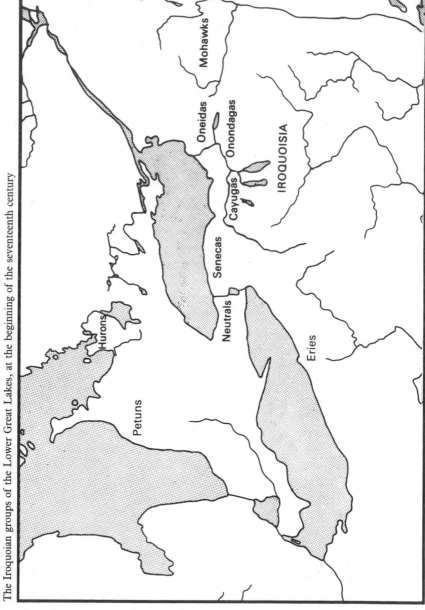

The Iroquoian groups of the Lower Great Lakes, at the beginning of the seventeenth century

Trudel, *Introduction to New France*, p. 28.

the Dutch on the Hudson River and the bypassing of the St. Lawrence would have ruined the fur-trading colony. As it was, only in the short run did the dispersal of the Hurons hurt the colony's economy.

In the long run, the dispersal economically helped New France, since the Hurons were replaced as the suppliers of foodstuffs to the northern Algonquians. Historian John Dickinson has noted how a large market now existed for New France's agricultural products.[4] In the 1650s the majority of the *engagés* began to stay in the colony after their contracts had expired. Farming expanded, as did the French fur trade.

The French coureurs de bois (see chapter 3) began in 1653 to replace the vanquished Huron middlemen in the fur trade. They went inland to live with the Algonquians of the upper Great Lakes, or "Ottawa" as the French called them, and to take their furs to New France. In 1654 Médard Chouart Des Groseilliers and another Frenchman canoed into the interior, returning two years later with a rich cargo of furs. (Des Groseilliers' brother-in-law, Pierre-Esprit Radisson, accompanied him on later journeys, including one in 1659 to the far end of Lake Superior, where they heard of a "Bay of the North Sea," hundreds of kilometres to the north.) Canada depended on the export of beaver fur, and without it the colony could not have survived.

In the early 1650s New France suffered greatly and almost collapsed from the Iroquois attacks. A mere fifty men held Montreal, the advance guard of the settlements. Even at Trois-Rivières and at Quebec few went out to work their fields because of the ever-present danger. Between 1650 and 1653 thirty-two French settlers were killed by the Iroquois and twenty-two were captured. The Iroquois' use of guerilla war tactics, their avoidance of open combat in favour of ambush, and the speed and unexpected nature of their attacks demoralized many of the colonists. As Marie de l'Incarnation, the foundress of the Ursuline order in New France, recalled in a letter to her sister, the Iroquois "... made such ravages in their regions that we believed for a time that we should have to go back to France."

With the outbreak of war between the Iroquois and the Eries to the west, New France obtained a five-year truce with the Iroquois in the mid-1650s. However, fighting resumed in the late 1650s and early 1660s. For the French, the struggle took on the atmosphere of a holy war. By this time, though, the population had increased in number and the colony was no longer in such danger as it had been in the early 1650s. The population almost tripled, from 1050 permanent French residents at the end of 1651 to nearly 3300 in 1662. Thanks to new opportunities for farming in the colony, this increase was the highest for any ten-year period in the history of New France.

67

A RENEWAL OF THE IROQUOIS ATTACKS

In the late 1650s and early 1660s the colony developed effective measures against Iroquois attacks. A small detachment of soldiers patrolled the St. Lawrence from Trois-Rivières to Montreal, the most exposed settlement. The French organized militia units and erected stockades. They also came to realize that the Iroquois could best be fought using Indian tactics, and so adopted them.

The French took their first initiative against the Iroquois in the spring of 1660. The military force consisted of Adam Dollard Des Ormeaux, an ambitious young soldier recently arrived from France with sixteen other young Frenchmen, and Annaotaha, an experienced Huron warrior with several dozen warriors. They left Montreal with the intention of ambushing a small Iroquois war party on the Ottawa River. The Frenchmen and their Indian allies knew that each winter the Iroquois raided and hunted for furs in the Ottawa valley. They also hoped to trade with a large contingent of Ottawas who were expected to arrive that summer at Montreal.

To his horror, Dollard encountered an Iroquois invasion army. Instead of a small band of Iroquois hunters at Long Sault, northwest of Montreal, they faced three hundred warriors on their way to rendezvous with four hundred more who awaited them at the Richelieu River. The Iroquois besieged the hastily built Franco-Huron fort, then waited for reinforcements from the south before making the final assault. In the interim, some of the adopted Huron in the Iroquois camp persuaded a number of Huron with Dollard to join them. Since the French had turned over several Huron refugees to the Iroquois not long before, most of the Hurons felt no obligation to fight to the death.

Only five Frenchmen were alive when the Iroquois took the fort and one was tortured to death immediately. Although treated as prisoners, the Iroquois allowed the four surviving Hurons with the French to live, three of whom later escaped. From them the French learned of the incident.

Historian André Vachon has succinctly summarized the accomplishment of Dollard and his companions: they "diverted the Iroquois army temporarily from its objective in 1660, thereby allowing the settlers to harvest their crop and escape famine and allowing Radisson to reach Montreal safe and sound with a load of furs ..."[5] (In the late nineteenth and early twentieth centuries, French-Canadian historians resurrected Dollard as a national French-Canadian hero, and in French-speaking Quebec, May 24, or Victoria Day in English-speaking Canada, is known as Dollard Day).

The Iroquois raids continued. From 1660 to 1661, fifty-eight settlers were killed and fifty-nine captured. New France could not truly prosper unless the French stopped the Iroquois raids. Pierre Boucher, governor of Trois-Rivières, warned in 1663 of the constant danger: "... A wife is always uneasy lest her husband who left in the morning for his work, should be taken or killed and that never will she see him again."

68

Security finally came for the habitants when, in 1663, Louis XIV took control of the colony. The previous year he had sent one hundred troops and in 1665 dispatched another twelve hundred under veteran officers. The following year, in 1666, the French made two attacks on the Iroquois country in present-day New York State. On the second raid the French burned four Mohawk villages with all their winter food supply. Intimidated by the raid, the Iroquois who were also then involved in a war with the Susquehannock (Iroquoian-speaking Indians living in present-day Pennsylvania), made peace with the French in 1667. Twenty years of peace followed for New France. The truce finally allowed the colony to advance in the 1660s as dramatically as it had in the 1650s.

AN EARLY FRENCH IMMIGRANT

69

To put a human face on the immigrants who came to New France after the fall of Huronia and were able to enjoy the peace established by the truce of 1667, let us look at the experience of one man, Etienne Trudeau, of the city of La Rochelle in western France. This robust fellow, a master carpenter at eighteen, signed a contract for five years of military service in New France. Upon arrival in Montreal in 1659 he began service with the Sulpician Fathers, who had hired him. But three years later he and two others were ambushed by fifty Iroquois. They fought back bravely and survived the attack.

In 1667, the year of the Iroquois peace treaty, the now twenty-six-year-old Etienne married Adrienne Barbier, the daughter of a carpenter who was one of the original twelve colonists to arrive at Montreal in August 1642. Etienne and Adrienne had fourteen children; one child later settled in Louisiana, while three became voyageurs and went to the Great Lakes before their marriages. Etienne lived an active life as a farmer, carpenter, and stonemason. He died in 1712 at Montreal; his wife died several years later. Etienne Trudeau was the ancestor of all the Trudeaus of New France, including a ninth-generation descendant—Pierre Elliott Trudeau, prime minister of Canada from 1968 to 1979 and from 1980 to 1984.

The Iroquois and the French, 1667–1701

Very soon, the interests of the Five Nations and those of the French clashed, first in the west. To obtain furs the Iroquois sent raiding parties all the way to the Illinois country, but this activity interfered with French exploration of the Mississippi valley. The tribes in the Illinois refused to accept the Iroquois invitation to ally themselves with the Confederacy and turned to the French, who promised aid and protection. Each year relations between the Five Nations and the French became more discordant, as the Iroquois increased their raids against the Illinois Indians, now French allies.

At the same time that the Five Nations attacked the Illinois to the west, they attempted to improve their relations with the northern Algonquians in order to obtain their furs. This seriously troubled the French. The establishment of Hudson's Bay Company posts on James and Hudson Bays in the 1670s had already diverted some northern furs from the French. If the Five Nations took more furs from north of the Great Lakes, then New France would lose its leading export.

The Iroquois had colonized the north shore of Lake Ontario in the 1660s, and they used their settlements as bases for trading with the northern Algonquians. These developing trade links frightened the French, who established the post of Cataraqui or Frontenac (at present-day Kingston) in 1673 to control the trade at the eastern end of Lake Ontario. French policy north of the Great Lakes necessitated that the northern Algonquians be hostile to the Iroquois. Around 1680 the French also briefly maintained a fort at Niagara to control the trade at the western end of Lake Ontario.

The French themselves ended the truce with the Iroquois in the mid-1680s. They wanted the Five Nations to cease their attacks on the Illinois Indians and to put a stop to the shipment of northern Algonquians' furs to the English via the Iroquois. An attempted invasion of the Iroquois country in 1684 under the leadership of Governor Le Febvre de La Barre, proved a complete fiasco. When fever ravaged his troops and provisions ran out, he was forced to sign a humiliating peace treaty with the Iroquois, which led to his subsequent dismissal as governor.

In 1687 the French persuaded the Algonquians to join nearly two thousand French troops on a second expedition to the Iroquois country. The invaders burned a number of villages, destroyed cornfields, and looted graves. The war was now fully underway. In retaliation the Iroquois, supported by the English, in 1689 struck the French settlement at Lachine, about fifteen kilometres west of Montreal. According to a French account, fifteen hundred Iroquois laid waste the open country: "the ground was everywhere covered with corpses, and the Iroquois carried away six-score captives, most of whom were burned."

As in the early 1650s, Five Nations' warriors in the early 1690s prevented the French from farming, particularly in the area around Montreal. The habitants near Quebec had also to repell an English invasion fleet in 1690 (see chapter 6).

The early 1690s marked the high-water mark of the Iroquois' greatest success against the French, then their fortunes turned. The settlers (by necessity now skilled in the techniques of guerilla warfare) and fifteen hundred regular troops sent from France gained the upper hand. By 1693

J. Grasset S.t Sauveur inv: et del: J. Laroque Sculp:

Iroquois allant a la Decouverte

National Archives of Canada / C3165.

An eighteenth-century Iroquois warrior, an engraving of a sketch by Jacques Grasset St. Sauveur.

the Five Nations were suffering very heavy losses both from battle casualties and from disease; in the face of the Algonquians' attacks they could
no longer maintain their forward position on the north shore of Lake
Ontario. Their numbers fell from more than ten thousand in the 1640s to
less than nine thousand, despite massive adoptions of other Iroquoians.

IROQUOIS CHRISTIAN CONVERTS

The Iroquois were also weakened by the presence of Jesuit fathers in their
villages during the truce, especially in 1668–86. The priests attracted
Christian converts, particularly from among the Mohawks, to their mission
villages in the St. Lawrence valley. By 1682, 120–150 families moved to
the reserve at Sault Saint Louis (Caughnawaga) near Montreal, and by
1700 an established two-thirds of the Mohawks lived in Canada.

72

The formation of Christian factions among the Iroquois in present-day
New York State disrupted their communities. When ritual demanded, for
example, that Garakontié, a leading Christian convert, recite "the genealogy and origin of the Iroquois ... he always protested [the Jesuit *Relations* report] that what he was about to say was merely a formula which
is usually followed on such occasions, but that it was not true; in fine,
that all he would relate about the creation of the world was simply a story,
and that Jesus was the sole Master of our lives."

Many of the Jesuits' converts were recently adopted Huron and other
prisoners, a fact that indicates the Five Nations had not yet had enough
time to assimilate all of those they had hastily adopted. In the mid-1660s
several Jesuit missionaries established that adoptees constituted two-thirds
or more of those in many of the Iroquois villages. The recently adopted
Iroquois no doubt weakened the unity of the Five Nations' communities.

THE MIGRATION OF THE ALGONQUIANS SOUTHWARD

With the Five Nations in such a vulnerable state, the Algonquians migrated
southward from Lake Superior and the north shore of Lake Huron to
reoccupy extensive lands near the former Huron, Petun, and Neutral
homelands. By coming south the Algonquians acquired rich new hunting
and fishing grounds, and some acquired a new name. The English colonists
on the Atlantic Coast termed all the newcomers in the area bounded by
Lakes Ontario, Erie, and Huron either Chippewa or Ojibwa. But they
reserved a new name, Mississauga, for the Ojibwa on the north shore of

Lake Ontario. In 1640 the Jesuit fathers had first recorded the term *omisagai* (Mississauga) as the name of an Algonquian band near the Mississagi River on the northwestern shore of Lake Huron. For unknown reasons the French, and later the English, applied this name to all the Algonquians settling on the north shore of Lake Ontario. Only a tiny fraction of these Indians could have been members of the actual Mississauga bands, but once recorded in the Europeans' documents, the name was the one most commonly used. The Ojibwa, of course, continued to call themselves by their own name of "Anishinabeg," meaning men or human beings.

PEACE ESTABLISHED, 1701

The English made peace with the French in 1697. This truce led the Iroquois to consider once again their own conflict with the French. In 1700 they made an offer to the French, who convened a council with them at Montreal. Combat fatalities, the exodus of Roman Catholic converts to New France, and the inroads of disease had all greatly weakened the Iroquois. The Five Nations had approximately 2570 warriors in 1689 and by 1700 only 1230, or one-half their former number.

The Iroquois made peace with the French and thirteen western tribes in August 1701. To ensure the Iroquois' continued existence as a buffer between the English colonies and New France, the French allowed some northern furs to be traded with them. In turn the Iroquois promised their neutrality in any future colonial war between France and England.

In the short term the Iroquois had seriously hindered the expansion of New France. The very existence of the colony was in question after the dispersal of the Hurons, and the Iroquois raids in the early 1650s on the tiny French settlements in the St. Lawrence valley. Yet, in the long term the destruction of Huronia actually contributed to New France's growth. With the removal of the Hurons as the great provisioners to the Algonquians this export market opened to the French colonists. Agriculture finally became more profitable and New France began to grow in the late 1650s and early 1660s.

The French began in the same period to enter the interior themselves to trade directly for the Algonquians' furs. A new class of intermediaries, the coureurs de bois, arose—men who helped to reinforce the existing Franco-Algonquian alliance. Together the French and their Algonquian allies defeated the Five Nations in the late 1680s and 1690s. The peace treaty of 1701 marked the end of the great Iroquois resistance to French expansion.

NOTES

[1] Paul A.W. Wallace, *The White Roots of Peace* (Philadelphia, 1946). John C. Mohawk has written a "Prologue" to the most recent reprinting of *The White Roots of Peace* (Saranac Lake, New York, 1986), pp. xv-xxiii.
[2] John Webster Grant, *Moon of Wintertime: Missionaries and the Indians of Canada in Encounter since 1534* (Toronto, 1984), p. 24.
[3] Bruce G. Trigger, *Natives and Newcomers: Canada's "Heroic Age" Reconsidered* (Kingston, 1985), p. 335.
[4] John A. Dickinson, "Les Amérindiens et les débuts de la Nouvelle-France," *Canada ieri e oggi*. (Bari, Italy, 1986), vol. 3, p 100.
[5] André Vachon, "Dollard Des Ormeaux," in *Dictionary of Canadian Biography*, vol. 1 (Toronto, 1966), p. 274.

Related Readings

R. Douglas Francis and Donald B. Smith, *Readings in Canadian History: Pre-Confederation*, 2d ed. (Toronto, 1986), includes Bruce G. Trigger, "The French Presence in Huronia: The Structure of Franco-Huron Relations in The First Half of the Seventeenth Century," pp. 15–44. W.J. Eccles, "Society and the Frontier," pp. 85–101 outlines the Indians' influence on the French.

BIBLIOGRAPHY

A number of studies exist on the relationship of the People of the Longhouse and the French. William Fenton provides an overview in "The Iroquois in History," in *North American Indians in Historical Perspective*, edited by Eleanor Burke Leacock and Nancy Oestreich Lurie (New York, 1971), pp. 129–68. Bruce Trigger's summary in *Natives and Newcomers: Canada's 'Heroic Age' Reconsidered* (Montreal, 1985) is the most up to date. Francis Jennings reviews the period from the seventeenth century to 1744 in *The Ambiguous Iroquois Empire* (New York, 1984). A new study of the Iroquois and their relations with neighbouring Indian groups is Daniel K. Richter's and James H. Merrell's *Beyond the Covenant Chain: The Iroquois and their Neighbors in Indian North America, 1600–1800* (Syracuse, N.Y., 1987).

Paul A.W. Wallace relates the story of the founding of the League of the Iroquois in *The White Roots of Peace* (Philadelphia, 1946). A shorter version by the same author entitled "Dekanahwideh," appears in the *Dictionary of Canadian Biography*, vol. 1: 1000–1700 (Toronto, 1966), pp. 253–55. Christopher Vecsey comments on other versions in "The Story and Structure of the Iroquois Confederacy," *Journal of the American Academy of Religion*, 54 (1986): 79–106. Anthony F.C. Wallace, son of Paul

A.W. Wallace, has written a full study of one of the Iroquois tribes in *The Death and Rebirth of the Seneca* (New York, 1969).

A good short summary of the Jesuits' contact with the Hurons is contained in Henry Warner Bowden, *American Indians and Christian Missions* (Chicago, 1981), pp. 59–95. This can be supplemented by John Webster Grant's *Moon of Wintertime: Missionaries and the Indians of Canada in Encounter since 1534* (Toronto, 1984). S.R. Mealing has edited *The Jesuit Relations and Allied Documents* (Toronto, 1963), a one-volume anthology of selections from the *Jesuit Relations*. For additional French views of the Iroquois, see *Word from New France: The Selected Letters of Marie de l'Incarnation*, translated and edited by Joyce Marshall (Toronto, 1967).

Several articles are also very useful for an understanding of the French and the Iroquoians: John A. Dickinson, "Annaotaha et Dollard vus de l'autre côté de la palissade," *Revue d'histoire de l'Amérique française*, 35 (1981–82): 163–78; John A. Dickinson, "La guerre iroquoise et la mortalité en Nouvelle-France, 1608–1666," *Revue d'histoire de l'Amérique française*, 36 (1982–83): 31–54; John A. Dickinson's "Les Amérindiens et les débuts de la Nouvelle-France," in *Canada ieri e oggi* (Bari, Italy, 1986), vol. 3, pp. 87–108; Anthony F.C. Wallace, "Origins of Iroquois Neutrality: The Grand Settlement of 1701," *Pennsylvania History*, 24 (1957): 223–35; Richard Haan, "The Problem of Iroquois Neutrality: Suggestions for Revision," *Ethnohistory*, 27 (1980): 317–30. Daniel K. Richter, "War and Culture: The Iroquois Experience," *William and Mary Quarterly*, 3rd series, 40 (1983): 528–59; Daniel K. Richter, "Iroquois versus Iroquois: Jesuit Missions and Christianity in Village Politics, 1642–1686," *Ethnohistory*, 32 (1985): 1–16.

Marcel Trudel reviews the French colony from 1645 to 1663 in *The Beginnings of New France, 1524–1663* (Toronto, 1973). The best treatment of Dollard is that by André Vachon in the *Dictionary of Canadian Biography*, vol. 1, pp. 266–75. For the growth of settlement in New France during the 1640s and 1650s, see Lucien Campeau, "Le peuplement de la Nouvelle-France, operation civilisée," in *La vie quotidienne au Québec* (Sillery, Québec, 1983), pp. 107–23. The story of the Trudeau family in Canada appears in Thomas J. Laforest, *Our French-Canadian Ancestors* (Palm Harbour, Fla., 1981). Useful maps showing France's inland expansion appear in Volume 1 of the *Historical Atlas of Canada*, edited by R. Cole Harris (Toronto, 1987).

75

CHAPTER FIVE

Province de France

From the 1650s onward the small French colony in the valley of the St. Lawrence grew steadily. A new market for French farm produce had opened among the Algonquians after the scattering of the Hurons in 1649–50. French traders entered the interior to gather and bring out the furs, thus expanding the trade. Decades of warfare with the Iroquois forged a sense of unity among the settlers. More than seventy years of intermittent struggle with England's American colonies, from 1689 to 1760, also helped to fashion a new Canadian identity.

During the course of one decade the French Crown strengthened the colony's economic infrastructure and established a political structure that lasted nearly a century. Three men transformed New France politically between 1663 and 1672: King Louis XIV; Colbert, the king's minister of the marine; and Jean Talon, the first intendant, the official responsible for the civil administration of the colony. They tried to make the St. Lawrence valley into La Nouvelle France—a new France overseas—but the attempt failed. By the late seventeenth century the habits and the mentality of the French began to change in the North American setting. A new people, the *Canadiens*, emerged.

Colbert's Dream of a Compact Colony

In 1661 Louis XIV, at the age of twenty-two, assumed full responsibility for the control of his kingdom of eighteen million subjects. The supremely confident young man decided to act as his own prime minister as soon as Cardinal Mazarin, his chief advisor, died. Louis XIV became the Sun King, from whom all power descended and to whom everything returned. He believed himself God's lieutenant upon earth and wanted to command all of Europe's admiration.

Jean-Baptiste Colbert served as one of the king's most loyal advisers. Colbert, a draper's son, acted as Cardinal Mazarin's trusted agent in the last years of his life. The minister of the marine, or to use the more modern term, the minister of colonies, devoted himself entirely to the king.

As the minister responsible for France's overseas possessions, Colbert attempted to make mercantilism succeed. The colonies were to be used to increase France's strength and the glory of Louis xiv. From New France the minister wanted not only furs but also timber and ship masts (which France had to import from Scandinavia and Russia) and minerals. Finally, he worked to develop a trade relationship between New France, the French possessions in the Caribbean, and France itself. From the St. Lawrence valley the French could export fish, wheat, peas, and barrel staves to the French West Indies. In return, the islands would export rum, molasses, and sugar to France, which would then send its textiles and manufactured goods to Canada.

New France had to become more self-sufficient before the master plan could succeed. Colbert dreamed of making New France into a much more self-reliant, defensible colony, with a prosperous agricultural base in the St. Lawrence Valley and its own basic industries. The minister wanted it to become a "compact colony," one centred in the St. Lawrence valley, without unnecessary forts and outposts distant from the valley. He opposed western expansion. First, though, he had to make the new royal province capable of defending itself. The dispatch of regular troops in the mid-1660s, including one of the better units in the French army, the Carignan-Salières regiment of nearly eleven hundred men, accomplished this goal.

The Iroquois made peace in 1667, and upon the disbanding of the regiment in Canada, four hundred troops elected to stay in the colony. They were located at the colony's weakest point, along the Richelieu River between Lake Champlain and the St. Lawrence—the Iroquois' invasion route. With the establishment of peace, Colbert's programme to transform New France into a profitable and well-populated colony based in the St. Lawrence valley could begin.

Reform of the Seigneurial System

In fashioning this new royal province of France the minister of the marine reformed the seigneurial system. French immigrants to the valley of the St. Lawrence were familiar with the seigneurial system, since it was the basis of land tenure in France. Peasant settlers, or *censitaires*, depended on a seigneur, or lord, who in turn was himself a vassal of the king. Title to all the land rested with the king. To obtain his fief or estate the seigneur first declared himself a vassal of the king. The soil belonged to the seigneur, but the mineral or subsoil rights and all oak trees on the property belonged

77

TYPICAL LAYOUT OF A SEIGNEURIE

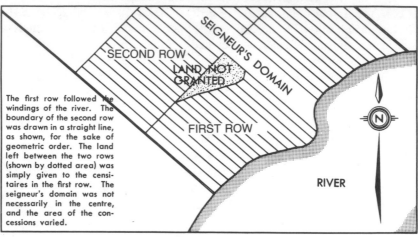

The first row followed the windings of the river. The boundary of the second row was drawn in a straight line, as shown, for the sake of geometric order. The land left between the two rows (shown by dotted area) was simply given to the censitaires in the first row. The seigneur's domain was not necessarily in the centre, and the area of the concessions varied.

Cornell, Hamelin, Ouellet, Trudel, *Canada, Unity in Diversity*, p. 56.

to the king. The system expanded after 1633–34, when the Company of One Hundred Associates (see chapter 3) granted more than fifty seigneuries of varying size along the St. Lawrence between Quebec and Montreal. In return for their large rectangular estates fronting on the river and usually extending into the foothills behind, the seigneurs undertook to bring out the *censitaires*, or habitants, as they were better known, who in turn paid them rent and dues.

Under royal government the intendant, among his other administrative duties, granted seigneuries and supervised the seigneurial system. Jean Talon, on his arrival in 1665, declared uncleared seigneuries forfeited. Actual occupancy became a condition of all future grants. Talon and his immediate successors also kept the size of the seigneuries relatively small to prevent the rise of a class of large landowners who might challenge royal authority. By 1700 the Crown had ceded almost all the river front from Montreal to below Quebec. Nearly two hundred seigneuries were open for rural settlement by 1715.

THE OBLIGATIONS OF THE SEIGNEURS AND THE CENSITAIRES

The intendant had to ensure that the seigneurs and *censitaires* fulfilled their mutual obligations. The seigneur had to clear some of his seigneury, maintain a manor house, and reside there or have a responsible person living there throughout the year. He had to make land grants of up to eighty hectares to any genuine settlers who applied. Finally, on part of their land they had to establish a flour mill for the use of their *censitaires*, and a few maintained a court of law to settle minor disputes.

The *censitaries* also had responsibilities. They had to clear the lands granted them and pay to their seigneur the *cens* (a small cash payment) and *rentes* (another money payment). Together, these two different charges amounted to less than one-tenth of the *censitaires'* annual income. In a few seigneuries they might also owe the seigneur the performance of the *corvée*, or compulsory work day. The Crown also required them to serve on a *corvée* for a day or two a year, doing general maintainance work on any seigneurial roads or bridges. By having accepted a grant of land the habitants had to maintain that portion of road which passed through their farms. As members of the militia, the *censitaires* also owed military service to the Crown.

Under royal government the settlers became part of a well-organized social unit, gaining free title to a tract of land. In time a manor house for the seigneur, a church, and a mill might be built on the seigneury. That many seigneurs in pioneer times lived and worked as their habitants did, blunted the social distinctions of Old France. In the colony's early years, in fact, a small number of enterprising and ambitious habitants themselves became seigneurs. However, as historians Louise Dechêne and Fernand Ouellet argue, social distinctions became important as the seigneuries became heavily settled, and the opportunity for social mobility declined.

79

Growth of Settlement

To populate the seigneuries Colbert and Jean Talon tried to build up the French population of the colony, particularly the number of women. In Montreal in 1663, for example, there was only one marriageable woman for eight marriageable men. Most widows remarried within a year of their husband's death.

THE KING'S GIRLS

Colbert sought women strong enough for work in the fields, and those with a good moral character. At first the French Crown selected orphanage girls, but when they proved not rugged enough, they recruited young healthy country girls. Many were not much over sixteen. In the mid- and late 1660s French ships carried hundreds of the *filles du roi* ("king's girls") to Quebec, where the Ursulines and Hospital sisters looked after them. In all, the state sent nearly eight hundred "king's girls." The king even provided dowries—"the king's gift"—usually consisting of clothing or household supplies.

The girls, kept under supervision in one place, chose their husbands themselves, most of them within two weeks after arrival. A young man in search of a wife had to deal first with the "directress" who was in charge of the girls, and declare his possessions and means of livelihood.

As there were so many men seeking brides, the women had a good deal of choice. Usually they sought first to find out if the suitor had a farm. Even if the young man had begun a farm, a difficult life awaited these women, whose marriage contract bound them for life. They faced relentless work in clearing and maintaining their new family farms, for the women in New France toiled in the fields alongside the men.

The severity of Canadian winters also came as a shock to the young French women. Fortunately, though, by the time of the arrival of the *filles du roi* the French settlers had made many adjustments to winter conditions. Life was much more comfortable. The settlers now slaughtered animals at the onset of winter and hung the meat in icy cellars. By eating fresh meat and vegetables throughout the winter they conquered scurvy. They also constructed houses by digging cellars first, which helped to hold the heat. Innovatively, they began to build fireplaces in the centre of their houses, improving the heating efficiency and reducing heat loss. They introduced roofs with steep angles that readily shed the snow. In the late seventeenth century the settlers introduced another improvement—iron fire boxes that produced four times more heat than conventional fireplaces. Barns were built larger to store fodder for the winter season and to keep domestic animals inside during the coldest weather.

To make the settlers' life easier, Colbert sent livestock to Canada, at the Crown's expense. In 1665 the first horses arrived. The Indians, who had never seen such animals, called them the "moose of France." Horses thrived in the colony. The habitants developed a particular fondness for them, and by the eighteenth century even the poorest tried to keep one.

THE ENGAGÉS

In the mid- and late 1660s the Crown sent annually to the colony several hundred *engagés*, or indentured workmen. Bound by a contract or *engagement* to an established farmer for three years they received a modest wage. They were nicknamed "36 months," since after that period they became free. Apparently, beginning in the 1650s, more than half stayed in the colony after their term of service expired. The system proved advantageous to both the seigneur, who used them to help clear his land,

and to the *engagé*, who gained valuable knowledge of local conditions before he began farming on his own.

THE SETTLEMENT OF THE ST. LAWRENCE VALLEY

Although many immigrants died from disease, either on the voyage or in the colony itself, New France's population grew rapidly, from roughly three thousand in 1663 to almost ten thousand a decade later. By 1672, nearly four thousand men and women had been sent to Canada at the Crown's expense. French immigrants settled the land on both sides of the St. Lawrence from below Quebec to Montreal, and they cleared more land east of Montreal along the Richelieu River.

The St. Lawrence remained the colony's main thoroughfare, both in summer by canoe or small boat and in winter by sleigh over the ice. Everyone wanted frontage along the water highway and to be close to one another in the event of Iroquois attacks. Around Quebec the shores of the St. Lawrence already looked like one unending, sprawling village street, with the *censitaires'* whitewashed farmhouses huddled closely together and their long, narrow farms often twenty times as long as they were wide.

81

Much was achieved by the French government in the first decade of royal government from 1663 to 1672. The women sent out in Colbert's great wave of immigrants quickly married and produced large families. In the late seventeenth century the state encouraged births with what might be termed Canada's first baby bonuses. Couples with ten living children received three hundred *livres* a year, while those with twelve obtained four hundred. The imbalance in the ratio of males to females was corrected by the turn of the century, when the sexes were then roughly equal in number. Despite disasters, such as the smallpox epidemic of 1701 that killed one thousand people, New France's population increase continued to be extremely high: every twenty-five years the population doubled, almost entirely from the high birth rates, rather than from immigration.

THE RISE OF A *CANADIEN* IDENTITY

By 1700 the residents of the colony called themselves *Canadiens*; some families had been in Canada for two or three generations already. A new French people, increasingly conscious of their separation from the metropolitan French in France, had come into being. They had even begun to speak a *parler canadien-français*, a language with its own distinct expressions to describe Canadian realities: *poudrerie* (drifting or powdering of snow), *cabane à sucre* (a cabin used at maple sugar time), and Indian words such as *canoe* and *toboggan*.

Thus, at the end of the seventeenth century a common Canadian French had evolved. In the seventeenth century, France had many regional dialects; in fact, what would later be called Standard French was still developing in Paris and the surrounding area. In the St. Lawrence valley, however, the regional dialects eventually died because the newcomers did not establish separate linguistic communities. The Standard French of the period, with some Canadian words and phrases, dominated.

Colbert's Administrative Reforms

To mark New France's new status as a royal colony, Colbert established a new authoritarian political structure modelled on that of the French provinces. At the top level of authority was Louis XIV, but the king delegated enormous powers to his ministers, particularly to Colbert. In effect, the government of New France resided with the minister of the marine, assisted by his *commis*, or secretary (the equivalent of a twentieth-century deputy minister in Canada). Colbert made policy on the advice of his *commis* and the colony's administrators. The most senior administrator was the governor general, who symbolized royal authority in New France. He and two other important officials, the intendant and the bishop, constituted the ruling triumvirate in the colony.

82

THE GOVERNOR

In New France the governor general was, almost without exception, a noble and a soldier. The Crown clarified the powers of the office after Louis de Buade, Comte de Frontenac, clashed repeatedly in the late 1670s with the magistrates of the Sovereign Council (which functioned as the colony's supreme court), and the intendant. Thereafter, whenever he entered into their jurisdictions, he had to justify his actions to the minister of the marine. Colbert made it quite clear that the governor should leave the work of the officers of justice alone, unless convinced that those same officers were neglecting their duties. The governor's real task was to ensure that the other officials discharged their responsibilities honestly and efficiently.

The governor also had complete control over military affairs and diplomatic relations with the neighbouring Indian tribes and the English colonies to the south. The administration of Daniel de Rémy de Courcelle, governor of New France from 1665 to 1672, was marked by important

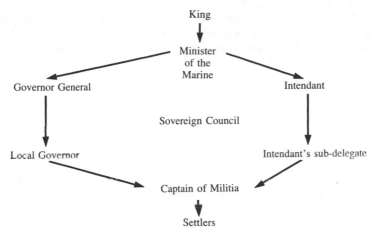

King

Minister
of the
Marine

Governor General   Intendant

Sovereign Council

Local Governor   Intendant's sub-delegate

Captain of Militia

Settlers

Adapted from Trudel, *Introduction to New France*, p. 156.

campaigns against the Iroquois. His successor, the Comte de Frontenac (1672–82, and 1689–98) also spent much of his time dealing with the Indian nations and with the English colonies.

Two of the most celebrated governors in the eighteenth century were Philippe de Rigaud de Vaudreuil (1703–25) and his son, Pierre de Rigaud de Vaudreuil de Cavagnial (1755–60), the only Canadian-born governor of New France. The towns of Montreal and Trois-Rivières also had local governors and town majors answerable to the governor general. These officials' functions were mainly military.

THE INTENDANT

Second to the governor was the intendant, the official responsible for justice, public order, and finance. In France the king appointed intendants for each province. They were generally bureaucrats with sweeping powers, who were appointed to apply the orders from the king and his ministers. The intendant was a skilled administrator with a good educational background and usually extensive legal training.

In New France the intendant urged the habitants to clear more land and experiment with new crops like hemp and flax. In times of war the intendant had many other military duties to perform. He paid, fed, and clothed the troops and kept them supplied with arms and munitions. While the governor decided the military measures to be taken, the intendant provided the necessary supplies and labour. He was also responsible for the construction and maintenance of fortifications. As the population increased, the Crown appointed deputy intendants, answerable to the intendant at Quebec, at Montreal, Trois-Rivières, and later, Detroit.

The governor and intendant quarrelled constantly in the early years of royal government, largely because of their overlapping powers. These conflicts led the minister to define ever more clearly their respective roles and those of the other justice officers. Although the governor remained the supreme authority, the new definitions of authority considerably enhanced the powers of the intendant. He quickly, for example, became the dominant figure in the Sovereign Council. Although ranked behind the governor and the bishop, the intendant came to preside over the council meetings. At the meetings the members never made motions or took votes; this meant, in effect, that the tribunal's verdicts were those of the presiding officer acting on the other members' advice. Three of the best-known intendants of New France were Jean Talon (1665–68, 1669–72), Gilles Hocquart (1731–48), and François Bigot (1748–60).

THE BISHOP

The bishop played a role in the political life of the colony, but lacked the powers he had enjoyed immediately before 1663. Frère Luc's famous portrait of François de Laval, the first bishop, completed around 1670, shows an austere man with a long thin face, a long nose, compressed lips, and a stern chin.

When the Sovereign Council was first established, the bishop ranked only behind the governor. He initially shared with him the responsibility of selecting the other council members from among the leading colonists, but after he clashed with the governor the bishop lost his right to share in the selection of councillors. After the removal of this privilege the bishop's influence declined, and his attendance at the council became infrequent. The Crown respected the social and the religious role of the church, but it did not want it to become a political rival in the colony.

Laval was followed by the even more puritanical Jean-Baptiste de La Croix de Chevrières de Saint-Vallier (1688–1727), who served for nearly forty years. He favoured a severe morality and waged war against drunkenness, blasphemy, dancing, and immodest dress. (Laval had spoken against women appearing in church wearing fashionable gowns that revealed naked arms and bosoms, but St. Vallier went further and tried to stop women wearing low-cut gowns in their homes.)

85

Musée du Séminaire de Québec, Québec.

Portrait of Bishop François de Laval (1623-1708); attributed to Claude François (Brother Luc) (1614-85); circa 1672. Bishop Laval, the first bishop of New France, directed the diocese of Quebec from 1659 to 1684.

THE SOVEREIGN COUNCIL

The Sovereign Council (Superior Council after 1703) was both a law-making and a judicial body. It legislated and heard criminal and civil cases. Appeals could also be heard from lower courts. The members of the tribunal sat around a large table, with the governor, bishop, and intendant at the head, the governor in the centre, the bishop on his right, and the intendant on his left, surrounded by the councillors. As the amount of litigation in the colony increased the council restricted itself to its legal functions, and the intendant enacted legislation.

THE LOWER COURTS

The lower courts in Quebec, Montreal, and Trois-Rivières stood below the Sovereign Council. The judges of these inferior courts applied the municipal legislation drawn up by the Sovereign Council, for example, regulations on street traffic, road maintenance, the disposal of garbage, and fire prevention. A few of the most populated seigneuries also had seigneurial courts, which heard minor civil disputes. In 1663 the law for the area around Paris, the custom of Paris (*coutume de Paris*), officially became the colony's legal code. Today's civil code in Quebec evolved from this "law of Canada."

In reforming the system of justice in New France, Colbert took several measures to insure that justice would be provided with minimal expense. First, he banned lawyers from practising in the colony; citizens argued their own civil cases in court. Notaries—not lawyers—drew up legal contracts. By 1700 the colony supported four notaries at Quebec, three at Montreal, and one at Trois-Rivières. Second, to ensure that justice remained inexpensive, the Crown established a tariff of fees that could be charged by legal officials, from judges down to bailiffs. All fees were very modest.

The operation of the courts was the same as in France. When a crime was found to have been committed, the local magistrate or the attorney general of the Sovereign Council ordered an exhaustive investigation to gather all the evidence and make an intensive study of it. The judge—or a member of the Sovereign Council delegated by the attorney-general—interrogated anyone thought to have knowledge of the crime. If the evidence revealed a suspect, that person was apprehended and put in jail. The judge or attorney general then interrogated the prisoner under oath who, at this point, still had not been informed of the charge against him.

This questioning and the taking down of statements was known as the *question ordinaire*. If, in important cases, the defendant being questioned proved reluctant to talk, torture could be used to extract testimony. This procedure was the *question extraordinaire*; it was employed against at least thirty men and women during the century of royal government.[1] The *maître des hautes oeuvres* or master of the means of torture, bound boards to the defendant's shins, inserted wedges, and then struck them with a hammer, painfully crushing the bones of the accused. After each hammer blow the interrogators restated their questions until they were convinced that the prisoner was telling the truth. As the legal historian Douglas Hay

86

wrote: "If the truth had to be sought in the bones, nerves and sinews of an unwilling witness, that was unfortunate; but ... a lawyer considered it much as a surgeon would his exploratory operation."[2]

If the Sovereign Council heard the trial, the attorney general received all the evidence and testimony, laid it before the court, and added a summation. The members of the council subsequently discussed the report and gave their opinions. The intendant then delivered the verdict. The sentence was carried out either the same day or within a day or two.

THE CAPTAIN OF MILITIA

Colbert also established another institution, the office of captain of militia. In 1669 the intendant organized the entire male population between sixteen and sixty into militia units. He formed a company in each parish and appointed a captain from among the most respected habitants to command it. The office carried with it no salary, but it did bring considerable status and prestige; the captains became the most respected men in their communities. In addition to calling up the militia for military service, they had other important civilian functions. The captains acted locally as the intendant's agents, communicating certain of his regulations and ordinances to the habitants and seeing that they were carried out. They also ordered the *corvées* for work on bridges and roads. During a *corvée* even the local seigneur came under the militia captain's command. This new office thus prevented the seigneurs from becoming too powerful, as they were subordinate to the militia captains. Through the captains the people could make their wishes or complaints known to higher officials.

PUBLIC MEETINGS

Colbert made no provision for local self-government. New France would contain no municipal governments, no mayors or town councils. The people on their own could not call a meeting or public assembly. Government came from above, not from below. Even the magistrates of the Sovereign Council were appointed and paid stipends, and were dependant on governor and intendant.

The only elected office in the late seventeenth century (and for the remainder of the French regime) was that of church warden. Under royal government the power of the Crown was uncontested. Yet some flexibility existed. On occasion the governor and intendant did make efforts to obtain the views of the people on issues that affected the general interest. Seventeen such assemblies were held between 1672 and 1700. On at least one of these occasions, the intendant subsequently acted to meet the wishes of the assembly. Thus, the people of New France did have a limited say in the administration of their affairs, and, while not bound to do so, the authorities could legislate in accordance with their views. (Later, more adjustments were made. In 1709 in Quebec and in 1717 in Montreal the governor and intendant also permitted the merchants to establish chambers of commerce. These bodies were asked to nominate one of their number to inform the governor and intendant of measures to promote commerce in their towns).

ROLE OF THE CHURCH UNDER ROYAL GOVERNMENT

At the beginning of the period of royal government Louis XIV and Colbert feared the excessive authority of the clergy in New France. The Jesuits, in effect, had run the colony for thirty years. The governor and the intendant were instructed to make the church subordinate to the authority of the state. After 1663 the king himself nominated the bishop. The Crown had an important voice in the church's administration as it contributed forty percent of the colonial church's finances. These subsidies were thus used as a means of controlling the church.

The Failure of Colbert's Plan for a "Compact Colony"

Having set up a new administrative structure, Colbert sought capable men to fill the senior posts. These men, he hoped, would establish a self-reliant, or "compact colony," in the St. Lawrence valley. Talon, a man of about forty who had previously been an intendant in France, began investigating New France's economic possibilities: discovering what the soil would grow, surveying the forests, and sponsoring expeditions to search for minerals. He also tried to develop a ship-building industry in the colony. The Crown sent skilled ship carpenters, tarmakers, blacksmiths, and foundry workers as well as the necessary supplies. They even built three ships, but the industry never became profitable. The imported skilled workers demanded high wages. Iron had to be imported and the industry required heavy capital outlays. Ships cost much more to build in Canada than in France, and the programme was curtailed.

Another setback to Colbert's plans arose from the failure to develop a large overseas trade with the West Indies. The loss of two of Talon's ships at sea also helped to end the experiment. Moreover, the handicaps were great—New France's ships could sail south only in the summer months, which is the hurricane season in southern waters. The French ships also had to run the gauntlet of English privateers in wartime, and other nations' privateers infested the waters at all seasons. Finally, the Canadians had to compete with New England mariners, who could sell the same wheat and fish at a lower price all year round. For all these reasons, then, New France failed to obtain any real foothold in the West Indies' market.

Of the industries in New France, fishing offered the greatest promise. Colbert gave it every possible assistance, providing subsidies for the necessary equipment and keeping French duties on the Canadians' fish as low as those placed on fish brought to France by French fishermen. But once again the Canadian fishermen faced several disadvantages, the foremost being the lack of salt in the colony. French fishermen could take their catches from the Grand Banks and sell them for a lower price in France than could Canadian fishermen. Despite large expenditures of energy and money, in the end New France's fishing industry really only supplied the colony's needs.

89

One of Talon's enterprises, though, did make a strong beginning—a brewery at Quebec. Cheap beer brewed at Quebec proved popular. Other industries he promoted included the production of hats and shoes. Unfortunately for Colbert's hopes, however, everything Canada produced could be obtained more cheaply elsewhere, except perhaps for furs and beer.

In 1672, the year Jean Talon left the colony, the infant industries died and the further dispatch of *filles du roi* ended. The Crown allocated no further funds because France began a costly war with the Dutch. As Colbert stated in June 1673: "His Majesty can give no assistance to Canada this year on account of the great and prodigious expense to which he has been put for the maintenance of more than 200 000 men and a hundred ships." New France had to look after itself. It returned to its dependence on the fur trade, which remained the main economic activity.

Colonial administrators in New France also contributed to the failure of Colbert's "compact colony" ideal. The first prominent governor, Louis de Buade, Comte de Frontenac, in the 1670s openly favoured the expansion of the fur trade. As business historian Michael Bliss wrote: "The idea that people with power should *not* use it to enrich themselves is a very modern notion. In the seventeenth and eighteenth centuries virtually all administrators of government—in Britain, France, and all their colonies—expected to gain personally from possession of their offices."[3]

Privately, officials in the colony used their positions to advance their own interests. Frontenac sent out expeditions to open up new fur trading territory and did little to promote economic development in the St. Lawrence valley. Fortunes could be made in the fur trade, at least until the mid-1690s, when the amount of beaver exported to France far exceeded what the market could absorb.

Economic Development in New France in the Eighteenth Century

In the eighteenth century, particularly in the period of peace in the St. Lawrence valley from 1713 to 1744, attempts were made to duplicate Colbert's attempts to diversify the economy. This time they were successful. The number of flour mills increased by 50 percent in 1719–1734 to more than a hundred (from 76 to 118). The fishing industry also grew, with fish and seal oil becoming export products. Gilles Hocquart, the intendant, established tanneries at Quebec, Lévis, and Montreal. Apart from a refusal to send tradesmen to Canada to weave flax and hemp and a rejection of the idea of hat-making in New France, the state favoured new economic initiatives in New France.

The Crown worked, for example, to improve transportation. A road link was essential for farmers to take their growing surpluses to market. In 1737 the intendant completed the first royal highway connecting Montreal and Quebec, which greatly facilitated travel. While a return trip by water from Montreal to Quebec might take several weeks, the trip by coach over the King's Highway could be completed in as little as nine days. The highway opened up to settlement new lands north of the St. Lawrence. The road became the colony's lifeline when the British fleet controlled the St. Lawrence in the summer of 1759.

90

PRIVATE INDUSTRY

Private citizens also worked to develop the industrial resources of the colony. Lack of capital and skilled labour and high transportation costs, however, left few products that could be made in New France and sold profitably in or outside the colony. Beginning in the 1720s Canadian businessmen established small shipyards along the St. Lawrence. The Intendant Gilles Hocquart helped with subsidies and tried to build on this economic growth by establishing state-owned shipyards. Canadian workers were to be employed in sailmaking, rope manufacturing, tar works, foundries, sawmills, and tool and machinery making.

Unwisely, though, the intendant promoted the building of large ships, even though Canada's resources were better suited for small ones. The royal shipyard at Quebec constructed fifteen warships, six of which were five hundred tonnes or more (one ship, the *Saint-Laurent*, carried sixty cannon) but labour costs proved too high. In the 1750s the royal shipyard built and launched only two naval vessels.

Canada's first heavy industry, the St. Maurice forges near Trois-Rivières, was established in 1729, but under its second owner serious technical errors and lax administration caused its ruin. By 1741 the company's directors declared themselves bankrupt, at which point the Crown, which had given large subsidies, intervened. Production under royal administration fluctuated greatly from year to year, but for a few years profits were reported. The ironworks employed about one hundred workers, who produced sizeable quantities of cooking pots, pans, soup ladles, stoves, as well as cannon and cannonballs.

AGRICULTURE

Agriculture replaced the fur trade as the leading employer in the colony, greatly changing the colony's economic structure. Three out of four Canadian families farmed by 1700. As in the English colonies the virgin soil's high productivity and the unlimited supply of land led farmers to avoid the intensive agricultural methods of Europe. The chronic labour shortage also encouraged farmers to increase their production by clearing more land rather than farming intensively. From 1706 to 1739 the Canadian population increased 250 percent, and the amount of land cultivated by 430 percent. Wheat generally occupied about three-quarters of the farm land in cultivation, so the colony became self-sufficient in wheat and flour (wheat, in fact, made up one-third of the colony's exports by the 1730s). The habitants also grew peas, oats, rye, barley, and maize. Surprisingly, the vegetable that in the early nineteenth century became the staple food of the habitants' diet was not grown in the colony: it was the English who introduced the potato to the St. Lawrence valley after 1760.

91

Market conditions limited the production of both produce and livestock. The towns of New France were not large, and many town dwellers kept their own gardens and livestock. But an increase in the population and the opening up of an export market in the eighteenth century improved the situation. Flour, biscuit, and peas were exported regularly to the new French fortress at Louisbourg on Cape Breton Island and to the French West Indies. The habitants needed to produce a surplus to pay church tithes and seigneurial dues and to purchase the things they could not make themselves.

The Society of New France in the Eighteenth Century

By the eighteenth century about one-quarter of New France's inhabitants lived in towns. The royal officials and military officers dominated life in Quebec, Montreal, and Trois-Rivières. In terms of social ranking, the senior administrators in New France stood at the forefront of society. The

92

National Gallery of Canada, Ottawa.

Château-Richer. This painting by Thomas Davies (c. 1737-1812), completed in 1787, portrays typical habitant farm buildings on the shores of the St. Lawrence east of Quebec City.

metropolitan French occupied many of the seats of the Sovereign Council and the top posts in the civil service hierarchy. At the local level, however, the greater number of judges were Canadian born.

THE MERCHANTS

The merchants or bourgeois, often connected indirectly or directly with the fur trade, constituted another important group in New France. In the 1950s and 1960s this social group was the focus of much debate among historians. Did New France really have a number of solid French Canadian entrepreneurs? Was there an active bourgeoisie in the colony? Some historians, among them Maurice Séguin, Guy Frégault, and Michel Brunet, argued that indeed it existed; others, such as Jean Hamelin and Fernand Ouellet, denied that it had. Among other factors, the existence of monopolies and state control over the economy, Hamelin and Ouellet contended, stunted the development of a national bourgeoisie. This question assumed great importance in view of the British Conquest. Was the effect of the Conquest to remove French Canada's dynamic entrepreneurial class, or did such a class ever exist?

Although a conclusive answer is not possible, it can be said that the metropolitan French appear to have controlled the biggest commercial operations connected with the profitable wholesale trade. They had the necessary funds and contacts to obtain adequate supplies in France. These French merchants provided most of the imported manufactured goods at Louisbourg and Quebec. About two-thirds of the colony's external trade was handled by French merchants and their Quebec agents.[4] The Canadian merchants dominated the smaller-scale retail trade, however. Thus, while much work remains to be done on this subject, a picture emerges of a strong metropolitan French presence in large-scale commerce and of a French-Canadian dominance in smaller-scale trading.

In the eighteenth century the fur trade was carried on by scores of small partnerships. The companies usually consisted of three or four partners who obtained from the authorities a three-year lease on the trade at a particular fur-trading post. (At Niagara, Detroit, and Michilimackinac, however, the French military commanders controlled the fur trade.)

93

The members of the partnership shared the profits or the losses, according to the percentage of the capital they had subscribed. The partners obtained trade goods from the large Montreal merchants, usually on credit at 30 percent interest. These large French merchants marketed the furs through their agents at home in France.

WOMEN IN COMMERCE

Women in eighteenth-century New France frequently ran small businesses that sold cloth, clothes, furs, brandy, and utensils. During their husbands' absence in the interior, the fur traders' wives and daughters often looked after their stores and accounts. A number of the merchants' wives, as widows, later continued their late husbands' businesses. Well-versed in the affairs of her fur trader husband, Marie-Anne Barbel decided to continue his business after his death in 1745. She also expanded upon his real estate holdings and began a pottery works. Until the Seven Year's War ruined her fur trade operation she was one of Quebec's well-to-do merchants. Much of her property was destroyed in the British bombardment of Quebec's Lower Town in 1759.

Other women who began successful commercial careers include Agathe de Saint-Père, Madame de Repentigny, who headed a textile firm—New France's first—in the early eighteenth century. This energetic businesswoman ransomed nine English weavers held prisoner by the Indians and hired them to teach Canadian apprentices the trade. Soon she had twenty looms operating, which turned out coarse cloth and canvas. Madame de Ramezay operated a sawmill, a brick factory, and a tile works. Her daughter Louise de Ramezay was the owner of a flour mill, a tannery, and sawmills.

THE *ENGAGÉS* IN THE FUR TRADE

Below the middle-sized French Canadian merchants stood the small traders and the voyageurs or *engagés*. The male and female merchants carried the products of the country to the town, and vice-versa; the voyageurs, under contract as *engagés* (as was increasingly the case after 1700), travelled thousands of kilometres from the St. Lawrence valley.

Every year, 400–500 people received permission to enter the fur trade around the Great Lakes or in the Upper Mississippi valley. Possibly as many as five to six times that number went without permission. Little is known of these people. According to the historian Gratien Allaire, the majority were recruited around Montreal.[5] His research also reveals that the *engagés* tended to be habitants seeking to supplement their farm incomes, and they came from rural areas.

94

TRADESPEOPLE

The colony had about two thousand trades workers by the 1740s. The most numerous workers in the construction industry trades were carpenters and masons; in transportation, navigators and carters; and in the food industry, bakers and butchers. As a rule, craftsmen worked in small workshops often attached to their homes and owned all their own tools. Often the French authorities accused *Canadien* workers of being headstrong and insubordinate, their self-confidence and independence being unappreciated by the administrators from Old France, where the average person had little, if any, personal freedom or opportunity for personal advancement.

THE HABITANTS

The most numerous group in the colony was the habitants. By the 1740s the oldest seigneuries had two (in some cases three) rows of farms stretching back from the river. Although many farmers produced just enough for their subsistence, an estimated one-half produced a surplus. The habitants paid no direct taxes (apart from the occasional tax for local improvements), whereas in France the peasantry paid between one-third and one-half of its income in taxes. The habitants' tithes were only half the usual rate in northern France.

The majority of the habitants apparently ate well, with meat served almost every day. Pork and game, particularly venison and wild hare, were the early staple meats. Gradually, though, wild game came to be relied on less and less as it became harder to obtain near the settled areas. The pig, however, remained a mainstay of the habitant's diet due to that animal's ability to turn anything edible, from acorns to kitchen scraps, into usable cuts of meat. As the old folk saying in both France and New France ran, "You can eat everything but the squeal." Fish was also part of the core diet of the French settlers, as was buckwheat, a hardy cereal used to make bread, pancakes, and porridges. Maple syrup was the chief source of sweetening in the colony.

95

Vegetables from the garden, peas and fèves (the large tough-fibred beans from Normandy that were brought to the St. Lawrence valley), were favourites. The dried peas and beans could be stored for years and then made into tasty soups. As they absorbed well the flavour of either smoked or salted pork fat, the habitants used pork freely in their recipes for pea soup and baked beans.

The *Canadiens* also enjoyed such fruits as apples, plums, and cherries. Apple trees from the northwest of France thrived in the cool moist climate. Wild fruits, especially raspberries, red and black currants, and cranberries were to be had for the picking.

As for drink, wealthy habitants could obtain tea and coffee from the traders, but these goods were costly. Milk, in contrast, was cheap and plentiful. Cider was drunk at all meals. The well-to-do could afford wine imported from France, while the habitants drank the cheap beer brewed in the colony or beer that they brewed themselves.

Farmers in New France detested being called "peasants," as the Finnish traveller Pehr Kalm noted in 1749: "The gentlemen and ladies, as well as the poorest peasants and their wives, are called Monsieur and Madame." The habitants had more personal freedom than their counterparts in France. The royal officials in New France repeatedly complained that the independent-minded Canadians always pleased themselves and paid little attention to the administrators' directives.

The habitants' lives centred on their farms, which they cultivated with their families' help. The *curé* and the captain of militia were the habitants' links with the outside world. As in France, the *curés* were responsible for the registration of births, deaths, and marriages.

THE NOBILITY

The nobility kept alive the military and aristocratic values of Old France in Canada. In general, the sons of the nobles became military officers, obtaining commissions in the *troupes de la marine*, or colonial regular troops. The military was a very important element in the community. Every year the Crown spent large sums for the maintenance of soldiers in New France. About fifteen hundred regular French troops garrisoned the posts during the early eighteenth century.

Within the army, tension existed between the French and the Canadian-born officers. In the army, as in the militia, Canadian leaders enjoyed a moral authority over the Canadian troops that French officers lacked. Unlike the French, Canadian troops preferred to fight a different type of war—what would be called in the twentieth century a guerilla war.

96

The Clergy in New France

During the years of royal government, the church suffered from an acute shortage of personnel. Particularly in the years of the great migration from France in the late 1660s and early 1670s, there were not enough priests to serve the growing populace. As late as 1683 the intendant reported that three-quarters or more of the habitants heard mass only four times a year. The shortage of priests remained a serious problem to the end of the French regime.

The parish priests played a very important role in the community; one that has been aptly described by the sociologist Jean-Charles Falardeau: "The Canadian curés were pastors of communities lacking resources, organization and most of the time, local leaders. They soon became also the real leaders of these communities."[6]

Yet historians like W.J. Eccles and Cornelius Jaenen, while not denying the church's central role, moderately distance themselves from such an interpretation. They stress that the people of New France showed a surprising independence towards any political direction by the church. When, for instance, the Crown decided after the imposition of royal government that the populace would pay tithes for the support of a secular clergy, the bishop stipulated that it be at the rate of one-thirteenth of the produce of the land. The people protested on the grounds of their poverty. The bishop reduced his demand to one-twentieth, but eventually he had to accept only one twenty-sixth of their grain (wheat, rye, barley, and oats). To make up the difference between what the tithe produced and the *curés* needed, the Crown then had to provide the clergy with annual subsidies. Only when more land came into production in the early eighteenth century did many of the parish priests become relatively well off.

The frequent *ordonnances* of the intendant provide further proof of the independence of the *Canadiens* to the clergy. Repeatedly he directed the inhabitants of various parishes to behave with more respect towards their *curé*. The intendant sought to stop their practice of walking out of church as soon as the priest began his sermon, standing in the lobby arguing, brawling during the service, and even bringing dogs into church.

As Eccles points out, however, religion still did mean a great deal to the colonists, despite these signs of lack of respect for the clergy. Statistics collected by the demographer Jacques Henripin on the conception dates of children born in the colony indicates this. The number of conceptions steadily increased through the winter until a very sharp decline occurred in April, followed by a sharp rise peaking in July, followed by a decline to the level of the preceding winter months for the rest of the year. As Eccles writes: "Obviously, the Canadians abstained from more than the pleasures of the table at that time, and this could only have come about because they were heeding the precepts of their church."[7]

97

THE CHURCH AND PUBLIC WELFARE

For what today would be called social services, the church enjoyed un-questioned respect in the community. A major contribution of the clergy to life in the colony came from their involvement in teaching, nursing, and other charitable work. In 1760 the nearly 100 diocesan or parish priests in the colony were assisted by 30 Sulpicians (a religious order which began work in the colony in 1657), 25 Jesuits, 24 Récollets (who had returned in 1670), and more than 200 nuns belonging to six religious communities. During the early history of New France the church established the first clerically administered social institutions; these endured, in many cases, into the twentieth century.

Since schooling was the preserve of the church in the colony, all the religious communities assumed some responsibility for the education of the colonists' children. The parent religious orders in France and the Crown founded the schools.

Along with education, the church provided various welfare services and maintained charitable institutions. Three women's religious communities and two men's communities became involved in this work. Each of the three principal towns of Canada had a Bureau of the Poor, which served as a relief centre and employment agency. Those too elderly or infirm to work or take care of themselves were placed in institutions at Montreal or Quebec, along with the chronically ill, the insane, and women of "loose morals," the latter put there to be reformed by the hospital nuns. To help pay for these institutional services the church in 1663 held about one-tenth of the seigneurial lands in the St. Lawrence valley. By the 1750s it held one-quarter of the land.

POPULAR RELIGION

Popular religion remained strong in France and in New France. Many *Canadiens* in the rural areas believed firmly in magic and witchcraft. On a winter's night tales of flying canoes, of werewolves, and of encounters with the devil, were told to generations of Canadian children. These tales, though, were harmless, in contrast with the real belief in sorcerers. Frequently the clergy were called on to exorcise suspected sorcerers with prayers, candles, and holy water. Individuals who today would be recognized as suffering from mental illness were then believed to be possessed of demons. Even the clergy supported the principle that anyone believed to have been a sorcerer should not be buried in sanctified ground. New France, however, never knew the hysteria that swept through part of New England in the 1690s, such as in Salem with its witchhunts. No executions occurred in New France for occult practices.

THE CANADIANIZATION OF THE CLERGY

Just as the regular colonial army became "Canadianized," so gradually did the clergy. The training of a native-born Canadian secular clergy had long been an objective of the church. The seminary at Quebec accepted seventy-five students, most of whom were not required to pay fees or the cost of room, board, and clothing. The Sulpicians also operated a boys' school in Montreal, and the Jesuits operated a college at Quebec.

During the eighteenth century the parishes in New France came to be increasingly staffed by Canadians. Canada had in 1760 about one hundred parishes, most of them run by diocesan clergy, about four-fifths of whom were Canadian. Tensions, though, existed between the Canadian and the French clergy. In the early eighteenth century, for example, Bishop St. Vallier agreed with the intendant of the time that a metropolitan Frenchman be appointed dean for the cathedral, since the Canadians were reluctant to submit to their superiors' authority. In the grip of internal problems, and still experiencing a shortage of priests for all its parishes, the church withdrew somewhat its former support of Indian missions.

The Amerindian Population

The settled areas of Canada also contained a small non-French population. Several thousand Indian refugees lived in five major reserves in the St. Lawrence valley: the Hurons at Lorette near Quebec; the Abenakis from present-day Maine at St. François, east of Montreal; and the Iroquois at Caughnawaga (Kahnawake), St. Regis, and the Lake of Two Mountains (both west of Montreal).

Historian Peter Moogk has noted that these Christian Indians raised French children.[8] Frequently, illegitimate children born to *Canadiennes* were given to the Indians, rather than let babies die of exposure (in New France infanticide was a capital crime). Indians also raised American children who had been taken as captives on Franco-Indian raiding parties and were subsequently adopted into the respective tribes.

99

AMERINDIAN AND BLACK SLAVES

In Canada a slave class existed. From the late 1680s Indian slaves from the Upper Mississippi valley began arriving in New France on a regular basis. These *panis* (or Pawnees, a term used even though the slaves were taken from many other tribes as well as from the Pawnee) were sold to the French by other Indians. Blacks captured in raids on the English colonies or brought in from the French West Indies also increased the number of slaves in the colony. The rare black slaves sold at an average price twice as great as the more numerous Indian captives, because they had greater resistance to disease than the Indians.

The Canadians traded slaves like cattle, at the marketplace or at auction. Slavery, which was an urban phenomenon, enjoyed great popularity among the governors of New France: Rigaud de Vaudreuil, governor from 1703 to 1725, owned eleven slaves; the Marquis de Beauharnois, in office from 1726 to 1746, owned twenty-seven.

Merchants, traders, and the clergy were the biggest slave owners. Indian and black slaves worked at the convents and hospitals operated by nuns in Quebec and Montreal. There were approximately four thousand in French Canada between the 1680s and about 1800. They lived short lives: for Indian slaves the average age at death was about eighteen, and for Blacks, twenty-five. But it should be remembered that the life expectancy in France at this time was about twenty-five years.

By 1754 New France's French population had reached fifty-five thousand. What had begun as an offshoot of Old France became a new community in Canada. Little by little the French had become *Canadiens*, with values, manners, and even attitudes that differentiated them more and more from metropolitan Frenchmen. The *Canadiens* resented the assumption of superiority by the military and ecclesiastical leaders of old France. The French officer Louis-Antoine de Bougainville, who came to Quebec in 1757, noted the increasing differences between Frenchmen and *Canadiens*: "We seem to belong to another, even an enemy nation."[9]

NOTES

[1] André Lachance, "Tout sur la torture," *Le Magazine Maclean*, décembre 1966, p. 38.
[2] Douglas Hay, "The Meanings of the Criminal Law in Quebec, 1764–1774," in *Crime and Criminal Justice in Europe and Canada*, edited by Louis A. Knafla (Waterloo, 1981), p. 77.
[3] Michael Bliss, *Northern Enterprise: Five Centuries of Canadian Business* (Toronto, 1987), p. 44.
[4] Ibid., p. 70.
[5] Gratien Allaire, "Fur Trade Engagés, 1701–1745," in *Rendezvous: Selected Papers of the North American Fur Trade Conference, 1981*, edited by Thomas C. Buckley (St. Paul, Minn., 1984), p. 22.
[6] Jean-Charles Falardeau, "The Seventeenth-Century Parish in French Canada," in *French-Canadian Society*, vol. 1, edited by Marcel Rioux and Yves Martin (Toronto, 1964), p. 27.
[7] W.J. Eccles, "The Role of the Church in New France," in *Essays on New France*, edited by W.J. Eccles (Toronto, 1987), p. 37.
[8] Peter N. Moogk, "*Les Petits Sauvages*: The Children of Eighteenth-Century New France," in *Childhood and Family in Canadian History*, ed. Joy Parr (Toronto, 1982), p. 27.
[9] Bougainville quoted in Guy Frégault, *Canada: The War of the Conquest*, translated by Margaret M. Cameron (Toronto, 1969), p. 64. On this important point see the comments of George G.F. Stanley in *New France: The Last Phase, 1744–1760* (Toronto, 1968), p. 272.

100

Related Readings

R. Douglas Francis and Donald B. Smith, *Readings in Canadian History: Pre-Confederation*, 2d ed. (Toronto, 1986) contains a number of articles that deal directly with this topic: W.J. Eccles' "Society and the Frontier," pp. 85–101; John F. Bosher, "The Family in New France," pp. 101–11; and Guy Frégault, "Canadian Society in the French Regime," pp. 148–60.

BIBLIOGRAPHY

For a study of the domestic life of New France in the late seventeenth and early eighteenth centuries, see W.J. Eccles, *Canada Under Louis XIV, 1663–1701* (Toronto, 1964), and his "Social Life in New France," in the Canadian Museum of Civilization's *Canada's Visual History Series*, vol. 28; and Dale Miquelon, *New France, 1701–1744* (Toronto, 1987). Developments in France are reviewed in Pierre Goubert's *Louis XIV and Twenty Million Frenchmen* (New York, 1970). Two helpful surveys of New France in the eighteenth century are the chapter by Jacques Mathieu, "Un pays à statut colonial (1701–1755)," in *Histoire du Québec* (Montréal, 1976), pp. 183–230, and the beautifully illustrated *Taking Root: Canada from 1700 to 1760* by André Vachon, with the assistance of Victorin Chabot and André Desrosiers (Ottawa, 1985). Useful guides for the period 1663–1760 are provided by W.J. Eccles, *The Canadian Frontier, 1534–1760* (Toronto, 1969); and W.J. Eccles, *France in America* (New York, 1972); and Marcel Trudel, *Introduction to New France* (Toronto, 1968). In *Northern Enterprise: Five Centuries of Canadian Business* (Toronto, 1987), Michael Bliss reviews the economic life of New France.

A number of important articles by W.J. Eccles on New France in these years have been republished in his *Essays on New France* (Toronto, 1987). Terence Crowley, in " 'Thunder Gusts': Popular Disturbances in Early French Canada," *Historical Papers/Communications Historiques*, 1979, pp. 11–32, reviews civil discontent in the colony. Louis Dechêne describes Montreal in the eighteenth century in "La croissance de Montréal au XVIIIe siecle," *Revue d'histoire de l'Amérique française* 27 (1973/74): 163–79; this article appears in English translation as "The Growth of Montreal in the 18th Century," in J.M. Bumsted, ed., *Canadian History Before Confederation*, 2d ed. (Georgetown, Ont. 1979), pp. 154–67. *101*

For further information on other aspects of the social history of New France see the following historical pamphlets published by the Canadian Historical Association: Marcel Trudel, *The Seigneurial Regime* (Ottawa, 1956); W.J. Eccles, *The Government of New France* (Ottawa, 1965); and Cornelius J. Jaenen, *The Role of the Church in New France* (Ottawa, 1985). Two accounts of the seigneurial regime are William Bennett Munro's now-dated *The Seigneurs of Old Canada* (Toronto, 1922); and Richard Colebrook Harris, *The Seigneurial System in Canada: A Geographical Study* (Madison, 1966). The legal historian Douglas Hay comments on French law in New France in his article, "The Meanings of the Criminal Law in Quebec, 1764–1774," in *Crime and Criminal Justice in Europe and Canada*, edited by Louis A. Knafla (Waterloo, Ont., 1981), pp. 77–110. Historian André Lachance reviews the question of torture in his "Tout sur la torture," *Le Magazine Maclean*, décembre 1966, pp. 36–39, 41–42. Jean-Charles Falardeau's "The Seventeenth-Century Parish in French Canada" appeared in Marcel Rioux and Yves Martin, eds. *French-Canadian Society*, vol. 1 (Toronto, 1964), pp. 19–32. An interesting article on witchcraft is Jonathan L. Pearl's "Witchcraft in New France in the Seventeenth Century: The Social Aspect," *Historical Reflections*, 4 (1977): 191–205. The best short summary of the fur trade is that by W.J. Eccles, "Fur Trade," in *The Canadian Encyclopedia* (Edmonton, 1985), vol. 2, pp. 704–05. On the *engagés*, see Gratien Allaire, "Fur Trade Engagés, 1701–1745," in *Rendezvous: Selected Papers of the North American Fur Trade Conference 1981*, edited by Thomas C. Buckley (St. Paul, Minn., 1984), pp. 15–26. Marcel Trudel has written a short history of slavery in New France in

"Ties that Bind," *Horizon Canada*, number 18 (1985): pp. 422–27. A short article on the French language in Canada, written by the linguist Gaston Dulong, appears in *The Canadian Encyclopedia* (Edmonton, 1985), vol. 2, p. 696. For a view of New France in 1749, see Pehr Kalm's *Travels in North America*, 2 vols. (New York, 1966) for his descriptions of Canadian life and customs. A delightful account of early French Canadian food and cooking customs is Jay A. Anderson's "The Early Development of French-Canadian Food Ways," in *Folklore of Canada*, edited by Edith Fowke (Toronto, 1976), pp. 91–99.

For the activities of women in New France, consult Micheline Dumont et al., *Quebec Women. A History* (Toronto, 1987); the article by Jan Noel, "New France: Les femmes favorisées," in *The Neglected Majority: Essays in Canadian Women's History, volume 2* edited by Alison Prentice and Susan Mann Trofimenkoff (Toronto, 1985), pp. 18–40; and Lilianne Plamondon "A Businesswoman in New France: Marie-Anne Barbel, The Widow Fornel," in *Rethinking Canada: The Promise of Women's History*, edited by Veronica Strong-Boag and Anita Clair Fellman (Toronto, 1986), pp. 45–58. Peter N. Moogk reviews the children of eighteenth-century New France in *"Les Petits Sauvages,"* in *Childhood and Family in Canadian History* edited by Joy Parr (Toronto, 1982), pp. 17–43.

Two valuable historiographical articles on the economic and social history of New France are Serge Jaumian and Matteo Sanfilippo, "Le Régime seigneurial en Nouvelle-France: Un débat historiographique," *The Register*, 5, 2 (Autumn 1984): 226–47; and Robert Comeau and Paul-André Linteau, "Une question historiographique: Une bourgeoisie en Nouvelle-France?" in *Economie québécoise*, edited by Robert Comeau (Montréal, 1969), pp. 311–23. Serge Gagnon's *Quebec and its Historians: The Twentieth Century* (Montreal, 1985), contains several interesting historiographical essays on New France. For biographies of the leading individuals in New France, see *Dictionary of Canadian Biography*, vols. 1–4 (Toronto, 1966, 1969, 1974, 1979); and for valuable maps of the St. Lawrence colony consult, the *Historical Atlas of Canada*, vol. 1, edited by R. Cole Harris (Toronto, 1987).

CHAPTER SIX

The Anglo-French Struggle for a Continent

At approximately the same time that the French founded Quebec, England 　*103*
established several Atlantic colonies that, by the end of the century, en-
circled New France. The first English colonies were Virginia, 1607; Newfoundland, 1610; and Massachusetts, 1620. Others followed on the Atlantic
seaboard, and in 1664 the Dutch colony of New Netherlands passed into
English hands and was renamed New York. The English also sponsored
expeditions into the huge inland sea north of New France. Henry Hudson
led the English expedition that in 1610–11 first located the immense body
of water the size of the Mediterranean Sea. A little over a half-century
later an English company established a string of fur-trading posts around
Hudson Bay.

Conflict arose between England and France in the late 1680s when the
two empires confronted each other in the interior of the North American
continent. Contrary to Colbert's directives, New France in the 1670s and
1680s had established forts around the Great Lakes to the Mississippi
River. Even after the fur trade became uneconomical in the mid-1690s,
the French resolved to stay for strategic reasons. The French, in fact,
subsidized the fur trade to retain their military alliance with the inland
Indian tribes. European claims to the contrary, the Indians remained the
sovereign powers beyond the St. Lawrence valley and the Appalachian
Mountains.

Founding of the Hudson's Bay Company

The English preceded the French in the area north of New France in
1610–11. Henry Hudson had just returned from a voyage in the Dutch
service to the river that now bears his name in New York, when English
financial backers sent him on an expedition to discover the Northwest

Passage. In early June 1610 he entered an ice-bound strait previously noted in the 1570s and 1580s by the English Arctic explorers, Martin Frobisher and John Davis. He navigated his tiny vessel successfully through the channel and into the inland sea, both of which were later named after him. Although he and his men spent a terrible winter on the east coast of James Bay, the following spring the determined captain announced that the search would continue. His crew mutinied and seized the middle-aged Hudson, his son, and seven others, setting them adrift to die in a small boat on James Bay. Eight of the twelve mutineers returned alive to England, where they falsely reported that the expedition had found the Northwest Passage. The Welsh navigator Sir Thomas Button crossed Hudson Bay in 1612 but failed to find Hudson or a passage to the Indies.

Other English expeditions followed until 1631, when it became clear that even if a Northwest Passage existed, it would not be commercially viable as a trade route. Since both the Dutch and the English had already begun to make the longer but less hazardous journey around Africa to India and China, the lure of the Northwest Passage diminished. There was no recorded sea voyage into Hudson Bay from 1632 to 1668, the year that Médard Chouart Des Groseilliers and Zachariah Gillam, a New England sea captain, completed the fur-trading mission that led to the formation of the Hudson's Bay Company.

Ironically, two renegade French coureurs de bois, Pierre-Esprit Radisson and Médard Chouart Des Groseilliers (Mr. Radishes and Mr. Gooseberry, as the English translated their names), had directed the English to the rich fur country south of Hudson and James Bay. Finding no support in New France for their plan of trading in this area the two went over to the English.

In 1668 a group of English merchants under the patronage of Prince Rupert, a cousin of King Charles II, sponsored Groseilliers's expedition that was to winter on Hudson Bay and return with a cargo of fur. The enterprise proved so successful that in 1670 Charles II gave the Hudson's Bay Company exclusive trading rights and property ownership to all the lands within the area drained by the rivers flowing into Hudson and James bays (nearly half the area of Canada today); in return, their only payment was to be the gift of two elks and two black beavers whenever an English monarch visited the territories. No one consulted the Indians about this charter to "Rupert's Land," since the English did not regard the non-Christian Indians as having any land rights.

French Expansion to the North and West

The English now threatened New France's fur trade from two sides—the upper Hudson River valley and Hudson Bay. The collapse of the Huron trading system in 1649 left a vacuum and greatly facilitated the English establishment on Hudson Bay. In response, the French in the early 1670s dispatched overland expeditions to Hudson Bay, Lake Superior, and the Mississippi River, to establish French claims to these areas.

Frontenac, the impoverished French nobleman who became governor in 1673, openly promoted further westward expansion. In this adventure his great ally was René-Robert Cavelier de La Salle, a daring and ambitious fur trader. Both Frontenac and La Salle knew that a fortune in furs awaited the first Frenchman to reach the Indians in the Mississippi valley. In pursuit of this goal La Salle went to France and obtained official sanction to explore the Mississippi valley. Early in 1682 La Salle reached the Mississippi delta, where he raised the royal arms of France. The French explorer then made a solemn declaration claiming all the land drained by the Mississippi River and its tributaries for the King of France and named the huge valley Louisiana, after Louis XIV. La Salle's own attempt to found a colony in Louisiana ended with failure—and his assassination in 1687—but Louisiana was successfully founded twenty years later.

The merchant fur traders continued to pay little heed to the surviving royal edicts forbidding trade with the Indians in the interior. In the mid-1670s Montreal traders built Michilimackinac at the junction of Lakes Michigan and Huron, which became the starting point for the fur trade along the Upper Mississippi and beyond Lake Superior. Soon French trading posts dotted the entire area from the Ohio River to Lake Winnipeg and northward to Hudson Bay. The exodus of Canadians to the west could not be stopped.

In 1681 Colbert admitted defeat. A royal edict granted amnesty to all coureurs de bois, provided that they return to the colony immediately. The great minister instituted a new permit system but, with his death in 1683, did not live to see its subsequent failure. Jacques-René de Brisay de Denonville, governor of New France in the late 1680s, was reliably informed that some six hundred coureurs de bois were in the interior, away from the colony.

War with England's American Colonies

The successors to Frontenac, who had been recalled in 1682, faced an increasingly difficult military situation in the 1680s. The Hudson's Bay Company was successfully established on Hudson Bay, and after the French ended their truce with the Iroquois in the mid-1680s, the Five Nations (with the encouragement of the English) again resumed their raids on New France. The colony was thus caught between two opposing forces. Few in number and scattered over a vast area, the French realized more than ever the importance of co-operation with their Algonquian allies. The coureurs de bois, the very Frenchmen that Colbert had so opposed, became the colony's greatest strength because they could be used to revitalize France's native alliances in the interior.

The Iroquois raid in 1689 on Lachine, a settlement west of Montreal, launched in retaliation for a French attack on several Iroquois villages two years earlier (see chapter 4), led to a new round of conflict between the French, the Iroquois, and the Iroquois' allies, the English colonies. Sent back to New France as governor in 1689, Frontenac immediately launched Canadian and Indian hit-and-run raids against the English settlements. At Schenectady, New York, and Salmon Falls, New England, the French and Indian raiding parties broke into homes and scalped men, women, and children as they struggled out of their beds; others were cut down as they ran out of their burning houses.

La petite guerre, the war of ambush and surprise, had begun. It was waged by the Canadian militia and their Algonquian allies under the direction of regular French officers. For nearly a decade the war continued, until the Treaty of Ryswick in 1697 between England and France gave four years of peace. But in 1701, the very year that New France's conflict with the Iroquois ended, war broke out again with England.

FRANCE'S NEW NORTH AMERICAN STRATEGY, 1701

France developed a new North American strategy in 1701 and held to it for the remainder of the French regime. Economically, Canada was a complete liability on France's economic balance sheet. With a glut of furs in France the fur trade had ceased to be of any economic benefit. Rather than retreat from the Great Lakes and Mississippi valley, the French resolved to remain for strategic reasons. To keep the Indians in the French alliance they would, if necessary, subsidize the fur trade in the interior so that the Indians would curb the westward expansion of the English. France had to prevent the English occupation of the region between the mountains and the Mississippi river, for if the English succeeded in settling the interior, their numbers would greatly increase and England's wealth and power grow.

The empire the fur traders had created was to be retained for non-economic reasons. No more attention was paid to Colbert's idea of a "compact colony" on the banks of the St. Lawrence. The French now began preparations for a chain of posts linking the Great Lakes to the Gulf of Mexico. Louis XIV also ordered a settlement, Détroit (the straits) to be built at the narrows between Lakes Erie and Huron. The new fort was to bar English access to the northwest and maintain French control of the Upper Great Lakes. With their Indian allies the French planned to contain the English to the coastal strip between the Alleghenies and the Atlantic.

New France's Weaknesses in Wartime

The war that began between the English colonies and New France in 1689 was only resolved in 1760—more than three-quarters of a century later. In the initial struggle New France had three main handicaps. First the colony's population was small—the English colonists, in fact, outnumbered the French by nearly twenty to one. A second weakness of the tiny colony lay in the precariousness of its economy. Only one real export industry existed—the fur trade, and it was extremely vulnerable in wartime when the transport of furs from the interior could be cut off. New France had a third telling weakness: war made agriculture unusually vulnerable to disruption. Even in good years the habitants produced only a small surplus. In wartime they had a deficit, because militia service pulled the habitants off the land. It also meant increased dependence on French food and war materials at a time when the sea lanes to and from France became vulnerable to English attack.

107

New France's Strengths in Wartime

New France's small population, the difficulty of transporting its one major export product in periods of war, and its inability to feed itself during war time all were serious. The French colony did, though, have a number of advantages.

POLITICAL UNITY

Effective political leadership was the colony's first advantage. The reforms of 1663 left New France a unified command structure in times of war, with the chain of command very clear. Subject only to annual review, the governor had complete control over the marshalling of the colony's resources, its negotiations with the Indians, and the planning of the colony's war strategy.

NEW FRANCE'S NATURAL DEFENCES

In the 1690s nature provided New France with a second strength—natural defences. The Adirondacks of New York, the Green Mountains of Vermont, and the White Mountains of New Hampshire and Maine all protected the French colony from a direct attack from the south. Two of the three gates to the St. Lawrence, the river itself (closed half of the year by ice), and the Hudson River–Lake Champlain–Richelieu River waterway could be sealed. Quebec commanded the St. Lawrence River and a system of forts existed on the Richelieu (later to be complemented by fortifications at the southern end of Lake Champlain). The only gateway that could not be effectively shut off was the western approach from Lake Ontario—the Iroquois proved this in 1689 with their lightning raid on Lachine.

108

THE IROQUOIS' CONTRIBUTION

Inadvertently, the Iroquois represented the third strength of New France: they had trained the French in guerilla warfare. A cadre of tough and versatile French raiders emerged from the wars with the Iroquois in the Illinois country, men who became Frontenac's most-valued troops in his raids against English frontier settlements in New England and New York. These Frenchmen matched the success of the Iroquois' devastation at Lachine.

NEW FRANCE'S ALGONQUIAN ALLIES

France's Algonquian Indian allies constituted her fourth great asset. The French had very close trading (hence military) ties with the Abenakis from Maine, many of whom had sought refuge in Canada and with the Micmacs and Malecites in the Maritimes.

France also had loose alliances with the Great Lakes Algonquians: the Ojibwa, Ottawa, Potawatomi, Miami, and Illinois. Moreover, the Canadian fur traders and fort commanders, unlike the land-hungry English settlers, cultivated the friendship of the Algonquians by giving the Indians gifts and presents. While the English benefitted from the Iroquois' support in the 1680s and 1690s, the majority of the Amerindian groups in northeastern North America sided with the French.

THE DIVISIONS AMONG THE ENGLISH COLONIES

Another great advantage for the French arose from the divisions among the English colonists in the late seventeenth century. A great deal of friction existed in English America, arising in part from differences in origin and religion. Not all the colonies even felt the French danger; for instance, the southern colonies of the Carolinas, Virginia, Maryland, and Pennsylvania believed themselves quite safe behind their mountain barriers. New York and Massachusetts shielded Rhode Island, Connecticut, and New Jersey. In the north, really only two highly populated colonies—Massachusetts and New York—supported the struggle.

Of the two English colonies that fought New France, New York might have proved Canada's match but for the fact the colony's non-Indian population was divided in the 1690s between the descendants of the original Dutch colonists and the new English settlers. The Dutch in the north showed little enthusiasm for offensive operations in the name of the English king, and consequently New York posed little threat to New France. Massachusetts, though, did launch a naval attack on Quebec in 1690.

NEW FRANCE'S "LUCK"

New France's final great advantage over the English came through what, for a better word, might be termed luck. Sir William Phips of Massachusetts, after taking Port-Royal in Acadia in 1690 (see chapter 7), returned to Boston to take command of a naval expedition of over thirty vessels with twenty-three hundred men. Fortunately for the survival of Canada, Phips' ships took two months to reach Quebec. En route smallpox had broken out and swept through his ranks. They also arrived at Quebec late in the season. Fearing entrapment in the ice, Phips withdrew after consuming almost all of his powder in bombarding the Quebec citadel.

Luck, if it could again be called that, intervened again in the second round of the contest, which began in 1702. The English and French fought the second conflict largely as a rerun of the previous war, without any conclusive blows being delivered by either side until 1711. In that year England decided to make a final, decisive strike against New France. An armada under Sir Hovenden Walker was organized, and England supplied 5300 troops, building up the armada's strength to nearly 6500, while 2300 troops on land worked their way up the Lake Champlain route. New France was thus invaded by a force three times as large as had attacked her in 1690. In numbers the invasion force equalled one-half of the total French population in the St. Lawrence valley. Fortune again intervened on the side of the Canadians. In the fog and gales of the mouth of the

St. Lawrence the English lost ships and nearly 900 men. The Walker expedition turned back.

The Treaty of Utrecht, 1713

The Treaty of Utrecht in 1713 settled the war, one in which the French did suprisingly well. From 1682 to 1713 they waged a determined campaign to expel the English from Hudson Bay. In the first round of conflict, Pierre Le Moyne d'Iberville defeated the English in several sea expeditions. At the close of the second round in 1713 the French held York Factory, the most important Hudson's Bay Company post, on Hudson Bay. They retook Port-Royal in Acadia, retained Detroit and their forts on the Great Lakes, and by founding Louisiana, consolidated their position in the Mississippi valley. Although casualties are difficult to estimate, it appears that New France and its Indian allies inflicted casualties at a ratio of at least three to one, yet the peace treaty did not reflect this success.

110

New France paid Louis XIV's debts at the bargaining table at Utrecht. On account of its military losses in Europe, France had to make concessions elsewhere, and Louis XIV decided to make them in North America. To regain some of its losses in Europe, France ceded all claims to Newfoundland, except for fishing rights on the north shore. It gave up its claims on Hudson Bay. The French recognized British suzerainty over the Iroquois Confederacy, which the British later interpreted to mean that commerce with the Indian nations in the west was now open to English traders as well as the French. They also surrendered French control over what the English called Nova Scotia, handing the major French Acadian settlements over to the English. Without having lost a single major battle, the Canadians lost the Treaty of Utrecht.

Military Preparations, 1713–44

New France's governor, Philippe de Rigaud de Vaudreuil, began preparations for another round of military conflict with the English in 1713. From the late 1660s on, the entire male population from sixteen to sixty served in the militia, with each parish, large or small, furnishing a company. The French government also had more than six hundred troops in the colony in 1714 to complement the roughly forty-five hundred militia. New France's great military advantage still lay in its ability to mobilize its citizen army quickly.

New France's loss of the St. Lawrence gateways of Acadia and Newfoundland was a serious strategic loss. France, though, still held on to Cape Breton Island. In 1717 the French attempted to redress the situation

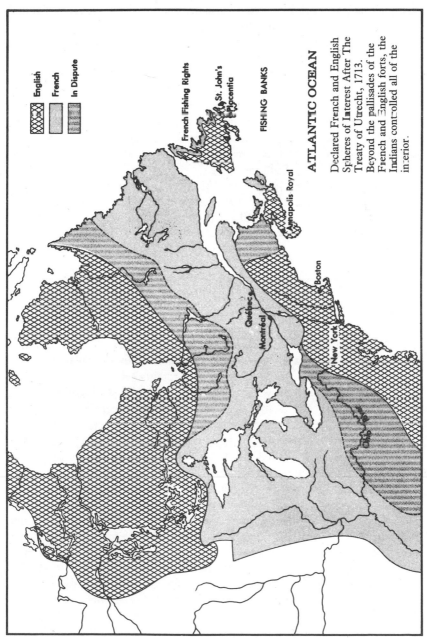

ATLANTIC OCEAN

Declared French and English Spheres of Interest After The Treaty of Utrecht, 1713. Beyond the pallisades of the French and English forts, the Indians controlled all of the interior.

English
French
In Dispute

French Fishing Rights
St. John's
Placentia
FISHING BANKS
Annapolis Royal
Boston
Québec
Montréal
New York

111

Cornell, Hamelin, Ouellet, Trudel, *Canada, Unity in Diversity*, p. 38.

by constructing at Louisbourg a military fortress to rival that at Gibraltar. Although essentially a garrison town, Louisbourg also became an important fishing port and a vital commercial centre fur trade between France, Quebec, and the West Indies. It became one of the busiest ports in colonial America—fourth only to Boston, New York, and Charlestown.

To protect the major towns in the St. Lawrence valley, Vaudreuil built fortifications at Quebec and Montreal. The French also moved to strengthen their military position on the Great Lakes and on Lake Champlain. When the French learned in 1719 that the colony of New York intended to establish a fort at Niagara (which could cut the trade links between New France and Louisiana), Vaudreuil requested permission from the Iroquois to build a "house" on their western boundary and erected a fort. The English responded by building Fort Oswego at the eastern end of Lake Ontario. As a counterbalance the French then constructed Fort Saint-Frédéric on Lake Champlain, at the narrows of the lake near its southern end. Saint-Frédéric now closed off the main invasion route into Canada from New York.

112

THE WAR AGAINST THE FOX INDIANS

While the Canadians were strengthening their military position on Lakes Ontario and Champlain they became involved in an Indian war west of Lake Michigan. The Fox tribe, wishing to retain their position as middlemen in the fur trade, prevented the French from making direct contact with the Dakota (Sioux), the Fox's neighbours and enemies immediately to the west. Friction with the French turned into open warfare from 1714 to 1717. The first campaigns only temporarily checked the Fox, with whom conflict again broke out in 1728. On this occasion, for the first and only time in the Great Lakes area, the French aimed at wiping out the hostile group by inciting incessant attacks by the Fox's Indian neighbours. The French authorities decided that the Fox should all be killed or sent as slaves to the West Indies. It proved impossible, as the Fox retreated and regrouped in present-day Wisconsin. In 1737 the French authorities conceded the futility of continued military action against the tribe and granted them a pardon.

French strength in the interior rested on its "gift diplomacy." Each year at Detroit, Niagara, Michilimackinac, and other posts around the Great Lakes and Lake Winnipeg (where Pierre Gaultier de Varennnes et de La Vérendrye established posts in the 1730s and 1740s, see chapter 18), the French gave their Indian allies "presents"—guns, ammunition, and supplies. The Indians regarded the annual gifts as a form of rent for the use of the land on which the French forts stood and also as a fee for

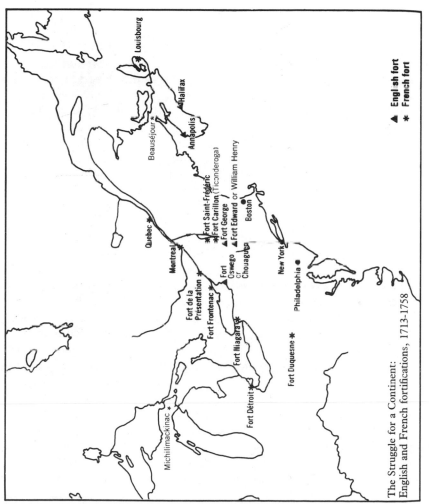

The Struggle for a Continent:
English and French fortifications, 1713-1758

Trudel, *Introduction to New France*, p. 88.

the right to travel across their territory. The Indians remained in complete possession of their lands and limited French rule to the tiny confines of their trading posts.

THE OUTBREAK OF WAR AND THE FALL OF LOUISBOURG

Apart from the war with the Foxes to the west and the Micmac raids against the British in Nova Scotia, the period 1713–44 was relatively peaceful. This tranquility ended in 1744 with the outbreak of war in Europe between France and England. The business community of New England welcomed the opportunity of attacking Cape Breton (Ile Royale). If it fell, they could secure a monopoly of the North Atlantic fisheries as well as eliminate the French privateers based on Louisbourg, who had caused havoc among the New England fishing and trading fleets. Governor William Shirley of Massachusetts organized an expedition of more than four thousand colonial militia to attack the French fortress. In spite of the long years spent on construction, the invaders found the walls on the town's southern and northern flanks extremely weak. The defenders also lacked adequate provisions and munitions. The attackers bombarded the town heavily for nearly seven weeks, reducing it to ruins. Finally, with no help expected from France, the defenders surrendered.

Louisbourg's fall caused great anxiety in Canada and revealed the precariousness of France's position in the interior. It opened the gates of the St. Lawrence, clearing the way to Quebec. Fortunately for New France, England could not mount an invasion of Quebec in 1745. Prince Charles Edward Stuart, "Bonnie Prince Charlie," had just rallied his Highland forces in Scotland. Until the English defeated Prince Charles at Culloden Moor in April 1746, they could not send troops elsewhere.

The French realized the fortress's importance. They attempted to retake Louisbourg in the summer of 1746, assembling a force of seven thousand. The naval expedition, though, proved to be one of the most unfortunate ever undertaken by the French. In Nova Scotian waters scurvy and smallpox took a terrific toll of the men onboard. On October 5 it was reported that nearly six hundred men had died and fifteen hundred more were too weak to do anything. The fleet returned to France without having obtained a single one of its objectives, at the cost of thousands of dead.

The continued possession of Louisbourg by the English had very serious consequences for the French. The fall of the fortress meant that British privateers had an open season on French trading ships. This prevented the supplies of ammunition and trade goods so badly needed for the Indian trade from reaching the interior.

The disruption of normal trade between France and Quebec led to the defection of many of France's Great Lakes Indian allies. An Indian conspiracy arose in 1747 in the Wyandot (Huron) village of Sandusky on Lake Erie, not far from Detroit, with many Algonquians joining the Wyandot. Fortunately for France, hostilities with England ceased in 1748 and the French could rush trade goods to the interior, ending the Indian hostility.

France now knew that without their great Atlantic port it would lose the interior of North America, perhaps the St. Lawrence valley as well. In order to regain Louisbourg, they sacrificed during the peace treaty negotiations at Aix-la-Chapelle their conquests in the Netherlands as well as the city of Madras in India.

Rivalry in the Ohio Country

The Treaty of Aix-la-Chapelle in 1748 proved only a glorified ceasefire, with the next clash to come in the Ohio country. The governor of New France refused to concede this strategic region (the natural highway to the west), to the English. Governor Roland-Michel Barrin de La Galissonière authorized the dispatch of a military expedition to the Ohio in 1749. Pierre-Joseph de Céloron de Blainville, the veteran commander at Detroit, commanded the mission. To deter the Pennsylvanians from trading in the region west of the Alleghenies and in the Virginians' settlements, Céloron recommended the construction of a chain of forts to connect Lake Erie with the Ohio River.

In 1753 the Marquis Duquesne, the new governor of New France, made the occupation of the Ohio a top military priority. Even though the cost in money—and lives—would be high, the English had to be stopped. That same year he sent a French military expedition to clear a route from Lake Erie to the forks of the Ohio River, and the following year he commanded French soldiers to build Fort Duquesne at the forks of the river.

As early as November 1753 Virginia's governor received British authority to use force, if necessary, to oust the French from the king's dominions; Virginia considered English territory to include the area at the forks of the Ohio. In early 1754 the governor sent George Washington, a twenty-two-year-old Virginia militia officer, and a number of Indian allies to expel the French. In the late spring of 1754 Washington's party of militiamen and Indians ambushed a small French detachment sent to order them to withdraw from the area. The Virginians killed the officer in command and nine of his men. These were the first deaths in what became a larger war. The Seven Years' War thus began in America two years before the first shots were fired in Europe.

After the clash Washington quickly withdrew about one hundred kilometres from Fort Duquesne to a temporary fortification that the Virginians called Fort Necessity. The French quickly prepared an attack on the Virginian "assassins." Under cover from a nearby woods a force of five hundred French, Canadians, and Indians opened fire on the Virginians and soon overpowered them. The French allowed George Washington and the Virginians to return home, and their defeat brought all the wavering Indian bands into the French alliance.

New France at the Outset of The Seven Years' War

By the mid-1750s New France had built up its military strength considerably. The population of Canada had tripled since 1713, to more than fifty-five thousand in 1755. Moreover, new farmlands had been cleared along the Richelieu River, southeast of Montreal; along the Ottawa, northeast of Montreal; and along the Chaudière, south of Quebec. More manpower could be called up and more farm produce provided. Finally, transportation had improved over the last half century. Road-building allowed expansion back from the waterfront, thereby facilitating better communication. All these developments were definite strengths for the colony.

Many weaknesses also existed. First, New France suffered from the precariousness of its elongated frontier; it took a year to exchange letters between Quebec and New Orleans. To protect French interests the crown built a string of forts from Louisbourg to Fort Duquesne, but many of these outposts were simply trading posts grown into wooden forts. Second, the Franco-Algonquian alliance was precarious. The Canadians could hold the interior only as long as they retained the support of the Great Lakes Indian tribes. In 1747 the French learned how the Indians would react if French trade goods did not reach the interior. Third, although the population of New France increased greatly to over 50 000, the population of the American colonies was more than one million. American settlement extended nearly two hundred kilometres from the coastline. Fourth, although the eight thousand militia of the colony could be quickly called up, few of them knew the guerilla techniques for the forest warfare that their grandfathers and great-grandfathers had mastered. Fifth, the growing friction between the French and the Canadian-born in the army officers' ranks weakened New France.

A sixth weakness of New France lay in its economy—in wartime the colony could not feed its more than three thousand regular troops, as well as the varying numbers of Indians and militia who had to be supplied, at least while on service. Another problem arose as well: the need for manpower to harvest crops made it impossible for the French to go on lengthy offensives.

More troubling than all these shortcomings was the new unity of the American colonies. The co-ordination of strategy under a British com-

116

mander-in-chief did much to draw them together. In addition, the colonists wanted to defeat New France to end the border raids and open up the rich farmlands of the Ohio valley. Nine colonies with larger populations than New France gave the English colonists a manpower advantage of nearly twenty-five to one. The foodstuffs available to them were enormous. In 1755 the governor of Pennsylvania claimed that his colony alone could export enough food to provide for an army of one hundred thousand. Pennsylvania's iron industry already competed with the iron industry of the mother country.

New France's Successes, 1754–57

In its early years, however, the war for North America went badly for the British. In 1755, General Braddock planned a four-pronged offensive aimed at taking four French forts: Duquesne, Niagara, Saint-Frédéric, and Beauséjour (the latter on the Isthmus of Chignecto between Nova Scotia and present-day New Brunswick). Since France and Britain were still officially at peace in 1755, Braddock's offensive did not aim at the conquest of New France but merely the rolling back of France's empire in North America.

117

Braddock himself took command of the assault on Fort Duquesne, with a strike force of 1000 regulars and 1500 colonial troops. It took two months for the force to make its long march over the mountains—to clear roads and drag cannon and supplies. The spirits of the advance column of 1450 men were high when they finally arrived within fifteen kilometres of Fort Duquesne. Then came an ambush. The French and their Indian allies unleashed a barrage of gunfire at the scarlet-coated regulars and blue-coated Virginians, inflicting 1000 casualties. Braddock himself was killed and his army destroyed.

Immediately after news of the defeat at Duquesne arrived, the British postponed their expedition against Fort Niagara. In the attack on Fort Saint-Frédéric in the Lake Champlain area they did no better than a draw. Governor Pierre de Rigaud de Vaudreuil de Cavagnial (the Canadian-born son of Governor Philippe de Rigaud de Vaudreuil) immediately built Fort Carillon at the northern end of Lake George. Carillon, so named because it was where the falling waters produced the sound of bells, became New France's first line of defence for the St. Lawrence valley.

In Acadia the Anglo-Americans scored their only clear-cut success. Thanks to the assistance of Thomas Pichon, a traitorous French officer, Fort Beauséjour fell and with it, French Acadia. The fall of Beauséjour cleared the way for an attack from Halifax on Louisbourg and for a drastic measure—the expulsion of the Acadians, then approximately ten thousand strong, from peninsular Nova Scotia (see chapter 7).

Apart from Beauséjour, the French and their Indian allies thus humiliated the larger English colonies and the British army in 1755. The newly-appointed governor, the Canadian-born Marquis de Vaudreuil, wanted to keep up the momentum, fighting where the Canadians and the Indians excelled—in the forest. Terror struck the frontier settlements of Pennsylvania, Maryland, and Virginia. In 1756 Vaudreuil sent out more than two thousand Indians and Canadians in raids from Fort Duquesne. These raids spread by the end of the summer to the Carolinas. Canadian cadets, or junior officers, led the Indian war parties. The Canadian guerilla bands caused so much terror in Virginia and Maryland that these two colonies stayed out of the war to the north until 1758, fearing that the raids might trigger slave uprisings.

The French gained control of the Great Lakes by capturing Fort Oswego in 1756. The following year Vaudreuil attempted to take Fort William Henry, south of the French stronghold of Carillon (or Ticonderoga as the English termed it). It was a more difficult challenge, as Fort William

118 Henry—unlike Oswego—lay at the end of a short and easy supply line and, in fact, could be reinforced speedily from Albany. In addition, grain shortages were severe and persistent in Canada, and the limited provisions would not permit a long seige of the English fort. A final problem arose as well: the growing rift between Governor Vaudreuil and the lieutenant general, the Marquis de Montcalm, the new French military commander in Canada. Fort William Henry did fall, but Montcalm refused to march against Fort Edward, the English post on the Hudson River twenty-five kilometres to the south.

For Vaudreuil, offence was the only defence, but Montcalm opposed such a strategy. He wanted to see a concentration of French and Canadian troops in the St. Lawrence valley in order to protect Montreal and Quebec against the next English invasion. The French ministry resolved the dispute by putting Montcalm over Vaudreuil in military matters.

Britain Gains the Upper Hand

The entire aspect of the war changed in 1757 with the accession to office of William Pitt the elder, a self-styled saviour of the British Empire. The new prime minister inspired a nation suffering defeat to make a greater effort and made the American war and the conquest of Canada his major objectives. The British offensive of 1758 came in the same four localities as 1755, but on this occasion with rather different results. Braddock's previous offensive had clearly succeeded in only one. The campaign of 1758 succeeded in three of the four.

Several factors explain the change in England's fortunes. First, Pitt decided in 1758 to commit large numbers of regular soldiers to America, men reliable under fire in set-piece European-style battles. Second, by

1758 the Royal Navy's blockade of France was so effective that there were no more major "escapes" of French support squadrons to Canada. Lastly, Pitt greatly increased Britain's financial commitment to the war. More men, more ships, and more money made a significant difference in British fortunes in 1758 and 1759.

FRANCE'S REVERSES IN 1758

The first English objective in 1758 was Louisbourg which, because of the effectiveness of the British blockade on France, now lacked the protection of a fleet. The thirteen thousand attackers outnumbered the defenders three to one. To the British the important factor was speed. Louisbourg had to be taken quickly for Quebec to be captured in the same season. The defenders, however, held out for seven weeks, just long enough to rule out an expedition against Quebec in 1758.

119

The successful French defence at Carillon also served to prevent an attack on Canada in 1758. At Carillon, Montcalm with 3500 men faced 15 000, the largest English army yet to serve in North America. Although he won, the French success had its price. Indirectly it cost the French both Fort Frontenac on Lake Ontario and Fort Duquesne in Ohio. As almost all the troops available in the colony had been concentrated at Carillon, Fort Frontenac, with its small garrison and inadequate walls, could not be defended against an English attack. The French destroyed the important post in August 1758. They also abandoned Fort Duquesne. When an English army of seven thousand came within a few kilometres of Fort Duquesne, the French garrison blew the fort up and retreated. The English renamed the site "Pittsburgh," after their prime minister.

The largest single explanation for the English success in 1758 was the Royal Navy, which blockaded Canada. The navy allowed the English colonies to obtain troop reinforcements and supplies, and New France was deprived of any major outside assistance. In 1759 New France faced odds of nearly three to one in ships, four to one in soldiers, and ten to one in money.

NEW FRANCE IN 1759

The year 1759 proved harsh for New France. Pitt's determination to take the French colony became an obsession. With the great resources England had in America it could attack at both Quebec and Carillon in equal strength. New France, however, with its limited resources, had to concentrate its strength in the most vital area—Quebec. At the capital white-haired men and beardless boys turned out to defend their homeland. All told, the Franco-Canadian army that gathered at Quebec in the summer of 1759 numbered between 12 000 and 15 000. From a population of only some 60 000, this was an extraordinary mobilization.

JAMES WOLFE AT QUEBEC

James Wolfe, thirty-two years old, a first-class regimental commander, ambitious and covetous of reputation, commanded the British invasion force sent against Quebec. He had performed very well at Louisbourg, and Pitt gave him a splendid professional army; all the troops had previous American experience. The strike force of 4000 included some of the best units in the British army. In all, the gigantic invasion fleet had 13 500 men. With the help of a gifted officer named James Cook, whose skill in locating the St. Lawrence River channel later made him one of the world's greatest seamen, the entire fleet was conveyed up to Quebec in three weeks without a single grounding.

The French defenders at Quebec faced several defensive problems in the summer of 1759. First, the city walls on the western side facing the Plains of Abraham had no gun emplacements, seriously weakening the city's defence. Second, the French made another monumental error: they left undefended the south bank of the river opposite the city, and shortly after their arrival the British established batteries there. From the Lévis heights they bombarded and largely destroyed the city. Worse still, under cover of this fire, the Royal Navy could transport their ships up the river beyond Quebec. In effect, the British army could land either above or below Quebec for an assault on the walled town.

All that summer inland French-held garrisons continued to fall into enemy hands. By the end of June 1759 the British reoccupied Fort Oswego. Fort Niagara succumbed to a British attack in late July. The French had now lost control of Lakes Ontario and Erie, and the Ohio country. In addition, the French abandoned Fort Carillon and Fort Saint-Frédéric and retreated northward to the head of Lake Champlain.

The Canadian historian C.P. Stacey aptly called James Wolfe a "Hamlet-figure"—a good soldier but one who had enormous difficulty making up his mind.[1] This was his first independent command, and he could not decide where to attack. After several weeks of indecision he made up his mind to strike Montcalm and his forces at Montmorency, just east of Quebec. Wolfe's frontal attack on the French army's entrenchments failed and the British retreated. The English commander spent the remainder of the summer burning to the ground fourteen hundred stone homes and manor houses in the Quebec area.

THE BATTLE OF THE PLAINS OF ABRAHAM

Wolfe knew that he had to obtain a foothold on the north shore and then force Montcalm into an open, European-style battle. Haste was essential, for the naval expedition had to leave the St. Lawrence before the onset of winter. Then luck intervened: the British found a passage, Anse au Foulon, now also known as Wolfe's Cove. From the small cove a narrow path led up the steep cliffs sixty metres high. Believing it to be impossible for the invasion force to climb the heights on the tiny path, the French had left it lightly guarded. Incredibly, they had also failed to establish a password for a French convoy expected to bring supplies on the night of September 12–13.

Right up until the landing Montcalm believed that Wolfe's attack would come on the other side of the city or on the centre, never at Anse au Foulon to the west. The British achieved complete surprise, as the French sentries on the shore believed that the boats gliding past them belonged to the French convoy expected that night (in fact, the convoy had been cancelled). The British commander placed his few French-speaking officers in the forward vessels; in the dark, they answered the sentries' challenges satisfactorily. On the morning of September 13 the British landed near the cove, a half-hour before morning broke. Three waves of landing ships reached the shore in total darkness. The advance party, two abreast, then walked up the steep pathway and, without detection, gained the summit of the cliffs.

A long succession of risks taken all worked out in Wolfe's favour: the difficult naval landing succeeded and his advance guard overpowered the French post, securing a foothold above the cliffs. Wolfe had taken an enormous chance—if the French sentries had identified the British in time they could have sounded the alarm, and the French could have easily picked off the advance guard as they climbed the summit.

By the daybreak Wolfe deployed 4500 highly trained British troops on the Plains of Abraham, the grassy field close to the unarmed western walls of the citadel. At this point, Montcalm made a fatal mistake. Without waiting for Colonel Louis-Antoine de Bougainville to arrive with 3000 regulars stationed at Cap Rouge about fifteen kilometres upstream, Montcalm rushed into battle with 4500 men, half of his available forces. About 8 o'clock that morning Bougainville learned of the enemy landing, but by the time he reached Quebec the conflict was over.

The battle lasted less than half an hour. As the French marched out the British held their fire. Wolfe knew the value of precise, accurate, and concentrated firepower. He had deployed three-quarters of his men in a single line. The British waited silently until the French army, also 4500 strong, was but forty metres away. Then the British officers gave the order, "Fire." The muskets roared, and a second volley followed, covering the ground with French dead. When the British regulars charged with fixed bayonets, the Canadian and French troops broke ranks. Wolfe, leading a picked force of grenadiers, was shot down and died on the battlefield. In the confusion after Wolfe's death the French army escaped to Quebec. Mortally wounded in the battle, Montcalm died the next day in Quebec. The British suffered about 650 casualties and the French roughly the same. On September 17, Quebec, short of provisions, soldiers, and weakly fortified on its western side, opened its gates to the English after the defeated French army had retreated.

122

NEW FRANCE'S FINAL YEAR, 1759–60

The loss of Quebec was a serious blow to the French, but they still controlled all of the valley of the St. Lawrence, with the exception of Quebec and its outskirts. Their army was intact. Everything now depended on which ships would arrive first in the spring. The French planned to launch a spring offensive to co-ordinate with the arrival of ships from France.

Before the ice left the rivers in April the Chevalier de Lévis, the new French commander, marched his 7000 troops to Quebec. James Murray, the British commander, had experienced a terrible winter, one in which he had seen scurvy reduce his garrison to about 4000. Lévis defeated him at Ste-Foy, immediately west of the city, near today's location of Université Laval. This battle proved bloodier than the Plains of Abraham, with losses of about 850 casualties on the French side and nearly 1100 on the English.

Victorious Lévis, Montcalm's successor, proceeded to besiege Quebec. Short of ammunition and supplies, Lévis and New France eagerly prayed for French ships to reach Quebec. But British seapower had dealt a final fatal blow to the French navy at Quiberon Bay in November 1759. No seaborne French invasion of England would be forthcoming. The English ships arrived first at Quebec in mid-May, and no French ships were sighted. Lévis had to raise his seige, with the rest of the year's operations being a forgone conclusion.

At Montreal that September Lévis and 2000 troops confronted 17 000 British and American troops coming from three directions. After the French

National Gallery of Canada.

"The Death of General Wolfe." The most famous portrayal of the Battle of the Plains of Abraham was painted by the American artist Benjamin West—eleven years after it happened. In actual fact only about four men were with the general when he died.

capitulated on September 8, 1760, the British took possession of Montreal and Canada passed into British hands.

Was the fall of New France inevitable? Many historians argue that it was. I.K. Steele, for instance, concludes his study, *Guerillas and Grenadiers. The Struggle for Canada, 1689–1760*: "The British Army and the Royal Navy beseiged Canada with an overwhelming military force. France could not send a force to lift the siege and, after a stout defence, Canada fell to fortune's favourite—the biggest army."[2] Yet, at least one leading historian of New France disagrees. W.J. Eccles presents a contrary view in his *France in America*: "Had Montcalm not employed such disastrous tactics at Quebec on September 13, 1759, the fortress city would not have fallen; instead the British army might well have been destroyed."[3] Thus, over two centuries after the event, the historical controversy over the fall of New France continues.

In 1760 the *Canadiens* would have had little time for such discussion. Disarmed and obliged to swear an oath of allegiance to the British King they awaited the announcement of their ultimate fate. Many feared that Britain would deport them all, just as she had expelled the Acadians from their homeland.

NOTES

[1] C.P. Stacey, *Quebec, 1759: The Siege and the Battle* (Toronto, 1959), p. 171.
[2] I.K. Steele, *Guerillas and Grenadiers. The Struggle for Canada, 1689–1760* (Toronto, 1969), p. 134.
[3] W.J. Eccles, *France in America* (New York, 1972), p. 208.

Related Readings

Two articles in R. Douglas Francis and Donald B. Smith, *Readings in Canadian History: Pre-Confederation*, 2d ed. (Toronto, 1986), are useful for this topic: W.J. Eccles, "The Preemptive Conquest, 1749–1763," pp. 126–48; and Guy Frégault, "Canadian Society in the French Regime," pp. 148–60.

124

BIBLIOGRAPHY

For an overview of French expansion into the interior of North America and New France's conflict with the English colonies, see W.J. Eccles, *The Canadian Frontier, 1534–1760* (Toronto, 1969), and *France in America* (New York, 1972); also, his *Essays on New France* (Toronto, 1987). Marcel Trudel briefly reviews French westward expansion in "Planting Flags," *Horizon Canada*, number 24 (1985): 560–65.

Four excellent volumes on the military events of the late seventeenth and eighteenth centuries are: I.K. Steele, *Guerillas and Grenadiers. The Struggle for Canada, 1689–1760* (Toronto, 1969); George F.G. Stanley, *New France: The Last Phase, 1744–1760* (Toronto, 1968); C.P. Stacey, *Quebec, 1759: The Siege and the Battle* (Toronto, 1959); and Guy Frégault, *Canada: The War of the Conquest*, translated by Margaret M. Cameron (Toronto, 1969). The *Dictionary of Canadian Biography* (Toronto, 1966–) also contains important biographical sketches; of particular interest are C.P. Stacey's "James Wolfe" in vol. 3: 1741–1770, pp. 666–74; and W.J. Eccles' "Louis-Joseph de Montcalm," pp. 458–69, in the same volume—and W.J. Eccles, "Pierre de Rigaud de Vaudreuil de Cavagnial," pp. 662–74, in vol. 4: 1771–1800. The best summaries of the two respective armies in the 1750s appear in vol. 3 of the *Dictionary of Canadian Biography*; see the essays by W.J. Eccles, "The French Forces in North America during the Seven Years' War," pp. xv–xxiii; and C.P. Stacey, "The British Forces in North America during the Seven Years' War," pp. xxiv–xxx. An overview of Louisbourg is J.S. McLennan's *Louisbourg from its Foundation to its Fall, 1713–58* (London, 1918). Students will enjoy the five well-crafted biographies in Christopher Moore's *Louisbourg Portraits* (Toronto, 1982). For an American perspective on the final struggle for the continent, see *Prehistory to 1789*, vol. 1 of Samuel Eliot Morison's *Oxford History of the American People*, 3 vols. (New York, 1972).

Valuable maps on the Seven Years' War and the battles for Quebec, 1759–60, are contained in the *Historical Atlas of Canada*, vol. 1, edited by R. Cole Harris (Toronto, 1987).

125

CHAPTER SEVEN

The Acadians

The name Acadia was first used by the French to distinguish the eastern or maritime part of New France from the valley of the St. Lawrence, or western portion, which they called Canada. Under French rule Canada and Acadia remained separate colonies. Just where the border of Acadia ended and that of Canada began was never clearly defined, but certainly Acadia included present-day New Brunswick, Nova Scotia, and Prince Edward Island. Its fate was to be located on the frontier between English- and French-dominated areas.

Since France's interests lay largely in Canada, with its fur trade and its agricultural settlement centred in the St. Lawrence valley, Acadia was largely neglected. Little contact existed between the two colonies, even before Acadia passed to England by the Treaty of Utrecht in 1713. Gradually, a cultural distinctiveness emerged between the Acadians and the French Canadians despite their common French origins and shared Roman Catholic faith. By the mid-eighteenth century the Acadians had become a people distinct from both the French Canadians and the French. Yet with the outbreak of war with France in 1754, the English regarded them as a threat to British Nova Scotia, and in 1755 they deported the Acadians from their homeland.

Beginnings of French Acadia

The roots of French Acadia go back to 1604, when the French wintered on an island in the St. Croix river, and then again in 1605 and 1606 at Port-Royal. With Champlain's founding of Quebec in 1608, however, France's colonization efforts became focussed on Canada, although French interest in Acadia never waned entirely.

Jean de Biencourt, Sieur de Poutrincourt, a French nobleman, came out with the first expedition of 1604 and left in 1607. In 1611 Poutrincourt brought back his family, several settlers, and two Jesuit priests, Pierre Biard and Enemond Massé. But Poutrincourt's settlement failed after Samuel Argall, a Virginia pirate, struck from his base at Jamestown and destroyed Port-Royal. Argall's attack ruined Poutrincourt's French investors, and *Acadie*, as an European settlement, almost completely vanished until the 1630s.

After Argall's attack in 1613 France and England showed little interest in this isolated Atlantic region. Although in 1621 Acadia was granted to a Scot, William Alexander, he did not establish a Scottish colony there until 1629. About seventy settlers came to Port-Royal, but with the exception of one or two families who elected to remain, they left three years later when the Treaty of Saint-Germain-en-Laye restored Acadia to France.

With the arrival of Governor Isaac de Razilly in 1632, France began its first serious attempt to colonize Acadia. Many of the settlers came from the regions of Poitou, Aunis, and Saintonge on the west coast of France, near the Atlantic port of La Rochelle. Acadian names are easily recognizable today: Dugas, Gaudet, Landry, and Aucoin were among the earliest arrivals, followed by Leblanc, Cormier, Gallant, Légère, Saunier, and Arsenault, Boudreau, Comeau, Robichaud, Thériault, and Thibodeau.

Labourers skilled in harvesting salt from the salt marshes joined the contingent of several hundred colonists. In Acadia they used their skills to build dikes to reclaim the fertile land that the Bay of Fundy's strong tides flooded twice a day. The colonists spread their dwellings out around bays and through the valleys, rather than clear the forested upland areas.

Razilly's death in 1636, though, proved catastrophic for the colony. Years of strife and confusion followed as three of his successors claimed Acadia. In 1640 Charles de Menou d'Aulnay, Nicolas Denys, and Charles de Saint-Etienne de La Tour governed their own territories and claimed the exclusive right to trade. A small civil war broke out. The conflict was bloody and bizarre, and did not end until La Tour killed d'Aulnay and married his widow! In 1654 the struggle between France and England again reached Acadia, which lay as a wedge between their expanding empires. The English in that year re-conquered Acadia and held it until 1670. They chiefly saw it as a strategically located fishing zone and fur-trading area.

Acadian Society in the Late Seventeenth Century

During the occupation the Acadians first developed a spirit of accommodation rather then confrontation with their English rulers. On account of the need to know English some Acadians learned to speak that language.

The generation of Acadian children born between 1654 and 1670 had little or no knowledge of France.

The Acadians developed a unique identity, with strong family kinship patterns. Although the settlers had come from different areas in France, once settled here, they intermarried with the original French inhabitants and developed a family network that crisscrossed the colony.

Within Acadian society the family and the church, rather than the seigneurial system, became the most powerful institutions. The Crown granted seigneuries at Port-Royal, Beaubassin (the first major village settled after Port-Royal), and along the St. John River, but the seigneurs had practically no influence on the settlers' daily life. In the St. Lawrence valley an intendant enforced the system, but in Acadia there was none. Nor did the English compel obedience to the seigneurs during their occupation of the region.

The Acadian church, in contrast, was an important influence. No one religious order dominated Acadian development but the Jesuits, Capuchins, Récollets, and Sulpicians took part in religious and educational work among the Acadian population. The Acadians often consulted the priests, who in many cases acted as unofficial judges in disputes among the inhabitants. The clergy, however, did not rule the settlements. As in New France in the eighteenth century, the clergy in Acadia did not have unquestioned authority.

RELATIONS WITH THE INDIANS

From the first years of the colony, the Acadians maintained good relations with the resident Micmac Indians. The Acadians utilized the tidal flats, lands of little interest to the Indians. Unlike the New England settlers, who antagonized the Indians by seizing their lands and clearing away the forests, the Acadians posed no threat. As a result, many of the early French took Indian wives. The community at La Hève, for example, on the southeastern coast of what is now Nova Scotia, was a Métis settlement. Until after the deportation of 1755 there was always at least one Acadian family in most settlements where one partner, usually the woman, was a Micmac or Malecite (from present-day western New Brunswick).

THE GROWTH OF THE COMMUNITY

The population of Acadia grew rapidly through natural increase rather than through immigration. The absence of war, famine, or epidemics such as typhoid, smallpox, and cholera accounted for the rapid growth. At Port-Royal the average Acadian couple usually married in their early twenties, and had ten or eleven children; most of whom survived to adulthood. The population itself doubled every twenty years—a faster rate than in New France. By 1670 the colony had a population of about 400–500. The list included the Melanson brothers, men of Scottish ancestry, and a Roger Kuessy (or Caissey) of Irish descent. In all, there were only two other foreign names: Granger, of English origin; and Mirande(a), of English and Portuguese origin respectively.

Although Port-Royal was the largest settlement, there were other small outlying communities around the Bay of Fundy and along the eastern coastline of present-day Nova Scotia (see page 146). Acadian settlements began in the 1670s and 1680s at Beaubassin (Amherst), Grand Pré (Wolfville), and Cobequid (Truro). With the addition of about forty families brought out after 1671, the colony expanded to more than eight hundred in 1686.

129

Blood ties, common beliefs, and a system of mutual aid and solidarity united the first Europeans in Acadia. These Acadians developed their own speech patterns and an amalgam of a variety of dialects—mostly French, a few English, one or two Indian, blended into a whole by the Acadians' distinctive life and their need for a special vocabulary to describe it.

By the end of the seventeenth century the Acadians established themselves in the region's fertile and easily worked marshlands. Judging from the names they gave their settlements along the Bay of Fundy and the Isthmus of Chignecto, which connects present-day Nova Scotia to New Brunswick, they were contented—Beaubassin (Beautiful Pond), Cocagne (Land of Plenty), and a settlement near Port-Royal with the name of Paradis Terrestre (Earthly Paradise or Garden of Eden).

Acadia and Massachusetts

The Acadians traded southward to New England rather than westward to Canada or eastward to France. In many respects the colony on the Bay of Fundy become more an economic satellite of Boston than of Versailles. Acadian governors proved powerless to prevent the entry of American merchants and fishermen to the area. British merchants had such a flourishing business, in fact, that they built warehouses at Port-Royal. There they bought furs and the Acadians' surplus grain (wheat and oats) in return for products from the West Indies, such as sugar, molasses and rum, and manufactured goods from Europe—knives, needles, dishes, and cloth. The Acadians themselves went to Boston to sell their wheat and furs, bringing back cloth, tobacco, and pipes. Even Louis-Alexandre Des Friches de Meneval, governor of Acadia, in the late 1680s bought stockings and shoes in Boston for the French garrison at Port-Royal.

NEW ENGLAND AND ACADIA AT WAR

The Bostonians, however, wanted political as well as economic control. When war broke out in Europe in 1689, the New Englanders obtained their opportunity. Under William Phips an invasion force of seven hundred New Englanders attacked Port-Royal in 1690. They easily overpowered Governor Meneval and his garrison of one hundred troops and devastated Acadia's capital. Repulsed later that year at Quebec, the New Englanders held on to Acadia for seven years until the signing of the Treaty of Ryswick in 1697, when France regained it (see chapter 6).

130

With the outbreak of war in Europe in 1702, Acadia once again became easy prey for sea-faring raiders from New England. Despite the repeated attacks and looting (Port-Royal was attacked unsuccessfully once in 1704 and twice in 1707), the Acadians, with little help from France, held their ground against the English until 1710. In that year, determined to conquer Acadia, Britain supplied New England with money, arms, munitions, and naval aid; the colonies provided additional men and supplies.

An expedition of thirty-four hundred men and thirty-six ships arrived at Port-Royal in September 1710. Against this invasion force the French governor had a ramshackle fort held by less than three hundred men. The French resisted for three weeks, then accepted the inevitable and surrendered in mid-October. The Treaty of Utrecht in 1713 put to rest the question of ownership of the Nova Scotia peninsula. Acadia became Nova Scotia, and the English changed the name of Port-Royal to Annapolis Royal.

An Acadian Nova Scotia, 1713–54

The English administrators of Annapolis Royal immediately faced an important problem: how should an English minority govern a French majority? They tried to bring large numbers of American settlers to the Bay of Fundy, but few came. After the signing of the Treaty of Utrecht, the English had to accept the inevitable—that the Acadians would remain the colony's majority because the New Englanders would not come north. The English now required that the Acadians become British subjects. In reality, however, the Acadians had little contact with their new Protestant rulers, and Nova Scotia remained a French and Roman Catholic colony.

By the Treaty of Utrecht Louis XIV obtained certain guarantees for the

Acadians. One clause stipulated that they had the right to leave Nova Scotia and settle elsewhere. Originally, they had one year in which to make up their minds, but this was later changed to allow a slightly longer time period. Then rivalry for the allegiance of the Acadians began. France had retained one territory in the Gulf of St. Lawrence that it expected to develop—Ile Royale (Cape Breton Island). Anxious to establish a strong colony, the French tried to attract the Acadians, who sent representatives to inspect the lands. But the delegates reported negatively on Cape Breton's rocky soil and its frequent fog. Few liked the idea of having to commence pioneering once again, to leave their rich lands and comfortable houses. The English tried to prevent the Acadians from leaving by forbidding them to construct boats or sell their property and cattle. From the English vantage-point, French immigration to Cape Breton would only reinforce the French presence and weaken Nova Scotia, which would lose successful farmers and their livestock. The Acadians might also destroy their home-steads and the restraining dikes as they left.

131

THE OATH OF ALLEGIANCE

The English administration sought above all to make the Acadians swear an oath of allegiance. The practice of asking the inhabitants of a country to make an oath of loyalty was customary whenever a new monarch succeeded to the throne or after a war. On five separate occasions the governors of Nova Scotia tried to force the Acadians to swear an oath. Each time the Acadians insisted on remaining neutral. As a border people in a land coveted by powerful neighbours, the Acadians wanted to proceed cautiously.

Finally, in 1717 the Acadians worked out the terms on which they would remain under British government: first, their adherence to Catholicism was to be respected; and secondly British officials were to recognize that they lived in Indian territory and that they would suffer Indian attacks by aligning themselves militarily against the French, the Indians' allies. The British agreed in 1730, only demanding that a simple oath be taken:

> "I sincerely promise and swear on my faith as a Christian that I will be utterly loyal, and will truly obey His Majesty King George the second, whom I recognize as the sovereign lord of Acadia or Nova Scotia. May God so help me."

Thereafter, most Englishmen spoke of Acadians as "the Neutrals" or "the neutral French," the term the Acadians applied to themselves. The Acadians saw this as a victory and made the required statement. In 1730 they had every reason to believe that the British authorities agreed to their terms for staying in Nova Scotia, that they had gained exemption from bearing arms and from fighting in future wars against either the French or the Indians.

THE ACADIANS' GOLDEN AGE

For the next thirty years the Acadians prospered. Their high birth rate led to a phenomenal population increase. From approximately twenty-three hundred in 1714 their total population increased in forty years to an estimated thirteen thousand. The Acadian population spread into settlements along the present-day New Brunswick shoreline, as well as to Ile Saint-Jean (Prince Edward Island). In the 1730s the Acadians further expanded into areas of present-day Nova Scotia that had been surveyed and reserved for future English immigration.

132

The Acadians spent their time and energies as they had always done—in developing their lands and in fishing, hunting, and trading. Charles Morris, the surveyor general of Nova Scotia, visited Beaubassin at the mouth of the Bay of Fundy in 1748 and left a vivid description of the Acadians' country: " ... a Number of Villages built on gentle rising Hills interspers'd with Gardens and Woods the Villages divided from each other with long intervals of marshes and they at great distance bounded by Hills covered with Trees the Natural growth of the Country. Here may be seen rivers turning and winding among the Marshes then Cloath'd with all the variety of Grain."

The Acadian communities relied on their local priest or on the village patriarch to solve their problems of land boundaries, cattle theft, and other legal matters. The text of the Treaty of Utrecht had guaranteed them the free exercise of Catholicism, "insofar as the laws of Great Britain allowed." Although this guarantee was a contradiction because English laws prohibited, or at least made very difficult, the practice of Roman Catholicism in Britain, the British authorities in Nova Scotia allowed a much broader interpretation of the clause and permitted the Acadians religious freedom.

England's tolerant policy allowed the Church of France to minister to both the French and Micmac populations. The missionaries gained great influence among the Micmacs, who numbered about one thousand in the early 1740s in peninsular Nova Scotia; probably another thousand lived on the Ile Saint-Jean, Cape Breton, and the mainland side of the Bay of Fundy. By the first half of the eighteenth century the Roman Catholic religion had become an integral part of the Micmacs' identity. Abbé Pierre Maillard developed a Micmac alphabet, allowing the Micmacs to learn selected prayers and chants and the catechisms. Abbé Jean-Louis Le Loutre, who arrived in 1738, enjoyed considerable respect among both the Acadians and the Micmacs at Beaubassin.

THE NEUTRAL ACADIANS

The Acadians faced another challenge to their neutrality in 1744, when war again broke out between the English and French. They proved their loyalty by remaining neutral. News of the capture of Louisbourg by the New Englanders in 1745 led the Acadians to adhere even more closely to their neutrality until the struggle ended in 1748. For their policy of neutrality, they earned the wrath of both antagonists. As historian Naomi Griffiths notes: "In 1748, the Acadians considered themselves Acadian, the French considered them unreliable allies, and the English, unsatisfactory citizens."[1]

Founding of Halifax

The peace treaty in 1748 restored the status quo. Louisbourg was given back to France, an act that greatly angered the New Englanders who had, at great expense and loss of life, captured it. England then felt obliged to fortify Nova Scotia, to make it a proper counter-balance to Louisbourg and a strong outpost of English power. The English had earlier committed themselves to making Nova Scotia an effective part of their North American empire. They now sought to make the Acadians into completely trustworthy subjects, to populate Nova Scotia with Protestant settlers, and to replace Annapolis Royal with a new military and administrative centre.

The new governor, Edward Cornwallis, then thirty-six years old (he was the uncle of the Lord Cornwallis who surrendered to the Americans at Yorktown in 1781) proceeded to transport two thousand colonists to the port the Micmacs knew as "Che-book-took" (at the biggest harbour), a name the English rendered as "Chebucto." Cornwallis renamed it Halifax, after the Earl of Halifax, the president of the Board of Trade and Plantations, a committee of Crown appointees in London who handled the administration of Britain's North American colonies until 1768.

In 1750–51 the British also brought in approximately fifteen hundred "foreign Protestants," largely Germans who they settled at Lunenburg on the south shore of the peninsula, within easy reach of Halifax. British authorities transferred the seat of government from Annapolis Royal to Halifax, and for the first time in more than thirty years Nova Scotia's Protestant population surpassed two hundred. Cornwallis also introduced British institutions and laws, and he fortified the new settlement to equal the strength of Louisbourg. These measures, together with the construction of roads to the Acadian settlements and the introduction of a large English garrison, completely changed the balance of power in the colony.

Simultaneously, the French decided to strengthen their position in what is now New Brunswick. While the English were constructing Halifax and bringing Protestant immigrants into the colony, the French increased their garrison at the mouth of the St. John River and occupied the Chignecto Isthmus, building Fort Beauséjour in 1751. Beauséjour protected their overland communications from Canada to Louisbourg. At the same time, the French at Louisbourg used every possible means to retain the Indians in their alliance, and to promote conflict between the Micmac and the English. The Micmac needed little prompting since the English, without consulting them, had encroached upon their favourite hunting grounds.

THE MICMACS AND THE ENGLISH

134   Years of Micmac raids and harassment followed, with many of the attacks taking place at sea, for the Micmac had purchased European longboats after their first contact with French fishermen. Oar-propelled or under open sail, these boats enabled the Micmac to travel the coastal waters and make short sea voyages. From 1713 to 1760 the Micmac captured at least eighty English trading and fishing boats.

The Micmacs viewed the founding of Halifax in 1749 as a serious encroachment on their lands, and French missionaries as Abbé Jean-Louis Le Loutre encouraged the Micmacs in Nova Scotia to resist. From Louisbourg the Indians obtained the necessary arms, money, and presents for their war of resistance on the English, which they declared in September 1749.

The English had quickly antagonized the Indians. Gifts were fundamental to Indian diplomacy, but the English initially refused to accept the idea of presents as rent for the use of the Micmacs' land. They assumed that under the Treaty of Utrecht, France had ceded title to Acadia and that the lands now belonged to King George I.

After the outbreak of Indian raids Cornwallis proposed drastic measures. One plan was to recruit fifty rangers locally, another hundred from Boston, and to send them throughout the entire province to kill Micmacs. On October 2, 1749, the English governor issued his proclamation commanding all "to Annoy, distress, take or destroy the Savages commonly called Mic-macks, wherever they are found." In wartime the French paid the Indians for English scalps brought in, just as the English paid for Indian scalps. Cornwallis again promised payment and added that any person found helping the Indians would this time be treated as if one himself.

Cornwallis' drastic measures, however, never went into effect. London advised a milder policy, adding that experience in other parts of North America had indicated that "gentler Methods and Offers of Peace have more frequently prevailed with Indians than the Sword, if at the same Time, that the Sword is held over their Heads."

BRITAIN'S GROWING ANXIETY ABOUT THE ACADIANS

As frontier incidents and Micmac raids increased, Cornwallis became ever more wary of the Acadians in Nova Scotia. In 1749 the governor commanded them to swear an oath of allegiance—this time without conditions. Those who refused had to leave Nova Scotia. But when the Acadian delegates replied negatively to Cornwallis' ultimatum, he did nothing, preferring to wait until British power became stronger in Nova Scotia. Such false threats made it difficult for the Acadians to take the menace of deportation seriously.

The Acadians entered a period of much greater strain in the early 1750s. Between 1500 to 2000 Acadians left peninsula Nova Scotia by choice or by coercion (many were forced by French raiding parties to move to French territory north of the isthmus). Everyone was certain that war between France and Britain would soon break out once again. Yet four-fifths of the Acadians who remained in the colony believed that the governor, by his refusal to remove them, had acquiesced; that like other English governors before him, he accepted their "neutral" status.

When Charles Lawrence became lieutenant governor of Nova Scotia in 1753 the Acadians expected the situation to remain the same. This time, however, the Acadians were completely wrong, for Lawrence believed it was necessary to make Nova Scotia a safe British colony. First and foremost, Colonel Lawrence was a soldier. Like most soldiers, he knew allies and enemies, not "neutrals." To him, the Acadians posed a definite threat in the event of another full-scale war. But in the early months of 1754 Lawrence felt expulsion unjustified; he believed that if the British confronted the Acadians firmly, they would yield and agree to the oath.

Expulsion of the Acadians

The outbreak of war in North America in 1754 and General Braddock's campaign in 1755 completely altered the military situation as well as Lawrence's view of the Acadians. In June 1755 Colonel Robert Monckton, with a force composed largely of New England troops, captured Beauséjour and the rest of the French garrisons in the Isthmus of Chignecto. Sufficiently impressed by the English victories, the Indians stopped their attacks. This allowed Lawrence to turn his attention to the Acadian question.

In July Lawrence ordered representatives of the Acadian people to

135

appear before the Halifax Council which advised the Governor. Lawrence probably believed that the Acadians would capitulate quickly and make the unqualified oath of allegiance to the British Crown. Fearful of how weak the British position in Acadia really was, the council (which was dominated by military officers) made it quite clear that they insisted upon an unqualified oath. (Perhaps as well some of the twelve council members eyed the Acadians' rich lands along the Bay of Fundy; there were profits to be made in the evacuations, as well as in the resettlement of New Englanders in Nova Scotia.) The council asked the two thousand New England volunteers still in Nova Scotia after the military action along the Bay of Fundy that spring to remain in Nova Scotia a little longer. Then on July 23, two days before the first of the Acadian delegates from the villages arrived in Halifax, the news reached the town of Braddock's defeat in the Ohio country. Nova Scotia's need for the Acadians to make a declaration of unequivocal allegiance to Britain became all the more urgent.

136

The Acadian delegates presented their case before the council members, arguing that they always had been loyal to George II and would willingly present to the English all their firearms as proof of their loyalty. Although they were prepared to abide by the oath they had sworn earlier, they would not take a new one. They asked to be considered as a neutral people pointing out that between 1713–55 they had never fought for France. Throughout the entire discussion none of the delegates foresaw the catastrophe impending if they refused to swear the required oath. They underestimated the determination of Lawrence's council.

The final confrontation came on Monday, July 28. After hearing the delegates one last time, the council reached a decision. It endorsed the deportation of all Acadians under British jurisdiction who refused to take the unqualified oath. Like the French, the English saw the Acadians as French and not as a separate, distinct people.

Since the mid-seventeenth century New England had argued for this solution. It would have been more merciful if the decision to oust the Acadians had been made in 1713, when they were less numerous. But Nova Scotia's governors were all reluctant to strengthen their French rivals. In the general hysteria after Braddock's defeat the British prepared to remove them. The Acadians' fate passed into the hands of two thousand hostile, anti-Catholic New England recruits working under the instructions of Lieutenant Governor Charles Lawrence.

THE DEPORTATION BEGINS

The deportation began immediately after the council's decision. Lawrence attempted initially to prepare carefully for the evacuation, providing adequate cabin space and allowing ample provisions for the duration of the journey. But the evacuation was brutal and poorly planned. Lawrence's troops, including those commanded by Colonel Robert Monckton, the victor at Beauséjour, burned houses and barns to deprive those who escaped of shelter. Within hours, the work of over a century of toil was turned to ashes.[2]

THE DESTRUCTION OF ACADIAN SOCIETY

The expulsion destroyed Acadian society. It broke up communities and dispersed closely knit families. Some fought back, although largely inceffectively. Abbé François Le Guerne, who remained in what is now southern New Brunswick until August 1757, reported that women and children took to the woods to escape deportation, to flee from the English soldiers who had burned their property to the ground. Some eighty-six Acadians escaped from Fort Lawrence by digging a tunnel from their barracks in their prison camp. On board a ship bound for the American colonies an Acadian group seized their captors, sailed back to the Bay of Fundy, then fled overland to the upper reaches of the St. John River. Most Acadians in Nova Scotia, however, were expelled in 1755.

137

Many died in the deportation. The English first herded them together at Annapolis Royal, Grand Pré, Beaubassin and other settlements. As sending Acadians to Cape Breton or Canada would only serve to build up the French militia in the two French colonies, the English decided to disperse them among the Thirteen Colonies.

The major loss of life came on board the ships bound for American ports. Storms at sea, a shortage of food and drinking water, and poor sanitary conditions meant that many boats lost more than one-third of their passengers. The *Cornwallis*, which left Chignecto with 417 Acadians on board, docked at Charleston, South Carolina, with only 210 still alive. For eight years the expulsions continued, until 1762, although Lawrence's participation was ended with his death in October 1760.

The British military occasionally sent ships from the same village to different destination points. Inevitably, family members were separated. Massachusetts, New York, Pennsylvania, Maryland, Virginia, the Carolinas, and Georgia all received Acadians. For the most part, the Americans provided support and tried to settle them in various small towns and villages, but these efforts were largely unsuccessful. Despite all prohibitions to the contrary, the Acadians, footsore and half-clad, wandered from town to town, looking for family and friends. They remained outsiders in the communities where they were settled. The mortality in the American colonies was great. An estimated one-third of those deported died from

138

National Archives of Canada / C-73709.

The reading of the proclamation (expelling the Acadians) at Grand Pré, 1755.
C.W. Jefferys has imaginatively re-created the scene.

diseases that had been practically unknown to them before 1755—small-pox, typhoid, and yellow fever.

It is extremely difficult to estimate the number of Acadians expelled in 1755–63. Some historians consider that as many as 10 000 people were displaced; others put the figure around 6000. The historical geographer, A.H. Clark, has shown that the Acadian population in peninsular Nova Scotia could not have been less than 10 000 in 1755 and was probably closer to 12 000. The majority of those exiled (roughtly 7000) were sent away in 1755. Before the policy officially ended in 1762, another 2000–3000 were deported.

The Acadians from peninsular Nova Scotia were split into small groups. Some escaped to Ile Royale (Cape Breton) and Ile Saint-Jean (Prince Edward Island), only to be rounded up after the British took these two islands. (Of the two thousand captives taken on Ile Saint-Jean in 1758, seven hundred drowned when three of the transport vessels were lost at sea.) About fifteen hundred Acadians also fled to New France to establish homes near Quebec, Trois-Rivières, and Montreal. Others made their way to Saint-Pierre and Miquelon, the two small islands off the coast of New-foundland that France had retained under the peace treaty of 1763.

139

THE ACADIANS IN LOUISIANA

Approximately twenty-five hundred Acadians eventually made their way to Louisiana. The first group, numbering three hundred, arrived in 1764-65. Some of them initially sought refuge at Saint-Domingue or present-day Haiti, the French sugar island, but many fell victim to the climate and to disease.

Although now a Spanish colony, Louisiana's main language was French and the colony was officially Catholic. Like the Bay of Fundy area, Louisiana had large marshes that needed draining—work at which the Acadians excelled. About seven hundred Acadians from Maryland and Pennsylvania arrived in Louisiana by ship between 1766 and 1770. The largest single migration of Acadians to Louisiana—nearly sixteen hundred people—came after seven years' exile in England and more than twenty in France in 1785.

THE ACADIANS IN FRANCE

The one thousand Acadians sent to Virginia in 1756 were immediately dispatched to England, the Virginians arguing that the Acadians were British subjects and entitled to England's support. They spent seven years in internment camps in England until France took them in 1763. About one-quarter died from an epidemic of smallpox during their first summer in England.

Many of the Acadians who settled in France in 1763 had difficulty adjusting to French society, which suggests strongly that, although they spoke French and practised Roman Catholicism, they were a people separate from the French. Acadians were not accustomed to the limitations that restricted the life of the eighteenth-century Frenchman: the *corvée* and restrictions on travel within the country. The way of life in France was alien to them. As one perceptive French lawyer noted, the Acadians were used to a bountiful country where the land was easily cultivated. At home they had eaten bread, butter, meat, and drunk milk; in France they looked down upon fish, vegetables, and cider.

Not finding comfortable homes in France, seven shiploads of Acadians left in 1785 for New Orleans. Charles III, the Spanish king and cousin of France's monarch, Louis XVI, invited them to Louisiana. A small number of Acadians remained on Belle-Ile-en-mer, an island off the coast of Brittany where the French had attempted to establish some of the exiles. Nearly sixteen hundred—just over two-thirds of the Acadians then in France—left. Today, Louisiana has more than a million descendants of the Acadians, or Cajuns (a word derived from *Cadien*).

140

THE RETURN OF SOME ACADIANS

Once permission was given in 1764 for the Acadians to resettle in Nova Scotia, a steady stream of wanderers returned. As the Halifax authorities had set aside the Acadians' farms for New Englanders, they could not settle on their old lands, which were occupied by 12 500 English-speaking newcomers. In all, perhaps 3000 Acadians returned.

By 1800 the Acadian population in Nova Scotia numbered 8000, a result of high birth rates rather than the return of more exiles. They were now concentrated around Baie Sainte-Marie in western Nova Scotia (south of Digby) and around Chéticamp and on Ile-Madame on Cape Breton Island (see page 146). They also settled around Malpeque on Ile St. Jean (now termed by the English, Prince Edward Island). Since the best vacant lands were in present-day New Brunswick, especially along its east coast, the majority went there.

In isolated areas in Nova Scotia, New Brunswick, and Prince Edward Island the Acadians again built self-contained communities. Although many made a living from these lands, it was at a much lower standard than what they had known on their well-developed farms before 1755.

Buffeted about for a generation, from 1755 to the late 1780s, the Acadians finally established a new Acadia but one that was much less cohesive than the old one. They tried to rebuild their shattered communities but many family units had been broken up. In the new Acadia the church, as one of the few surviving institutions, acquired an authority and influence greater than in the old Acadia. Priests became more central than ever before community life.

It became customary in Acadian villages for old people to recount their memories and experiences of the deportation. The expulsion became the unifying event of Acadian experience. The tradition remained in unwritten form until Henry Wadsworth Longfellow, an American poet who first heard the story in the early 1840s, recorded it in his poem *Evangeline*. The story centres on Evangeline Bellefontaine, a seventeen-year-old *Acadienne* who is separated in the deportation from her lover Gabriel Lajeunesse. When, after a lifelong search, she finds him again, he is a broken old man. As she holds him in her arms, he dies. *Evangeline* confirmed for Acadians that they were a unique people with an identity of their own.

In 1979 Antonine Maillet, Acadia's great novelist, wrote a more convincing tale, *Pélagie-la-Charrette*. This is the story of an unconquerable woman, Pélagie, who, after the expulsion, spent a decade travelling in a *141* cart drawn by a cow. With others she met along the way, she journeyed from Georgia back to Acadia. "When they built their carts," Maillet wrote, "they were just families. By the time they returned to Acadia they were a people."

How ironic that the first European group to establish itself successfully in the present-day Maritime provinces received such treatment. But the Acadians were living in an area contested by two great European powers. Geography isolated them from their natural allies—the Canadians in the valley of the St. Lawrence; geography also made the region in which they lived an extension of New England. The Acadians tried to maintain a balance between the two competing powers by keeping a strict neutrality. They succeeded for more than a century, until wartime hysteria won out and the British expelled the "neutral French." The first successful European settlers in the present-day Maritime provinces became its outcasts. Only with great difficulty did the Acadians later re-establish *la nation acadienne*, not in Nova Scotia, the land of deportation, but in New Brunswick, the land of their return.

NOTES

[1] Naomi Griffiths, *The Acadians: Creation of a People* (Toronto, 1973), p. 37.
[2] Ironically, the name of Robert Monckton—although now without the "k"—is borne by the chief Acadian community.

Related Readings

Naomi Griffith's article, "The Golden Age: Acadian Life, 1713–1748," reprinted in R. Douglas Francis and Donald B. Smith, *Readings in Canadian History; Pre-Confederation*, 2d ed. (Toronto, 1986), pp. 111–24, is a valuable introduction to the topic. Information on the Micmacs in Acadia appears in the essay in the reader by L.F.S. Upton, "Contact and Conflict on the Atlantic and Pacific Coasts of Canada," pp. 438–48.

BIBLIOGRAPHY

142

Two good summaries of Acadian history are John Bartlet Brebner's *New England's Outpost: Acadia Before the Conquest of Canada* (Hamden, Conn., 1965; first published 1927), and Naomi Griffiths, *The Acadians: Creation of a People* (Toronto, 1973). Andrew H. Clark provides a historical geographer's view in *Acadia: The Geography of Early Nova Scotia to 1760* (Madison, Wis., 1968). See also Naomi Griffiths' "The Acadians," *Dictionary of Canadian Biography*, vol. 4: 1771–1800 (Toronto, 1979), pp. xvii–xxxi. Jean Daigle's account, "Acadia, 1604–1763: An Historical Synthesis" in *The Acadians of the Maritimes*, edited by Jean Daigle (Moncton, 1982), pp. 17–46, is very useful. *The Acadian Exiles* by Arthur G. Doughty (Toronto, 1964; first published 1915) is still worth reading. Guy Frégault's sixth chapter, "The Deportation of the Acadians, 1755–62," in *Canada: The War of the Conquest*, translated by Margaret M. Cameron (Toronto, 1969), pp. 164–200, provides a French-Canadian historian's interpretation of events in Acadia in the 1750s.

Several interesting articles on the Acadians are included in Phillip A. Buckner and David Frank, eds. and comps., *Atlantic Canada Before Confederation*, vol. 1: *The Acadiensis Reader* (Fredericton, 1985): Gisa Hynes, "Some Aspects of the Demography of Port-Royal, 1650–1755," pp. 11–25; Naomi Griffiths, "Acadians in Exile: The Experiences of the Acadians in the British Seaports," pp. 26–43; and Graeme Wynn, "Late Eighteenth-Century Agriculture on the Bay of Fundy Marshlands," pp. 44–53. Also useful is Naomi Griffiths, "The Golden Age: Acadian Life, 1713–1748," *Histoire Sociale/Social History*, 17, no. 33 (1984): 21–34. Robert G. Leblanc provides a short review of the expulsion in "The Acadian Migrations," *Canadian Geographical Journal*, 81 (July 1970): 10–19. For the Acadians' arrival in Louisiana, see Carl A. Brasseaux, "A New Acadia: The Acadian Migrations to South Louisiana, 1764–1803," *Acadiensis*, 15 (1985): 123–32. The history of the Micmacs in Acadia under French and British rule is recounted in Olive Patricia Dickason, "Louisbourg and the Indians: A Study in Imperial Race Relations," *History and Archaeology*, 6 (1976): 1–

206; and L.F.S. Upton, *Micmacs and Colonists: Indian–White Relations in the Maritimes, 1713–1867* (Vancouver, 1979). The story of the founding of Halifax is told in Thomas H. Raddall's entertaining *Halifax: Warden of the North*, rev. ed. (Toronto, 1971).

The story of the Acadians since the expulsion is reviewed by George F.G. Stanley, "The Flowering of the Acadian Renaissance," in *Eastern and Western Perspectives*, edited by David Jay Bercuson and Phillip A. Buckner (Toronto, 1981), pp. 18–46; and by Léon Thériault in, "Acadia, 1763–1978: An Historical Synthesis," in *The Acadians of the Maritimes*, edited by Jean Daigle (Moncton, 1982), pp. 47–86. Thomas R. Berger provides a lively review of the Acadians' past and present in "The Acadians: Expulsion and Return," in *Fragile Freedoms: Human Rights and Dissent in Canada* (Toronto, 1981), pp. 1–25. Biographical portraits of seventeenth- and eighteenth-century Acadians appear in the *Canadian Dictionary of Biography*, vols. 1–4 (Toronto, 1966, 1969, 1974, 1979). Maps of Acadian marshland settlement and of the Acadian deportation and return appear in the *Historical Atlas of Canada*, vol. 1, edited by R. Cole Harris (Toronto, 1987). Donald Lemon's *Theatre of Empire* (St. John, 1987) contains many valuable maps of the Maritimes.

143

CHAPTER EIGHT

Nova Scotia and the American Revolution

After the British conquest of Canada the Thirteen Colonies slowly advanced towards independence. The new United States, however, would not include all of British North America. Nova Scotia, the new colony of Prince Edward Island (created in 1769), the island of Newfoundland, and the former French colony of Quebec would stay within the Empire.

Prince Edward Island had no difficulty in deciding the stand it would take. The small isolated island, with a total settler population of only one thousand recent British arrivals and Acadians, wanted to keep its ties with Britain. As for Newfoundland, its Anglo-Irish population looked eastward to Britain rather than southward to the Thirteen Colonies, and it wanted to remain within the Empire.

Nova Scotia, which then comprised the whole of present-day Nova Scotia and New Brunswick, had perhaps the most difficult time deciding whom to support, for the "fourteenth colony" had the closest links with New England. It may seem puzzling that the Nova Scotians did not join their fellow Americans in 1776, since about 60 percent of its approximately twenty thousand inhabitants were New Englanders with strong economic, cultural, and political ties with their former home. Why, then, did Nova Scotia not become the fourteenth state in the American union?

New England's Outpost

Once Louisbourg was captured and dismantled, Americans began moving north. The British authorities wanted to attract loyal Protestant settlers in order to prevent the return of the deported Acadians. In October 1758 Governor Lawrence issued a proclamation throughout British America that invited settlers to claim the empty Acadian farmlands. The circular described Acadia's eighty thousand hectares as "Plowlands producing Wheat,

Rye, Barley, Oats, Hemp, Flax ... cultivated for more than a Hundred Years past, and never fail of Crops, nor need manuring." The Nova Scotian government promised to pay for New Englanders' transportation and give grants of forty hectares of land to each family head and twenty hectares for each additional family member.

In crowded, heavily settled southeastern Massachusetts, eastern Connecticut, and Rhode Island the invitation had great appeal among the poorer farmers. Hundreds of fishermen wanting to locate closer to the Grand Banks also came. By the end of 1763 thousands left New England and sailed to Nova Scotia.

Most of the immigrants went to the Annapolis Valley in peninsular Nova Scotia, to lands cleared and diked by the Acadians before their deportation, and around the Bay of Fundy to the area around Cumberland, near present-day Sackville, New Brunswick. A much smaller number entered the St. John River valley, forming small frontier communities at the mouth of the river and at Maugerville, which extended thirty kilometres along the lower St. John River. By the time the Loyalists arrived in 1783, the region of Nova Scotia north of the Bay of Fundy had approximately three thousand French- and English-speaking settlers.

145

At the same time the Americans migrated to the forested lands north of the Bay of Fundy, hundreds of Acadians returned. In 1764 the British government permitted them to settle in Nova Scotia, providing that they disperse throughout the colony. Many returned not to their farms now occupied by New Englanders but to the Bay of Chaleur, on the present-day border between Quebec and New Brunswick. The settlement of Caraquet became a focal point for the region. Other Acadians lived on farms along the lower St. John River.

The New England farmers and fishermen worked to create a new English-speaking Nova Scotia. Yet the lack of roads between the settlements prevented regular communication. As historian George Rawlyk notes: "On the eve of the American Revolution, Nova Scotia was little more than a political expression for a number of widely scattered and isolated communities."[1]

Other immigrants came to Nova Scotia in the 1760s and 1770s. In addition to the 5000 or so Yankees, some 2000 Ulstermen from Ireland, more than 750 Yorkshiremen from England (many of whom settled on the Isthmus of Chignecto), and in 1773 nearly 200 Scots (who settled at Pictou) arrived. They joined the original British residents at Halifax, the 1500 or so Acadians, and the 1000 or so "foreign Protestants," largely Germans, who resided south of Halifax in the area around Lunenburg. New Englanders constituted about 60 percent of Nova Scotia's total population of nearly 20 000 in 1776.

146

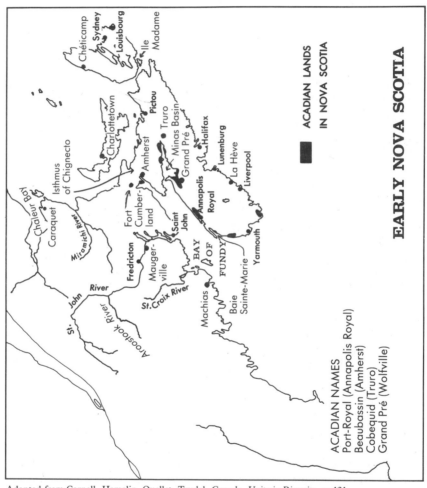

EARLY NOVA SCOTIA

ACADIAN LANDS
IN NOVA SCOTIA

ACADIAN NAMES
Port-Royal (Annapolis Royal)
Beaubassin (Amherst)
Cobequid (Truro)
Grand Pré (Wolfville)

Adapted from Cornell, Hamelin, Ouellet, Trudel, *Canada, Unity in Diversity*, p. 121.

THE IMPORTANCE OF HALIFAX

Halifax, the colony's capital and only urban centre, housed the military establishment and published the province's only newspaper. The upper level of Halifax society centred on the governor, his senior officials, and a group of merchants who had grown rich from army and navy contracts; a handful of smaller merchants and professional people also lived in the colony's capital. The rest of the population consisted of poor fishermen, carpenters, mechanics, and labourers.

Nova Scotia was given an assembly in 1758, but few rural members could afford the honour of taking their seats as unpaid members. A small clique of Halifax merchants controlled both the assembly and the governor's council. So influential were the merchants that they secured the recall of Governor Francis Legge. Sent out in 1773, the would-be reformer attempted to expose the spoils system operating in the colony by the large Halifax merchants. The merchants protested to London, arguing that if Legge were not removed, Nova Scotia would join the American Revolution. Already fearful of developments in the Thirteen Colonies, London overlooked the evidence of corruption unearthed by Legge and ordered the governor home in early 1776.

147

THE IMPACT OF THE AMERICAN REVOLUTION

The rhetoric of the American colonies in 1775–76 found an audience in rural Nova Scotia. Many New Englanders in Nova Scotia resented the fact that in the late 1750s they had been promised constitutional rights and liberties similar to those enjoyed in New England, where the townships had considerable local autonomy. At annual town meetings the voters elected their officers and decided local issues. But in Nova Scotia in the 1760s this form of township democracy was not practised; instead, London intended to build a truly royal government, not a republic as Massachusetts had been. The merchant-controlled assembly in Halifax, which strongly supported the governor, worked to eliminate local township government. It appointed justices of the peace to administer the local areas and did not allow the election of township officials.

As the troubles escalated in the Thirteen Colonies, outer settlements began holding town meetings similar to those being held in other colonies. When Governor Legge called out one-fifth of the provincial militia in November 1775 and levied new taxes to meet the cost, petitions from the settlements of Truro, Cumberland, and Onslow voiced opposition to military service. The Chignecto settlers objected to the new tax and to the idea that the governor might force them to "march into different parts in

Arms against their friends and relations." Like the Acadians of twenty years earlier, most of the Nova Scotian settlers sought neutrality. Yarmouth, for example, responded to the governor's request with the following statement.

> "We were almost all of us born in New England, we have Fathers, Brothers, & Sisters in that country, divided betwixt natural affection to our nearest relations, and good Faith and Friendship to our King and Country, we want to know, if we may be permitted at this time to live in a peaceful State, as we look on that to be the only situation in which we with our Wives and Children, can be in any tolerable degree safe...."

Realizing the seriousness of the discontent, Legge wisely retreated and promptly suspended compulsory military service, and allowed the militia to stay at home unless an actual invasion occurred, and he cancelled the new taxes. This declaration effectively neutralized much of the discontent that existed in the colony.

Support for the Revolution

The communities farthest from Halifax showed the greatest enthusiasm for the American cause. The town of Mathias on the vaguely defined border between Nova Scotia and Maine, the Maugerville settlement on the lower Saint John River, and the Chignecto–Cumberland region at the head of the Bay of Fundy became active centres for support of the Revolution. Jonathan Eddy, a New Englander who farmed in the Chignecto region, took the lead in the development of a revolutionary movement in his area. In the summer of 1775 a few vocal revolutionaries operating out of tiny Machias, a few kilometres west of the St. Croix river in Maine, proposed to General Washington that they would invade Nova Scotia if backed up by a force of one thousand soldiers and four ships. Washington, aware of the enemy's strength at sea, refused to launch an attack. Although rebuffed by George Washington, the Continental Congress, and Massachusetts, Jonathan Eddy still was convinced that the New Englanders settled in Nova Scotia were ready to revolt. Rashly, he and his supporters in Nova Scotia decided to act on their own. Having raised an invasion force of about 180 men and having received some ammunition and supplies from Boston, Eddy attacked Fort Cumberland (the reconstructed French fort of Beauséjour). He had no artillery and his force was smaller than the number of soldiers defending Fort Cumberland. Few New Englanders in the isthmus openly supported Eddy's poorly trained, undisciplined, and badly led army. With the arrival of British reinforcements, Eddy's troops fled in disorder, and the English burned the homes and barns of Eddy's supporters. In the summer of 1777 British naval vessels entered the Bay of Fundy and rapidly took control of the area.

Eddy's attempt to capture Fort Cumberland failed for a number of reasons. Historian John Bartlet Brebner points out that Washington clearly saw the Americans had "little energy or material available for side shows, no matter how admirable the cause and its proponents,"[2] and so they refused to support an invasion. British military power, in particular the Royal Navy, also discouraged the Americans from making the attempt. Brebner believes the American's lack of a navy to be the central explanation for the revolutionaries' defeat in Nova Scotia. As he argues the Nova Scotians supporting the revolution, "could make no headway because their friends in the rebellious Colonies had no navy and because they themselves could not assemble from the scattered settlements an effective force for unassisted revolt."[3]

149

THE INDIANS' RESPONSE TO THE REVOLUTION

The English also obtained the neutrality of most of the thousand or so Micmacs and Malecites who held the balance of power north of the Bay of Fundy. They adopted the French techniques of gift diplomacy to win the Indians' neutrality, giving food, medicine, and ammunition. Pierre Tomah, a Malecite chief, later announced that he was "half English and half Boston and would not lift up the hatchet." To the local Indians, Britain also seemed to be the stronger power, particularly after it extended its control over the Bay of Fundy and captured the coastline of northern Maine from the Americans. Thanks to the Indians, the upper St. John valley was recognized as being in the British zone at the end of the war.

GROWING ANTAGONISM TO THE AMERICAN REVOLUTIONARIES

In the same years that the Americans consolidated their hold on the former Thirteen Colonies, Nova Scotia moved in a different direction. Raiding by American privateers had made a number of once-sympathetic Nova Scotians antagonistic to the American revolutionaries. No substantial Nova Scotian settlement except Halifax seemed to have completely escaped land raids by American sea raiders, who seized anything they could carry away. On a raid on Annapolis Royal the privateers even stole the shiny buckles from ladies' shoes.

The attacks alienated wealthy citizens in ports like Yarmouth, Lunenburg, and Liverpool. Annapolis Royal and Liverpool launched their own retaliatory raids against American shipping. By 1781 settlements in the Minas Basin and Bay of Fundy area, which in 1775–76 had opposed increased taxes for military defence, willingly accepted militia service and taxes to meet the cost of defence.

Henry Alline and the New Light Movement

The unwillingness of the New Englanders in Nova Scotia to support the revolution may be explained by what has been called the "missing decade" thesis.[4] These recent immigrants held many New England values and still possessed an attachment to their old homeland, but they had been absent during a crucial decade in New England's political development. They had no doubt heard the revolutionary rhetoric of the early 1770s about the growing British oppression and the need to defend New Englanders' liberties, but these hard-pressed settlers were more preoccupied by the need to clear land and to develop the fisheries. They wanted only to be left alone by both the political agents from Maine and those from Halifax.

150

Yet during this period of acute disorientation and confusion they needed direction. In the late 1770s and early 1780s a religious rather than a political gospel monopolized the attention of Nova Scotians. They became part of a great religious revival, one which centred around a charismatic young man named Henry Alline.

HENRY ALLINE

In Nova Scotia most of the New England immigrants belonged to the Congregational church. Henry Alline, who was born and raised in Rhode Island in 1748, belonged to this tradition. Henry received his early education at Newport, an education that ended at age twelve when his family moved to Nova Scotia in 1760. They settled in one of the richest farming areas in the colony—the Minas Basin, near present-day Windsor. He received no further schooling, for no school existed in his township. Nor was there a church. Religion was preserved through family prayer, Bible reading, and religious discussions at home. As the oldest son, Henry worked long hours in the fields. Only in the winter months, from December to April, could he pursue his programme of reading and studying. Relying on his own reading of the Bible, the young New Englander believed in a personal religion of the heart. He came into contact with an evangelical group known as the "Separate Congregationists" who, like him, emphasized the need for an intensely emotional conversion experience—the necessity for the "New Light."

In 1776, at the age of twenty-eight, Henry Alline began his itinerant preaching career. From the reminiscences of one of his early listeners we have a full physical description of him: he was of "middling size; straight, and very thin; of light complexion, with light curly hair, and blue eyes, with a solemn expression"; his dress was "neat but plain." In conversation he did not talk "about the world at all, except as urged by necessity." "Mighty in prayer," he was "a good singer and loved singing."

The preacher initially confined his activities to Minas Basin, but three years later three Annapolis Valley churches ordained him as an evangelist. Convinced that God had selected him to carry His message, Alline travelled constantly, seldom spending more than a few days in any one township or locality. The evangelist often rode as much as sixty to eighty kilometres in a day, bringing religion to the rural people. His willingness to preach under all conditions struck a responsive chord among rural Nova Scotians, then still struggling on the brink of survival. They heard Alline's message and honestly believed that Nova Scotia had become the new centre of Christendom.

151

Clergymen of the established churches dismissed Alline as a semi-literate layman without credentials. But the psychological uneasiness of having pulled up roots elsewhere to settle in Nova Scotia predisposed many of the colonists to listen to the fiery preacher. They contrasted Alline's behaviour with that of other clergymen, who seemed more concerned with regular salaries and physical comfort. Alline's message filled a spiritual vacuum in the frontier areas.

Nova Scotia's New England communities chose political neutrality and worked during the years of the Revolution to perfect their spiritual condition. Alline's religious revival diverted their attention away from the revolutionary struggle to religious questions. He convinced many Nova Scotians that they were performing a special role—bringing the world back to God; that Christ merited Nova Scotians' allegiance, not George III or the revolutionists.

The charismatic preacher returned to New England to bring back the purity of the Christian Gospel. He died of tuberculosis in New Hampshire in early February 1784, leaving behind him in Nova Scotia scores of disciples and hundreds of followers. In the years that followed, his manuscript journals were copied and recopied by hand and circulated among his followers until published in 1806. George Rawlyk regards them as "one of the two or three most illuminating, honest, introspective accounts available concerning the spiritual travails of any eighteenth-century North American mystical evangelical."[5] His disciples later became members of the Baptist church and carried on the teachings of the "Apostle of Nova Scotia."

The Loyalists

A substantial number of the colonial elite in the Thirteen Colonies opposed the American Revolution and remained loyal to Britain. Many of these individuals objected as strongly as the insurgents to British attempts to impose taxation and administrative restrictions, but other factors kept them loyal to the king. The Loyalist elite felt that a greater threat to freedom than King George III was the people. As the Reverend Mather Byles stated: "Which is better—to be ruled by one tyrant three thousand miles away or by three thousand tyrants one mile away?" The elite believed that the British connection guaranteed a richer—and a freer—way of life than the colonists could provide for themselves.

Loyalists came from the ruling class, many of whom had a vested interest as colonial office holders in keeping the status quo. They also came from every other class and race, occupation, religion, and geographical region of the original Thirteen Colonies. Members of religious and cultural minorities, however, had a higher proportion of Loyalists than among the population at large. Not having yet joined the mainstream American society, recent immigrants from Europe (Germany, Holland, and the British Isles) and from the religious minorities (such as the French Huguenots, Maryland Catholics, and Quaker pacifists) held on to the British connection out of fear of increased American power. The Indian tribes, particularly the Iroquois, looked upon the Crown as the lesser of two evils, since it might slow down the advance of the American settlers westward. Blacks saw an opportunity to free themselves by joining the British and fleeing their owners.

Persecution of the Loyalists began as early as 1774, when neutrality in the approaching struggle became more and more difficult to maintain. Appropriately, the term "lynch law," an informal system of law enforcement, originated to describe the treatment of Loyalists in Virginia. A favourite pastime was tarring and feathering outspoken Loyalists: the victim was stripped naked, smeared with a coat of tar and feathers, then paraded through the streets.

With the passing of the Declaration of Independence the local revolutionary committees stepped up their activities. According to historians Wallace Brown and Hereward Senior, the committees' means of persuasion "ranged from mild social pressure to murder."[6] On a legal level the various states disenfranchised, put in prison, banished, and fined "Tories" and confiscated their property as well. In Loyalist-controlled areas outrages were also committed against, and restrictions of civil liberties imposed on, those believed to be supporters of the Revolution.

THE LOYALISTS' DEFEAT

The Loyalists were strongest in New York, partly because the British occupied the city after the Battle of Long Island in the autumn of 1776, and partly because New York had an aristocratic social structure. Many of the colony's high officials and wealthy merchants sided with the Crown. The Loyalist party was weakest in Connecticut, Massachusetts, and Virginia. Historians now estimate that approximately 20 percent of the white American population of 1776 (approximately half a million people) became Loyalists.[/] Some fled to coastal areas controlled by British troops, but the majority remained in the insurgents' area. Those who kept silent and paid their taxes were left unharmed.

The decisive battle of the war was fought on October 19, 1781, when Lord Cornwallis surrendered his army of seven thousand at Yorktown, Virginia. This battle really ended the revolutionary war, although the general peace was only made two years later.

For many Loyalists, the two years between the disaster at Yorktown and the final signing of peace proved the worst time of all. As the war wound down and the British began to evacuate southern ports like Wilmington, Charleston, and Savannah, to which the Loyalists had fled for protection, the persecution reached new levels. Several of the newly independent states subjected the Loyalists to double and triple taxation, and Congress invited the states to confiscate property. Physical violence against Loyalists continued. It became clear that Britain had to do something for the Loyalists. The British continued to hold New York City and Long Island, and many Loyalists (at one point, 30 000) assembled there, awaiting evacuation.

At the peace negotiations the American commissioners agreed that no further persecutions of Loyalists would take place. But while Congress urged the states to grant restitution and amnesty, it had no power to enforce its requests. Except in one or two states, every clause in the Treaty of Paris relating to the Loyalists was abrogated repeatedly. When news of the preliminary peace reached the United States in the spring of 1783, the proscriptions, confiscations, and harassment began again.

The Great Migration to Nova Scotia

A great migration of thousands of Loyalists and their families began even before the peace treaty. Both during and after the war, the more influential Loyalists, such as royal officials, wealthy merchants, landowners, and professional men, and high military officers sailed for England to press their claims for compensation. The humbler element decided, for the most part, to settle in the remaining British colonies in North America.

Traditionally, the number of exiles has been estimated at 100 000, but this figure is probably inflated. Wallace Brown and Hereward Senior believe that British North America received more than 50 000 white, black, and Indian Loyalists; Bermuda no more than a hundred; the Bahamas about 2000; the British West Indies about 4000; and a few settled on the Mosquito Coast (now Belize, Central America). The British Isles received approximately 10 000, with a small number (mainly Germans), returning to the Rhine Valley. The overwhelming majority of the Loyalists were white, Brown and Senior note, but there were also approximately 6000 or so black Loyalists who migrated to the Maritimes, Sierra Leone, the Bahamas, and the West Indies. Some 2000 Iroquois Indians also left New York. In all, 70 000 people—more than the entire population of New France at the moment of conquest—left the United States.[8]

The Loyalists favoured Nova Scotia over Quebec, with its French-speaking Roman Catholic population, at a ratio of roughly two to one.

Nova Scotia's fisheries, its large tracts of empty land, and the potential trade with the West Indies were well known. Nova Scotia, too, was the shorter trip by sea. Small groups of Loyalists had been finding their way to Halifax since 1775. The evacuation of New York in 1783, though, led to an unanticipated invasion. On April 26, 1783 the first or "spring" fleet set sail, carrying no less than seven thousand men, women, children, and servants. Half the vessels went to Port Roseway on the south shore of Nova Scotia and the other half to the mouth of the St. John River. They went ashore at St. John on the 18th of May, now celebrated in New Brunswick as "Loyalist Landing Day." Other fleets followed in the summer and autumn.

The Loyalists usually left New York in groups, either as the remnants of the old provincial regiments who had fought beside the British or in "companies" formed by the authorities, each with an appointed captain. Other groups were self-generated. The majority who came to Nova Scotia had to leave the newly independent United States on account of their commitment to the Crown during the war. Joining the Loyalists, however, were about two thousand British regulars accompanied by a thousand women and children. Some of the poorer people in New York left to better their lot and were not necessarily Loyalists. On the ships were several hundred foreign troops and recent immigrants who had served in Loyalist units.

THE LOYALISTS' ARRIVAL

The voyage from New York to either Halifax or to the mouth of St. John usually took from one to two weeks, depending on the winds and the navigators' skill. About 14 500 people, or one half of the migrants, went to what became New Brunswick in 1784; about the same number went to peninsular Nova Scotia, 400 to Cape Breton, about 500 to Prince Edward Island, and a few families settled in Newfoundland. The British government provided the families with free land, provisions, and building materials.

The largest group of those who made their way to Nova Scotia came from New York, and then New Jersey, with some southerners. Surprisingly, the smallest group came from New England. As historian Neil MacKinnon notes: "The New England states seem to have been represented more by quality than quantity, leadership than numbers."[9] He estimates that of those who came to Nova Scotia, at least 40 percent came from New York State, 15 percent from the other middle colonies (particularly New Jersey), 20 percent from New England, and about 25 percent (black and white) from the southern colonies.

Arrival proved a mixed blessing. At St. John the colonists found that almost no preparations had been made to receive them. No shelter had been prepared, provisions were in short supply, and the land along the river was not yet surveyed. One Loyalist woman later recalled her thoughts immediately after landing: "I climbed to the top of Chipman's Hill and watched the sails disappearing in the distance, and such a feeling of loneliness came over me that, although I had not shed a single tear through all the war, I sat down on the damp moss with my baby in my lap and cried." (This same individual became the grandmother of Sir Leonard Tilley, one of New Brunswick's Fathers of Confederation.)

The largest and most unsuccessful Loyalist settlement was at Port Roseway (now Shelburne), about 150 km south of Halifax. The French name, Port Razoir (for the razor clams in the area), became Roseway. By 1784 the population reached ten thousand, making the town the largest in British North America. About half of Nova Scotia's three thousand black Loyalists settled in Shelburne's suburb of Birchtown. But the following year the population sharply declined, shrinking to six hundred by 1815. The inexperienced Loyalist settlers picked Shelburne for its magnificent long, narrow harbour, but it had little else; the soil and timber were poor, its inland communications primitive, its whaling and fisheries disappointing.

THE BLACK LOYALISTS

For the black Loyalists there were far more disappointments than the conditions at Shelburne. Among their ranks were men and women who had heeded the British proclamation of 1779, that offered freedom to any slaves who left their American masters and rallied to support the Crown. One of the runaways was Henry Washington, a former slave of General

George Washington. Some Blacks had taken part in combat; others had served as spies, pilots, guides, nurses, and personal servants. Assuming equality with the white Loyalists, the free black Loyalists expected to receive government grants of land and provisions. Most, however, received no land and those who did, found themselves in possession of rocky tracts. Few obtained any provisions. Out of necessity many of the landless had to, in the words of one of their number, "cultivate the lands of a white man for half the product, which occupies the whole of our time." Finding their prospects poor and objecting to the servile jobs they had to take, almost half of the black Loyalists left Nova Scotia in 1792 to join a free black colony in Sierra Leone in West Africa.

Many of the white Loyalists also found economic conditions in Nova Scotia difficult. In one stroke the colony's population almost tripled, and the resources of "Nova Scarcity" (as the first refugee Loyalists termed the province) were insufficient to meet the demand. Not surprisingly, many soon left peninsular Nova Scotia. Some went to Upper Canada, others to England, many back to the United States, and a large number to what was then western Nova Scotia, soon to be named New Brunswick.

Founding of New Brunswick

The privations and sufferings of the American refugees on the north shore of the Bay of Fundy were considerable, as so little had been done before their arrival. The future Loyalist leaders of New Brunswick subsequently began a partition movement to have the section north of the Bay of Fundy removed from the jurisdiction of the Nova Scotian governor, John Parr, and made a separate Loyalist province. Loyalists argued that the distance of the St. John settlements from Halifax made it difficult to transact business with Nova Scotia's distant capital. Since Halifax had so prospered economically during the struggle, they did not want to be under the rule of Nova Scotia, which they felt had done little for the war. Without admitting as much they also realized that the creation of a new colony would provide administrative offices for themselves.

In the summer of 1784 Britain met their request and created the new colony of New Brunswick. Colonel Thomas Carleton, the younger brother of Sir Guy Carleton, accepted his appointment as the colony's first governor, a position he held for thirty years. In 1785 the major settlement at the mouth of the great river was named St. John. Colonel Carleton gave the new capital approximately one hundred kilometres north of St. John the name of Fredericktown (the "k" and "w" were dropped shortly thereafter), in honour of Prince Frederick, second son of George III.

Thomas Carleton selected Fredericton as the capital to promote inland settlement. Moreover, the up-river location had a distinct military advantage, as Carleton's two regiments of British troops could be garrisoned there and be safe from a sudden coastal attack. The fear of an American attack was a real one, because the Americans claimed one-third of the province.

The Treaty of Paris of 1783 established the Saint Croix River as the boundary between Maine and New Brunswick. Unfortunately, identification of the river was unclear because three rivers flowed into Passamaquoddy Bay. The Americans pressed for the most easterly river as the boundary. Fifteen years later, however, New Brunswick won its case by establishing that Champlain and de Monts had wintered in 1604-05 on Dechet's Island at the mouth of the most westerly river, which was indeed the true Saint Croix. They confirmed the site by conducting excavations on the island and revealing the ruins of the buildings as described by Champlain in his journal. New Brunswick thus emerged in roughly the form its founders had dreamed for it.

157

BUILDING A LOYALIST PROVINCE

The Loyalist immigrants in New Brunswick came from all levels of society, and most did not have a superior education. Slowly the Loyalists built a new society in the St. John valley. It was hard work even for the affluent, for New Brunswick had a severe shortage of labour. All who came to the province preferred to work for themselves and not for others. As W.S. MacNutt, the New Brunswick historian, wrote: "Judges of the Supreme court and other Loyalist patricians took to the fields to raise the fruits and vegetables necessary to livelihood."[10] Along the lower and middle reaches of the St. John a series of largely self-sufficient agricultural communities developed. The town of St. John became the major urban centre, with a population of thirty-five hundred in 1785.

Ironically, the very people whose allegiance retained western Nova Scotia for the Crown suffered the most. With the coming of the Loyalists, vast portions of the Indian's hunting and fishing territories were encroached upon; the British claimed the land as Crown land and did not make purchases from the Indians. The Royal Proclamation of 1763 (see chapter 9) was observed in Upper Canada, under which the British negotiated land surrender treaties with the Indians but not in the Maritime colonies. As historian Leslie Upton points out, the Micmacs and Malecites in 1782 "were no longer of account as allies, enemies, or people." The correspondence connected with the arrival of thirty thousand immigrants contains "not one word about the Indians who would be dispossessed by the new settlers."[11]

The Loyalists in Prince Edward Island

Several hundred Loyalists travelled to Prince Edward Island. They constituted about one-fifth of the population. In Nova Scotia and New Brunswick the Loyalists were—eventually—looked after by the authorities and supplied with free land, government timber, and tools. On Prince Edward Island (as it was renamed in 1798) they became victims of treachery and duplicity.

In 1767 the British government, in a curious experiment, gave the entire island and many parts of Nova Scotia away. The system vaguely resembled that of the seigneurial system. The land on the island was first divided into long belts of land, stretching from north to south. It was chosen by lot until all sixty-seven townships of roughly eight thousand hectares each had been granted to soldiers, politicians, and courtiers favoured by the British government. Each new landlord had to pay a small annual fee or quitrent for his land, and promise to bring over settlers. Elsewhere, the government of Nova Scotia later practised *escheat*, the process of cancelling the large land grants. But Halifax could not end the grants on the island, as the owners had protected their lots by having the island established as a separate colony in 1769.

To attract Loyalists to their lands, the large landed proprietors assigned certain areas of their lands for colonization. They promised Loyalists grants of land with secure titles. But once the Loyalist settlers on the island had cleared their lands, erected buildings, and planted orchards, the proprietors denied written title deeds to those who wanted to become freeholders rather than tenants. Many obtained no redress and left in disgust without obtaining title. Those who remained fought for seventy-five years for justice.

As late as 1860 the issue still troubled island politics. Only in that year did a land commission recommend that free grants be made to those who could prove that their ancestors had been attracted to the island under the original promises made to the Loyalists.

Nova Scotia

Nova Scotia, its land area reduced now to the peninsula, stood cut off from the Thirteen Colonies. (With the arrival of a late migration of Loyalists into Cape Breton Island in 1784, that island became a separate colony.) The ancestral home of many of Nova Scotia's inhabitants became a foreign country. In the early 1780s the hatred on both sides remained very strong. Gradually, though, the Loyalists' animosity to the newly independent United States receded. Communication began to be resumed in the late 1780s as time wiped out bitter memories of the years of struggle. Ties with relatives and friends had not been entirely broken. Letters and visits to and from the United States became more frequent. A number of Loyalists returned to the United States in the late 1780s, particularly when Britain decided to allow half-pay officers to receive their pensions while living outside the Empire. With time, American anger against the Loyalists subsided and the returning Loyalists found a cordial welcome. Cadwallader Colden, for example, a grandson of a royal lieutenant governor of New York, returned from self-imposed exile and later was elected mayor of New York City.

Slowly, the Loyalists and the New Englanders in the Maritimes lost their Yankee customs, except for one—Thanksgiving, celebrated in late autumn. It is today the only mark of the Pilgrims on Canada's calendar. The Americans became Maritimers.

One important cultural trait, though, did remain. While certain American customs disappeared many of the speech patterns in English did not. The New Englanders and the Loyalists were speakers of American English, which by the time of their arrival in the Maritimes in the mid- and late-eighteenth century was noticeably different from British English. Consequently the English speech community that developed in the Maritimes was, in most respects, North American and not British.

159

The Loyalist made a considerable impact on the province of Nova Scotia and Prince Edward Island. Their arrival led to the creation of two new colonies—New Brunswick and Cape Breton Island (to 1820). Among the Loyalists were American colonists of many different class, ethnic, racial, and religious backgrounds. Regardless of those divisions, the Loyalist legacy contributed to a deep affection for Great Britain in what became Maritime Canada. One might add that it contributed a respect for evolution—rather than revolution—in the development of Maritime government.

NOTES

[1] George A. Rawlyk, "The American Revolution and Nova Scotia Reconsidered," *Dalhousie Review*, 43 (1963–64): 379.
[2] John Bartlet Brebner, *The Neutral Yankees of Nova Scotia* (Toronto, 1969; first published 1937), p. 285.
[3] John Bartlet Brebner quoted in Rawlyk, "American Revolution," p. 380.
[4] The thesis was first advanced by Gordon Stewart and George Rawlyk, *A People Highly Favoured of God* (Toronto, 1972); see especially pp. 3–4 and 43–44.
[5] G.A. Rawlyk, *Ravished by the Spirit: Religious Revivals, Baptists, and Henry Alline* (Kingston, 1984), p. 13.
[6] Wallace Brown and Hereward Senior, *Victorious in Defeat: The Loyalists in Canada* (Toronto, 1984), p. 16.
[7] Paul H. Smith, "The American Loyalists: Notes on Their Organization and Numerical Strength," *William and Mary Quarterly*, 3rd series, 25 (1968): 269.
[8] The estimates of the Loyalists' numbers are taken from Brown and Senior, *Victorious in Defeat*.
[9] Neil MacKinnon, *This Unfriendly Soil: The Loyalist Experience in Nova Scotia, 1783–1791* (Kingston, 1986), p. 59.
[10] W.S. MacNutt, *New Brunswick: A History, 1784–1867* (Toronto, 1963), p. 70.

[11] L.F.S. Upton, *Micmacs and Colonists: Indian-White Relations in the Maritimes, 1713–1867* (Vancouver, 1979), p. 78.

Related Readings

For articles of interest on this topic in R. Douglas Francis and Donald B. Smith, *Readings in Canadian History: Pre-Confederation*, 2d ed. (Toronto, 1986), see George A. Rawlyk's "The American Revolution and Nova Scotia Reconsidered," pp. 234–46; and W.G. Shelton's "The United Empire Loyalists: A Reconsideration," pp. 246–55.

BIBLIOGRAPHY

160

The major events in the American Revolution are reviewed in Samuel Eliot Morison's *Oxford History of the American People*, vol. 1: *Prehistory to 1789* (New York, 1972). On the Loyalists, see Christopher Moore, *The Loyalists: Revolution, Exile, Settlement* (Toronto, 1984); Wallace Brown and Hereward Senior, *Victorious in Defeat: The Loyalists in Canada* (Toronto, 1984); and Robert S. Allen, *The Loyal Americans: The Military Role of the Loyalist Provincial Corps and their Settlement in British North America, 1775–1784* (Ottawa, 1983). For an estimate of the number of Loyalists, see William H. Nelson, *The American Tory* (Boston, 1964); and Paul H. Smith, "The American Loyalists: Notes on Their Organization and Numerical Strength," *William and Mary Quarterly*, 3rd series, 25(1968): 259–77.

For a general overview of Maritime history in this period, see W.S. MacNutt's *The Atlantic Provinces, 1712–1857* (Toronto, 1965), pp. 76–102. Nova Scotia's response to the American Revolution is reviewed by John Bartlet Brebner in *The Neutral Yankees of Nova Scotia* (Toronto, 1969; first published 1937). George A. Rawlyk examines the question of the Nova Scotians and the Revolution in depth in *Nova Scotia's Massachusetts: A Study of Massachusetts–Nova Scotia Relations, 1630 to 1784* (Montreal, 1973); see also his "Revolution Rejected: Why did Nova Scotia Fail to Join the American Revolution?" in *Emerging Identities: Selected Problems and Interpretations in Canadian History*, edited by Paul W. Bennett and Cornelius J. Jaenen (Scarborough, Ont., 1986), pp. 133–57.

For information on Henry Alline and his New Light Movement, consult Gordon Stewart and George A. Rawlyk, *A People Highly Favoured of God: The Nova Scotia Yankees and the American Revolution* (Toronto, 1972); J.M. Bumsted, *Henry Alline* (Toronto, 1971); and George A. Rawlyk, *Ravished by the Spirit: Religious Revivals, Baptists, and Henry Alline* (Kingston and Montreal, 1984).

Two bibliographical guides to writings on the Loyalists and their influence on the Maritimes' development are Robert S. Allen, *Loyalist Literature: An Annotated Bibliographic Guide* (Toronto, 1982) and J.M. Bumsted, *Understanding the Loyalists* (Sackville, N.B. 1986). The impact of the Loyalists in New Brunswick is reviewed by Ann Gorman Condon in *The Envy of the American States: The Loyalist Dream for New Brunswick* (Fredericton, 1984). W. Stewart MacNutt reviews the same subject in the opening pages of *New Brunswick: A History, 1784–1867* (Toronto, 1963). Neil MacKinnon examines the Loyalists' first decade in Nova Scotia in *This Unfriendly Soil: The Loyalist Experience in Nova Scotia, 1783–1791* (Kingston, 1986). An earlier article by MacKinnon, "The Changing Attitudes of the Nova Scotian Loyalists towards the United States, 1783–1791," has been reprinted in Phillip A. Buckner and David Frank, eds. and comps., *Atlantic Canada Before Confederation*, vol. 1: *The Acadiensis Reader*: (Fredericton, 1985), pp. 118–29. Thomas Raddall's *Halifax: Warden of the North*, rev. ed. (Toronto, 1971) contains a lively review of the impact of the revolution and the Loyalists on Halifax. J.M. Bumsted's *Land, Settlement, and Politics on Eighteenth-Century Prince Edward Island* (Kingston, 1987), focusses on developments in Prince Edward Island.

161

For information on the Maritime Indians during the American Revolution, see L.F.S. Upton, *Micmacs and Colonists: Indian-White Relations in the Maritimes, 1713–1867* (Vancouver, 1979); and for the Malecite, Richard I. Hunt's sketch of Pierre Tomah in the *Dictionary of Canadian Biography*, vol. 4: 1771–1800 (Toronto, 1979), pp. 735-736. The experience of black Loyalists is described in *Horizon Canada*; see "On the Way to Africa," by Sylvia D. Hamilton, number 54 (1986): 1292–96. James W. St. G. Walker's *The Black Loyalists: The Search for a Promised Land in Nova Scotia and Sierra Leone, 1783–1870* (New York, 1976) is the most important secondary source on the subject. Eleven portraits of Loyalists, including Phyllis R. Blakeley's "Boston King: A Black Loyalist," appear in Phyllis R. Blakeley and John N. Grant, eds., *Eleven Exiles: Accounts of Loyalists of the American Revolution* (Toronto, 1982). Maps of the Maritimes in the late eighteenth century appear in Donald Lemon's *Theatre of Empire* (St. John, 1987).

CHAPTER NINE

The Aftermath of the Conquest in Quebec, 1760–74

162   Most historians have agreed on the nature of the immediate effects of the Conquest. In their appreciation of the longer-term repercussions, however, they have engaged in fierce debates. Their analyses, especially those of French-speaking historians, have varied widely because they have stressed different aspects and asked different questions. What happened to the church? What became of the traditional elites? What were the effects on French-Canadian participation in Quebec's economy? How did life change for the habitants? Historians' evaluations have also differed because they have written at different periods and thus used different frames of reference.

In the aftermath of the rebellion of 1837/38, the nationalist François-Xavier Garneau, recognized as French Canada's first major historian, portrayed the Conquest as a tragedy, the beginning of his people's "sufferings and humiliations."[1] But in 1905, historian Benjamin Sulte, who revered British liberties, concluded that, on the contrary, it signified the passage from "a reign of absolute subjection under the Bourbons to the free and untrammelled life of constitutional government."[2]

Many clerical historians, their eyes firmly fixed on the excesses of the French Revolution, suggested that, by conquering the colony, the British saved Quebec from the atheism of republican France. Canon Lionel Groulx, whose historical writings spanned more than six decades of the twentieth century, also viewed the Conquest as a catastrophe. He felt the events of 1759 paralyzed French Canada's normal economic, social, and cultural development.

In the 1960s, historians such as Maurice Séguin and Michel Brunet argued that New France's bourgeoisie had been "decapitated" (though admittedly not in Jacobin fashion) by the Conquest; the return to France of many of the colony's bourgeoisie inevitably condemned French Canada to economic inferiority. Yet other historians doubt that a significant bourgeoisie actually existed prior to the Conquest or, like Fernand Ouellet, tend to attribute the relative economic decline of the French in Quebec to the French Canadians' values and ways of doing business (see chapter 5). Perhaps historian Susan Mann Trofimenkoff's comment is the most telling: "Conquest is like rape."[3] Still, no consensus exists on the nature of the impact of the Conquest, although there was surely no more significant event in French Canada's history.

The Capitulation

With thousands of British troops massed at the gates of Montreal in early September 1760, the Marquis de Vaudreuil, governor general of New France, saw no hope in continuing the struggle. Wishing to spare the colony further devastation and bloodshed, he resolved to surrender and set about drawing up the conditions to offer the attackers. Certain of victory, however, General Jeffery Amherst, the British commander-in-chief, was not about to accept indiscriminately all the demands of the losers; in particular, he refused to accord the French the honours of war. Vaudreuil capitulated anyway, thereby bringing upon himself the wrath of the French government, which was apparently far more interested in the fate of the French army than in that of the *Canadiens*. Then, on September 22, 1760, Britain established military rule over Quebec by a proclamation issued by General Amherst. The British Conquest thus became a reality, at least militarily. But until the final peace treaty the ultimate fate of the colony—whether it would be retained or restored to France—was not determined.

163

Wartime conditions were painful for the 70 000 *Canadiens* living in the St. Lawrence valley. Quebec City was in ruins. During the prolonged siege of that fortress in the summer of 1759, Wolfe's troops also laid waste the south shore of the St. Lawrence as far as Kamouraska, 150 km to the east. Major George Scott, in charge of the expedition, reported that he had burned nearly a thousand "solid constructions." The next year James Murray continued the ravages at Sorel and elsewhere. This devastation resulted in such severe food shortages that Murray, named military governor of the district of Quebec after the surrender, had to intervene to force merchants to sell hoarded grain stocks at uninflated prices.

The terms of capitulation proved mild, from the *Canadiens'* viewpoint. They had feared worse, since their bishop warned them in 1756 that, if they lost, they would suffer the Acadians' fate. Perhaps the British were practising enlightened self-interest rather than magnanimity, but the results were the same. Rather than encourage New France's inhabitants to depart for some other French colony, the British wanted to make them loyal subjects of the Crown. The conquerors did refuse to guarantee the perpetuation of French laws, customs, and institutions, but His Majesty's new subjects retained their "entire peaceable property and possession of

National Archives of Canada / C11043.

The capitulation of the French to the British, Montreal, September 1760. The Canadian artist, A.S. Scott, has re-created the scene as it might have looked, as the French turned their arms over to the British, and surrendered New France.

their goods, noble and ignoble, moveable and immoveable." They could also continue to practise the Roman Catholic religion. Priests and female—but not male—religious orders could continue to perform their functions.

Colonials wishing to return to France could do so. Thus, of the twenty-two hundred French troops still part of Vaudreuil's desertion-plagued army, about three-quarters sailed home with their officers. Another two thousand French and *Canadiens*, including the richest members of colonial society, also crossed the Atlantic. New France thus lost its political and military elites.

War and its aftermath disrupted the colony's economy. Some merchants returned to Europe. Others were forced into bankruptcy. François Havy and Jean Lefebvre, French Huguenots, started transferring their assets from Quebec to La Rochelle when the Seven Years' War officially broke out in 1756. Hostilities made it virtually impossible for them to ship their furs across the sea, and after the battle of Ste-Foy, the French government's decision to suspend payments on all colonial paper money consummated their ruin. Moreover, the shelling of Quebec's Lower Town had destroyed much of the property of the local merchants. Marie-Anne Barbel (see chapter 5), for example, who had administered the lucrative trading post at Tadoussac after the death of her husband, Louis Fornel, lost numerous properties in which she had invested her capital, including a general store that she maintained at Place Royale. For her and others suffering similar losses, as historian Lilianne Plamondon has shown, the Conquest was disastrous.[4]

The Conquest also placed the Roman Catholic church in a delicate and precarious position. First, the church suffered substantial property losses during the military campaign; then, numerous ecclesiastics returned to France. When Monseigneur Pontbriand, Bishop of Quebec, died in June 1760, he left no successor. Without a bishop, new clergy could not be ordained. Worse, the Church of England now became the established church and the colony's Roman Catholic church could no longer count upon the government to support it financially and legally.

The Proclamation of 1763

The Treaty of Paris, signed in 1763, formally ended the Seven Years' War. France ceded Canada to the British, who were not really sure that they wanted it. During the discussions of the terms of peace, Prime Minister William Pitt allegedly pleaded with his cabinet: "Some are for keeping Canada, some Guadeloupe. Who will tell me what I shall be hanged for not keeping?" For reasons of security, Britain decided to retain Canada. The following year civil rule began, and the three military districts of Montreal, Trois-Rivières and Quebec were united into the province of Quebec, with James Murray as governor.

The peace treaty confronted Britain with a dilemma in North America. It now administered a large French population whose loyalty could only be doubtful in the event of renewed war with France. The new colonial masters thus hoped that the French population might be quickly assimilated—that is, protestantized and anglicized. Assimilation could only succeed, though, if large numbers of New Englanders migrated north, and they did not. Quebec's climate appeared too harsh and there was little desire to live among a "foreign" population with strange laws and customs. Prospective colonists much preferred to move west.

Thus, by the outbreak of the American Revolution, the habitants were not only still very Catholic and French, they were also, thanks to an astonishingly high birth rate of at least 55 per thousand, much more numerous. British concern for security in the face of mounting tension in the American colonies soon forced a major revision of imperial policy towards Quebec and the French Canadians. The change was put into statute law in the Quebec Act, adopted by the British Parliament in 1774.

PONTIAC'S RESISTANCE

The treatment of the French-speaking Roman Catholic *Canadiens* was not in 1763 a major problem for Britain. Indeed, the proclamation dealt as much with growing unrest in the west as with Quebec. The administration of the vast territories acquired south of the Great Lakes and west of the Allegheny Mountains required a new policy for dealing with the Indians, who resented the increasing encroachment of settlers upon their lands.

Indian bitterness over land-grabbing by British Americans had been growing since the French surrender in 1760. Pontiac, a discontented Ottawa chief in the Detroit region, organized a pan-Indian confederacy to oppose the British. The discontent arose as well from a fundamental difference in French and English policy towards the Indians (see chapters 6 and 7). In contrast to the French's "gift diplomacy", the English on the Atlantic seaboard pursued a system of making treaties or outright purchases for the Indians' land. They made payments only once. After their conquest of the interior, the British put a halt to their enemies' policy of making generous annual payments to the Indians.

Sir William Johnson, superintendent of northern Indians, understood the need for payments to the Indians for the use of their land. He urged a return to the French policy of supplying ammunition and presents, but General Amherst refused and paid dearly for his stubbornness. In May 1763, the Indians attacked the British garrisons throughout the upper Mississippi and Ohio River basins. The Indians captured every British fort west of Niagara, with the exception of Detroit.

166

Several factors then led the Indians to make peace. By autumn, Indian morale began to decline as Detroit remained in English hands and the Indians had to resume their hunting to bring in winter food supplies. The halt in the fur trade hurt as the Indians ran short of ammunition. To quell resistance, the English at Fort Pitt (Pittsburgh) gave the Indians a present of two blankets and a handkerchief from the garrison's smallpox ward. Whoever handled the material would inhale the deadly bacteria spores that the cloth released into the air. Then word of the peace treaty signed between the French and the English finally arrived, signifying that the Indians would not receive French military aid from Louisiana. Finally, in 1764, the British military expeditions effectively put an end to the Indian resistance. The individualism of various tribes having reasserted itself, Pontiac's confederacy was broken.

Yet the conflict with the Indians did justify British plans, already laid out by the Board of Trade and Plantations in London, to appease the Indians. The Proclamation of 1763, issued by the British in October at the height of the troubles, set aside a huge reserve west of the Allegheny Mountains for "the several nations or tribes of Indians with whom we are connected, and who live under our protection." The British agreed that they did not own the territory and that they had no right to colonize it without prior purchase by the Crown and the consent of the respective Indian band. Colonial governors were forbidden to make any land grants or engage in any surveying in this area. Trade relations were to be strictly managed by London.

This "ambitious programme of imperial control," as historian Pierre

Tousignant describes the proclamation,[5] was thus the first legal recognition by the British Crown of aboriginal rights. Events soon showed, however, that without a substantial British military presence in the interior, the policy was unenforceable, for thousands of land-hungry Americans pushed over the mountains into the fertile Ohio country.

The *Canadiens* After the Proclamation of 1763

In creating the Indian territory the Royal Proclamation drastically reduced Quebec's territory to a rough quadrilateral along both sides of the St. Lawrence River extending from what is today eastern Ontario to Gaspé (see page 180). It also provided the new province with governmental institutions, among them a council to assist the governor.

Other stipulations gave the *Canadiens* good reason to worry about the future: as Roman Catholics, they were to be excluded from all offices. Elected assemblies were promised, with a view to attracting English Protestant immigrants from the New England colonies. While awaiting the expected wave of settlers that would permit the British to remake Quebec into an English colony, those few English-speakers already living in Quebec could rely on "the enjoyment of the benefit of the laws of our realm of England."

167

The *Canadiens* occasionally expressed dissatisfaction with the conditions imposed by the British. As before, some habitants attempted to avoid unpaid *corvées* required for roadworks by taking the wheels off their wagons. Moreover, they protested whenever the question of enlistment in the militia was raised. There were also complaints about the functioning of the judicial system after military government ended in 1764. Historian A. L. Burt shows that, prior to that date, the British used the militia captains as "the hands, the eyes, the ears, and the mouth of the government."[6]

As magistrates, these militia captains relied on the *coutume de Paris*, or French civil law, to reach their decisions. With the coming of civil government, however, they were cast aside and replaced by Protestant justices of the peace and bailiffs. These new law officers administered English law, seized homes for minor debts, and frequently jailed debtors. Inept justices of the peace were even accused of deliberately stirring up feuds so that they might charge fees to settle them. Sir Guy Carleton, who was sent to Quebec as lieutenant governor in 1766, commented wryly on the competence of some judges: "Not a Protestant butcher or publican became bankrupt who did not apply to be made a justice."

The legal disorder in the colony proved so great that Murray soon felt obliged to waive the laws disqualifying Roman Catholics from serving on juries or preventing Roman Catholic barristers from practicing in courts. Unfortunately, there are no written statements by the habitants themselves about their response to those reforms. Certainly, though, the governor's tolerance of Roman Catholic lawyers and jurors (and his allowance of some use of French civil law) helped to pacify the habitants. Governor Murray was possibly correct in assuming that the *Canadiens* wanted "nothing but that plenty which the ravages of the war have deprived them of to make them entirely happy."

With the return of peace and reasonably good weather, agricultural production, notably of wheat, increased. So did both the marriage and birth rates of the habitants—a sure sign of better times.

Although the time was hardly a golden age, survival was possible in British-ruled Quebec. Pressures on the land in the old seigneurial region along the St. Lawrence were not yet intense and new concessions could be had with relative ease. Nor did the habitants feel threatened by a rise in the "foreign," English-speaking population: excluding soldiers, there were barely five hundred British in the colony in 1765.

168 Moreover, the presence of British troops prevented any serious thought of uprising. Nor could the French population expect any help from overseas. In a realistic assessment, Murray commented that the *Canadiens* "hardly will hereafter be easily persuaded to take up arms against a nation ... who will have it always in their power to burn or destroy."

URBAN LIFE

It is more difficult to judge the degree of satisfaction among urban dwellers, particularly those of modest circumstances. Even the term "urban" has to be put into context. Quebec, the largest centre, boasted scarcely more than seven thousand citizens in 1765; Montreal had barely five thousand. Beyond the new frontiers, the Detroit area contained perhaps another two thousand *Canadiens*.

Although these townspeople had access to certain goods and services that their country cousins lacked, they suffered important disadvantages. Wage workers, for example, had to contend with the seasonal nature of much employment.

Disease and fire also caused untold misery. Epidemics due to contaminated water supplies and poor hygiene took many lives, especially those of the old and the very young. Fires devastated urban areas. On May 18, 1765, Montreal suffered a third great conflagration when a fire that began near the waterfront destroyed more than a hundred houses, and provoked an acute housing crisis. The town was rebuilt, but the rising cost of land within the small city, with the ensuing increase in rents, pushed less-affluent citizens, such as artisans and labourers, beyond the town walls. Although the bourgeois rebuilt their homes from stone, the poor continued to use wood, which was much cheaper. In spite of ordinances requiring regular sweeping of chimneys and forbidding the use of wooden shingles, fires continued to take a heavy toll.

THE OLD ELITES

The colony's traditional elites—the seigneurs and the clergy—faced difficult times after the Conquest. The seigneurs, many of whom had lived in town, were obliged to rely on the revenue from their seigneurial land and even to live there, but sparsely populated seigneuries produced precious little income. The seigneurs also lost their privileged links with the state as well as their military commissions with the end of the French Regime.

169

Yet Carleton entertained ambitions for this group, whom he mistakenly viewed as having great influence with the habitants. Recognizing that the "nobles" had been deprived of "their honours, their privileges, their revenues and their laws," he recommended that the British show them sympathy in order to assure their loyalty. His views attracted considerable support in London, and by 1771 additional royal instructions assured the perpetuation of the seigneurial system.

James Murray found policy in regard to the Roman Catholic church more difficult to apply. Not that there were any attempts to close the churches; indeed, both the articles of capitulation and the Treaty of Paris granted freedom of worship, though only "so far as the laws of Great Britain permit." Roman Catholics had clearly become second-class citizens.

During the war Murray was strongly antipathetic to the Catholic church and identified the clergy as "the source of all the mischiefs which have befallen the poor Canadians." He obviously entertained considerable doubts over the church's loyalty. Many priests, particularly the members of male religious orders like the Jesuits and the Sulpicians, were French-born and thus were to be looked upon with suspicion. Moreover, London had instructed Murray to take measures to ensure that the *Canadiens* "may by degrees be induced to embrace the Protestant religion, and their children be brought up in the principles of it."

In time, however, Murray came to manifest a pragmatic attitude towards the Catholic church. He realized that, even with all the support of the colonial administration, the handful of Protestants presently in the conquered colony had no chance of converting the *Canadiens*. He also judged that the church enjoyed considerable influence with the habitants. By avoiding openly oppressing Roman Catholics and indeed rewarding loyal priests, the British might even be able to rally the church and make good use of it as an ally. In the meantime, Murray and his officials intended to keep a watchful eye upon church activities and administration.

PRECARIOUS STATE OF THE CHURCH

The period immediately following the Conquest was a trying one for the church. Numbering approximately 170 at the Conquest, the Catholic clergy declined, through deaths and departures, to only 138 by 1766. Male communities were forbidden to recruit. The British army was quartered at the Jesuit property at Quebec, and the fate of the wealthy Sulpician community in Montreal was in doubt.

The female orders, with about two hundred members in 1760, seemed to enjoy greater tolerance, perhaps because most of the nuns had been born in Canada or because their hospital and other social assistance work were judged necessary by the new authorities. In fact, the nuns were obliged to give priority to caring for wounded soldiers, though they were explicitly warned to leave their patients' souls alone. Nevertheless, the community of the Hôpital Général de Québec verged on bankruptcy and that of the Montreal hospital, the Hôtel-Dieu de Montréal, envisaged returning to France. Anxious to consolidate good relations with the British, the Ursulines at Quebec elected as their superior Esther Wheelright, an American captive who had been rebaptized Marie-Joseph and had become an Ursuline nun forty-five years earlier.

The most delicate problem that had to be solved was the replacement of Monseigneur Pontbriand, who died in 1760. Murray's instructions from London indicated that the "Popish hierarchy" should not be re-established. But after the New Englanders failed to come north, the governor needed someone with whom he could deal as the leader of French-Canadian society. For the aristocratic Murray, it was quite natural that such a leader come from the church. He was thus ready to accept a "superintendent of the Romish religion." However, when the Quebec cathedral chapter chose Etienne Montgolfier, superior of the Sulpicians, as bishop, both Rome and Murray balked. The chapter then selected Jean-Olivier Briand, vicar general of the diocese of Quebec.

With Murray's support and some rule-bending, the nominee sailed for London to lobby the British government for a job he declared he did not want. After obtaining London's approval, Briand went to France where Rome, conveniently forgetting the manner in which he had been selected, named him bishop. In June 1766, six years after Pontbriand's death, the Canadian church at last had a new head.

With a bishop installed, priests could now be ordained, though training them was another matter. Ecclesiastical discipline could also be more easily maintained; indeed, a firmer hand at the helm was necessary. Too many priests had committed serious offences against discipline, and other petty breaches of the rules were even more common. Nor were the faithful above reproach. Monseigneur Briand ceaselessly bemoaned wayward members of his flock who "confessed Christianity with their mouths while contradicting it by their conduct." Exasperated, he sometimes wondered if he would not have been happier ministering to a single parish.

Co-operation with the British brought the church obvious benefits. Bishop Briand even obtained a gratuity from the governor for his "good behaviour." But the British exacted a high price for their concessions. In reality, the governor had chosen the bishop—a significant limitation of ecclesiastical authority. When Briand was finally permitted to name his co-adjutor (a process that took fully eight years), Carleton forced him to choose a man five years his senior who would attempt to run the diocese from the seclusion of his presbytery on the Ile d'Orléans. When Briand named priests to *curés*, he sought Murray's approval. When he solicited the governor's approbation to recruit foreign priests, Murray refused.

171

The governor used the church as a means of communicating with the general population. Pastoral messages in support of the state were forthcoming when Murray so desired. Priests made government announcements from the pulpits and on the church steps. Briand even offered prayers for King George III. To his critics, who thought him overly obliging, he replied that the British "are our rulers and we owe to them what we used to owe to the French." Briand was trying to gain time until the situation of the church improved.

THE COMMERCIAL ELITES

Several hundred merchants involved in a wide variety of commercial pursuits including the fur trade, vied for influence in Quebec. Many of these merchants were French-speaking; some, however, were English-speaking, having arrived after the conquest from Britain or the American colonies. They quickly carved out for themselves an important place in the local economy.

The respective fates of the two groups have long nourished historical controversy. On one side, historian Hilda Neatby maintains that French-speaking merchants had no difficulty in adjusting to British rule; they could get the credit they needed and, far from being worse off after the Conquest, participated in the general prosperity.[7] On the other side, Michel Brunet sees the Conquest as establishing a new set of rules that placed the French at a decided disadvantage. For his part, Fernand Ouellet admits that the French merchants did suffer a relative decline but asserts that they themselves were much to blame for it: they were too individualistic to build up the powerful associations that would have enabled them to remain competitive, and they were too conservative in their investments. Nevertheless, as Dale Miquelon has demonstrated, British investments in the fur trade as well as in other sectors had surpassed French investments by the early 1770s.[8]

The difficulty of trade relations with France forced Canadian merchants to adapt to the new conditions. A few continued to import French merchandise to be sold in Canada. Others, like François Baby, successfully made arrangements to shift their commercial relations from France to England. But most French-speaking merchants possessed only meagre financial resources with which to undertake the post-Conquest struggle for control of the fur trade, the most dynamic sector of the economy. Moreover, the army usually chose British or American traders to supply its posts.

172   British merchants also appeared to benefit, as José Igartua has shown, from less obvious types of favouritism. When shipping space was scarce, for example, they were able to get their shipments aboard government vessels. They also appeared more at ease in lobbying governments, both in Quebec and in London, in favour of their interests. The English merchants were used to the competitiveness that accompanied British trade policy, while in New France trade had been well ordered and state-regulated. Still, the French did enjoy one advantage: the Great Lakes Indians preferred doing business with French families, like the Cadots (Cadottes), St. Germains and Grignons, who had intermarried with them, and had Métis families.

Conflict Between the Merchants and the Governor

Although English-speaking merchants did benefit from the new context, they did not necessarily enjoy the favour of the aristocratic colonial governors. The arrogant Murray, for example, clearly preferred gentlemen like the French-Canadian seigneurs (with whom he could converse in excellent French) to English tradesmen, whom he considered "the most cruel, ignorant, rapacious fanatics who ever existed."

In return, the merchants viewed Murray as a despot. They condemned him for the strict controls he imposed on the fur trade, conveniently ignoring the fact that British policy severely limited the governor's options. They denounced him for being too conciliatory towards the colony's French-speaking Roman Catholic population, who happened to constitute more than 95 percent of the total, and they agitated for an assembly in which no Catholic would be allowed to sit. Finally, they petitioned the king for Murray's recall. Murray's troubles were compounded by the fact that, in the colony, authority was divided between himself, as civilian governor, and Ralph Burton, as military commander. Friction between the two, who formerly were warm friends, rapidly intensified. Murray sailed for England in June 1766, and even though he succeeded in clearing his name and officially remained governor until 1768, he never returned to Quebec.

Murray's successor, Sir Guy Carleton, appeared to want to do a better job of redressing the merchants' grievances. He endorsed Britain's decision to lift the constraints imposed upon the fur traders and to leave control of trade relations with the Indians to the colonial governments. Canadian merchants were pleased but began to complain increasingly of competition from wealthier traders from New York and Pennsylvania. Moreover, in responding to the merchants' complaints concerning Quebec's laws, taxes, and system of justice, Carleton could not overlook the necessity of ensuring the loyalty of the overwhelming majority of the population who, he prophesied, would people this country "to the end of time," barring some unforeseen catastrophe. Before long, the merchants vigorously censured his moderate policies and his sympathy for the seigneurs and higher clergy.

173

The Quebec Act

From the late 1760s, pressures in North America began to force London to consider changes in its administration of Quebec. Within the colony itself a tiny but vocal minority, mostly merchants, urged England to grant Quebec the liberties it had given the Thirteen Colonies. This group was convinced that appointed officials from London, many of them army officers, were incapable of recognizing that the commercial class constituted the very backbone of the colony and thus merited special consideration. French merchants supported some of their grievances, particularly in opposition to the seigneurs' own pretentions, but language and religion constituted a barrier to common action. While English-speaking merchants demanded that British commercial law apply to the colony, *Canadiens* agitated in favour of a return to "our customs and usages." The English felt that, by right of the Conquest, only Protestants should occupy administrative positions in the colony. For the *Canadiens*, only equality between the king's old—that is, British—subjects and his new, French-speaking Roman Catholic subjects was acceptable.

THE QUEST FOR SECURITY

For Britain, security in North America was paramount. The Quebec Act of 1774, which spelled out Britain's new policy, extended Quebec's frontiers into the Ohio region. The British hoped by this means to put an end to the virtual anarchy and ferocious competition among traders that plagued the territory. Quebec's economy depended far more on furs than New York's, and giving the west to Quebec would thus preserve the economic balance. London also viewed annexation to Quebec as a wise decision, since the St. Lawrence traders and merchants had generally maintained good relations with the Indians; furthermore, they appeared to be the only traders capable of successfully meeting French rivalry on the Mississippi.

Not surprisingly, the extension of Quebec's boundaries embittered the Americans (see page 180). They viewed it as a measure that continued to seal off the west, officially closed since the Proclamation of 1763. They also resented the recognition that the act bestowed upon the colony's despised "papists," that is, the Roman Catholic church: it conceded "the free exercise of the religion of the Church of Rome" and recognized firmly the right of the Catholic church to collect tithes. The "tyrannical" act figured prominently among the grievances of the Americans when they launched their rebellion in April 1775.

174

The Quebec Act also put into law the significant concessions already made by Murray and by Carleton to the seigneurs. Generally speaking, it retained the application of English criminal law but reintroduced French civil law with regard to property. This was an attempt to resolve the uneasy coexistence of two completely different legal systems.

The return of French civil law enraged the merchants but pleased the seigneurs. Britain now legally confirmed the existence of the seigneurial system and gave it a much-needed boost through the restoration of seigneurial dues.

Finally, this new constitution for Quebec substantially modified the structures of government in the province. It established an appointive legislative council that could make laws with the governor's consent. The governor could suspend or remove councillors. Significantly, these councillors could be Roman Catholics, since the act introduced a special oath that eliminated references to the doctrine of transsubstantiation, or to royal supremacy over the church.

While pleased with the colony's new boundaries, the English merchants were furious that Parliament had denied them the elective assembly for which they had so often petitioned. The only plan put forth during the debate preceding the Quebec Act had been for an exclusively Protestant body. The British Parliament refused to place the colonial government in the hands of a few hundred English merchants, nor was it willing to countenance the establishment of a representative assembly that would be dominated by French-speaking Roman Catholics whose race and religion made them quite untrustworthy in the eyes of British Protestants.

The higher clergy and seigneurs may well have looked upon the Quebec Act as a veritable charter of French-Canadian rights, but for the habitants the legal recognition given to the tithe and seigneurial dues was probably disappointing. Nevertheless, restoration of their system of colonization, which enabled the habitants to obtain land without having to purchase it, no doubt pleased them.

SECRET INSTRUCTIONS

The Quebec Act cannot be fully appreciated without considering the secret instructions that accompanied it and in many ways contradicted it. The instructions required the governor to weigh the possibility of law reform that would gradually introduce English civil law. They also explicitly detailed plans to subordinate the church to strict state control. Appeals to any "foreign ecclesiastical jurisdiction"—that is, the pope—were forbidden. Protestant ministers could at some future date collect tithes from Roman Catholics. Clergy were to be permitted to marry. The government was to survey the bishop in the performance of all his official functions and regulate seminaries. The religious communities were to disappear, with the Jesuits being given an extra push through the outright suppression of the order and the confiscation by the state of all its holdings. When the British had carried out all of these initiatives, the church itself would gradually wither away. That, at least, was the hope of the authors of the secret instructions.

175

Bishop Briand appears to have learned of these proposals, and they must have horrified him. Had all his efforts to improve the lot of the church in the years since the Conquest and to establish it as the leading French-Canadian institution been to no avail? Were the British now going to push for the full Protestantization of the colony?

Carleton reassured Briand that he disapproved of the instructions and intended to ignore them. Understandably, Carleton's major preoccupation was with the security of the colony he governed. His conservative and aristocratic bias led him to favour the clergy and the large landowners, who would support the government during the American invasion. Carleton's preferences, though, brought him to exaggerate the influence of these elites on the general population. But did he have an alternative? Had he chosen to promote the objectives of the largely anti-French and anti-Roman Catholic English merchants and thus deliberately attempted to undermine the colony's traditional social institutions, would he have had any greater success with the rather independent-minded habitants?

Fifteen years after the Conquest, official British policy towards the new colony of Quebec was thus modified for a second time. Publicly, Britain gave the appearance of yielding to French and Catholic desires. George III declared that the act would have "the best effects in quieting the minds and promoting the happiness of my Canadian subjects." The French could now play at least a minority role in the administration of the province. The Quebec Act also showed that the British believed the Roman Catholic church was powerful and held considerable sway over the *Canadiens*. There was no quick way in which to anglicize and protestantize a colony that had attracted but a few hundred English-speaking Protestant immigrants, largely merchants. Not that the British rejected assimilation as their ultimate aim; it was simply not a realistic policy in 1774. A year later, with the outbreak of revolution to the south, it was even less feasible. Eventually, with the arrival of thousands of Loyalists who wished to cast their lot with Britain, the hopes of the assimilationists would revive. But for the moment, Quebec's population remained overwhelmingly French-speaking and Roman Catholic.

176

NOTES

[1] François-Xavier Garneau, *Histoire du Canada* 8th ed. (Montréal, 1945), volume 6, p. 82.
[2] Benjamin Sulte, cited in Ramsay Cook, *The Maple Leaf Forever: Essays on Nationalism and Politics in Canada* (Toronto, 1971), p. 102.
[3] Susan Mann Trofimenkoff, *The Dream of Nation: A Social and Intellectual History of Quebec* (Toronto, 1982), p. 31.
[4] Lilianne Plamondon, "A Businesswoman in New France: Marie-Anne Barbel, the Widow Fornel," in *Rethinking Canada: The Promise of Women's History* edited by Veronica Strong-Boag and Anita Clair Fellman (Toronto, 1986), pp. 45–58.
[5] See his essay, "The Integration of the Province of Quebec into the British Empire, 1763–91; Part I: From the Royal Proclamation to the Quebec Act," *Dictionary of Canadian Biography*, vol. 4, (Toronto, 1980), pp. xxxii-xlix.
[6] A. L. Burt, *The Old Province of Quebec* (2 vols., Toronto, 1968; first published 1933), 1:28.
[7] Hilda Neatby, *Quebec, the Revolutionary Age, 1760–1791* (Toronto, 1966), 23ff.
[8] José Igartua analyses this debate in "A Change in Climate: The Conquest and the *Marchands* of Montreal," *Canadian Historical Association Papers* (1974): 115–34.

Related Readings

R. Douglas Francis and Donald B. Smith, *Readings in Canadian History: Pre-Confederation*, 2d ed. (Toronto, 1986) contains three important articles on this topic: Fernand Ouellet, "The Legacy of New France Restored to Favour," pp. 191–203; Michel Brunet, "French Canada and the Early Decades of British Rule, 1760–1791," pp. 203–16; and José Igartua, "A Change in Climate: The Conquest and the *Marchands* of Montreal," pp. 216–32.

BIBLIOGRAPHY

Although now half a century old, A. L. Burt, *The Old Province of Quebec* (Toronto 1933, reprinted Toronto, 1968) is the standard general work for the post-Conquest decades. Hilda Neatby added new research in her work *Quebec: The Revolutionary Age, 1760–1791* (Toronto, 1966). See also Pierre Tousignant's useful essay, "The Integration of the Province of Quebec into the British Empire, 1763–91; Part I: From the Royal Proclamation to the Quebec Act," *Dictionary of Canadian Biography*, vol. 4: 1771–1800, pp. xxxii-xlix.

On the impact of the Conquest, see Michel Brunet, *La présence anglaise et les Canadiens: études sur l'histoire et la pensée des deux Canadas* (Montréal, 1964); Cameron Nish, ed., *The French Canadians, 1759–1766: Conquered? Half-conquered? Liberated?* (Toronto, 1966); Dale Miquelon, ed., *Society and Conquest: The Debate on the Bourgeoisie and Social Change in French Canada, 1700–1850* (Toronto, 1977). For recent examinations of the historiography of the Conquest, consult Claude Couture, "La Conquête de 1760 et le problème de la transition au capitalisme," *Revue d'histoire de l'Amérique française*, 39 (1985/86): 369–89; and S. Dale Standen, "The Debate on Social and Economic Consequences of the Conquest: A Summary," in *Proceedings of the Tenth Meeting of the French Colonial Historical Society, 1984*, edited by Philip P. Boucher (Lanham, Md., 1985). Finally, the major figures of these years all have biographies in various volumes of the *Dictionary of Canadian Biography*, an essential tool for this and other periods. For important maps of the Province of Quebec in this period, see the *Historical Atlas of Canada*, vol. 1, edited by R. Cole Harris (Toronto, 1987).

The following book and articles provide a good introduction to the native history of the period: Howard H. Peckham, *Pontiac and the Indian Uprising* (Chicago, 1971; first published 1947); W.J. Eccles, "Sovereignty Association, 1500–1783", in his *Essays on New France* (Toronto, 1987), pp. 156-81; Jacqueline Peterson, "Many roads to Red River: Métis genesis in the Great Lakes region, 1680–1815", in *The New Peoples: Being and Becoming Métis in North America*, edited by Jacqueline Peterson and Jennifer S.H. Brown (Winnipeg, 1985), pp. 37–71.

177

CHAPTER TEN

The Impact of the American Revolution on Quebec, 1774–91

178   For Quebec, the American Revolution had the impact of a second British conquest. The capitulation of the French in 1759–1760 did not lead to the arrival of a sizeable English-speaking population in the province. The Revolution did. The American victory forced those colonists who wanted to live under the British flag or who had supported Britain during the Revolution to move to Nova Scotia and Quebec. In Quebec's case, the flight of 12 000–15 000 Loyalists gave the province a significant English-speaking minority. This peaceful invasion set the stage for the heightened ethnic tensions that followed.

As for the Indians, they were in no way concerned with this "family feud" among the British. The Six Nations Confederacy council declared its neutrality, but it could not avoid being later drawn into the struggle. Most tribes of the Confederacy living south of Lake Ontario favoured the British, and thus at the war's end had to migrate northwards, as "Loyalists." Other tribes inhabiting the western portion of the colony below the Great Lakes found themselves living on American soil. For them, the American victory opened up the settlement of their lands and signified the collapse of the Indian reserve policy, spelled out in the Proclamation of 1763 and strengthened by the Quebec Act of 1774. In the intensifying competition between Indians and settlers, the Indians could only momentarily resist the American advance, and move themselves further west or north.

The French Canadians and the American Invasion

From the early 1770s American radical propaganda denouncing British tyranny, lauding elective institutions, and proclaiming the people's rights and liberties circulated widely in Quebec. American agents roamed the countryside, appealing to the French Canadians to choose between making the rest of North America their "unalterable friends" or their "inveterate enemies." French-born expatriate Fleury Mesplet, sent to Quebec by Benjamin Franklin, set about printing and distributing pamphlets on liberty. He took up residence in Montreal where, except during the years he spent in prison, the founder of *The Gazette* defended democratic ideals, first American, and then after 1789, French.

The Continental Congress in Philadelphia decided early in the revolutionary war to invade Canada to prevent the British from concentrating their forces there and then sweeping down into the colonies. In September 1775 Washington's armies advanced into Quebec by way of Lake Champlain and Maine, and the French Canadians were compelled to choose sides. Both church and seigneurs, who were supporters of a traditional order which the American revolutionaries clearly threatened, urged the habitants to support the British cause and indeed to enlist. They had strikingly little success, however. When Carleton proclaimed martial law and summoned the militia the result was strong resistance and even mob violence. The experience embittered Carleton, who had written scarcely a few months earlier that the French Canadians were rejoicing over the Quebec Act and that "a Canadian regiment would complete their happiness."

179

CARLETON'S ROLE

After abandoning Montreal to the Americans in late November 1775, Carleton fled to Quebec, narrowly escaping the advancing American forces. He was not optimistic over Quebec's possibilities of successfully holding off the besiegers. As he put it: "We have so many enemies within, and foolish people, dupes to those traitors (i.e. the American rebels) ... [that] I think our fate extremely doubtful, to say nothing worse."

The Americans, for their part, were certain of success. General Richard Montgomery boasted that he would eat Christmas dinner in Quebec City or in hell. In fact, he ate it in neither place: he was killed attempting to scale the walls of the city on New Year's Eve.

In London the British government made preparations for an expedition to relieve Quebec. George III, whose mental instability had not yet prevented him from appreciating the course of events, declared that "when such acts of vigour are shown by the rebellious Americans, we must show that the English lion when aroused has not only his wonted resolution, but has added the swiftness of the racehorse." Five months later, in May 1776, a fleet of British ships sailed up the St. Lawrence, and the ill-equipped and demoralized Americans departed hastily.

Several British politicians demanded Guy Carleton's recall for neglecting

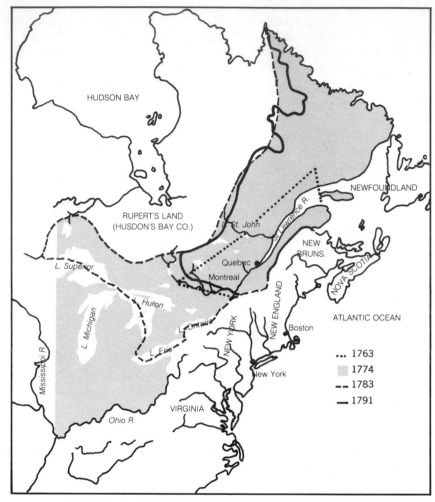

HUDSON BAY

RUPERT'S LAND
(HUSDON'S BAY CO.)

NEWFOUNDLAND

St. John

St. Lawrence R.

NEW
BRUNS.

180

L. Superior

Quebec

Montreal

NOVA SCOTIA

L. Michigan

Huron

L. Ontario

NEW YORK

NEW ENGLAND

Boston

ATLANTIC OCEAN

L. Erie

Mississippi R.

New York

... 1763

1774

-- 1783

— 1791

VIRGINIA

Ohio R.

Edgar McInnis, *Canada: A Political and Social History* (4th ed., Toronto, 1982), p. 161.

The Old Province of Quebec, 1763-1791

to prevent the American retreat up the Richelieu and for not retaking the important fortress of Ticonderoga on Lake Champlain in preparation for the invasion of the Hudson valley. Historian A. L. Burt also believed that the governor's inaction "ruined the campaign of 1776 and possibly altered the outcome of the war."[1] Actually, Carleton did try to march after the Americans but his troops, after weeks spent on crowded transport ships, needed frequent rest. Moreover, they appear to have consumed too many fresh vegetables and were plagued with an outbreak of the "flux." The British also lacked supplies, again through no fault of Carleton's. According to historian R. A. Bowler, Carleton may have been overprudent, but he does not seem to have made strategical errors, and he should certainly not receive all the blame for the failures of the campaign.[2]

In 1777 the British conceived a plan to crush the revolt by striking down from Quebec to New York City, thus cutting the rebellious colonies in two. These hopes were dashed when a numerically superior American force surrounded and defeated the British at Saratoga, north of Albany. Thereafter, the British launched no further large-scale expeditions southward from the St. Lawrence.

The alliance of France with the American colonies in February 1778 changed the face of the war. A secret clause of the arrangement stipulated, though, that France should not invade Canada or Acadia; the Americans wanted no restoration of New France to France. Louis XVI hoped that a British Canada, by posing a continual threat to the Americans, would ensure the latter's dependence on France. Clearly, neither France nor the United States wished the other to possess Canada.

181

AMBIVALENCE OF THE HABITANTS

During the American expedition into Canada, many habitants seemed, if not to have welcomed the invaders, at least to have given them support. These folk may have been swept up by the Americans' heady notions of liberty and equality; probably they listened more readily to the Americans' denunciations of tithes and seigneurial rents, both firmly established by the Quebec Act. But linguistically and religiously the invaders were akin to the conquerors—not to the conquered, and there was little love lost for the *Bostonnais*. Like the Indians, the habitants felt little interest in this struggle, and most preferred to keep their neutrality as long as possible. When American fortunes improved and American soldiers were willing to pay good prices for supplies, the habitants sympathized with them. However, when the invaders failed to take Quebec and the long winter siege dragged on, and when—even worse—they began paying for their provisions with paper money or simply not at all, the liberators' popularity fell precipitously.

With the retreat of the Americans, many French Canadians who had given them aid now had to submit to British exactions and, in some cases, retribution. Throughout the war, military *corvées*, previously levied under the French regime, were still common, with the habitants being called upon to furnish and transport materials for various construction works. Nor were they even paid for their labour unless they were artisans. The correspondence of Frederick Haldimand, appointed governor of Quebec in 1777, shows that desertions from the military *corvées* were frequent and that, to avoid paying for the labour, the governor imposed fines and prison sentences on recalcitrant workers.

The church, too, attempted to reassert its authority. Bishop Briand worked hard to secure the repentance of those who had sided with the

Americans. "I stand firm," he wrote in September 1776. "The rebel must retract publicly before being admitted to the sacraments, even at the hour of death." A hard core of intractable rebels remained. One, asked on his deathbed to recant, was reported to have spat back at the priest, "You sound like an Englishman." Having uttered these words, he turned his back and died.

Those habitants left in peace in the war years did benefit from a tripling of agricultural prices. In part, speculators caused this inflation by going out into the countryside and buying up crops. In an effort to control prices, the government intervened, just as it had in earlier days, by prohibiting exports and hoarding, but its initiatives were opposed by commercial elements connected with the grain trade, and thus proved generally unsuccessful.

The rise in prices did encourage the habitants to clear and sow new land to increase production of wheat and other farm products. Prosperity reached the countryside, but the towns suffered greatly as prices for flour and other basic necessities soared. Harvests were generally abundant but, in view of war needs, most of the crops were sold on the local market. Thus grain exports to both the West Indies and to Britain fell off considerably.

182

The American Revolution and the Indians

If the *Canadiens* had been threatened and cajoled by both sides in the struggle, so were the Indians, particularly the Six Nations Confederacy. The cost of their involvement in the conflict was heavy: the League, which was several hundred years old, collapsed, and the Mohawks lost their lands along the Mohawk River and elsewhere. Britain's defeat forced two thousand Indians to abandon their homelands and migrate to what became Upper Canada.

After the defeat of Pontiac, the British cultivated good relations with the Indians to ensure their military assistance. William Johnson, a large landowner in the Mohawk Valley, who spoke Mohawk, and who served as the northern superintendent of Indian affairs, was greatly instrumental in carrying out this policy. Johnson, whose companion was Molly Brant, Joseph Brant's sister, played an important role in the lengthy negotiations that took place after the Proclamation of 1763 and Pontiac's rebellion and that were designed to define a boundary for the Indian territory. After his death in 1774, his successor and nephew, Guy Johnson, argued that the placement of Indian territory within the province of Quebec (by the Quebec Act), showed the British government's solicitude for its Indian subjects and its desire to protect their territory from white settlement.

In 1775 the British instructed Guy Johnson to pressure the Iroquois to "take up the hatchet against His Majesty's rebellious subjects." Johnson failed, however, to neutralize American efforts to enlist the aid of the Oneidas and Tuscaroras, among whom an American Congregationalist minister had made converts. Johnson then came to Montreal and attempted to build up support for the British cause among the Iroquois of Caughnawaga (Kahnawake) near Montreal, and St. Regis (Akwesasne), an Iroquois settlement on the St. Lawrence River about 100 kilometres west of Montreal, as well as in the Six Nations country to the south.

Thanks largely to the efforts of Joseph Brant, a war chief of the Six Nations with close ties with the Johnson family, the Mohawk and some Senecas supported the British. The Onondaga and Cayuga, though, declared their neutrality, while many Oneidas and Tuscaroras showed a preference for the Americans.

In 1779, however, American troops under General Sullivan invaded the Six Nations territory, indiscriminately punishing the Iroquois by burning crops and destroying villages. These attacks on the hitherto neutral Onondaga and Cayuga brought them over to the British side. One thousand Iroquois warriors retaliated by burning and pillaging American farms throughout the immense territory between the Ohio and Mohawk rivers.

By 1782, with the British on the verge of final defeat, Frederick Haldimand, the governor of Quebec instructed commanders to limit themselves to purely defensive actions. The Indians, however, were not prepared to capitulate and only with difficulty did Haldimand's orders prevail.

183

THE INDIANS AND THE RETURN OF PEACE

Peace came, first in preliminary fashion at the end of 1782 and then finally in September 1783 with the Treaty of Paris. The Indians were not mentioned in the treaty, and the British recognized as American the area south of the Great Lakes. The Iroquois, though, had never acknowledged direct British sovereignty over their territory or the Crown's right to dispose of it. Outraged, Brant and the Indians were described as being prepared to "defend their own just rights or perish in the attempt ... they would die like men, which they thought preferable to misery and distress if deprived of their hunting grounds." John Johnson (William's son) who had just replaced his first cousin Guy as Indian superintendent, went with much trepidation to Niagara. To mollify the Iroquois and the Great Lakes Indians and to ensure that they would not turn upon their betrayers, Haldimand urged the British not to surrender immediately the western posts of Oswego, Niagara, Detroit, and Michilimackinac, now on American territory (see chapter 11).

Indian attempts to convince the Americans to recognize the boundary of the Proclamation of 1763 (and as later clarified in a treaty in 1768) proved fruitless because the Americans intended to open the eastern part of the Indian territory to white settlement. In fact, hundreds of settlers had already crossed the old line. The Indians thus had no choice but to cede extensive lands to the states of New York and Pennsylvania.

A disheartened Joseph Brant, backed by Johnson, prevailed upon Haldimand to grant new lands to the Iroquois in the area north of Lakes Ontario and Erie. In 1783–84 the Indian Department purchased vast tracts of land from the Mississauga, as the British called the Ojibwa on the north shore of Lake Ontario. It gave part of this territory (more than 300 000 ha along the Grand River valley) to the Six Nations "to enjoy forever." Joseph Brant personally received land at what is now Burlington, as well as a house and a military commission. His sister Molly was also given a house, and her daughters married English military men and officials.

184

Loyalist Immigration

During and after the revolution thousands of white Loyalists, bitterly denounced as un-American by the victorious revolutionaries, fled northward across the border. Haldimand was overwhelmed and, at least in regard to tardy arrivals, suspected that they were more often land-hungry immigrants rather than genuine Loyalists. Many came to Quebec from upper New York and New England. They would immediately have settled in what were to become the Eastern Townships had not Haldimand, unsure of the location of the international border and perhaps fearing to settle an English-speaking population along it, forbidden them to do so.

Only in 1791 was the ban finally lifted. The governor preferred that the Loyalists immediately move on to Nova Scotia, as he did not want them to settle on the seigneurial lands where, he feared, conflicts with the French might erupt. He did though encourage new arrivals to migrate to the western portion of the colony. The Crown bore the costs of transporting the Loyalists and after the agreements with the Mississauga, assisted the Loyalists in establishing their own farms (see chapter 11).

The arrival of the Loyalists encouraged those British administrators who wanted to make Quebec into an English-speaking colony. For the first time since the Conquest, an important contingent of English-speaking immigrants came. With their arrival Quebec's population of British origin increased to at least 10 percent of the total European population, estimated at about 160 000 in 1790.

Carleton, now Lord Dorchester, changed his mind about the *Canadiens* and showed a much more English outlook during his second tour of duty as governor from 1786 to 1796. He had been greatly disappointed by the habitants' failure to rally to the British cause and was convinced that they had not been governed with a firm enough hand. He took as his principal adviser William Smith, a loyalist from New York whom he named chief justice. Smith looked forward to the day when the French would be assimilated by further waves of English-speaking settlers from the United States.

Life of the Habitants

The departure of the Americans and the return of peace did not guarantee prosperity for the habitants. Agriculture, of course, depended largely on the weather and yields were highly uncertain. After a prosperous period in the mid-1770s came several very lean years. Drought ruined the crop in 1779 and the harvests of the early 1780s were also poor, spoiled by late springs or early autumn frosts. Only in the mid-1780s did the situation improve, and then not for long. Rust or smut resulted in a serious drop in production in 1788, and the important surplus of 1787 had already been shipped away before the extent of the damage was realized. The results were catastrophic. In the wake of the shortage, prices more than doubled and both the urban and rural poor suffered. Many died from famine, particularly in the Montreal area. Not until 1791 did harvests finally climb back to pre-war levels.

185

Increased production necessitated larger markets, both at home and abroad. Fortunately for the colonial economy, the accelerating pace of industrialization, urbanization, and population growth in Britain meant that that nation would buy virtually all surplus grain available in Canada. In the aftermath of the American Revolution and the Napoleonic wars in Europe, Canada's economy became ever more closely integrated into the imperial economic system.

Even in relatively prosperous times, illness haunted the habitants. On several occasions they fell victim to smallpox, typhoid fever, and other diseases transmitted through the water supply. In the disastrous epidemic of 1784 the death rate climbed to an extremely high 45 per 1000. The government, for its part, expressed only the vaguest interest in public health. Medical practitioners in the colony (most with no diploma) numbered but a few dozen in the late eighteenth century. The majority of them were English speaking and lived in towns, at a time when 80 percent of the population was rural. Moreover, the number of inhabitants per doctor was rising sharply and the colony had no school of medicine to train new doctors. The profession lacked prestige, except perhaps for medical officers in the army. In addition, doctors seem to have had difficulty both in finding clients and in getting paid, since newspapers often contained notices placed by doctors requesting payment.

Merchants and Commerce

Most of Quebec's inhabitants survived by cultivating the land, but the fur trade was the province's principal source of commercial wealth. The grain trade fluctuated wildly, sales of fish products declined, and wood exports were just beginning to enter a period of dramatic expansion. In the late 1780s, however, furs contributed more that half of total exports. Yet the fur trade was undergoing a revolution. Government regulations in wartime, such as the preference accorded military cargoes on transport ships, had provoked numerous complaints from traders. The revolutionary war obviously caused Albany's decline as a centre for fur exports to Britain, thus boosting the fortunes of the Montreal traders. Then, in 1794, after the British finally relinquished the Ohio country to the Americans, the Montreal merchants quickly lost an enormously productive region and now had to look westward.

186   More importantly, industry was becoming concentrated in the hands of fewer and fewer traders. The new barons of the North West Company, formed in the early 1780s, were almost all English speaking. The French, who tended to work alone or in small associations, were gradually pushed out; by 1789 they supplied only 15 percent of the trade goods sent into Indian country. The surviving *Canadien* merchants could not pay the capital investment required for expeditions to the western posts. But French Canadians continued to provide most of the labour used in the trade.

At the same time, relations between the merchants and the colonial authorities went from bad to worse. The merchants' bitterness towards the Quebec Act intensified and they petitioned London for its repeal. They maintained the province needed an elected assembly to defend their interests. As well, they demanded the granting of English commercial law that would liberate them from French custom and usage. They sought recognition of legal rights, such as the right to trial by jury in civil cases, to protect them from the arbitrary authority exercised by the governor and appointed officials. The merchants also managed to arouse the ire of several public officials whom they personally attacked. Although the government did make some effort to redress their grievances, Haldimand felt that most merchants were making their representations without considering the rest of society.

The Traditional Elites

In his relations with the merchants, Haldimand was simply treading the well worn path of hostility already established by Murray and Carleton. All three were conservative, authoritarian, and generally unwilling to share power in the colony with any group. After 1786, however, Carleton came under Loyalist influence. All three had a legislative council at their disposal to which they appointed mostly government supporters, including some French-speaking seigneurs. The governors also had a few close advisers, such as the chief justice and the attorney general; many of them were inept and few had any sensitivity towards the colony's French-speaking majority.

Virtually the sole preoccupation of the governors in this troubled period was security. They treated the French seigneurial and clerical elites with a certain deference. They assumed that these elites controlled the *Canadiens*, and they favoured individuals they viewed as belonging to the upper ranks of society. All three were deeply suspicious of the ambitions of the colony's Anglophone merchants and were thoroughly unimpressed by the latter's political pretensions.

187

SEIGNEURS

Historians have emphasized the governors' sympathies for the colony's traditional elites. The Quebec Act helped confirm the social and economic status of the seigneurs. Some, such as the military engineer Gaspard-Joseph Chaussegros de Léry, the military officer René-Amable Boucher de Boucherville, and the businessman François Baby were named to the Legislative Council; several others received civil service or judicial appointments. When Carleton re-established the militia in 1777 seigneurs like Baby, who had been loyal to Britain during the American invasion, regained their traditional military role.

The growth of Quebec's population and of wheat production should have brought the seigneurs important economic benefits. The development of new lands and investments in roads and mills, however, required capital that most seigneurs did not possess. Seigneuries, therefore, began to pass into the hands of the British, to individuals like Gabriel Christie, whose five properties assured his family material security with minimal risk.[3] By 1784 more than one-quarter of the seigneuries, including the most lucrative, had British owners. The *censitaires* remained almost exclusively French, with English-speaking settlers preferring the freehold system of land tenure. Thus, despite the declining prestige of the seigneurs, the system itself appears to have served as a bulwark against assimilation.

The seigneurs belonging to Carleton's councils often voted together as a sort of conservative French party, resisting plans for immigration and for the conversion of seigneurial grants to freehold tenure. When talk of enacting a new constitution that would introduce a popularly elected assembly increased in the late 1780s, seigneurs like Baby and Boucher de Boucherville pleaded against setting up a body that would surely boost the fortunes of the Anglophone merchants and thus endanger religion and property.

After the establishment of the Assembly, though, several seigneurs ran for office and, except for the merchants, they constituted the most numerous group in Lower Canada's first elected house. They also tended to speak of themselves as the representatives of the French-Canadian nation, although French-Canadian merchants hotly disputed this claim. Moreover, a slowly rising group of professionals, at first comprising a few notaries and lawyers, more frequently challenged the seigneurs' attempts to assume leadership.

THE ROMAN CATHOLIC CHURCH

188

The church proved a much more complex problem. It was loyal to the Crown during the American Revolution, but the British authorities tried to prevent it from becoming too strong and independent. Also, many of the strongly Anglican administrators of the colony scorned "Romanism" and hoped that the French might eventually convert to Protestantism. While waiting for this transition, they did not intend to support the Roman Catholic church's institutions.

Ecclesiastical succession continued to pose a serious problem. Briand resigned in 1784 so that his assistant, co-adjutor Louis-Philippe Mariauchau D'Esgly, then seventy-four years old, might become bishop and choose his own co-adjutor before he died. D'Esgly picked the relatively youthful Jean-François Hubert, but Haldimand, then in England, was furious at not having been consulted. London then demanded that the old and senile Etienne Montgolfier be named in place of Hubert, but Montgolfier refused. Hubert was finally accepted and became bishop upon D'Esgly's death in 1788. Lord Dorchester then imposed as co-adjutor the ambitious and worldly Charles-François Bailly de Messein, a strongly pro-British cleric whose relations with Hubert were often sorely strained.

The church confronted other equally serious problems, among them the perennial question of clerical recruitment. At the Conquest, Quebec had three priests per thousand people. By 1788 this ratio had declined to only one per thousand; seventy-five parishes were without priests and the bishops seriously worried about the quality of parish religious life. The government opposed any attempts to relieve the shortage by bringing in priests from France, except when the plans came from the governor himself.

Male orders like the Jesuits and Récollets were still prohibited from recruiting and together accounted for only sixteen priests in 1790. Although female communities could continue to recruit, in practice they received few candidates because of their insistence on a dowry. The number of nuns in 1790—about 230—was scarcely higher than in 1760. Church officials lamented the lack of discipline in the communities, complaining of nuns who were discourteous to their superiors, who maintained small business operations for their private needs, and who played cards too much.

British interference ensured the Canadianization of the clergy. Of sixty-four new priests appointed in 1784–92, fifty-eight had been born in Canada. The government did not persecute the Roman Catholic church in the usual sense of the term, but it did intervene constantly in church affairs in an effort to weaken and control the institution.

In the late eighteenth century, the church made an important contribution to Quebec's cultural heritage through the work of artists and sculptors hired to create religious art for churches. The Baillargés, founders of a dynasty that long occupied a predominant place in Quebec's art and architecture, executed the interior decoration of the reconstructed Cathedral of Quebec. Philippe Liébert, a painter and sculptor, devoted his considerable talents to church decoration in the Montreal region. Goldsmiths like François Ranvoyzé showed imagination and versatility in the fabrication of hundreds of chalices and other religious objects.

189

Towards the Constitutional Act of 1791

The church showed little interest in the colony's constitutional future; the merchants discussed it with increasing urgency. They wanted an assembly, preferably controlled by the province's tiny English-speaking minority. They saw themselves as responsible for economic growth and thus deserving of greater political power. Attorney General James Monk agreed that any assembly would have to overrepresent the English to avoid French domination. But Chief Justice William Smith felt that the English element had to be strengthened through immigration before representative government could be established.

Many French-Canadian merchants and professionals also desired an assembly, since the French, as the majority, hoped to control this part of government. The merchants and professionals tried to persuade the habitants that an assembly would decide on the *corvées* and on militia laws—the implication being that a French-dominated legislative body would be unfavourable to both. But the seigneurs, who linked their interests and privileges to the maintenance of the status quo, warned that an assembly could be dangerous for the colony, for it might tax land. Moreover, the seigneurs were outraged by the prospect of their tenants becoming their political equals with the advent of elections.

Petitions and counter-petitions circulated. In reality, the great majority of the province's 150 000 "new subjects" (the *Canadiens*) probably had little understanding of and even less interest in the question. Their main preoccupation was simply in subsisting, an objective not easily attained in these often difficult years.

Although not thoroughly familiar with social conditions in Quebec the imperial government had to arbitrate often contradictory pressures and draw up the new constitution. William Grenville, secretary of state for the colonies, drafted the Constitutional Act of 1791 that provided for the division of the province into two sections, Upper and Lower Canada, with the upper part possessing an English-speaking Loyalist majority. The reasons for the partition of Quebec were not economic or geographic, for the colony functioned as a single unit. Rather, Westminster's motivation was, as Grenville explained, to reduce "dissensions and animosities" among two "classes of men, differing in their prejudices, and perhaps in their interests."

190

Institutional Changes

The major new institution established in both Canadas was the elective Assembly. Besides giving a voice to the population, this body could raise money through taxes for local expenditures, thus reducing the burden on the imperial treasury. At the same time, wary of what had happened in the American colonies, London moved to place the assembly under strong executive control that would apply restraint if the people's representatives got out of hand. Members of the Legislative Council, the assembly's upper house, were appointed for life. Its membership was intended eventually to be hereditary, like that of the British House of Lords. Thus the "right men", that is, landowners, would be assured of a place of power. The Executive Council, also composed of appointed officials, was the governor's personal cabinet. It was to advise the governor, who could dissolve the assembly if it proved too stubborn. The governor enjoyed extensive veto powers and a measure of financial autonomy, thanks to the revenues from the Crown lands set aside by the Constitutional Act of 1791. (Other lands were reserved for the maintenance of a "Protestant clergy," intended to mean the Church of England.) Yet this remarkably equilibrated construction soon condemned Lower Canada's government to increasingly frequent and severe bouts of paralysis.

On account of property qualifications in England at this time, relatively few people could vote in elections. Essentially the same qualifications applied to Lower Canada, but because of that colony's very different social structure, the great majority of habitants obtained the right to vote. Still, suffrage was not universal. Most urban labourers and domestics were disqualified because they neither owned property nor paid sufficient rent.

The property qualification eliminated the great majority of women from the rolls although only in 1834 did the Assembly specifically disenfranchise women. This happened because Papineau and his party, the *Patriotes*, believed that electoral violence had attained such a point that "the public interest, decency, and the natural modesty of the sex" required that women not witness such scenes; also, they did not always like the way that women voted!

The electoral arrangements disappointed Lower Canada's English Protestants. They had petitioned so often for an assembly from which the French would have been excluded, or at least in which there would be an English-speaking majority bolstered by further immigration. Montreal merchant Adam Lymburner lobbied in London for an arrangement in which the towns (which contained a large majority of the English-speaking element, but only a small minority of the total population) would get half the seats. His avowed aim was to avoid putting the House in the "power of ignorant and obstinate men" who held "the absurd idea that it is the landholders' interest to oppress commerce." In fact, although the towns obtained only ten of the fifty seats, nearly 60 percent of the representatives elected in 1792 were well-established merchants who could afford to travel to Quebec and sit as unpaid legislators.

191

With the Constitutional Act of 1791, Quebec obtained its third constitution in fewer than thirty years. The American Revolution and the arrival of thousands of Loyalists had made change imperative. Reactions to the new legislation varied widely. In Britain there was satisfaction that the new colony of Upper Canada would be free to grow under British law and British liberty, and that the French majority in Lower Canada, confined to the House of Assembly, could do little damage. Some, like William Pitt, even hoped that the French, seeing the British system at work in Upper Canada, would gradually adopt English laws and customs. In the meantime, no force would be required.

Certain Lower Canadian groups, like the seigneurs, professionals, and merchants, thought they could use the new institutions profitably. Most disappointed as a group were undeniably Lower Canada's ten thousand English. The Constitutional Act of 1791 led to their separation from the growing English-speaking population in the new colony of Upper Canada. Moreover, the English-speaking inhabitants of what now became Lower Canada obtained few of the reforms for which they had agitated and did not even succeed in getting the Quebec Act repealed. The only real compensation offered was the provision for the freehold system of land tenure in the area outside the seigneurial zone, in what became the Eastern Townships. Moreover, they were unsure of what to expect from the Assembly. The maintenance of a strong executive in British hands was but small consolation to the merchants. After all the government had been in British hands since 1760—and yet the merchants were more often than not at loggerheads with the colonial administrators. Nevertheless, regardless of political changes, their economic power was increasing. In 1791 they had reason to be optimistic towards the future.

NOTES

[1] A. L. Burt, *The Old Province of Quebec* (2 vols., Toronto, 1968; first published 1933), 1:218.
[2] R. Arthur Bowler, "Sir Guy Carleton and the Campaign of 1776 in Canada," *Canadian Historical Review*, 55 (1974): 131–40.
[3] Françoise Noël, "La gestion des seigneuries de Gabriel Christie dans la vallée du Richelieu (1760–1845)," *Revue d'histoire de l'Amérique française*, 40 (1987): 561–82.

192

Related Reading

As with chapter 9, the following articles from R. Douglas Francis and Donald B. Smith, *Readings in Canadian History: Pre-Confederation*; 2d ed. (Toronto, 1986), will also be helpful for this topic: Fernand Ouellet, "The Legacy of New France Restored to Favour," pp. 191–203; and Michel Brunet, "French Canada and the Early Decades of British Rule, 1760–1791," pp. 203–16.

BIBLIOGRAPHY

Hilda Neatby's synthesis, *Quebec: The Revolutionary Age* (Toronto, 1966), reviews the political developments. Chapters 4 and 5 of Fernand Ouellet's *Social and Economic History of Quebec* (Toronto, 1980) are also very useful. On the American invasion, see Robert M. Hatch, *Thrust for Canada: The American Attempt on Quebec in 1775–1776* (Boston, 1979); George A. Rawlyk, *Revolution Rejected, 1775–1776* (Scarborough, Ont., 1968); and George F. G. Stanley, *Canada Invaded, 1775–1776* (Toronto, 1973).

L. F. S. Upton, ed., *The United Empire Loyalists: Men and Myths* (Toronto, 1967), contains useful documents, while David V. J. Bell, "The Loyalist Tradition in Canada," *Journal of Canadian Studies*, 5 (1970): 22–33, evaluates the impact of the Loyalists. The best study on the Six Nations is by Barbara Graymont, *The Iroquois in the American Revolution* (Syracuse, 1972). Church history is examined by Marcel Trudel in "La servitude de l'Eglise catholique du Canada français sous le régime anglais," *Canadian Historical Association Report*, 1963, pp. 42–64, and Jean-Pierre Wallot, "Religion and French-Canadian Mores in the Early Nineteenth Century," *Canadian Historical Review*, 52 (1971): 51–94. Information on women in late eighteenth century Quebec appears in Micheline Dumont et al.,

Quebec Women. A History (Toronto, 1987). Pierre Tousignant studies the genesis of the Constitutional Act in "Problématique pour une nouvelle approche de la constitution de 1791," *Revue d'histoire de l'Amérique française*, 27 (1973): 181–234. The *Dictionary of Canadian Biography* (Toronto, 1966-) includes sketches of merchants, statesmen, Indians, seigneurs, artists and other personalities.

CHAPTER ELEVEN

Britain's First Inland Colony, Upper Canada, 1791–1815

Since the 1970s Toronto and other Ontario towns and cities have celebrated the first Monday in August in honour of John Graves Simcoe, the first lieutenant governor of Upper Canada. Simcoe Day honours the British war hero who, after the American Revolution, did all in his power to create a new British colony, in his words, with "a Superior, more happy, and more polished form of Government" than that of the United States. In some respects Simcoe occupies the same position in Ontario as Champlain in Quebec. The founder of New France worked to make the St. Lawrence valley into a viable French colony, and Simcoe spent four years constructing a lasting framework for the first British inland colony. His successors, with the possible exception of Isaac Brock, who saved Upper Canada from American capture during the War of 1812, failed to come up to his standard of leadership.

The Anishinabeg

At the close of the 1770s few European settlers lived in the present-day southern Ontario peninsula. The Algonquian Indians in the area had seen French forts established on the fur trade routes at Niagara, Detroit, and Michilimackinac, but never in the interior. After the conquest of 1760 the English maintained these forts but made no attempt to begin settlements in what would soon become Upper Canada. Yet, by the outbreak of the War of 1812, seventy-five thousand Europeans occupied the area, outnumbering the native population by roughly ten to one.

THE EARLY LAND PURCHASES

The Proclamation of 1763 (see chapter 9) recognized the Great Lakes area as Indian country, which the Indians first had to surrender to the Crown before settlement could proceed. Until the early 1780s present-day southern Ontario was the home of three closely related tribes: the Ojibwa (Chippewa), Ottawa (Odawa), and Algonquin—the three Algonquian tribes who called themselves the "Anishinabeg," meaning true men, or true human beings.

Sir Frederick Haldimand, the governor of Quebec from 1778 to 1784, arranged for the purchase of the land from the Mississauga, as the British called the Anishinabeg along the north shore of Lake Ontario. To provide land for the Loyalists at Fort Niagara, the British paid the Mississauga in 1781 "three hundred suits of clothing," for a strip of land six and a half kilometres wide on the west bank of the Niagara River. In a second agreement the Indians surrendered all the land from roughly present-day Gananoque to the eastern end of the Bay of Quinte, extending back from Lake Ontario, "as far as a man can travel in a day." This was in exchange for clothing for all of their families, guns, powder, and ammunition for the winter's hunt and "as much coarse red cloth as will make about a dozen coats and as many laced hats." Other purchases followed, until the British believed in 1788 that they had obtained title to the entire Niagara peninsula and the whole north shore of Lake Ontario, except for a large tract between the head of the lake (present-day Hamilton) and Toronto. The British regarded the transactions as simple real-estate deals—complete title to the surrendered area in exchange for trade goods, paid on a once-and-for-all-time basis.

195

Why did the Mississauga accept these conditions? First, the Mississauga were dependent on European trade goods, which they expected the English to give annually, as the French always had. Second, they did not believe they were selling the land once and for all. While the Indians believed that they owned the land, their pattern of ownership and use differed from that of the British in the late eighteenth century. Among the Great Lakes Algonquians, an individual family could use a recognized hunting ground, fishing place, or maple sugar bush, but as soon as they ceased to go there, it reverted to the collective ownership of the entire band. For the Anishinabeg the initial sale was to tenants for the use of the land during good behaviour. Third, the Mississauga had a small population of one thousand, all divided into a dozen or more separate bands along the five hundred kilometres of lakefront. They could only have resisted their British allies with great difficulty. Thus, weakly organized, reliant on European trade goods, and believing they were receiving presents in perpetuity for the use of their land, the Mississauga agreed to the proposals.

Arrival of the Loyalists

The Loyalist refugees who arrived in large number on the north shore of Lake Ontario in 1784 were nearly all destitute. The Crown provided them with substantial help, bearing the costs of transporting them to their new home, and providing them with large amounts of free land, as well as provisions, clothing, tools, seed, and shelter.

The land was allotted according to status and rank. Each family head could receive 40 ha, with an additional 20 ha for each family member. Non-commissioned officers could claim 80 ha, field officers 400 ha, captains 280 ha. Subalterns, staff, and warrant officers were allowed 200 ha.

Loyalist settlements appeared throughout the province. About four thousand Loyalists settled in the townships along the St. Lawrence–Bay of Quinte area by the autumn of 1784. Since many of them had been farmers in the old colonies, they adjusted quickly transforming the forest into orderly farms and settled communities. They harvested their first real crop in the autumn of 1786, at which time government rations ended. Between 1787 and 1789—depending on the settlement—occurred the notorious "hungry years," when severe drought caused crop failures. Drought struck the upper St. Lawrence in 1787 and Niagara in 1788. Fortunately, it only lasted one year in each area, and good harvests the following year saved the settlers.

196

Next in size to the St. Lawrence–Bay of Quinte settlements was that at Niagara. During the war Niagara had been a haven for the Loyalists of the frontier districts of Pennsylvania and New York. Only a relatively small number of Loyalists settled on the northwestern shore of Lake Erie and in the towns of Sandwich (within the present-day boundaries of Windsor) and Amherstburg. In 1796 the population of these two towns greatly increased when Detroit passed into American hands. Many of Detroit's French citizens, wishing to retain their British allegiance, crossed to the Canadian side and became Loyalists.

Some Loyalists settled in the neighbouring lower Thames River valley (below present-day Chatham) once the Crown purchased the land from the Anishinabeg in 1790. The Long Point peninsula of Lake Erie was the last major centre of white Loyalist settlement, the majority of its inhabitants having originally settled elsewhere.

IROQUOIS LOYALISTS

Approximately two thousand Iroquois Loyalists came to Upper Canada, leaving behind an equal number of their people. Of those that came across the border, the majority followed Joseph Brant to the Grand River valley.

They were mostly Mohawk, Cayuga, and Onondaga who had fought for Britain. Brant chose the location because of its proximity to their allies, the Seneca, who decided to remain in western New York; and also to the Upper Great Lakes Indians, whom he aspired to lead in a Great Lakes Indian Confederacy. A small group of some hundred Mohawks who were antagonistic to Brant followed Chief John Deseronto and settled on a tract on the Bay of Quinte.

Anxious to retain the Indians' support in the event of another war with the Americans, the British provided the Six Nations people on the Grand River with a church, a school, a sawmill, a gristmill, and an allowance for a schoolmaster, and £1500 as general compensation for their war losses. The Mohawks on the Bay of Quinte also obtained a school along with a schoolmaster and a church. In keeping with Indian Department policy all the Indians received annual presents and, like the other Loyalists, clothing, tools, and provisions.

197

Loyalist Settlements

By the early 1790s the region west of Montreal had received many additional settlers. Historian Bruce Wilson has estimated that in 1785 approximately 7500 Loyalists (5500 white and 2000 Indian) lived in the area and by 1791, 20 000 to 30 000. From the St. Lawrence up the Ottawa River to the Rideau, new settlements were established. They extended over fifteen kilometres around the Bay of Quinte and formed a narrow strip along the Lake Ontario shore from the Bay of Quinte to York, where farms extended twenty-five kilometres up Yonge Street.

Settlers, mostly from rural New York and Pennsylvania, now occupied the narrow strip of good land below the escarpment around the Niagara peninsula and part way up the Lake Erie shoreline. From the concessions along the front of the Detroit River, settlement began to move along the south shore of Lake St. Clair, and the lower Thames River valley began to receive settlers.

LIFE OF THE LOYALISTS

Most early Loyalists to Upper Canada were poor. Not until the wave of immigration from New Brunswick in the 1790s did Upper Canada receive what might be termed a Loyalist elite, composed of families like the Robinsons, the Jarvises, and the Ryersons. These early Loyalists lived in military tents until they had built their first homes, usually comfortable

198

National Archives of Canada / PA-237054.

York, 1804, capital of Upper Canada, by Elisabeth Francis Hale. The painting shows the tiny settlement of 435 persons, hemmed in by the surrounding forest. Today's Front Street in Toronto was then the water's edge.

dwellings but very humble. They preferred sites by the lakes and rivers—the first highways before roads were built.

The average Loyalist home was a log cabin, with one or sometimes two rooms. These cabins had no cellar or foundation, the floor often being of earth. The cabin's dimensions were small, on the average no more than four metres by five metres, and sometimes three metres by four. The roofs were constructed of bark or small hollowed basswood logs, overlapping each other like tiles. Oil paper, not glass, usually covered the windows. Since bricks were not available, the chimneys were built of sticks and clay or rough unmortared stones. Sometimes there was no chimney, the smoke finding its way out through a hole in the bark roof. Clay and moss filled the chinks between the logs. Some sticks of furniture or family heirlooms might have survived the journey to Upper Canada, but the bulk of the furniture was handmade. The cooking was done at an open fireplace. In summer there were plenty of flies and mosquitoes in the houses. Field mice and rats (introduced from Europe) infested the towns.

199

Technically speaking, the Loyalist farms were seigneuries, since the Quebec Act applied to the western section of the province. Wanting to obtain the English freehold tenure land system, as well as British laws and institutions, these Loyalists petitioned the governor at Quebec for the English system. Lord Dorchester immediately increased by eighty hectares the size of Loyalist grants to the head of each family who had developed a farm. He also instructed that a registry be kept of all the names of the Loyalists, so that when sons of Loyalist settlers came of age they, too, would receive eighty hectares of additional land, as would daughters when they came of age or married. Unfortunately, colonial authorities soon overlooked Dorchester's two stipulations: that these grants would apply only to Loyalists' children already in the province, and the children had to occupy and improve the land granted. Instead, the officials gave away valuable land to absentee landholders and speculators.

THE CONSTITUTIONAL ACT OF 1791

The Constitutional Act of 1791 officially brought the colony of Upper Canada into existence. It provided for freehold tenure; in fact, all land was to be granted and not sold in Upper Canada. The settlers paid only the fees for the issuing and recording of the titles. In a curious phrase, the legislation also set aside the equivalent of one-seventh of all lands granted in the future, for "the Support and Maintenance of a Protestant Clergy." Unfortunately, just what was the "Protestant Clergy"—the Church of England only, or the Church of Scotland and other Protestant denominations as well—was not made explicit. Concern over these land reserves for the clergy led, within a generation, to great political controversy. The British government also set aside an additional one-seventh of all lands granted in the future. The revenues from the sale or rental of these Crown reserves might, it was felt, enable the colonial government to fund itself without recourse to the House of Assembly.

A "Truly British" Colony

John Graves Simcoe, an energetic and enthusiastic military officer then in his late thirties, became the first lieutenant governor of Upper Canada. The son of a naval officer who had died on Wolfe's expedition to Quebec in 1759, Simcoe was posted to America at the outbreak of the American Revolution, where he proved to be one of Britain's most successful commanders.

Simcoe did all in his power to make Upper Canada a home fit for Loyalist heroes and a centre of British power in North America. Believing that a minority had instigated the American Revolution and that many in the new republic remained actively loyal to England, he attempted to win other Americans back to their old allegiance. He believed that a new colony with "a free, honourable British Government," would remind Americans of what they had lost in leaving the empire and of the benefits if they returned.

Lasting evidence of Simcoe's plan to transform Upper Canada into a "little England" can be seen in his choice of place names. In 1793 the governor travelled through the colony, liberally choosing new designations. He went as far west as Detroit, confirming en route his choice of a site for the future capital at the place the Anishinabeg called "Ko-te-quo-gong" (At the Forks), at the headwaters of the Ashkahnesebe (Horn or Antler River). The governor renamed Kotequogong as London, and the river that the Anishinabeg had named because its branches reminded them of a deer's antlers became the Thames. He also travelled to Toronto (an Iroquoian name), which he named York. Intent on re-casting Upper Canada into a little England overseas, Simcoe now changed the names of the two major rivers in the Toronto area to the Humber and the Don, two rivers in northeastern England. When asked what he thought of John Graves Simcoe's contribution to the colony, Joseph Brant replied: "General Simcoe has done a great deal for this province; he has changed the name of every place in it."

The governor wanted the Anglican church, the established Church of England, alone to have the right of performing marriages in the colony. Only reluctantly did he agree that justices of the peace in remote areas might conduct marriage ceremonies, providing that they followed Church of England procedure. In the years to follow, Simcoe's and his successors' attempts to restrict to the Church of England the right to solemnize marriages caused great discontent, since the majority of the population belonged to other denominations. At times in the mid-1790s the results were amusing. An Anglican clergyman, the Rev. John Langhorne, announced at Ernestown (Bath), a village near Kingston, that since marriages performed by non-Anglican ministers were illegal, persons so married were at liberty to marry someone else. Two Lutheran couples took Langhorne at his word and requested to be married—with a switch in partners.[1]

Only in 1798 was the right to solemnize marriages extended to Lutheran, Calvinist, and Church of Scotland ministers—Methodists were excluded until 1831. The Upper Canadian administration regarded the Methodists, who had strong links until 1828 with their American parent church, as a dangerous American denomination.

Legislating a Colony into Existence   *201*

Simcoe established the new colony's initial institutions and laws, but first of all he placed the new colony on a firm military footing. War with the Americans threatened to break out over the British-held "western posts" (see chapter 10). By the peace treaty of 1783, Britain and the United States had agreed to an international boundary that ran through the upper St. Lawrence and through the Great Lakes, to the lands claimed by Spain in the Mississippi and Missouri river basins. The Americans had failed, however, as they had promised in 1783, to allow the Loyalists to return to their homes and to collect their legitimate debts.

Seizing upon this violation of the treaty, Britain refused to vacate the "western posts" of Oswego, Niagara, Detroit, and Michilimackinac. For defence purposes London allowed Simcoe to raise an infantry corps of some 425 officers and men, the Queen's Rangers (the name of his old Loyalist regiment in the Revolutionary War, for service in Upper Canada). The governor also had the Upper Canada Assembly pass a militia bill in 1793. It required all able-bodied men 16–50 years old to enrol and to attend parade drill for their local companies two to four times a year. By 1794 more than five thousand officers and men served in the militia.

THE ADMINISTRATION OF UPPER CANADA

Simcoe carefully structured his administration. Once he had established temporary headquarters at Newark (now Niagara-on-the-Lake), a small garrison on the west bank of the Niagara River, opposite Fort Niagara, he called for elections to the legislative assembly. As a product of the

English class system, Simcoe had some reservations about the social background of the assemblymen elected, describing them as "of a Lower Order, who kept but one Table, that is, who dined in Common with their Servants." Nevertheless, he was pleased that they supported his plans to fashion Upper Canada into a truly British province. For chief justice the new governor selected William Osgoode, a respected English lawyer.

The legislature created a judicial system. At the top stood the Court of King's Bench, the new superior court of civil and criminal jurisdiction. Within each district surrogate courts and a provincial court of probate were established. At a lower level, meetings for the courts of quarter sessions were organized. The justices of the peace presided over these and performed as well a wide range of administrative and judicial duties. At the township level the justices of the peace enjoyed considerable power, trying court cases, supervising road and bridge construction contracts, and issuing various licences, including one for taverns. As in Nova Scotia, township officials in Upper Canada were appointed, not elected as they were in New England.

202

Simcoe continued to introduce English place names. The four districts established by Lord Dorchester became the Eastern (Luneburg), Midland (Mecklenburg), Home (Nassau), and Western (Hesse). Legislation established district jails and court houses.

THE SLAVERY QUESTION

With Simcoe's full support, the legislature addressed another issue in its first sittings: the question of slavery. While the majority of black Loyalists and black slaves had gone to Nova Scotia after the Revolution, some black slaves were brought to Upper Canada. Joseph Brant, the Iroquois war chief, had black slaves, as did John Stuart, the first Anglican missionary at Kingston. By 1792 the Niagara district alone had an estimated three hundred slaves. Nevertheless, slavery proved unpopular. It was an expensive proposition in a northern area like Upper Canada. The short Canadian growing season ruled out such crops as cotton, which required a cheap, plentiful labour force. Also, owners had to feed, clothe, and house slaves throughout a long and unproductive winter. In addition, Simcoe and others found slavery abhorrent.

The legislature voted for the gradual elimination of slavery in the province. Slaves already in Upper Canada had to continue in that state until their death, but all children born in the future to female slaves in the colony were to be freed at the age of twenty-five; their children would be free from birth. No additional slaves could be brought to Upper Canada.

LAND GRANTS

Although anxious to eliminate the slave class—the lowest rung of society, Simcoe sought to create in Upper Canada what he considered the highest class: an aristocracy. He believed that he could legislate such an elite into existence through generous land grants. He allowed members of the executive and legislative councils to receive large grants of 1200–2000 ha; these grants were equivalent to those given the highest-ranked military officers. Their children, often quite numerous, could obtain 480 ha. His idea, however, rebounded on the colony. The recipients had no intention of becoming country squires, preferring instead to sell their estates profitably in the future. These grants locked up much valuable land and kept it out of settlers' hands. Furthermore, many of the so-called "late Loyalists," who arrived in the 1790s, were not really Loyalists; they had come in search of cheap land. Upper Canada lay on the advancing American settlement frontier, the natural migration route to northern Ohio, and even much of northwestern New York.

203

In 1794 Governor Simcoe broadened the standards and allowed all individuals who professed the Christian religion, whose pasts were respectable and law abiding, and who were capable of manual labour, to obtain eighty hectares of land, as long as they swore allegiance to the Crown. He knew that their North American agricultural experience would be valuable. But many of these settlers were not interested in Simcoe's plan for an elite British colony.

COMMUNICATIONS

As lieutenant governor Simcoe contributed to the improvement of communications in the colony. As a result of a tour in early 1793 he decided to build a military road from Burlington Bay to the Thames. The Queen's Rangers began work in the early summer of 1793 on the road designated Dundas Street, after Henry Dundas, then a secretary of state in the English cabinet. Simcoe believed that a second military road should be developed from York to Lac aux Claies (which he renamed Lake Simcoe in honour of his father), to ensure rapid communication with the upper lakes. In 1796 another party of Queen's Rangers began work on this project, called Yonge Street after Sir George Yonge, the British secretary of war.

These two military highways, Yonge and Dundas Streets, became the principal pathways for future generations of settlers. Both roads allowed settlers to begin farms inland at a time when most people clung tenaciously to the navigable waterways.

UPPER CANADA AFTER SIMCOE

John Graves Simcoe left Upper Canada in mid-1796. He served briefly in 1797 as the British governor of Saint-Domingue (Haiti). There the dedicated abolitionist found himself nominally protecting the human property of French Royalist plantation owners against the brilliant Toussaint L'Ouverture, an ex-slave who led a revolt to liberate all the slaves on the island. In 1806 Simcoe obtained the post of commander-in-chief in India, but he died before taking up the post.

While in Upper Canada Simcoe experienced many disappointments. He might well have considered the colony as something approaching the centre of the universe, but London did not. The home government turned down his schemes to build up the colony economically and militarily. His proposal to create a provincial university also received little support in London, as did his attempt to establish the Church of England in the colony under a bishop's tutelage. The hierarchical society he tried to construct did not materialize, but he at least established a community. As historian Gerald Craig wrote: "Simcoe had helped to nurse a new province into being, but its inhabitants, busy with their own projects and their own local affairs, showed only a tepid interest in the goals he had set for them."[2] He put Upper Canada on its feet, although the province was to choose its own directions.

The Indians of Upper Canada: A Displaced People

The Simcoe years have received considerable attention from Ontario historians. Less has been said of the resident Indian population, particularly the Mississauga Indians whom the Loyalists encountered on the north shore of Lake Ontario.

By the time of Simcoe's departure in 1796, the Indians had begun to realize what the early land purchases meant to the British: the whites denied them a right of way across their cleared fields. If the Indians camped on the white settlers' lands, the farmers shot the Indians' dogs. The tribal elders told the young people, such as Kahkewaquonaby (Sacred Feathers) or, in English, Peter Jones, a future native historian, that when the British first came they "asked for a small piece of land on which they might pitch their tents; the request was cheerfully granted. By and by they begged for more, and more was given them. In this way they have continued to ask, or have obtained by force or fraud, the fairest portions of our territory."[3] In 1805 and 1818 the Crown successfully pressured them to sell their last remaining tract, between Toronto and the head of the lake.

Other tragedies followed. From the 1790s to the 1820s smallpox, tuberculosis, and measles carried away almost two-thirds of the Mississauga at the western end of the lake. Their population dropped to two hundred in the 1820s, down from more than five hundred a generation earlier. The Iroquois as well experienced difficult times in the 1790s and 1800s as land sales eliminated a great deal of their reserve on the Grand River. Joseph Brant wanted white farmers to settle among the Iroquois on the Grand River and to teach them European agricultural techniques. The Iroquois war chief realized that with European plows the Indians could produce more on the available land. Yet not all the Grand River Iroquois agreed with Brant. They objected to the presence of the white people on their land and to the fact that by 1798, two-thirds of their land was already gone.

Growth of Settlement

Upper Canada's non-Indian population increased dramatically at the turn of the century. General Peter Hunter, who served as governor from 1799–1805, and Francis Gore, in office before the War of 1812, addressed the challenge of a rapidly expanding white settler population. Like Simcoe, they had to face the issue of granting land to late American settlers who claimed to be Loyalists. As long as the French and Napoleonic Wars continued, little hope existed of obtaining immigrants from Britain. At least these Americans had the necessary pioneer skills.

In the late 1790s to 1812 many "late Loyalists" came to Upper Canada. By 1812 the peaceful invasion put settlers on all the vacant townships along the north shore of Lake Ontario. Several townships also developed on Lake Erie. Although roads remained very few in number, communication and transportation along waterways allowed for the dispersal of settlement along an 800 km front in a period of less than twenty years.

THE PLAIN FOLK

Among the new immigrants were members of sects commonly termed the "Plain Folk"—Quakers, Mennonites, Dunkards, and Moravians. These religious sects opposed war, objected to taking oaths, and believed in a plain religion and plain dress. In most instances the Quakers were English in origin and the other groups largely German; because Quakers opposed all wars, these groups had remained neutral during the American Revolution.

The prospect of good, relatively cheap land, easily accessible by water, attracted the Plain Folk, as did the prospect of stability. Several years after the war the most radical revolutionaries in New York and Pennsylvania still persecuted them for their refusal to take oaths of allegiance. The old tolerance of colonial times had gone, and they sought to find it again under British rule in Upper Canada. Simcoe himself had welcomed Quakers to the province and declared they would be exempt from bearing arms.

The newcomers from Pennsylvania and New York made ideal farmers. Historian G. Elmore Reaman has noted their three great strengths: "They were physically equipped both in knowledge of what to do in the wilderness and the strength to do it; they came with money and equipment; and they aided one another, whether Quaker, Huguenot, Lutheran, or Mennonite."[4]

By 1800 large numbers of these Plain Folk settled in Upper Canada, many having trekked north in the heavy, broad-wheeled covered wagons, known as Conestoga wagons. Perhaps the greatest number selected the Niagara Peninsula on account of its accessibility to the Quaker, Mennonite, and Dunkard settlements in Pennsylvania. The Bay of Quinte became another favourite area for religious minorities, as did Yonge Street, particularly in Markham and Vaughan townships.

206

The Mennonites' largest settlement was in the difficult-to-reach Waterloo County, on land originally belonging to the Six Nations Reserve. The last area to receive settlers from Pennsylvania, Waterloo was the only locality in Ontario to retain the ethnic characteristics of its early settlers nearly two centuries later. The migration of the Amish directly from Germany in 1824 did much to strengthen the German character of the area, as did the later arrival of German Lutherans and Roman Catholics from Europe.

After three decades of settlement the population of Upper Canada reached seventy-five thousand in 1812. Four new administrative districts had been added to Simcoe's original four. Scattered along the St. Lawrence and Lakes Ontario, Erie, and St. Clair, the whites rarely settled more than a few kilometres into the interior.

The work of establishing farms and clearing new land took much of the settlers' time, leaving little opportunity for politics. No clear-cut alignments existed in the Assembly, and apart from one newspaper at Niagara, no opposition press existed. The newcomers from the United States outnumbered the old Loyalists and the few immigrants from Britain by four to one. Like the Acadians of Nova Scotia a century earlier, these Americans lived within a British colony without really understanding or belonging to it. The War of 1812 would—as did the Seven Years' War for the Acadians—press them to choose sides.

UPPER CANADA AND THE UNITED STATES

As long as Britain retained the western posts the outbreak of hostilities with the United States seemed inevitable. Simcoe, in fact, had hoped that the Indians south of the Great Lakes would defeat the Americans, which it appeared in 1791 they might. In that year they defeated General Arthur St. Clair, the governor of the Northwest Territory, killing six hundred Americans and forcing another fourteen hundred to flee for their lives across the Ohio. The Americans, however, responded by sending more soldiers to the borders of the Ohio country.

To shore up the defence of Detroit, Simcoe in 1794 authorized the construction of a fort near the mouth of the Maumee River on Lake Erie. The governor himself led the expedition that went deeply into American territory to establish the new fort. War seemed ever more likely in the summer of 1794 until the balance of power south of the Great Lakes suddenly changed. In late August the American general "Mad" Anthony Wayne defeated the Ohio Indians at the Battle of Fallen Timbers and put an end to Simcoe's dream of an Indian buffer state.

International developments also contributed to Britain's decision later in 1794 to hand over the western posts. As a result of its war with France, Britain badly needed to ease tension with the United States. In November 1794 the two countries signed Jay's Treaty, named for John Jay, the American Chief Justice who negotiated the treaty with the British. By its terms Britain agreed to evacuate the forts on the south shores of the Great Lakes to the United States in 1796. With Britain's imminent withdrawal, the Ohio Indians made peace with the Americans and ceded in the Treaty of Greenville (1795) their claims to most of the present-day state of Ohio. But the Indians' resistance to the American settlers' march westward continued.

CAUSES OF THE WAR OF 1812

In the first decade of the century Tecumseh, a Shawnee Indian chief, and his brother, a religious leader, assembled a formidable Indian Confederacy. In 1811 Tecumseh was in open war with the Americans. Many Ohioans, Tennesseeans, and Kentuckians, suspected—incorrectly—that the British continued to encourage and finance these Indian raids. Many aggressive and intensely patriotic Americans judged it time to eliminate the British. At the same time, the "war hawks," or American expansionists anxious to begin a war with Britain, argued that the United States could seize the fertile peninsula of Upper Canada.

Two direct provocations by Britain led President James Madison to support the pro-war party. In 1812 Napoleon's continental system closed all of western Europe, except Portugal, to British goods. Britain retaliated by imposing a naval blockade on France, preventing American ships from trading with France. Officially neutral in the struggle, the Americans called for freedom of the seas. What right had England to board American ships on the high seas and prevent them from trading on the continent? Madison considered this act the first provocation.

Britain also began to search American ships for British deserters. Thousands of British sailors had gone over to American vessels to obtain higher wages, better food, and better working conditions. Without regard for neutral rights, British cruisers stopped American ships on the North Atlantic and seized thousands of sailors, alleging that they were British deserters. If a man produced his easily obtained certificate of American naturalization the English ignored it, as their government did not recognize the right of a British subject to transfer allegiance to another country.

Earlier, in 1807, the United States had almost gone to war after a British ship fired on the *Chesapeake*, an American naval frigate, killing three and wounding eighteen aboard. The British then seized four men, three of whom turned out to be Americans. "Free Trade and Sailors' Rights" became the cry of many Americans. Forced, as he put it, to choose between war and degradation, Madison sent a message of war to Congress on June 1, 1812. Congress agreed and declared war against Britain.

UPPER CANADA'S SUCCESS IN 1812

Fortunately for the British, the Americans had a very faulty strategy of attack. In order of importance, Canada's key strategic points were Quebec, Montreal, Kingston, Niagara, and the Detroit River. The Americans chose first to attack the Upper Canadians east of the Detroit River, and then to strike at Niagara. Why their miscalculation? Throughout the first year of the war, the Americans believed incorrectly that Upper Canada's American population would welcome them as an army of liberation. Thomas Jefferson himself had assured Americans that the conquest of Upper Canada would be a "mere matter of marching."

Much of the credit for Upper Canada's success in 1812 is due to Major General Isaac Brock who had fought in the French wars in Europe and then been stationed in North America. Realizing the strategy that must be followed, Brock built up the province's fortifications, trained the provincial militia, and maintained good relations with the Indians. He knew that as soon as war broke out Upper Canada must take the offensive. The Americans had overwhelming superiority in numbers, but it would take them time to organize.

The Indians' military contribution best explains Brock's subsequent success. For the Great Lakes Indians, war did not break out in 1812; they had been fighting American frontiersmen for generations. Welcoming the outbreak of the second Anglo-American War in 1812, Tecumseh and hundreds of warriors joined the British in Upper Canada. The Indians

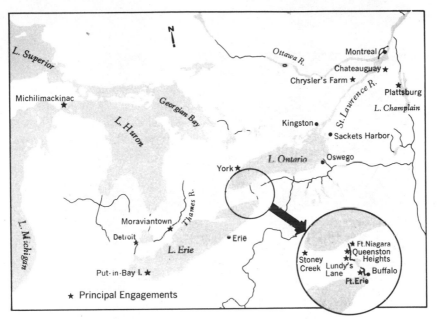

McInnis, *Canada*, p. 219.

The War of 1812

helped a small British force take Michilimackinac, the leading fur-trading post in the Upper Great Lakes; then Tecumseh and his warriors cut off the Americans' lines of communication with Detroit.

Only a few weeks earlier William Hull, the American commander at Detroit, had crossed the border near Windsor to issue a proclamation to the Upper Canadians: "You will be emancipated from tyranny and oppression and restored to the dignified station of freedom ... I come prepared for every contingency. I have a force which will look down all opposition. ... " Despite all his bluster, once he believed that Brock had five thousand Indians with him (he really only had about six hundred), General Hull surrendered without a fight. The fall of Detroit led to the loss of all the American territory west of Lake Erie.

Brock's unexpected victory at Detroit changed British fortunes overnight. He had proved that Upper Canada could be defended. Brock did so again in October at Queenston Heights, but at the cost of his life. An American sharpshooter shot the commander as he led a charge up the face of the heights. However, the attack succeeded. Five hundred Iroquois joined one thousand British regulars and six hundred militia in retaking the strategic heights. They captured nine hundred American prisoners.

Having lost one army at Detroit, the Americans had lost another in Niagara Peninsula. In 1840 a monument to Brock was built on the summit of the heights overlooking the battlefield, a reminder of his contribution to the successful defence of Upper Canada.

After the war a belief grew that the civilian soldiers had won the cam-

210

National Archives of Canada / C273.

Scaling Queenston Heights. The artist, John David Kelly (1861–1958), has re-created the famous battle.

paigns at Detroit, Queenston Heights, and other battle grounds. In reality this is quite false. Regular soldiers constituted the first line of Britain's defence of Upper Canada supplying the leadership and doing most of the fighting themselves. Throughout the war the Upper Canadian militia proved quite unreliable. Zeal for the fight always declined at harvest time or whenever news arrived of danger to the men's families from raiding parties. The British regulars remained the backbone of Upper Canada's resistance in 1812 and for the next two years of the war.

The Campaigns of 1813 and 1814

The darkest moment of the war for the Upper Canadians came in the summer of 1813. The Americans captured York and launched a second invasion of the Niagara Peninsula, forcing the British to withdraw to Burlington Heights at the head of the lake. Desertions grew and two members of the Upper Canada Assembly actually joined the Americans. Only a surprise attack by British regular troops at Stoney Creek, immediately south of Burlington Heights, dislodged the Americans and saved Upper Canada.

211

A second battle after Stoney Creek led to an American withdrawal from the Niagara Peninsula. Laura Secord, the daughter of Loyalists, provided the British with vital information. While the Americans were dining at her house at Queenston, she overheard some officers discussing a surprise attack against the British. The thirty-seven-year-old woman walked thirty kilometres from Queenston to Beaver Dams to warn them. Without downplaying Laura Secord's courage, Indian scouts had already informed the British of the American advance, but her information confirmed it. Two days later Iroquois from the Montreal area and from the Grand River ambushed the Americans. Shortly after the Indian victory at Beaver Dams, the American invaders withdrew from the peninsula.

The Americans fared better in the west once the American captain Oliver Perry defeated the British in an important naval battle on Lake Erie, which became an American Lake. The British then withdrew from Detroit. At Moraviantown, on the Thames River the Americans defeated the British regulars, the Upper Canadian militia, and the Indians. The Americans held on to southwestern Upper Canada until the end of the war.

Tecumseh was killed at Moraviantown on October 5, 1813. With his death his confederacy collapsed. Never again in the Lower Great Lakes area did the Indians constitute a serious military threat.

After Moraviantown the battle lines consolidated for the remainder of the war. The British in July 1814 defeated the Americans' last great attempt to capture Upper Canada, at Lundy's Lane in the Niagara Peninsula. Outside of Upper Canada, the British unsuccessfully took the offensive on Lake Champlain. In August 1814 a British expedition took Washington, burning the Capitol and the President's House (which, when rebuilt, was called the White House because the walls were whitewashed to hide the fire marks). The Americans halted the victorious British, however, at Baltimore. The only other major battle of the war (at New Orleans) took place after the peace treaty had been signed.

The war actually changed nothing. The peace treaty was based entirely on the status quo. But in one respect the war had a very profound effect contributing to the survival of a British Upper Canada: the unsuccessful and destructive attacks of 1812–14 had created anti-Americanism among the non-Loyalist settlers and also had promoted an Upper Canadian consciousness, a loyalty to the colony. Ironically, the American invasion helped to complete the work that Simcoe had begun. In the words of the Canadian historian A.R.M. Lower: "Upper Canada emerged from the War of 1812 a community, its people no longer Americans nor solely British subjects, but Upper Canadians."[5]

212

NOTES

[1] A.R.M. Lower, *Canadians in the Making* (Don Mills, Ont., 1958), p. 161.
[2] Gerald M. Craig, *Upper Canada: The Formative Years, 1784–1841* (Toronto, 1963), p. 41.
[3] Peter Jones (Kahkewaquonaby), *History of the Ojebway Indians* (London, 1861), p. 27.
[4] G. Elmore Reaman, *The Trail of the Black Walnut* (Toronto, 1957), p. 147.
[5] A.R.M. Lower, *Colony to Nation* (Toronto, 1957; first published 1946), p. 179.

Related Readings

The following essay in R. Douglas Francis and Donald B. Smith, *Readings in Canadian History: Pre-Confederation*, 2d ed. (Toronto, 1986) is of value to this topic: W.G. Shelton, "The United Empire Loyalists: A Reconsideration," pp. 246–55.

BIBLIOGRAPHY

For an understanding of early Upper Canada, Gerald M. Craig's *Upper Canada: The Formative Years, 1784–1841* (Toronto, 1963) is essential. The period immediately before the establishment of Upper Canada is reviewed by A.L. Burt in "The Loyalists," ch. 15 of *The Old Province of Quebec*, 2 vols. (Toronto, 1968; first published 1933), 2:76–115. Other sources on the Loyalists who settled in Upper Canada include Bruce Wilson, *As She Began: An Illustrated Introduction to Loyalist Ontario* (Toronto, 1981); James J. Talman, ed., *Loyalist Narratives from Upper Canada* (Toronto, 1946); and W. Stewart Wallace, *The United Empire Loyalists* (Toronto, 1922). Robert S. Allen's *Loyalist Literature: An Annotated Bibliographic Guide to the Writings on the Loyalists of the American Revolution* (Toronto, 1982) is a useful guide to the subject.

Simcoe's years in Upper Canada are reviewed in Stanley R. Mealing, "John Graves Simcoe," in *Our Living Tradition*, edited by Robert L. McDougall (Toronto, 1962), pp. 57–76; and "John Graves Simcoe," *Dictionary of Canadian Biography*, vol. 5:1801–1820 (Toronto, 1985), pp. 754–59. Malcolm Macleod examines Simcoe's defence policy in "Fortress Ontario or Forlorn Hope? Simcoe and the Defence of Upper Canada," *Canadian Historical Review*, 53 (1972): 149–78. Mary Beacock Fryer provides a popular overview of Upper Canada in "First Large-Scale Immigration 1784–1800," in *Loyal She Remains: A Pictorial History of Ontario*, edited by Mary Beacock Fryer and Charles Humber (Toronto, 1984), pp. 96–127.

213

The experience of the Six Nations in early Upper Canada is reviewed by Isabel Thompson Kelsay, *Joseph Brant 1743–1807: Man of Two Worlds* (Syracuse, 1984); and by Charles M. Johnston, ed., *The Valley of the Six Nations: A Collection of Documents on the Indian Lands of the Grand River* (Toronto, 1964); for the Mississauga, see Donald B. Smith, *Sacred Feathers. The Reverend Peter Jones (Kahkewaquonaby) & the Mississauga Indians* (Toronto, 1987). Daniel G. Hill's *The Freedom-Seekers: Blacks in Early Canada* (Agincourt, Ont., 1981) popularly summarizes the history of blacks in Upper Canada and in all of British North America. In *The Trail of the Black Walnut* (Toronto, 1957), G. Elmore Reaman tells the story of the "Plain Folk" and their arrival in Upper Canada.

A short summary of the War of 1812 appears in C.P. Stacey's essay, "The War of 1812 in Canadian History," in *The Defended Border: Upper Canada and the War of 1812*, edited by Morris Zaslow (Toronto, 1964), pp. 331–38. Pierre Berton has written two very readable accounts of the conflict: *The Invasion of Canada 1812–1813* (Toronto, 1980), and *Flames Across the Border 1813–1814* (Toronto, 1981). George F.G. Stanley provides the best scholarly account in *The War of 1812: Land Operations* (Ottawa, 1983).

For early maps of Upper Canada, see *Ontario's History in Maps*, edited by R. Louis Gentilcore and C. Grant Head (Toronto, 1984). Valuable portraits of early Upper Canadian figures are in the *Dictionary of Canadian Biography*, vol. 4:1770–1800, vol. 5:1800–1820, and vol. 6:1821–1835 (Toronto, 1979, 1985, 1987).

CHAPTER TWELVE

Upper Canada, 1815–40:
An Immigrant Society

In a quarter-century the population of Upper Canada expanded rapidly, from nearly one hundred thousand in 1815 to over four hundred thousand in 1840. The momentum continued into the 1840s, when the colony's population doubled to one million. Some of the new immigrants were from the United States but most were from the British Isles: Protestants from the north of Ireland, Roman Catholics from the south, Lowland and Highland Scots, Welsh and English. These immigrants brought new customs and attitudes that eventually mixed with those of the people already there. The newcomers settled the land, established and refined its political, social, and educational institutions, contributed to the colony's economic growth, and participated in its political movements. The British immigrants did much to distinguish Upper Canada still further from the American republic to the south.

Immigration and Settlement

After the War of 1812 the British government made every effort to encourage British immigration and, conversely, to discourage American immigration to Upper Canada. New laws prevented Americans from obtaining grants of land until they had resided in the province for seven years. Nevertheless, some Americans did come, including fugitive black slaves and free Blacks from the northern states. Most Blacks settled along the border, with the exception of 150 who settled in Oro township on the western shore of Lake Simcoe. Some became part of the general westward movement of the American frontier that carried American immigrants beyond Upper Canada to the newly opened lands in the Mississippi valley.

After 1815 the British settlers that Simcoe had so desperately wanted in the early years of the province finally arrived. Two factors account for the migration: peace and hard times. The end of the Napoleonic wars brought economic depression and unemployment to Great Britain, drastically reduced the army's demand for manpower, and made overseas travel less dangerous. For many people in crowded, post-war Britain, emigration seemed the answer to their problems.

The British government initially assisted the exodus with generous aid, similar to that first given the Loyalists. The assistance included the cost of transportation to the colony, free grants of land to each head of a family, rations for eight months or until established, agricultural supplies at cost, and a minister and school teacher on government salary for each settlement. This programme was at first intended mainly for demobilized soldiers and half-pay officers (those no longer in active service or retired).

By October 1816 more than fourteen hundred people had taken advantage of the offer to settle in Upper Canada, chiefly in the Lanark area in the eastern part of the colony. The government then extended aid to unemployed Scottish weavers and their families, who were being uprooted by the land enclosure system in Scotland. In 1820 two thousand government-assisted Scots settled in the Rideau district south of present-day Ottawa. Worse off than the Scots, however, were the Irish, forced from their land by high rents and taxes. In the early 1820s, some three thousand under government sponsorship came to settle in the Peterborough area.

In the mid-1820s the British government stopped aiding emigrants. The programme was considered too expensive and also unnecessary, since private charitable associations and landowners anxious to rid their estates of impoverished tenants assumed responsibility. Many of these immigrants ended up as paupers in Upper Canada, leading to the proliferation of public houses of industry or workhouses for the care of the destitute.

Upper Canada landowners also provided assistance in the hopes of profiting from this large group of potential settlers. Few were as successful as Colonel Thomas Talbot, who secured 2000 ha near St. Thomas in southwestern Upper Canada. He subsequently received 80 ha of adjoining land for each colonist he settled on a 20 ha lot of the original grant. Talbot eventually accumulated an estate of 8000 ha, making him one of the largest landholders in Upper Canada. In return, he settled thirty thousand people who cleared 200 000 ha of forest and swamp for farmland.

In 1826 the Canada Land Company began to settle approximately half a million hectares on the shores of Lake Huron. The colonization company obtained elsewhere another half-million hectares of Crown reserves and founded the towns of Guelph and Goderich.

THE VOYAGE OVERSEAS

Most immigrants came at their own expense. Only a few well-to-do could afford the £30 needed for first-class accommodation on an American

216

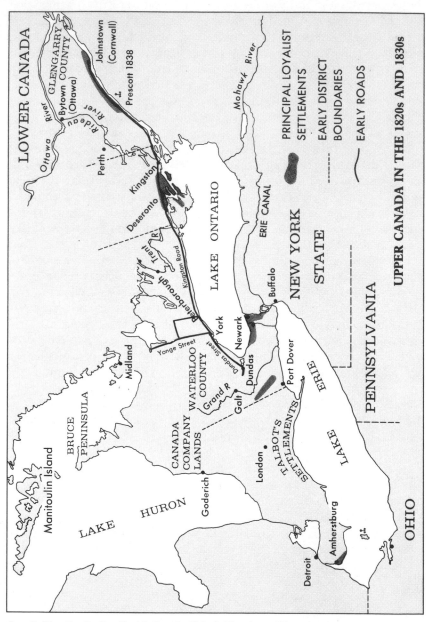

Cornell, Hamelin, Ouellet, Trudel, *Canada, Unity in Diversity*, p. 189.

frigate, which included a cabin with one or two bunks, a sofa, a window, and sumptuous meals. The remainder had to share a bunk in the steerage of crowded ships, or in the dank holds of timber ships.

Most immigrants never forgot their crossing of the Atlantic to the New World in a timber ship. Makeshift two-metre-square bunks stacked two or three tiers high lined the sides and ran down the middle of the vessel. The ship owners packed as many as 250 immigrants into a space 28.5 m long by 7.5 m wide and little more than 1.5 m high. Four people, often complete strangers, were crowded into a single berth to sleep. Food was often rancid, clean water and clean air non-existent. Not surprisingly, sickness was rampant, particularly cholera and typhoid. There were few doctors, and medical supplies were inadequate.

The immigrants had to endure these intolerable conditions for up to six weeks, and sometimes longer, under adverse sailing conditions. Many of them had already spent a week or two waiting on the dockside for the ship to sail or the right wind conditions. In his first novel, *Redburn*, Herman Melville describes how the emigrants talked of soon seeing America:

> The agent had told them that twenty days would be an unusually long voyage. Suddenly there was a cry of 'Land', and emigrants crowded a deck expecting America, but it was only Ireland.

Some never saw the New World; they died and were buried at sea. Many more arrived sick and debilitated, especially in the 1830s and 1840s, when cholera and typhoid spread through Britain and central Europe. One out of every twenty-eight immigrants to Quebec died on board ship during these two decades. Those wretched and bewildered immigrants lucky enough to survive the trip and remain healthy were met by unscrupulous "runners" or profiteers eager to take advantage of them. Then came the arduous overland journey to their new homes.

Nonetheless, for the strong, the new land carried a blessing. The constant need for labour in Upper Canada gave even penniless immigrants an opportunity to earn a living, to adjust to a freer society, and to save up for farms of their own. It took a lifetime for the average immigrant, lacking capital or labour, to clear a twenty-hectare farm and live comfortably. But in Upper Canada a landless labourer could at least become a landed proprietor—something nearly impossible in Britain.

THE NATIVE PEOPLES

The land came from the native peoples, a group already outnumbered ten to one by the non-natives by 1815. After the War of 1812 the Indians of Upper Canada made seven major land surrenders opening up much of present-day southern Ontario. Although the Indians now had a much greater understanding of the true nature and meaning of the land sales, their numbers were too slight to allow them to resist effectively. Secondly, the settled areas now divided the bands from one another, which helped to prevent any united response. Finally, much of their lands near the settlements had been ruined for hunting by the immigrant farmers, and the Indians needed support. In 1818 the government of Upper Canada had changed the method of purchasing the land, offering to pay annual payments or annuities in perpetuity to the Indians who sold their land, which was a more enticing offer than a simple one-time-only payment.

Indian migrants came northward to settle in Upper Canada. They came to escape the American government's decrees in the 1830s legislating that Indians east of the Mississippi must move west of the river. Several thousand Anishinabeg—Ojibwa, Odawa (Ottawa), and Potawatomi—took up residence in Upper Canada in the 1830s and 40s. Most of the Oneida, one of the Iroquois tribes remaining in New York State after the Revolution, also came around 1840 and purchased land on the Thames River west of London. Apart from one brief attempt by Governor Francis Bond Head in 1836/37 to re-locate the Anishinabeg of southern Ontario on Manitoulin Island (see page 216) on the north shore of Lake Huron (a proposal they vigorously opposed), the Upper Canadian Indians were allowed to stay on reserves in their old hunting territories.

Colonial Oligarchy: The Family Compact

British immigrants found much in Upper Canada that was familiar to them. The small, tightly knit elite popularly known as the "Family Compact," which controlled the leading positions in Upper Canadian society, jealously guarded its British character. Through political domination of the Executive Council—the governor's "cabinet"—and the Legislative Council (the upper house of the government), its members decided government policy and controlled the government's day-to-day operations. Through political patronage they appointed like-minded people to the local centres, thus creating smaller oligarchies throughout the province.

At the centre of the so-called Family Compact stood the Reverend John Strachan, cleric and educator. For more than two decades he acted as a leading adviser to the governors of Upper Canada. A humorous story circulated in the colony about Strachan's son: One day someone asked him, "Who governs Upper Canada?" "I do," he replied. When asked to explain, he answered, "I govern my mother, my mother governs my father, my father governs Upper Canada."

Around Strachan gathered a group of whom many were his former pupils. Members of this "old boy's network" had strikingly similar backgrounds and views. About half of the Compact consisted of descendants of the original Loyalist families, such as John Beverley Robinson, Christopher Hagerman, G.H. Markland, and John Macaulay. The other half included those who had come out from Britain as immigrants in the early years of the colony, like Strachan himself, William Allan and D'Arcy Boulton. Their role in the defence of the province during the War of 1812 heightened their determination to keep the province firmly within the British Empire. Upper Canada's strength came from its imperial connection, and the colony would weaken its position by becoming an independent nation or by forming part of a larger North American union. They believed that power had to remain in the hands of the governor and his appointed advisers. They agreed with Strachan that the colony needed the established Church of England to give a "moral underpinning to society." Finally, this elite believed in the economic progress of the province—to be directed by themselves—through commerce, canal building, settlement schemes, and banks.

219

Sir Peregrine Maitland, lieutenant governor from 1818 to 1828, reinforced the Family Compact's views of Upper Canada. He, too, favoured government through an appointed elite and readily allied himself with the members of the Executive Council. The governor and the Family Compact strengthened their hold on the colony through the Crown reserves.

By the 1820s, due to increased settlement during the immigration boom, the wealth from the Crown reserves had become substantial. These payments went directly to the governor and his Executive Council, much to the resentment of an emerging reform group in the elected Assembly.

The Clergy reserves became an even more contentious issue. In 1791 the British government had set aside one-seventh of the land in each township for the support of a "Protestant clergy" (see chapter 11). John Strachan argued against the claims of the non-Anglican sects for a portion of these "Protestant reserves." He held that clearly the Constitutional Act of 1791 had meant by the phrase, "Protestant clergy," the Anglican church, which he believed to be the state church in the province.

Religious Disputes

The first challenge to the Anglicans' ecclesiastical monopoly came from the Presbyterians. As the established Church of Scotland, they were allowed to share in the revenues of the Clergy reserves.

The Methodists subsequently launched an unsuccessful attack on the Anglicans' sole right to the revenues. This powerful and popular religious movement gained strength in Upper Canada with the influx of American immigrants. Its popularity rested on its appeal to a poor, backwoods frontier community. Through hymns, campfire meetings, and fervent preaching, Methodist preachers reached out to a population untouched by the more aloof and elitist Anglican church. The historian Fred Landon describes their camp meetings:

> Sometimes a wave of excitement would sweep over a gathering of this kind and as if moved by one impulse scores would rush to the altar, throwing themselves down, sobbing or groaning. This was the objective of the preaching and far into the night the ministers would move from group to group praying and exhorting the penitents.[1]

The Americans predominated in the movement until 1828, when the Upper Canadian Methodists separated from the American parent church to form their own Canada Conference. Using effective native preachers like the Mississauga Indian, Peter Jones, the Methodists converted two thousand Indians in Upper Canada to Christianity in the late 1820s. Indian and white Methodists built missions for Ojibwa-speaking converts at the Credit River twenty kilometres west of York and at Grape Island on the Bay of Quinte. The provincial government surveyed reserves and built other agricultural villages for Algonquian Indians, where the Indian hunters and fishermen were taught how to farm. (The British government in 1830 officially adopted a programme to promote the civilization and Christianization of the Indians.)

The growth of Methodism led to confrontation with the Anglicans. In 1825, Archdeacon John Strachan used the occasion of a funeral eulogy for Bishop Jacob Mountain of the Quebec Anglican diocese to make a vicious attack on certain "uneducated itinerant preachers." He described them as ignorant, incapable, idle, and, above all, disloyal, because of their emotionally charged and "republican" views.

The Methodists counterattacked through their promising young leader, Egerton Ryerson. Raised in an Anglican family but converted to Methodism, this twenty-three-year-old circuit-rider asserted the educated quality of the itinerant preachers, denied that Methodists were predominantly Americans with republican views, and challenged the legality of Strachan's position that the Church of England was the established church in the province.

Other Protestant denominations and sects appeared in the province. The Church of Scotland grew rapidly with Scottish immigration but soon came into conflict with American Presbyterians; the latter had settled mainly in the Niagara Peninsula and established an independent presbytery. Baptists, Quakers, Mennonites, Dunkards, Millerites, Campbellites, Christian Universalists, and Mormons also entered Upper Canada, creating greater religious pluralism. With the immigration of Irish Catholics, the Roman Catholic church strengthened its position.

220

Education

Religious disputes extended to education. Prior to 1815, only government-supported grammar schools existed in the province. These highly exclusive secondary schools catered to a limited number of well-to-do families. In 1816 a committee of the Assembly introduced the Common School Act, which allotted £6000 annually to state-supported, common primary schools for all children. Responsibility for building and maintaining the schools was to rest in the hands of local boards.

Strachan wanted these common schools under clerical control to counteract dangerous American tendencies, such as the use of American textbooks and American-trained teachers, but the Assembly successfully opposed the idea in favour of non-sectarian schools. It was a modest victory, however, since financial constraints reduced the annual appropriation to £2500 in 1820.

Lack of local funds kept the number of schools to a minimum, and existing schools lacked textbooks and properly trained teachers. Educational historian J.G. Althouse notes that "a teaching post was commonly regarded as the last refuge of the incompetent, the inept, the unreliable."[2] Only after the Act of Union was implemented in 1841 was a proper, province-wide, non-sectarian educational system established by that same young man who had confronted John Strachan in 1825—Egerton Ryerson.

221

Thwarted in his efforts for sectarian education in the common schools, Strachan directed his energy towards the grammar schools. These elite institutions, he believed, could offset the "Americanized" common schools. In 1819 he introduced legislation that required both an annual examination of all the grammar schools in the province and an annual report to the lieutenant governor. He also tried to introduce Andrew Bell's monitorial schools, an English system based on the teaching of church doctrines, but the Assembly voted down the suggestion and Strachan had to abandon the plan.

In an attempt to connect higher education with the Church of England, Strachan in 1827 helped draw up a royal charter to establish King's College, a provincial university, in the capital town of York. The university was to be closely affiliated with the Church of England through the hiring of Anglican professors and through a divinity school for training Anglican clergymen.

Once again, the Assembly opposed these "sectarian tendencies" and refused to support the provincial university. Strachan had to be content with a good preparatory school, modelled on the English classical schools and later known as Upper Canada College. King's College finally came into existence in 1843. By that time, the Methodists had already established their own university, Victoria College in Cobourg, and the Presbyterians had Queen's College in Kingston.

Social and Humanitarian Concerns

The first temperance societies in Upper Canada appeared in the Niagara Peninsula. Alcohol was a serious social problem contributing to family break-ups, poor work habits and output. Alcohol abuse also led to increased violence in society.

By the 1830s district temperance societies existed throughout the province, usually connected with the Methodist, Presbyterian, or Baptist churches. In 1839 the Upper Canadian temperance societies affiliated with the American Temperance Union. The temperance movement aimed at abstinence through self-restraint rather than through government legislation, in the belief that drunkenness was a personal problem requiring a personal solution.

Improved treatment of the insane and prison reform ranked with temperance as important social concerns in Upper Canada. On both issues, Upper Canadians took their lead from the United States. Dr. Charles Duncombe, an American-born reformer and member of the Assembly, formed and headed a three-man commission to examine current practices in the United States and to submit recommendations for Upper Canada. In two far-sighted reports in 1836 he advocated the separation of the insane into classes according to the nature and seriousness of their condition, urged a "mild and gentle treatment" without violence to the patients, and advocated a more enlightened attitude towards criminals, especially juvenile offenders.

Unfortunately, it was some years before his major recommendations came into effect. Before his reports could be implemented, Duncombe had to flee into exile for leading a revolt against the government in the western part of the province, in conjunction with William Lyon Mackenzie's assault on York in 1837.

Cholera, which entered the Canadas in the early 1830s with the British immigrants, posed an immediate and pressing social problem (see chapter 13). Near-panic conditions prevailed in the summer of 1832, between mid-June and mid-September, when the board of health recorded 273 deaths in York alone from the dread disease; in the province as a whole at least 550 people died that summer. Everywhere in the province, cholera became the primary concern. As one Upper Canadian complained: "Nothing is to be heard but the 'cholera'." The disease ran its course, only to return in 1834 and in the end caused nearly 350 deaths in Upper Canada.

222

Economic Developments

Mass immigration in 1815–40 contributed to economic growth. The expansion rested primarily on wheat farming, and agriculture thus became the backbone of the Upper Canadian economy. Historian John McCallum notes that "close to three-quarters of the cash income of Ontario farmers was derived from wheat, and wheat and flour made up well over half of all exports from Ontario until the early 1860s."[3]

Only timber rivalled wheat as the major export staple of Upper Canada. The timber trade was a by-product of farming, since settlers had to clear the forests before being able to farm the land. But only in the Ottawa valley, with its rich forests of pine and oak and easy access to the St. Lawrence, did lumbering become the primary industry.

Tension between French-Canadian and Irish lumbermen surfaced in the Ottawa valley. The *Canadiens* claimed that the Irish or "Shiners" worked for lower wages and therefore took jobs away from them. The Shiners came under the leadership of Peter Aylen, a millionaire who wanted to control the timber trade in the valley. Their feuds with the French Canadians, which became known as the Shiners' War, lasted intermittently from 1828 to 1843 and gave Bytown (renamed Ottawa in 1855) a rough-hewn image.

Wheat and timber required transportation networks. Roads were built by the Canada Company, the Talbot settlers south of London, and the military settlers in the Ottawa valley and Kingston area. Around York, a road system was developed to link the capital to outlying regions dependent on it for trade.

In the 1820s the first regular stagecoach line was established between York and Kingston. The service was erratic at first, since the coaches required anywhere from two to four days to complete a one-way trip. By the 1830s, however, daily service was available all year round. At the same time, coach lines along Yonge Street began to service the towns, villages, hamlets, and farming communities north of York (or Toronto as it became again in 1834).

CANAL BUILDING

The Great Lakes–St. Lawrence natural waterway provided an effective alternative means of transportation, but only if natural obstacles, notably Niagara Falls and the rapids at Lachine near Montreal, could be overcome. Canals offered a solution, and in 1825 the first canal was completed around the Lachine rapids. Canals also enabled small naval vessels to enter the heart of North America to defend against possible American aggressors. Trade and military protection thus provided an incentive for canal building.

The British and Upper Canadian governments largely paid for the two major canals constructed in the province in the 1820s and 1830s—the Rideau Canal and the Welland Canal. The British government wanted the

Rideau Canal to link Bytown (Ottawa) with Kingston for defence purposes. It put up the money for the entire cost of construction, which in the end amounted to £1 000 000, making it the costliest military work undertaken until then by the British government in defence of North America. The British also provided the engineering expertise for the enterprise.

Lieutenant Colonel John By of the Royal Engineers arrived in 1826 to oversee the project. Over a six-year period, By supervised a force of four thousand who worked at times sixteen hours a day, six days a week under the most gruelling conditions. Swarms of mosquitoes and blackflies plagued workers all spring and summer. In the swamps and marshes, swamp fever and malaria was rampant, caused by a heavy noxious mist arising from the decaying vegetable matter excavated after stagnant water was drained off. Trees were cut back in an effort to provide freer air circulation at the worksites, in keeping with the prevailing medical belief that malaria was caused by foul air (*mal aria*). More than five hundred men lost their lives in the work camps.

224

When completed in 1832, the waterway, threading through a series of lakes, was more than 210 km in length and contained forty-seven masonry locks. (The originals are still in operation today.) It proved to be an ambitious and expensive undertaking to meet an American attack that never materialized, but it nevertheless helped boost the economy of the eastern part of the province.

The incentive behind construction of the Welland Canal was strictly commercial. Yet once again the impetus for action came from the United States. Although a political boundary existed between the two countries after 1783, there was no economic boundary. Montreal and New York merchants competed for the monopoly of inland trade. In 1825 the Americans completed the Erie Canal, which linked the Great Lakes by water with the Hudson River and the ice-free port of New York. The new canal attracted much of the trade from the American West and much trade from Upper Canada. Great Lakes farmers found it cheaper and faster to ship via New York to Britain. New York rose to economic primacy in North America, with a population by the early 1830s of a quarter-of-a-million—roughly the size of Upper Canada's entire population. A young St. Catharines merchant and second-generation Loyalist, William Hamilton Merritt, dreamed of building a canal to bypass Niagara Falls and thus make the St. Lawrence–Great Lakes waterway system an effective rival to the Erie Canal. The government of Upper Canada eventually provided Merritt's company with a land grant and a loan of £25 000, while the British government agreed to underwrite one-ninth of the cost in return for the right of government ships to pass through the canal toll-free. In the end, Merritt's private project became, ironically, the biggest public project of its time. In 1829 Merritt completed the first Welland canal to join Lakes Ontario and Erie and avoid Niagara Falls.

EARLY BANKS IN UPPER CANADA

These major projects required large amounts of capital. This, in turn, meant the need for banks. Banks did not appear in Upper Canada until after the War of 1812. The early ones were branches of the Bank of Montreal. These branches soon proved inadequate to Upper Canadians, who desired their own banks. In 1819 the merchants of Kingston applied to the government to charter a provincial bank. Much to their dismay and anger, their appeal was denied in favour of a more recent one from prominent York merchants.

This Bank of Upper Canada came under government dominance. Nine of its fifteen directors belonged to Upper Canada's executive or legislative councils, while the government supplied more than one-quarter of the bank's stock. As historian Gerald Craig has concluded: "It is no exaggeration to say that the Bank of Upper Canada was a creature of the emerging Family Compact."[4]

225

The establishment of the first Upper Canadian bank at York rather than at Kingston indicated York's dominant position as the provincial capital. Through control of the wholesale trade to towns and rural areas within its radius of influence, York had become the most influential community in central Upper Canada. In population, York went from twelve hundred in 1820 to more than nine thousand in 1834, the year of its incorporation as the city of Toronto. Other towns such as London, Hamilton, Niagara, and Kingston controlled the surrounding rural areas. Conditions in the 1840s and 1850s further strengthened Toronto's dominance of Upper Canada.

Rise of a Reform Movement

The 1820s were a time of political polarization into conservative and reform camps. Led by the Family Compact, the conservatives favoured British political traditions, including the monarchical association and appointed legislative and executive councils. Economically, they endorsed enterprises such as the building of canals and the establishment of banks, which they believed would advance the commercial well-being of the province. The conservatives obtained strong support from the newly arrived middle- and upper-class British immigrants.

The reformers advocated political reform: generally, an elected legislative council or upper house and responsible government which, though it initially meant many things to many people, came to mean the choosing of the Executive Council from the members of the Assembly who could command the support of the Assembly. Economically, the reformers favoured agrarian measures, since they chiefly represented the farmers of the central and western areas of the province. They often opposed commercial enterprises such as canal building and banks, which they saw as being either expensive or of no benefit to farmers.

Thus, there developed in the province a situation which was roughly parallel to that in Lower Canada (see chapter 13). In both provinces many of the conservatives could be considered "reactionary" politically, but "progressive" economically, while the reformers were "radical" politically and "reactionary" economically.

GOURLAY AND MACKENZIE

226   Robert Gourlay, a Scottish immigrant to Upper Canada in 1817, initiated the first serious criticism of the Family Compact. Soon after his arrival, he complained about the tiny elite's control of the appointed Legislative Council. He favoured township meetings, like those in New England where people could express their grievances. Gourlay also advocated more power for the elected Assembly. These radical views, along with his attempt to stir up discontent, led to his prosecution and subsequent expulsion from Upper Canada in 1819.

This "banished Briton," however, left a legacy of political protest. Before his arrest, he circulated a questionnaire asking people to indicate what they believed to be the major problems in Upper Canada. He received a litany of complaints, from bad roads to incompetent land schemes and policies, including the Clergy and Crown reserves, and restrictions on American immigration. These complaints continued to be heard throughout the 1820s, especially among some members of the Assembly who called themselves "Gourlayites" and who attempted to carry on their leader's agitation. A Reform party began to take form in the Assembly in 1824.

William Lyon Mackenzie continued Gourlay's cause. He arrived in Upper Canada from Scotland in 1820. In 1824 he began, at Queenston, a newspaper, *The Colonial Advocate*, and dedicated it to the Reform case. His attacks on leading Upper Canadian families in his newspaper, which in 1825 he relocated in York, led the sons of prominent Family Compact members and their friends to break into his office the following year and throw his typesetting equipment into Lake Ontario. Such acts only made Mackenzie a hero to the reformers and strengthened his determination to continue his attacks. The Scottish immigrant also decided to contest a seat in the Assembly, which he won in the election of 1828.

That election returned the first Reform majority to the Assembly. Moderate Reformers such as John Rolph, Marshall Spring Bidwell, and William and Robert Baldwin, (father and son) led the new group. Yet the election of 1830 saw the Reformers lose their majority in the Assembly. This did not dampen their enthusiasm, however. They saw themselves accomplishing for Upper Canada what like-minded Reformers in Britain and in the United States were doing. In Britain, the Whig government of Lord Grey was agitating for reform and within two years introduced the Great Reform Bill to extend the franchise. In the United States, President Andrew Jackson led a democratic movement based on universal suffrage and the rotation of personnel in public office. So the Upper Canadian Reformers believed that they formed part of a greater progressive movement that would ultimately triumph.

Move to Rebellion

In the early 1830s William Lyon Mackenzie shifted to a radical reform position, chiefly as a result of a visit to the United States. In 1829 he had met President Andrew Jackson and had observed Jacksonian democracy. He returned to Upper Canada committed to the same ideals. Thwarted in his aspirations, he renewed his attacks on the political elite to the point where he was expelled from the Assembly, only to be re-elected and expelled three more times. In 1832 he visited England and met such British reformers as Jeremy Bentham, Richard Cobden, and John Bright. In London the fiery newspaper editor presented the complaints of the Upper Canadian reformers, as he saw them, to a sympathetic and receptive British government, which mistakenly believed that Mackenzie's views represented those of the majority of Upper Canadians.

Mackenzie's views were not even representative of the majority of Reformers. A rift occurred by the mid-1830s between a moderate wing led by Robert Baldwin and supported by Egerton Ryerson, and a radical wing under Mackenzie and John Rolph. The moderates did not want the American form of elective government that Mackenzie advocated. Instead they favoured the British plan of responsible government, that is, a government responsible to the Assembly.

After the Reformers regained control of the Assembly in 1834, the radical Reformers began taking action on their own. Mackenzie, just chosen as Toronto's first mayor as well as an assemblyman, was selected chairman of an assembly grievance committee that produced the famous Seventh Report on Grievances in 1835. It contained a wide-ranging attack on the existing system of colonial government and demanded an elective legislative council, an executive council responsible to the Assembly, and severe limitations on the lieutenant governor's control over patronage. A worried British government removed Lieutenant Governor John Colborne, whom it held largely responsible for the deteriorating political situation in the province.

The new governor, Sir Francis Bond Head, unexpectedly made a positive gesture to the Reformers in 1836 by appointing two of their members, Robert Baldwin and John Rolph, to the Executive Council. Then he negated the move by proceeding to ignore the Council's advice. The reformers on the Council resigned and persuaded their fellow members to follow suit. The Assembly censured the governor and then blocked the granting of supplies. He retaliated by refusing to approve any money bills. Then Bond Head dissolved the legislature and called an election for the early summer. He actively campaigned in the election for the Conservatives, warning that the battle was between American republicanism and the British connection.

Much to the chagrin of the Reformers, the Tories won the election. Their success could be attributed in part to Bond Head's intervention in the campaign and to his appeal to the loyalty of recent British immigrants. A large number in the colony sided with the governor and the Family Compact, fearing that the Reformers were dangerously radical and "republican." The Conservatives also used questionable tactics to influence the election: bribery, corruption, the careful selection of polling places, and the rapid enfranchisement of new British immigrants. Such action convinced Mackenzie and the radical Reformers of the impossibility of fair elections and peaceful reform.

In his newspaper, *The Constitution*, begun symbolically on July 4, 1836, Mackenzie cited the American Revolution as justification for direct action and reprinted Thomas Paine's *Common Sense*, which had sparked the movement for independence in 1776. A group of his followers issued a Toronto Declaration closely modelled on that of the American Declaration of Independence. It read in part:

> Government is founded on the authority and is instituted for the benefit of a people; when, therefore, any Government long and systematically ceases to answer the great ends of its foundation, the people have a natural right given them by their Creator to seek after and establish such institutions as will yield the greatest quantity of happiness to the greatest number.

Economic and social forces also contributed to unrest in the province. In 1836 a downturn in the economy occurred due to excessive speculation and over-expansion by business interests in the western world. In Upper Canada this led in turn to a tightening of credit by banks and even a recall of loans, which hit farmers especially hard. Such action only intensified Mackenzie's already deep distrust of banks. Along with hard financial times came a series of crop failures in 1835–37 that made some farmers in the region north of Toronto prepared to follow Mackenzie into rebellion.

In the western region of the province, around London, a separate group led by Dr. Charles Duncombe prepared to join them. News of the uprising of Lower Canadian *Patriotes* under Louis-Joseph Papineau, begun in mid-November, further encouraged rebellion.

The Upper Canadian Rebellion of 1837

Mackenzie set the date of the uprising for December 7. The previous Friday he printed a leaflet urging people to prepare to arm. Meanwhile, John Rolph claimed that the Toronto authorities knew of the rebels' plans and proposed an earlier date of December 4, before government preparations were complete.

During the evening and night of December 4, about five hundred ill-clad and poorly armed rebels—equipped with only muskets, pikes, pitchforks, and cudgels—gathered at Montgomery Tavern on Yonge Street (just north of present-day Eglinton Avenue) for the attack. The next day they marched down Yonge Street under the command of Mackenzie, who was wearing several overcoats buttoned to the chin, the better to protect him, he thought, from bullets. A truce party, including Robert Baldwin and John Rolph, met them, and Mackenzie explained the rebels' demands. At this point, Mackenzie was in command. Bond Head had only 250 volunteer forces and Mackenzie should have immediately marched on the city. Instead, he delayed.

It was not until later in the afternoon that he led 500–700 troops farther down Yonge Street towards the city. The rest was tragicomedy. Mackenzie's forces met a party of twenty led by Sheriff William Botsford Jarvis. The front rank of Mackenzie's men fired, then dropped to the ground to let the next rank fire over their heads. Those behind thought their front-rank men had been killed, and in panic they fled.

That same night reinforcements for the government side arrived from Hamilton. By Thursday, December 7, the Loyalist forces were 1500 strong. They marched up Yonge Street to attack Mackenzie's force of 500–600 stationed at Montgomery's Tavern. During the second battle the rebels were routed within half an hour. The Loyalist forces then burned the tavern and marched back to Toronto. "The march back," a journalist Samuel Thompson later commented, "was very leisurely executed, several of the mounted officers carrying dead pigs and geese slung across their saddle-bows as trophies of victory."

Mackenzie's ill-conceived and ill-fated rebellion was over. He escaped to the United States while some of his followers were captured. Among them were two leaders, Samuel Lount and Peter Mathews, who were later tried and hanged. In the western region of the province, Duncombe had by December 13 five hundred troops. Allan MacNab, a businessman, land speculator, and Loyalist leader, led an opposing group of five hundred Loyalists. Upon hearing word of Mackenzie's defeat, Duncombe's men

229

230

National Archives of Canada / C15388.

Mackenzie's men drilling, 1837. The historical illustrator, C.W. Jefferys, here shows a group of grim-faced country people, some armed only with pikes, preparing for the uprising.

began to desert the camp. When MacNab attacked on the morning of December 14, he found only a few rebels. Most had escaped to the United States, including Duncombe.

COUNTER-ATTACKS FROM THE UNITED STATES

From across the border the rebel leaders planned further attacks on the government of Upper Canada. They found eager support in the United States among those who saw the rebellion either as a Canadian version of the American Revolution—an attempt to end British tyranny—or as an opportunity to annex Upper Canada to the United States. Some of the rank and file simply saw it as an opportunity for loot and booty.

Mackenzie gathered together a motley band of supporters who occupied Navy Island on the Canadian side of the Niagara River, where they proclaimed a provisional government for Upper Canada. Upper Canadian officials retaliated by burning the *Caroline*, an American ship used to ferry men and supplies from the American side to Navy Island.

Mackenzie's supporters and American sympathizers crossed the border throughout 1838. The largest incident was the Battle of the Windmill near Prescott, Ontario, in November in which two hundred invaders barricaded themselves in an old windmill until forced to surrender. Thirty men were killed and the rest taken prisoner. The government hanged eleven for instigating and taking part in the battle. In the end, more than one thousand people in the province were jailed on suspicion of treason as a result of the rebellion.

231

Durham's Report

The Rebellion of 1837 in Upper Canada was a minor affair from a military standpoint, but together with the much more extensive uprising in Lower Canada (see chapter 13), it convinced Britain of the need for change. The Whig government under Lord Melbourne responded by relieving Bond Head of his post in early 1838 and sending out one of its most gifted politicans, Lord Durham or "Radical Jack," as he was nicknamed, to inquire into the affairs of the colony and report back to the British government. The Prime Minister gave Durham broader powers than any of his predecessors, including those of governor general of all the British North American colonies. He arrived in May 1838 and brought along with him an entourage of officials that included two able assistants, Gibbon Wakefield and Charles Buller, both well versed in colonial affairs.

Durham spent most of his five months in Lower Canada, but he made one short visit to Upper Canada, where he consulted with Robert Baldwin, one of the Upper Canadian Reform leaders. Despite the brevity of his stay in the Canadas the time spent was very important, for on it was based one of the most important documents in Canadian history—his famous *Report on the Affairs of British North America*, better known as *Durham's Report*.

In his report Durham made three main proposals. First, he recommended greater colonial self-government. He pointed out that local affairs should be colonial matters, and only the larger issues such as constitutional concerns, foreign relations, trade with Britain and other British colonies, and disposal of public lands, should be reserved by the mother country. Durham also believed that the colonial governor should choose his closest advisers, the members of the Executive Council, from the majority party in the Assembly, and that the governor should abide by the wishes of these elected representatives. While Durham may not have termed this "responsible government," it came to be considered as such.

Finally, Durham recommended a union of the two colonies of Upper and Lower Canada. Such a union was primarily designed to benefit Upper Canada, since it would improve trade for the inland colony and force Lower Canadians to assume part of the debt incurred by Upper Canadians during the building of canals. He saw such a union as the nucleus of an eventual larger union of all the British North American colonies, one which he highly favoured, and as a necessary precursor to the assimilation of the French Canadians.

232

Lord Sydenham, Durham's successor, implemented the recommendation for a union of the Canadas in 1840–41. Before it came into effect Sydenham resolved a long-standing disagreement in Upper Canada. He worked out an arrangement by which the two leading Protestant denominations—the Church of England (Anglican) and the Church of Scotland (Presbyterian)—would share half the proceeds of future sales of Clergy reserves while the other half would be divided among the other denominations, according to their numbers.

By the terms of the Act of Union of 1841, the capital of the new province became Kingston. English was to be the only official language of the Assembly, the united colony would assume the debt of Upper Canada, and the Assembly would consist of eighty-four members—forty-two from Upper Canada and forty-two from Lower Canada. Upper Canada officially ceased to exist. Instead, it formed part of a larger union of English and French Canadians that required considerable compromise to succeed.

A new era began in the history of the province, one that ultimately led to a wider union of all the British North American colonies, as Durham had envisioned.

NOTES

[1] Fred Landon, *Western Ontario and the American Frontier*, (Toronto, 1967; first published 1941), p. 125.

[2] Quoted in J. Donald Wilson, Robert M. Stamp, and Louis-Philippe Audet, eds., *Canadian Education: A History* (Toronto, 1970), p. 201.

[3] John McCallum, *Unequal Beginnings: Agriculture and Economic Development in Quebec and Ontario Until 1870* (Toronto, 1980), p. 4.

[4] Gerald M. Craig, *Upper Canada: The Formative Years, 1784–1841* (Toronto, 1963), p. 162.

Related Readings

Useful articles on this topic are contained in R. Douglas Francis and Donald B. Smith, *Readings in Canadian History: Pre-Confederation*, 2d ed. (Toronto, 1986): Jean Burnet, "Occupational Differences and the Class Structure," pp. 257–69; Peter A. Russell, "Upper Canada: A Poor Man's Country? Some Statistical Evidence," pp. 269–85; S.F. Wise, "Upper Canada and the Conservative Tradition," pp. 330–43; and John McCallum, "Urban and Commercial Development until 1850," pp. 365–83.

233

BIBLIOGRAPHY

The best overview of Upper Canadian society in 1815–40 is Gerald M. Craig, *Upper Canada: The Formative Years, 1784–1841* (Toronto, 1963). Also useful are the relevant chapters in J.M.S. Careless, ed., *Colonists and Canadians, 1760–1867* (Toronto, 1971): Michael Cross, "The 1820s," pp. 149–172; and G.M. Craig, "The 1830s," pp. 173–199. The experience of immigrating to British North America is best described in Helen Cowan, *British Emigration to British North America: The First Hundred Years*, rev. and enlarged ed. (Toronto, 1961). A shorter version is Helen Cowan, *British Immigration Before Confederation*, a Canadian Historical Association booklet (Ottawa, 1968). Also useful is H.J.M. Johnston, "British Immigration to British North America, 1815–1860," the Canadian Museum of Civilization's Canada's Visual History Series, vol. 8 (Ottawa, 1974), and Edwin C. Guillet, *The Great Migration: The Atlantic Crossing by Sailing Ship since 1770*, 2d ed. (Toronto, 1963).

On the Family Compact, see Robert E. Saunders, "What was the Family Compact?" *Ontario History* 49, (1957): 165–78, and reprinted in J.K. Johnson, *Historical Essays on Upper Canada* (Toronto, 1975), pp. 122–140. For the treatment of religion in the context of American immigration and political reform, see Fred Landon, *Western Ontario and the American Frontier* (Toronto, 1967; first published 1941). On education, see J. Donald Wilson, "Education in Upper Canada: Sixty Years of Change," in *Canadian Education: A History* edited by J.D. Wilson, R.M. Stamp, and L.-P. Audet (Toronto, 1970), pp. 190–213.

The importance of the wheat economy for Upper Canada is discussed in John McCallum, *Unequal Beginnings: Agriculture and Economic Development in Quebec and Ontario until 1870* (Toronto, 1980). Transportation developments and canal building in particular are briefly described in

Gerald Tulchinsky, *Transportation Changes in the St. Lawrence–Great Lakes Region 1828–1860*, Canada's Visual History Series, vol. 11 (Ottawa, 1974).

On the reform movement, besides Craig, *Upper Canada* and Landon, *Western Ontario* (both cited above), see Aileen Dunham, *Political Unrest in Upper Canada, 1815–1836* (Toronto, 1963; first published 1927). William Kilbourn's biography of William Lyon Mackenzie, *The Firebrand* (Toronto, 1956) is a lively account. On the discontent in western Upper Canada see Colin Read's *The Rising in Western Upper Canada 1837–38: The Duncombe Revolt and After* (Toronto, 1982) and, for the rebellion in general, Colin Read and Ron Stagg, eds., *The Rebellion of 1837 in Upper Canada* (Ottawa, 1985). The standard work on Lord Durham is C. New, *Lord Durham's Mission to Canada*, with an introduction by H.W. McCready (Toronto, 1963). Gerald Craig has edited and introduced an abridged version of Durham's Report in *Lord Durham's Report* (Toronto, 1963).

234　　The Amerindian history of the period is reviewed for the Iroquois in Charles M. Johnston, ed. *The Valley of the Six Nations: A Collection of Documents on the Indian Lands of the Grand River* (Toronto, 1964), and for the Mississauga and other Algonquian groups in Donald B. Smith, *Sacred Feathers. The Reverend Peter Jones (Kahkewaquonaby) & the Mississauga Indians* (Toronto, 1987), and James A. Clifton, *A Place of Refuge for all Time: Migration of the American Potawatomi into Canada, 1830 to 1850* (Ottawa, 1975). Ian A.L. Getty and Antoine S. Lussier, eds., *As Long as the Sun Shines and Water Flows* (Vancouver, 1983) contains several articles on the Indians of Upper Canada.

CHAPTER THIRTEEN

Rebellion on the St. Lawrence

The half-century between the partition of Quebec in 1791 and the union
of the two Canadas in 1841 is usually remembered for the political and
military events of the late 1830s. Certainly, the rebellion that broke out
at the end of 1837 and flared up again in late 1838 was the most sensational
occurrence of this period. The *patriotes*, or rebels, shouted revolutionary
rhetoric at mass meetings, laid plans to overthrow the British colonial
authorities, and took up arms. British troops intervened and brutally
crushed the revolts. In the aftermath, the colonial authorities hanged,
imprisoned, or exiled many *patriotes*; hundreds more fled. The uprisings
were much more widespread and violent than in Upper Canada.

Despite these dramatic events, the real revolution taking place in Lower
Canada lay in the transformation of the colony's economy, politics, society,
and institutions. These profound changes had some positive effects, but
they also contributed to the discontent that underlay the events of 1837/38.

Economic Revolution

At the close of the eighteenth century, Quebec entered a period of intense,
if uneven, economic growth, as Britain's industrialization and urbanization
created new markets for the colony's foodstuffs and resources. As the era
of the fur trade drew to a close, profits slumped because of contracting
sales abroad and ruinous competition at home. Yet some Montreal firms
succeeded in diversifying their interests and continued to prosper. Fur
trader Peter McGill, for example, also became a timber exporter, a shipowner, a forwarder of goods to Upper Canada, a banker, and a railroad
promoter.

The decline of the fur trade was more than offset by the rise of the
timber industry. Britain needed wood, especially to build ships. Napoleon's

continental blockade in 1806–12 cut Britain off from its traditional northern European suppliers and forced it to look to the North American colonies. The latter enjoyed a decided advantage in British markets when Britain abolished all tariffs on colonial timber. Largely because of this product, Lower Canada's exports quadrupled between 1807 and 1810; a large part of Lower Canada's population benefited from this wave of prosperity.

Other sectors of the economy underwent significant, though perhaps less spectacular, development. Ships were built at nearly eighty localities along the St. Lawrence. Quebec City had the biggest shipyards, and much of its production went overseas to Britain. Sawmills, candle and soap manufacturers, textile factories, flour mills, and an expanding construction industry all participated in this growth. Beginning with the Bank of Montreal in 1817, banks were established to supply credit to new enterprises and commercial initiatives.

236

Urban Life

The labour needed for resource exploitation and manufacturing was supplied by immigrants and by Lower Canada's rapidly growing population. Thanks to a birth rate that hovered slightly above 50 per 1000 throughout the period, the population rose from about 160 000 in 1790 to 650 000 in 1850. French Canadians began immigrating to the United States in search of the land or work they could not find at home.

Lower Canada's cities developed rapidly as centres of both wealth and poverty. In the early 1800s, Quebec City grew at an annual rate of more than 5 percent, with the poor settling in the suburb of St. Roch—much of which was destroyed by fire in May 1845. Most habitants had to pay seigneurial dues on their lots and in hard times they often accumulated debts. Though faced with vehement opposition, the government occasionally attempted to force payment of these debts. During one of these periodic crises, in the fall of 1838, rumours circulated that the workers of St. Roch intended to sneak up to Quebec's Upper Town to strangle the bourgeois while they slept. Barrels of gunpowder and stocks of ammunition were discovered, and for some time thereafter the anxious burghers kept the city gates locked day and night.

Montreal also grew quickly. British North America's premier city had 22 500 residents in 1825. The merchants, who were mostly English speaking, dominated the city. Formerly involved in the fur trade, they had diversified into the grain and timber trade and manufacturing. Montreal's workers made leather goods, clothing, barrels (used for transporting almost everything) and beer. To supply his Montreal brewery, pioneer industrialist John Molson brought seed barley from England and distributed it

237

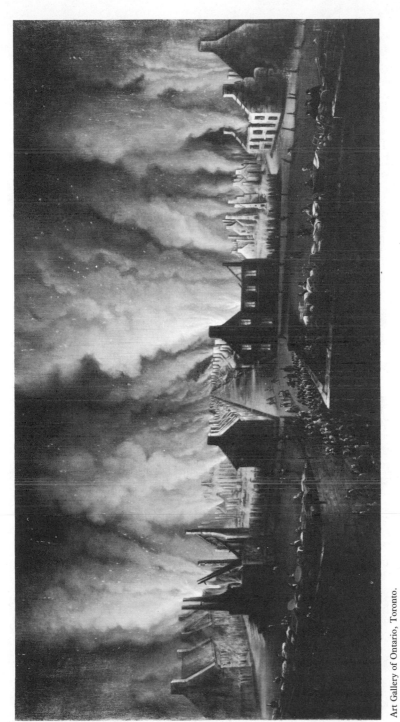

Art Gallery of Ontario, Toronto.

Fire at Quebec's suburb of St. Roch, 1845, by Joseph Légaré. Two fires that year left 22,000 people in Quebec City homeless. Urban fires were a constant menace.

among farmers. He also owned the first steamer on the St. Lawrence in 1809, sat in the Assembly and the Legislative Council, and was president of the Bank of Montreal.

Most workers were unskilled. Women and immigrants especially worked as domestics. Many workers were forced to spend 60 percent of their earnings to feed their family. There were no unions and legislation passed in 1802 authorized fines and prison sentences for striking workers. Few employers were French-speaking and their enterprises tended to be small. Those French Canadians who had money preferred to invest it in land and urban development.

CHOLERA EPIDEMICS

238

In these early decades of the nineteenth century, disease posed a serious threat to public health. This was particularly true in the towns, with their unhealthy living conditions and relatively concentrated populations. In 1832 the first of a series of cholera epidemics provoked a wave of panic among Canadians. The disease had spread from the delta of the Ganges River across Europe to Britain, being transmitted mainly through contaminated water supplies. Its attacks were sudden, extremely painful and very often fatal, with death coming within 48 hours, a result of complete dehydration of the victim's body. There was no cure. In fact, treatment of the disease must often have hastened death. Patients were bled, even when they were in a state of collapse. Doctors administered laxatives, although the patients were suffering from uncontrollable diarrhea. Leeches and blisters were applied to the stomach. Fortunately for the victims of both the disease and the proposed remedies, physicians commonly prescribed opium as a pain-killer.

The arrival in Canada of large numbers of immigrants, very often indigents from the British Isles, caused much concern. They had been migrating in large numbers to Lower Canada since 1815, although most went on to Upper Canada or the United States. Some 50 000 arrived in 1831. Many were steerage passengers who had spent weeks on the boats, in filthy conditions, and often near starvation. Worried about the threat to public health posed by these immigrants, the government of Lower Canada established a quarantine station on Grosse Ile, a small island in the St. Lawrence below Quebec. The measure proved ineffective since regulations could not be enforced and medical services were totally inadequate.

Conditions in Lower Canadian towns enormously assisted the spread of infection. Many houses were dirty and overcrowded, yards and streets were piled with refuse, and towns had open sewers. Slaughterhouses, often located in residential districts, simply dumped their waste into open water. In early spring 1832, the health board in Quebec City tried to force a general clean-up of streets, houses, and yards. Regulations that required homeowners to "scrape, wash and cleanse their premises and carry away all filth" proved to be unenforceable in the face of public indifference, if not outright hostility. In Montreal, city authorities simply sat back and waited for the expected attack.

Cholera struck Quebec City at the end of the first week in June. Hospitals overflowed with victims, while hundreds more lay in tents on the Plains of Abraham. Many panic-stricken residents fled to rural areas, often carrying the disease with them. To prevent despair, church bells were no longer rung for the dead after June 14. Police had to be called to enforce rapid burial of the deceased. By the end of October 1832, seventy-five hundred residents of Quebec and Montreal—more than one-tenth of the population of each city—had died.

The disease had important political, as well as economic and social, consequences. French Canadians, particularly in nationalist circles, hotly debated immigration policy; many, including the mayor of Quebec, blamed the British authorities for doing nothing to control the merchants and ship owners who profited by transporting immigrants. They also vigorously censured Lord Aylmer's administration for its inaction.

During a second, less severe outbreak of cholera in Quebec City in 1834, Aylmer fled to Sorel and most of the Executive Council took up more healthy residence in the country. Even the rich, however, were not spared; more through self-interest, perhaps, than from concern for the poor, they began to lobby for public health measures that, decades later, dramatically reduced the incidence of deadly diseases.

Rural Quebec

Nineteen out of twenty French Canadians in the early nineteenth century lived in rural areas, mainly on farms where they practised subsistence agriculture. Yet rural Quebec also underwent change. With the good harvests of the 1790s and early 1800s, many habitants had accumulated small surpluses of wheat that they sold to grain merchants for export abroad. For a short time, habitants saw their living conditions improve.

But yields varied enormously, and after 1815, crop failures were more frequent. Production on the best-located lands tended to drop after decades of cultivation without fertilization. New lands opened up for colonization, especially those near the Canadian Shield, proved rocky and infertile. Crop diseases and insects were a constant threat: the wheat midge, for example, almost completely destroyed the harvests of 1834–36.

Farmers also had to contend with conditions abroad. The War of 1812

239

severely disrupted the grain trade, and depression in Britain in 1815–20 caused prices to fall dramatically. Tariff barriers, like the Corn Laws of 1815, blocked the entry of colonial grain when the British price fell below a certain level. While Upper Canada boosted its production, Lower Canada had to buy wheat from its Upper Canadian competitors to meet its needs.

Historians agree that the 1830s witnessed a rapid deterioration of economic conditions, with famine reported in 1837. Some like Fernand Ouellet have blamed the habitant for failing to adopt more modern agricultural techniques such as crop rotation and for depleting soil nutrients while doing nothing to restore them. Others like Jean-Pierre Wallot and John McCallum contend that the habitants' alleged backwardness was the consequence, rather than the cause, of their economic plight, and that farmers in Upper Canada and in the northeastern United States were no more well-versed in sound agricultural methods. Climatic factors and disease, as well as overpopulation, also seem to have played a part. Lacking the capital to invest in commercial substitutes for wheat, habitants turned more and more to peas, potatoes, and barley in order to avoid starvation. Many in despair supported the organizers of rebellion in 1837.[1]

Alexis de Tocqueville, the French social philosopher, confirmed the existence of rural unrest during a visit to Lower Canada in the late summer of 1831. The Superior of the Sulpicians in Montreal assured him that there was no "happier people in the world than the French Canadians," and that they paid trifling rents and acquitted their dues to the Church "ungrudgingly and easily." But when de Tocqueville went out on horseback into the countryside around Beauport, near Quebec City, and spoke with the habitants, he found them worried about immigration, resentful of the seigneurs, and envious of the wealth that the tithe placed in the hands of some clergy.

The habitant had annual seigneurial dues to discharge, although the dues were notoriously difficult to collect. Those who bought land had to pay a heavy mutation fine or transfer fee to the seigneur. They were also obliged to grind their grain at the seigneur's mills—a lucrative privilege for the landed gentry. Historian Allan Greer asserts that this "feudal burden," while generally not crushing, made it difficult for the habitants to accumulate capital.[2] But in the crisis years of the 1830s, as the habitants' crops dwindled and their standard of living fell, their obligations must have weighed more heavily on them.

The Church

During this period, two groups vied to obtain influence and prestige among the habitants. On the one hand stood the Roman Catholic church, struggling to secure its independence from government dictates and implacably hostile to republican and liberal ideals. On the other was a new professional elite composed of notaries, lawyers, and doctors, growing at a much faster rate than the general population. This group endorsed increasingly nationalistic ideas, particularly on political issues, and tended to be critical of the church; its forum was the colony's Assembly.

At the turn of the century, the church's position in Lower Canada was far from assured. In spite of what has been written by clerical historians about the habitants' profound religiosity, Canada was not a theocratic society, and the clergy were neither very influential nor dominant. Contemporary accounts detail the spread of religious indifference and even of anticlericalism, particularly among the bourgeoisie. Liberals read the works of philosophers like Rousseau and Voltaire. As for the habitants, they did not challenge official dogma, although many were probably more superstitious and conformist than pious and fervent. They were also strong-minded and independent; continually they attempted to avoid paying tithes and other religious contributions and they feuded over pews, the location of new churches, and other matters of a material nature.

241

For its part, the clergy constantly complained of disorders and immorality although, admittedly, that was their duty. Travellers reported frequently that the *Canadiens* danced, gorged themselves, got drunk to prepare themselves for Lent which they scrupulously observed, then feasted again and got drunk to celebrate its passing. The church was even obliged to abolish several feast-days because of excesses, thus pleasing the British merchants who did not approve of these kinds of pleasures nor of the loss of time they entailed.[3]

To increase its influence within French-Canadian society, the Church needed more priests. Indeed, at this time, it faced a veritable crisis: the number of priests declined from about 200 to only 150 in 1760–1790 and then increased to somewhat more than 300 by the time of the Rebellion, but the population mushroomed from 70 000 to 500 000. Bishop Ignace Bourget of Montreal complained "there are not enough workers to help us cultivate the vine." Monseigneur Joseph-Octave Plessis encouraged the establishment of classical colleges and did succeed in increasing the number of vocations while Bishop of Quebec from 1806 until 1825.

The Church, however, entertained serious doubts about the value of universal primary schooling. Many *curés* did not want to spend parish money on schools and some saw education as dangerous. Monseigneur Jean-Jacques Lartigue, Bishop of Montreal, said of the habitants: "It is better for them not to have a literary education than to risk a bad moral education." As schools cost money and many habitants did not want to contribute to them, they agreed.

Some liberal French-speaking members of the Assembly saw education in a more positive light. So did the government, which in 1801 founded the Royal Institution for the Advancement of Learning (RIAL), a system of voluntary public education. The church, led by Plessis, was suspicious of the RIAL schools, since they were established by a Protestant government that still hoped for the assimilation and Protestantization of the habitants; the church, therefore, chose to ignore the schools and very few were established.

When in 1818 the Assembly set up a board of trustees to oversee education, Plessis refused to sit on this essentially English-speaking Protestant body. The board, however, did authorize separate religious worship, visits to the schools by priests, and French-language textbooks. It also appointed French-speaking Roman Catholic teachers in French-speaking areas of the province. Still, the local priests regarded the schools at best with indifference and sometimes with outright hostility. Many refused to become visitors, often on Plessis' orders.

In an effort to remodel educational legislation to make it more satisfactory to the church, the Assembly authorized the church to build its own schools, to be financed and directed by parish *fabriques* or councils. In the Legislative Council, Plessis urged state financing, but the government replied that, because of the Assembly's obstruction, no money was available. It was becoming more apparent, however, that French-speaking liberals favourable to non-confessional schools constituted as much a threat to clerical ambitions as Anglo-Protestant government officials. Indeed, in 1829 they supported a bill that gave control of schools to the Assembly and to local officials (syndics).

242

Within three years, many state-supported schools were built, leading to disputes between parish priests and town officials over their operation. But in 1836, in the face of church pressure, the Assembly abrogated the Elementary Schools Act. The way was now open for clerical control of education.

THE CHURCH'S RELATIONS WITH GOVERNMENT

The church's major triumph in these years was the achievement of real independence from government dictates. Until the 1830s, the government continued to interfere with the nomination of bishops but with decreasing success. When Monseigneur Bailly died in 1794, the governor gave Monseigneur Hubert a list of three names from which to choose a new coadjutor. But in 1825, it was Monseigneur Panet who submitted a list of three names to the governor, Lord Dalhousie. Furthermore, only one of the candidates had indicated that he would accept the position. A somewhat humbled Dalhousie finally agreed to the only choice. By 1840, ecclesiastical nominations became purely a church matter.

On the issue of parish appointments, church and state also clashed. Here again the government sought to affirm its supremacy, examining

lists of nominees and intervening occasionally but aggressively in the placement of priests. With the Constitutional Act of 1791, colonial administrators wanted amenable local clergy who could intervene to favour the
election of pro-government candidates. Sir Robert Milnes, sent to the
colony in 1799, prevented the entry into Lower Canada of French priests
whose loyalty he doubted in these years of war. Ultimately, though, the
church's use of its only weapon—passive resistance—brought it success.

The church also prevailed on the question of the division of the large
diocese of Quebec when, in 1836, Lord Gosford finally agreed to the
establishment of the diocese of Montreal. A grateful Monseigneur Lartigue
later wrote to Gosford to request his portrait "as a monument to your
good deeds in this country."

The colonial government's principal administrators in the early nineteenth century made plans to subvert the Catholic church. Herman Ryland, Prescott's profoundly anti-French and anti-Catholic secretary, hoped
to undermine its influence through a reform of the educational system.   *243*
Jacob Mountain, the Anglican Lord Bishop of Quebec, sought to raise
the prestige of his church by increasing its power while at the same time
decreasing that of the Roman church. Attorney General (later, Chief Justice) Jonathan Sewell, more moderate and more patient, wanted to diminish gradually the powers of the Catholic bishops and, by giving Plessis
and his co-adjutor pensions and seats in the councils, make them obedient
government servants. But by the time Sir George Prevost became governor
in 1812, a good part of the momentum had gone out of these ambitious
but dangerous projects. Plessis made it clear that an independent church
could be a powerful ally during renewed war with the Americans.

TOWARDS VICTORY

Undoubtedly, the local situation contributed to the church's ultimate victory in its long war with the state. Some governors were more willing to
be flexible than others and, perhaps, more realistic. For their part, many
church leaders were skilful diplomats who exploited every opportunity for
asserting the church's independence while at the same time giving the
government full co-operation and assuring British authorities of their un-
bending loyalty. In addition, the English rulers' hopes for converting the
habitants were fading. Groups like the Methodists, who used Swiss French-
speaking agents, attempted vainly to proselytize. Indeed, Protestants often
appeared more preoccupied with their own denominational rivalries. Anglican Bishop Mountain, for example, tolerated Presbyterian and Lutheran
ministers, but the Methodist clergy he disdained as "a set of ignorant
enthusiasts whose preaching is calculated only to perplex the understand-

ing and corrupt the morals, to relax the nerves of industry and dissolve the bonds of society."

International events also aided the church. The Canadian clergy's sound condemnation of the "anti-Christian" French Revolution certainly pleased the British authorities. Then, while Napoleon's military campaigns provoked new suspicions of all things French, the War of 1812 gave the church a welcome opportunity to preach loyalty through pastoral letters and sermons. Led by the clergy, loyal French Canadians praised the exploits of Charles-Michel de Salaberry and his militia, who forced a numerically far superior American force to retreat at the battle of Châteauguay in 1813. Here were French-speaking troops winning a glorious victory for the British—undeniable proof of loyalty. Governor Prevost could well declare, "The Catholic clergy are my firmest supports." As for the events of 1837, except in some parishes where the *patriotes* were well organized, they provoked additional manifestations of loyalty to the Crown, this time in the face of internal revolution.

244

The rise of the church in the early years of the nineteenth century took place partly at the expense of the colonial government, partly at the expense of the new professional elite. This latter group was the church's only serious rival in the struggle for support and influence within the French-speaking population. The Rebellion of 1837 brought this conflict to a head and sealed its issue in the church's favour. By 1840 French Canada's clerical elite was poised to enter a golden age.

The Professional Elite

The new professional class was not so fortunate. Many of its members were sons of small farmers and, as such, could scarcely base their social aspirations upon family wealth. Indeed, politics became an outlet for this group's ambitions. Espousing liberal, democratic, and, ultimately, republican ideals, it sought government reform through enlarging the powers of the Lower House and curtailing those of the executive. It was well aware of Lower Canada's colonial status and of French Canadians' lesser role in the economy and in government. These professionals thus aimed to become champions of national values, and they easily associated the interests of French Canada with those of their own class. Not surprisingly, they framed their declarations of battle in the name of the French-Canadian nation.

This new middle class aspired to replace the seigneurs and, to a degree, compete with the clergy as leaders of French Canada. Many of its members viewed the seigneurs as exploiting the habitants when they raised seigneurial *rentes*, especially when the growing population in the seigneurial zone and better prices for timber enhanced the value of the seigneuries, more than half of which had passed to British owners. The French-speaking seigneurs also appeared as collaborators who bowed to the British to gain lucrative appointments and pensions. Many notaries and lawyers also condemned the church for its support of Britain. Some were openly anticlerical, espousing the ideals of the French Revolution and American democracy. Monseigneur Plessis had denounced these radicals as early as 1809, accusing them of "tending to annihilate all principles of subordination and to set fire to the province."

Understandably, the French-speaking professionals who formed the backbone of the *Parti canadien* and, later, of the *Parti patriote*, had increasingly hostile relations with the British merchants. Well represented in the governor's inner councils, the really wealthy merchants numbered only a few hundred but as historian Donald Creighton has described them, they were "the most self-conscious, purposeful and assertive of all the Canadian social classes."[4] The merchants wanted to control Lower Canada's political institutions, in order to introduce new laws to promote economic growth, commerce, and transportation. Some even demanded the complete abolition of the seigneurial system. Naturally, they accused the Assembly's French-speaking majority of systematically blocking necessary change.

245

Members of the liberal professions anchored in rural Quebec had a very different view of Lower Canada's needs. Despite their political radicalism they were economic conservatives. While critical of many aspects of the seigneurial system they did see it as a rampart against English-speaking farmers (anxious to gain freehold title to their lands) replacing the habitant in the St. Lawrence valley. The professionals defended traditional agriculture, denounced the threat of commercial capitalism, and called for greater political autonomy for the colony. There even were many who favoured rebellion.

Assembly versus Governor

The Rebellion of 1837 marked the failure of the Constitutional Act as a system of government for Lower Canada. Actually, the Act's weaknesses had been apparent for over a generation. Since the turn of the century, the increasingly French and then *Parti canadien*-dominated Assembly had sought to strengthen the elective part of government and to weaken the all-powerful Executive whose members were appointed in London and in Quebec.

The causes of the Rebellion of 1837 in Lower Canada were more complex than those in Upper Canada because of the colony's ethnic division. In part, this struggle pitted the English against the French since Lower Canada's tiny English-speaking minority dominated the Executive Council and the Assembly represented the province's French-speaking majority. Yet the deterioration of French-English relations in the colony and the increasingly violent rhetoric on both sides did not prevent a small group of British Quebeckers from supporting the *patriotes*. Some were Irish Catholics who had an intense hatred of England. Others, like brothers Wolfred and Robert Nelson, both supporters of reform, endorsed *patriote* demands for an executive responsible to the Assembly.

The uprising was also, in many ways, a struggle between the haves and the have nots. The defenders of authority, tradition, and wealth, which included the Roman Catholic church and the seigneurs, faced the reformers in the Assembly, who affirmed that they represented the French-Canadian nation and the majority of the population. Yet, even this generalization needs qualification as the wealthy English-speaking merchants constantly attacked the economic status quo, and lobbied for the economic reforms they judged beneficial to the colony's commercial development. At the same time, as members of a small minority, they obviously felt threatened by the French majority. Although they had previously been devoted advocates of an elected assembly, they now defended their positions on the appointed executive and legislative councils. They could not countenance any political changes that would challenge their own economic dominance.

246

FINANCIAL QUESTIONS

In an effort to strengthen its role in government, the Assembly had for three decades sought a greater control over the colony's finances. Constitutionally, it alone could initiate money bills concerning taxes and expenditures, but the executive itself also possessed revenues from Crown lands, the military budget, and even from London that enabled it to distribute patronage in the form of positions, salaries, and pensions to its supporters. Moreover, the appointed Legislative Council could—and often did—refuse legislation that reached it from the Assembly. As a last resort, the governor disposed of extensive veto powers. Were the Legislative Council elective, the governor would no longer be able to fill it with his own people; popular control would thus be enhanced.

The Assembly's disagreements with the governor on these basic issues were frequent and heated. As early as 1805, for example, a bill designed to raise money to build prisons provoked a debate that showed the intensity of growing English-French conflict. French members favoured higher import duties, while British merchants wanted to tax the land. Agriculture was arrayed against commerce, French against English. When the Assembly voted for import duties, the merchants appealed first to the Legislative Council, then to the governor, finally to London. "If the [French]-Canadians succeed in building so many churches, why couldn't they pay for the construction of prisons?" they wondered. During this confrontation, a French-language newspaper, *Le Canadien*, was founded in November 1806. Edited by four members of the *Parti canadien*, it was intended to enable French Canadians to assert "the loyalty of their character and defy the designs of the opposition [British] party."

Relations between the Assembly and the governor further deteriorated during the mandate of Sir James Craig (1807–11). In the face of *Le Canadien*'s vitriolic attacks on the beneficiaries of patronage and government land policies, and influenced by advisers like the anti-Catholic Ryland, Craig embarked upon a "reign of terror." When vocal *Parti canadien* members annoyed him, he dissolved the Assembly. When the election returned an almost identical body, he dissolved it again and went out campaigning. After *Le Canadien* denounced him, he had the paper's presses seized and its editors thrown into jail on charges of treason. When the second election brought back a reinforced *Parti canadien*, he attempted to frighten it into behaving, and he largely succeeded. As a long-term solution to the problem, he recommended assimilation through a union of the provinces, large-scale British immigration, the subordination of the Roman Catholic church, and the abolition of "the representative part of government." Craig then left the province, to the relief of the French-Canadian populace.

247

The question of provincial revenues had produced a deadlock in relations between the Assembly and the governor by the 1820s. Louis-Joseph Papineau led the attack. Foremost among the leaders of the *Parti canadien* (called the *Parti patriote* after 1826), Papineau entered the Assembly in 1809 and became its speaker in 1815. As one who had been brought up on a seigneurie, and was himself a seigneur, Papineau defended the values of tradition, nation, and family. Yet, his education and political career had acquainted him with liberal thought. As the political crisis deepened after 1830, Papineau's early esteem for British institutions evolved into admiration for republicanism and Jacksonian democracy. Liberal in his religious views, he nevertheless viewed the Roman Catholic church as an important national institution, and he attended mass to set an example for his tenants. Here, indeed, was a "divided soul," as historian Fernand Ouellet has portrayed him.[5]

In 1828, believing that London would be more conciliatory once informed of the discontent in Lower Canada, the Assembly sent a petition bearing nearly 90 000 signatures and asking for curbs on the executive. But British politicians were convinced that a governor shorn of his powers would be unable to fulfil his constitutional obligations of responsibility to London.

Without saying as much, the *patriotes* were apparently pushing for independence. At a time when the empire still formed a single tariff unit, London refused to consider the idea. Worse, perhaps, an independent

Lower Canada might slide under the domination of the United States and risk pulling the rest of British North America along with it. Moreover, Britain's great interest in the emigration of its surplus population also made it imperative to retain the colony. In any case, Lower Canada's English did not want independence. As the *Quebec Gazette* editorialized in 1833: "Colonies biting the apple of independence will awake like Adam and Eve and find themselves naked."

RADICALIZATION

The British Parliament adopted what it hoped would be perceived as a compromise solution. It gave the Assembly control of all expenditures on the condition that it vote a permanent civil list to defray civil servants' salaries in the colony. But the mood among the *patriotes* was uncompromising. In 1834 they drew up the ninety-two resolutions, a veritable manifesto that the governor, Lord Aylmer, interpreted as nothing less than a declaration of independence. To help resolve the executive's financial problems, London established the British American Land Company and granted it more than 400 000 ha of land, in return for a commitment to build roads and make annual payments to the Crown. The company, however, showed little interest in colonization and much interest in speculation.

Internal political problems made the Lower Canadian question a very low priority for British politicians. The Whigs, then in power, opposed further concessions to Lower Canada's assembly; at the same time, they wanted to appear conciliatory. Procrastination in the form of an investigation seemed the wisest policy. Unimpressed, the London *Times* in 1835 viewed this commission, headed by the Earl of Gosford, as "a frivolous and toad-eating embassy ... , a temporizing mission, a bribe to the Radicals in the British Parliament to tolerate the Whig ministry."

Then, in March 1837, with the ten resolutions prepared by Lord John Russell, government leader in the British House of Commons, the Whigs announced an end to conciliation. The Colonial Office refused all of the Assembly's ninety-two resolutions. The government of Lower Canada would be able to defray its administrative costs from the consolidated revenue without needing the Assembly's approval. There would be no elective Legislative Council. The English-speaking minority's political influence would thus be preserved. The Executive Council, representing wealth and enterprise, would as before continue to be responsible to the governor alone, not to the Assembly.

Papineau and his party thus did not gain control over executive powers. So-called responsible government, that is, obliging the governor to choose his ministers from the majority in the Assembly, could not be reconciled with the colonial relationship; after all, the governor had to answer to London, not to the local assembly. Momentarily Canadian considerations were now forgotten until the events of November and December of that same year abruptly brought them back to the floor of Parliament.

The Lower Canadian Rebellions of 1837–38

When they received news of Russell's resolutions, the *patriotes* altered their tactics, since Britain apparently was not going to yield. For some, the time for revolt had arrived. More moderate views prevailed, though, and the plan agreed upon called for legal agitation that would bring the government to reconsider its positions. Revolution would be the ultimate recourse if this policy failed.

Throughout the tense days of summer and autumn 1837, the *patriote* *249* leaders worked on organization. They staged assemblies and collected funds. *Patriote* women established an association whose objective was "to assist, insofar as the weakness of their sex made it possible, in the triumph of the patriot cause."[6] In September an association with military sections, the *Fils de la Liberté*, was founded. At a public assembly at St. Charles in the Richelieu River valley east of Montreal, attended by perhaps four thousand people, *patriote* orators called for revolt. The meeting adopted resolutions that included a declaration of independence. Plans were elaborated to take Montreal and move on to Quebec.

Then the government issued warrants for the arrest of the principal *patriote* leaders who fled to the countryside south of Montreal, Papineau among them. The prospective urban uprising was suppressed.

After an initial skirmish at Saint-Denis on November 23 which the *patriotes* won, more British troops were called up. The fierce combat that ensued at neighbouring St. Charles was, however, catastrophic for the rebels, led by Wolfred Nelson.

Having pacified the Richelieu valley, Sir John Colborne, the former governor of Upper Canada, who had just become commander-in-chief of all British troops in the Canadas, turned his attention to the area north of Montreal where Amury Girod, a Swiss immigrant, and Dr. Jean-Olivier Chénier headed the resistance movement. News of the *patriotes'* defeat at St. Charles only hardened Chénier in his determination to "die fighting rather than surrender."

When Colborne approached St. Eustache in December 1837, Girod fled while Chénier and several insurgents took refuge in the church and other buildings. Some seventy *patriotes* including Chénier died by gunfire or were burned to death. The village was then put to the torch, as was nearby St. Benoît, which offered no resistance. One newspaper usually favourable to the British reported: "For a radius of 15 miles around St. Eustache,

National Archives of Canada / C-3653.

This scene, painted by M.A. Hayes, a British officer, shows British troops with *patriote* prisoners captured during the rebellion of 1837.

not a building escaped being ravaged and pillaged by these new vandals" who displayed "no feelings of humanity."

By the time news of the insurrection reached London, just before Christmas, many of the rebel leaders had found asylum in the United States, where they attempted to muster support and regroup. Then, in February 1838, Robert Nelson led an incursion across the border. As provisional president of Lower Canada, he declared Canada's independence from Britain before fleeing back to safety on the American side.

In November 1838, revolt broke out anew, this time southwest of Montreal. Colborne responded by proclaiming martial law, and his troops once again intervened. The rebellion was suppressed, though Colborne—nicknamed *"le vieux brûlot"* ("the Old Firebrand")—was to be long remembered for his ruthlessness.

Intense historical controversy has surrounded the principal actors in this drama. Conservative clerical historians lauded the role of churchmen like Bishop Lartigue who attempted to calm violent sentiment before it got out of hand. Others condemned the church for collaborating with the

Un Canadien Errant

Once a Canadian lad,
Exiled from hearth and home,
Wandered, alone and sad,
Through alien lands unknown.
Down by a rushing stream,
Thoughtful and sad one day
He watched the water pass
And to it he did say:

"If you should reach my land,
My most unhappy land,
Please speak to all my friends
So they will understand.
Tell them how much I wish
That I could be once more
In my beloved land
That I will see no more.

"My own beloved land
I'll not forget till death,
And I will speak of her
With my last dying breath.
My own beloved land
I'll not forget till death,
And I will speak of her
With my last dying breath."

Un canadien errant,
Banni des ses foyers,
Un canadien errant,
Banni de ses foyers,
Parcourait en pleurant
Des pays étrangers.
Parcourait en pleurant
Des pays étrangers.

Un jour, triste et pensif,
Assis au bord des flots,
Un jour, triste et pensif,
Assis au bord des flots,
Au courant fugitif
Il adressa ces mots,
Au courant fugitif
Il adressa ces mots:

"Si tu vois mon pays,
Mon pays malheureux,
Si tu vois mon pays,
Mon pays malheureux,
Va, dis à mes amis
Que je me souviens d'eux,
Va, dis à mes amis
Que je me souviens d'eux."

251

The English translation is printed with the permission of Edith Fowke, the translator.

"Un Canadien errant," one of Quebec's most famous folk-songs, was written by Antoine Gérin-Lajoie shortly after the uprisings of 1837/38. It relates the story of a *patriote* banished from Lower Canada after the suppression of the rebellions.

enemy. The *patriotes*, too, have been the subject of differing judgments. Modern-day nationalists have seen them as heroes who struggled for Quebec's independence. Others, like historian Fernand Ouellet, have described them as members of an ambitious professional elite, seeking political power and social prestige and often very conservative despite their revolutionary appearance. For example, Papineau was a conservative landowner, seigneur of Montebello, who nonetheless spoke fervently about American democracy. But his revolutionary rhetoric became more ambivalent over time and he denied with vehemence that he wanted revolution.[7] Half an hour after the beginning of the Battle of St. Denis, he fled to the American border.

That the *patriote* leaders, who were French-speaking merchants and professionals, had ambitions as a group, that they saw the welfare of the masses as a function of their own interests, is clear. Church leaders also had ambitions. So did seigneurs like Pierre de Boucherville, who calculated that, had the revolution been successful, he would have lost an annual revenue of five hundred louis (gold coin pieces). So did the English-speaking merchants who, although a small minority, largely controlled the colony's economy. So did the British administrators who believed that power should be entrusted to appointed officials, most of them English-speaking. So did the British Parliament that still felt that colonies should be, and could be, useful to the mother country. And so, finally, did the habitants, who had many ideas of what was wrong with their situation and of what might better their lot, especially for their poorest members, who constituted the great majority—perhaps 95 percent—of the insurrection's active sympathizers.

252

Consequences of the Rebellions

London chose to address the Canadian problem by forming a royal commission to visit both Lower and Upper Canada. The future historian, François-Xavier Garneau, appealed to the commissioner upon his arrival in Quebec: "Durham, close your ears to the counsels of vengeance; take upon yourself the defense of a helpless people." But Lord Durham was listening to other advice. Before he even left England, he had been lobbied by Canadian and British merchant groups who emphasized the ethnic aspect of the conflict; they urged union to save themselves from "the designs of the French faction, madly bent upon [the] destruction" of the rights, the interests and the property of Lower Canada's British population.

Durham's concern for economic development made him sympathetic to the merchants' views. In his report he drew attention to the "deadly animosity" between French and English: "I found two nations warring in the bosom of a single state; I found a struggle, not of principles, but of races." A union of the two Canadas would yield a clear English majority that immigration would further reinforce. As for the French, whom he viewed as innately inferior, he was convinced that they "when once placed, by the legitimate course of events and the working of natural causes, in a minority, would abandon their vain hopes of nationality." Union with Upper Canada would thus assure the assimilation of the French—the ultimate solution to ethnic conflict in Lower Canada.

The rebellion, then, brought Lower Canada to its knees and made it easy to overlook the enormous changes that the colony had undergone at virtually all levels since 1791. The colony lost its own government and was to be joined to Upper Canada in a union that the great majority of the

French did not want. Moreover, the avowed purpose of this union, as expressed by Durham, by British parliamentarians, and by Lower Canadian merchants, was to break the power of French Canada and eventually to assimilate it. But like the proponents of the Constitutional Act a half century earlier, the advocates of union proved to be poor prophets. So, too, were most of the French Canadians who viewed it so darkly.

NOTES

[1] John McCallum, *Unequal Beginnings: Agriculture and Economic Development in Quebec and Ontario until 1870* (Toronto, 1980), 25 ff.

[2] Allan Greer, *Peasant, Lord, and Merchant: Rural Society in Three Quebec Parishes, 1740–1840* (Toronto, 1985), 122–39.

[3] "Monseigneur, the Catholic Bishop. Joseph Octave Plessis, Church, State, and Society in Lower Canada: Historiography and Analysis" (Ph.D. thesis, Université Laval, 1980, 3 vols.)

[4] Donald Creighton, *The Commercial Empire of the St. Lawrence, 1760–1850* (Toronto, 1937), 23, quoted in Gilles Paquet et Jean-Pierre Wallot, "Groupes sociaux et pouvoir: le cas canadien au tournant du XIXe siècle," *Revue d'histoire de l'Amérique française*, 27 (1974): 539.

[5] Fernand Ouellet, *Louis-Joseph Papineau, A Divided Soul* (Ottawa, 1960).

[6] The original French text reads, "... concourir, autant que la faiblesse de leur sexe peut le leur permettre, à faire réussir la cause patriotique". Quoted in Micheline Dumont *et al.*, *L'histoire des femmes au Québec depuis quatre siècles* (Montréal, 1982), 145.

[7] Fernand Ouellet, "Papineau", *Dictionary of Canadian Biography*, vol. 10: 1871–1880 (Toronto, 1972), pp. 564–78.

253

Related Readings

Fernand Ouellet provides an important overview of the rebellions of 1837–38 in "The Insurrections", in R. Douglas Francis and Donald B. Smith, *Readings in Canadian History: Pre-Confederation*, 2d ed. (Toronto, 1986), pp. 313–27.

BIBLIOGRAPHY

Fernand Ouellet's *Lower Canada, 1791–1840: Social Change and Nationalism* (Toronto, 1979) is very useful for this period. His *Economic and Social History of Quebec, 1760–1850* (Toronto 1980), should also be consulted. Jean-Pierre Wallot and Gilles Paquet's research on social, economic and political history, often criticizing Ouellet's interpretations, provides a contrary view on several issues. See, for example, their article "The Agricultural Crisis in Lower Canada, 1802–12; *mise au point*. A Response to T. J. A. Le Goff," *Canadian Historical Review*, 56(1975): 133–61. Allan Greer, *Peasant, Lord, and Merchant: Rural Society in Three Quebec Parishes,*

1740–1840 (Toronto, 1985), suggests new insights. John McCallum's *Unequal Beginnings: Agriculture and Economic Development in Quebec and Ontario until 1870* (Toronto, 1980) and Michael Bliss's *Northern Enterprise. Five Centuries of Canadian Business* (Toronto, 1987) are also helpful.

James Lambert has made a notable contribution to social and religious history in his thesis, "Monseigneur, the Catholic Bishop. Joseph-Octave Plessis, Church, State, and Society in Lower Canada: Historiography and Analysis" (Ph.D. thesis, Université Laval, 1980, 3 vols.) Alexis de Tocqueville's Canadian journal offers a contemporary portrait of Lower Canada in the early 1830s; see Jacques Vallée, ed., *Tocqueville au Bas-Canada* (Montréal, 1973). The cholera epidemics are presented in Geoffrey Bilson, *A Darkened House: Cholera in Nineteenth-Century Canada* (Toronto, 1980).

For the events of 1837 and their origins, see Joseph Schull, *Rebellion: The Rising in French Canada, 1837* (Toronto, 1971) and Jean-Paul Bernard, *Les rébellions de 1838–1838* (Montréal, 1983). Jacques Monet, *The Last Cannon Shot: A Study of French Canadian Nationalism, 1837–1850* (Toronto, 1969) has useful material on both the Rebellion and its aftermath. Relations between Britain and Canada are analysed in Peter Burroughs, *The Canadian Crisis and British Colonial Policy, 1828–1841* (Toronto, 1972); Ged Martin, *The Durham Report and British Policy: A Critical Essay* (Cambridge, 1972); and Phillip Buckner, "The Colonial Office and British North America, 1801–50," *Dictionary of Canadian Biography*, vol. 8: 1851–1860 (Toronto, 1985), xxiii-xxxvii. For references to women in Lower Canada in the early nineteenth century see: Micheline Dumont *et al.*, *Quebec Women. A History* (Toronto, 1987). Individuals mentioned in this chapter are also studied in various volumes of the *Dictionary of Canadian Biography*.

254

CHAPTER FOURTEEN

The Union of the Canadas: Political Developments, 1840–64

The Act of Union adopted in July 1840 joined the two Canadas, now   255
rebaptized Canada East and Canada West. This act of the British Parliament gave the old province of Quebec its fourth constitution since the Conquest. The union had a short but stormy life. Indeed, many latter-day observers have seen it as simply a prelude to Confederation. After all, by 1864 perennial deadlock in the united province's Legislative Assembly led most of its members to agree to work towards the realization of a larger British North American Confederation.

Although ultimately a failure, the union could boast some political successes. As railway fever swept the nation's business community in the 1850s, solicitous politicians oversaw a multitude of costly and often competing construction projects. They fostered increased trade relations with the United States by negotiating a Treaty of Reciprocity, floated through on champagne, it was said, by Canada's suave governor general, Lord Elgin. They tried to stimulate industrial growth by instituting a protective tariff. In 1854 they finally abolished the seigneurial system in Canada East and even found a solution to the contentious Clergy reserves question in Canada West.

The union years also saw the resolution of another issue that for decades had been the source of constant feuding between the Assembly and the governor. Ten years after the failure of the rebellions, London accepted the principles of responsible government. Henceforth, the governor governed less; his ministers, who were responsible to the Assembly, made the decisions in his place.

Most significantly, French- and English-speaking politicians found common ground on which to co-operate in solving many major political questions. The need to construct a *modus vivendi* also helped restrain ethnic and religious bigotry. French Canada again escaped assimilation. In many respects, Canada East, like Canada West, led a separate existence and this separateness became more pronounced as the years passed.

French-English Relations

The Colonial Office in London originally intended to use union to punish the French and assure their subjugation, if not their eventual demise, as a linguistic group—of that French Canadians were convinced. English became the sole official language of parliamentary documents. The elective Assembly had an equal number of representatives from both halves of the colony, even though the largely French-speaking Canada East had 670 000 inhabitants and English-speaking Canada West only 480 000.

The Act of Union also created "one consolidated revenue fund," making Upper Canada's heavy debt burden the responsibility of the Province of Canada as a whole. Upper Canada could no longer by itself finance costly transportation facilities like roads and canals. It had already borrowed heavily in London, and only union with the much less debt-ridden Lower Canada could strengthen its position.

256   British financial houses operating in Canada who were worried about a series of bankruptcies regarded union as imperative. It would bring in higher revenues since the United Canadas could raise tariffs, a measure that Lower Canada, where most goods from Europe entered, could no longer block. It would also recognize that the two Canadas formed a common economic bloc.

Charles Poulett Thomson, Lord Durham's successor as governor general of Canada, had spent eight years on the Board of Trade. This hard-headed administrator knew that Canada had to be put on a sound financial footing to attract the necessary development capital. Investment would assure progress and make the appeal of the United States a little less enticing, thus warding off the constant threat of annexation. He also hoped that a substantial inflow of British immigrants would diminish the political and economic influence of French Canadians.

When the strong-willed and vain Thomson arrived in Canada in the autumn of 1839, his first task was to convince Upper Canada to agree unconditionally to the proposal for political union. He did not have to convince Lower Canada which would have no vote on the question of union. As Lord Melbourne, British prime minister, had written to Colonial Secretary Lord John Russell explaining his policy: "We feel that we cannot impose this union upon Upper Canada without her consent, and therefore we give her a choice. We give Lower Canada no choice, but we impose it upon her during the suspension of her constitution."

The union was officially inaugurated at the Château de Ramezay in Montreal on February 10, 1841. Thomson, now the new Baron Sydenham, declared: "Inhabitants of the Province of Canada: henceforth may you be united in sentiment as you are from this day in name!" Most French Canadians, though, were defiant and bitter. Pierre-Joseph-Olivier Chauveau, a future Quebec prime minister, condemned the British bankers whom he saw as the force behind union and prophesied: "Today a weeping people is beaten, tomorrow a people will be up in arms, today the forfeit, tomorrow the vengeance."

The French certainly had no reason to trust in the assurances of the anti-French Sydenham. Moreover, the Union simply had too many elements that they found objectionable. Augustin-Norbert Morin, a *patriote* of 1837 and reform leader Louis-Hippolyte La Fontaine's lieutenant in Quebec City, commented frankly in a letter to Toronto politician Francis Hincks: "I am against the Union and against the main features, as I think every honest Lower Canadian should be." John Neilson, an urbane bilingual Scot who owned the *Quebec Gazette*, formed a committee in the fall of 1840 to work for the election of representatives opposed to union in order to express by non-violent means "our reprobation of this injustice which is done to this Province." Unyielding opposition appeared to be the only path open to the French.

Sydenham, however, soon proved himself a master strategist, as capable as he was unscrupulous. Indeed, he won over most of Canada West to "his" party, with the exception of a few Family Compact Tories like Sir Allan MacNab (who judged the governor too sympathetic to the doctrine of responsible government), as well as some "Ultra Reformers" (who perceived him as too equivocal in his support of the same doctrine).

In Canada East, *le poulet* (the chicken), as the French disdainfully called Poulett Thomson, laboured under no illusions. He knew the French were hostile to him and would not support his candidates. Apart from areas with important English-speaking populations, he admitted: "We shall not have a man returned who does not hate British connexion, British rule, British improvements, and everything which has a taint of British feeling." This master political manipulator thus worked to assure the election of a maximum number of English-speaking members. He gerrymandered riding boundaries to eliminate French votes from certain districts and staged polls in English localities situated far from French-speaking towns. As returning officers for the polls he chose partisans, and he used British troops as well as Irish construction labourers to intimidate voters in the open voting (Canada only obtained the secret ballot in 1874). In La Fontaine's own district, thugs hired by the British candidate took possession of the polling place. Bitterly denouncing Sydenham's "law of the bludgeon," La Fontaine withdrew from the contest to avoid bloodshed and certain defeat. Not surprisingly, the governor won a comfortable working majority in United Canada's first legislature.

TOWARDS FRENCH-CANADIAN ACCEPTANCE OF UNION

Sydenham's heavy-handed tactics actually improved the chances for fruitful collaboration between reformers in Canada East and West. Since 1839 Francis Hincks, a pragmatic and ambitious Irish Protestant immigrant with a passion for journalism, business, and responsible government, assiduously cultivated good relations with La Fontaine. Hincks repeatedly assured the former *patriote* that, in return for co-operation in working towards responsible government, his followers would assist French-Canadian efforts to rid the union of objectionable features like official English unilingualism. Hincks concluded: "You want our help as much as we do yours." At first suspicious, La Fontaine finally responded by deciding to accept union and to work within it.

258   The particularities of politics in each section of the province created the conditions that brought most French Canadian leaders to work within the Union. The threat posed by the imposed link with Canada West made it necessary for the French to practise a great degree of electoral cohesiveness. After 1850, when a few extreme liberals from Canada East took their places in the Assembly, tensions between the left and the right increased among the French; nevertheless, this potential threat to the unity of the French *bloc* was successfully contained.

THE RISE OF A REFORM COALITION

Canada West's political spectrum was broad, featuring almost all shades of opinion, from Compact Tories on the right to Ultra Reformers on the left. Theoretically, in the early 1840s the French could have aligned with some of Upper Canada's extreme conservatives, Tories like Sir Allan MacNab. Like the French, they opposed union, but mutual animosities precluded even a *mariage de convenance*. An alliance between Reformers and French seemed far more natural, in view of the political goals of both groups throughout the 1820s and 1830s, and since then the rebellion had weakened the Reform movement and Lord Sydenham's ambiguous overtures had divided it.

It took time to establish this common front, however. Many so-called Reformers did not want to oppose the government, as the French had done, for fear of compromising the public-works projects promised for their districts by Sydenham and obviously desired by the voters. Hincks, at least until he, too, defected to the government side, and especially the more principled Toronto Reform leader Robert Baldwin, were virtually alone. Baldwin, for example, never succeeded in bringing the governor to appoint French-speaking members to the Executive Council. Essentially, then, when Sydenham died of lock-jaw in September 1841 (caused by an injury, the result of a fall from his horse), the French were quite isolated.

The French, however, could not long be ignored. Disappointed reformers returned to Baldwin's leadership. Sydenham's successor, Sir Charles Bagot, a highly successful diplomat, badly needed French support for his tottering government. Bagot's successor, Sir Charles Metcalfe, was likewise convinced that the anti-French assimilationist policies of the union were impractical, although he, too, believed that anglicization was an appropriate long-term policy.

These governors walked a tightrope in trying to govern without the aid of representatives of the French Canadians who formed nearly half the province's population. Yet they were conservatives, strong believers in the British connection, and in trying to appease the supposedly disloyal and rebellious French, they risked losing support among the English-speaking of both Canadas.

In addition, the governors had difficulty persuading the British government to renounce at least any immediate hopes for assimilation. Bagot told Colonial Secretary Lord Stanley that it was all very well to wait for immigration to "hem in and overwhelm French Population and French Power"; in the meantime, he had to solve pressing political problems by giving positions to French members and making other "concessions." Lord Stanley was horrified by this, and by Bagot's introduction of both Baldwin and La Fontaine into his government. On his deathbed, Bagot justified his conduct to his critics in London: "I had no choice in regard to [my measures] if the Union was to be maintained."

On the highly charged question of giving official status to the French language, Governor Metcalfe wanted to act before La Fontaine forced him to do so. Again, Lord Stanley vehemently disagreed since the Act of Union was designed "to promote the amalgamation of the French and English races" and to authorize bilingualism would be to abandon this goal. Only in 1848, three years after Metcalfe's request, did the British Parliament amend the Act of Union to end the proscription of the French language.

The achievement of responsible government did not curtail close co-operation between French-speaking and English-speaking politicians. It did signify the need to build new alliances, though. In the turbulent early 1850s, when the loosely organized reform group split into moderate and radical factions, most French-speaking members of the Assembly, the moderate *Bleus*, began to co-operate with Conservatives from Canada West to form governments. This coalition, symbolized by the close association of John A. Macdonald and George-Etienne Cartier, carried over into the post-Confederation period.

259

PERCEPTIONS OF UNION

By the end of the 1840s the position of the French appeared much stronger than it had just after union. For historian Mason Wade, this evolution represented an unqualified triumph: "Faced with the prospect of national extinction, the French Canadians closed their ranks and won the peaceful victory which insured their national survival."[1] Moreover, co-operation with anglophone politicians had proved not only possible but also desirable: the first hesitant steps towards "Canadian duality" had been taken.

Other historians, also preoccupied with the fate of the French, have been harsher in their judgments of union. For them, simply avoiding the worst possible outcome—assimilation—hardly constituted victory. There could be no real victory without equality, and union condemned the French to permanent inequality. Maurice Séguin, for example, views the union as a second conquest that the French had no choice but to accept.[2] It created a political entity in which the French demographically represented a declining minority. By 1851 Canada West, with 950 000 citizens, had a slightly larger population than the eastern portion of the province, where one-quarter were English-speaking. The French were also faced with political inferiority within institutions of government that were largely English-speaking. In addition, economic domination was a painful reality. Few leaders of industry or important merchants were French-speaking. As journalist Etienne Parent wrote: "Everywhere we let others take over the riches of our country."

260

The Coming of Responsible Government

The most important single factor in bridging the ethnic gulf during the 1840s was undoubtedly the arduous, but ultimately successful, struggle for responsible government. In 1840 recognition of this principle still appeared far off. The Act of Union concentrated enormous power in the hands of the colonial governor, named by London. The governor appointed for life the members of the Upper House, the Legislative Council. In Parliament he chose his advisers, dismissing and replacing them at will. He also held broad veto powers over bills adopted by the Legislature. Yet over the course of the union's first decade, the governor's powers were radically curtailed.

Responsible government came only after dramatic battles. The Colonial Office urged Canada's governors to avoid concessions lest things get out of hand in the colony and Canada agitate for independence. On his deathbed, Sydenham considered the issue favourably resolved, but his reign of "harmony" implied an active, and often unscrupulous, participation of the governor in politics. In contrast, Bagot, a conciliator, was willing to

SOVEREIGN

GOVERNOR

LEGISLATIVE COUNCIL   EXECUTIVE COUNCIL

LEGISLATIVE ASSEMBLY

THE PEOPLE

BEFORE RESPONSIBLE GOVERNMENT

SOVEREIGN

GOVERNOR

LEGISLATIVE COUNCIL   EXECUTIVE COUNCIL

LEGISLATIVE ASSEMBLY

THE PEOPLE

RESPONSIBLE GOVERNMENT

Cornell, Hamelin, Ouellet, Trudel, *Canada, Unity in Diversity*, p. 143.

Before the introduction of responsible government, the legislative assembly had no effective control over the executive council (above right) on whose advice the governor must act. With the introduction of responsible government, the executive council could remain in office only as long as it retained the legislative assembly's support.

261

risk appointing an executive council that would have the support of a majority in the Assembly. Taking into account the growing power of the French bloc in the Assembly, he invited La Fontaine to join his council. When the latter shrewdly demanded that Baldwin, too, have a place, the unhappy Bagot again yielded.

London was scarcely jubilant. The Duke of Wellington, Bagot's own uncle, called him "a fool." Colonial administrators expressed the strongest regrets—to which the governor replied that, had he acted otherwise, "Canada would have again become the theatre of a wide spread rebellion, and perhaps the ungrateful separatist or the rejected outcast from British dominion." Despite Bagot's apparent recognition of the principle that the administration could not govern without the support of the Assembly, there was still no guarantee that the governor might not some day dismiss his advisers if he disagreed with them and appoint others in their place. Moreover, Bagot's government, comprising a wide variety of personalities of various political hues, did not really constitute a ministry. Party government had not yet come to the province.

More to blame for this outcome was Sir Charles Metcalfe, who arrived in Canada as governor in March 1843 and was determined to work for the maintenance of the British connection. As the queen's representative, he did not intend to submit to La Fontaine, and he would certainly not commit himself to taking his advice. The Reformers' distribution of patronage and unseemly rush for jobs for their people greatly disturbed the governor. Metcalfe assured Lord Stanley that he would strive to get a majority in Parliament, that if he failed he would dissolve and try again, "and that if I fail then, still I cannot submit, for that would be to surrender the Queen's government into the hands of rebels, and to become myself their ignominious tool." Metcalfe proved every bit as steadfast as his confession of faith seemed to indicate. In the rancorous 1844 election, he did obtain a slim majority by inflicting a decisive defeat on the overconfident and "disloyal" Upper Canadian Reformers. He was, however, spectacularly unsuccessful in Lower Canada, where La Fontaine had built up an effective political machine.

The moderate regime that governed the colony from 1844 until 1847, led by the eloquent Conservative "Sweet William" Henry Draper as Attorney General for Canada West and virtual prime minister, succeeded in adopting several important pieces of legislation, including school acts for both Canadas, legal reform, and a permanent civil list of salaried officials. Technically responsible government did not yet exist for, although the Executive Council did have the confidence of the Assembly, the governor's powers remained far too broad. Moreover, Draper's attempts to build significant French support failed utterly. The old *patriote* Denis-Benjamin Viger agreed to work with him but was unsuccessful in gaining the support of influential individuals from French Canada.

262   The pace of events quickened with the arrival of Lord Elgin, the new governor general, in 1847. Convinced that only colonial autonomy could hold the empire together, the British government was now prepared to endorse responsible government, and it instructed Elgin to accept this principle and to behave in a strictly neutral fashion. The elections of 1848 produced a strong majority for La Fontaine's group in Canada East and a significant majority for Baldwin's Reform movement in Canada West.

The Reformers' victory achieved, Lord Elgin called on La Fontaine and Baldwin to form a government. Henceforth the governor assented to legislation adopted by Parliament, unless he judged it contrary to the interests of Great Britain. Elgin proved as much in 1849 when he agreed to sign, despite personal reservations, the bitterly controversial Rebellion Losses Bill, which compensated those who had lost property during the rebellions of 1837–38.

Responsible government thus moved Canada forward along the road to democracy and political autonomy. The voters, through their elected representatives, would now do the governing—or at least the male portion would, for in 1849 the Reformers amended the election law to exclude women from the franchise. In spite of the common law prohibition against female suffrage, a few women had voted. They had even helped a Tory win in 1844—an incident that the Reformers had not forgotten.

Ironically, after their hard fight to achieve responsible government and greater self-government from Britain, Canadian politicians imposed even tighter control over the Indian population of the Canadas. The government had established and surveyed reserves, but under the legislation adopted in the 1850s and 1860s, the Indians were given little opportunity to administer their remaining lands themselves.

The Annexation Movement

Following the achievement of responsible government, the years 1848–54 saw feverish political activity. When Lord Elgin sanctioned the Rebellion Losses Bill on April 25, 1849, the fury of Montreal's Tories exploded. A mob invaded the House of Parliament and put it to the torch, then stoned Elgin's carriage, ransacked La Fontaine's house, and rampaged through the town.

Canada West experienced considerable unrest, too. Baldwin and Mackenzie were burnt in effigy and Lord Elgin met a similar fiery condemnation from a Toronto mob. The Tories staged protest meetings to denounce the rewarding of "rebels" and "pardoned traitors", and thousands signed petitions demanding Elgin's recall. Said the *Brockville Statesman* of Her Majesty's representative: "Without peace there can be no prosperity, and that peace cannot be procured so long as his hated foot presses the free soil, or his lying lungs breathe the pure air of Canada."

263

For many Tories, this was French domination at its worst, and the British were bowing to it. At the same time, London's move towards free trade signified an end to imperial preferences. Exporters in the British North American colonies rapidly lost their relative advantage in British markets over other nations to which higher tariffs had previously applied. Britain's new trade policies thus pushed large sectors of Canadian commerce into depression. Shipping activity at Montreal declined by more than 40 percent between 1847 and 1849. Finding none of the much-vaunted benefits of the British connection, these Tories, who had hitherto proclaimed their loyalty and condemned traitors and rebels, now began to campaign for annexation to the United States.

In Montreal, the hotbed of annexationist sentiment, the English-language press published in October 1849 the manifesto of the Annexation Association. It was signed by 325 citizens, many of them well known in business circles. Early in 1850 the formation of the Toronto Annexation Association, supposedly embracing "a large number of the most respectable merchants and inhabitants of this city, of all parties and creeds," was announced.

Even French Canada displayed some interest in annexation, though obviously for entirely different reasons. Louis-Joseph Papineau's admiration of American democratic institutions and hatred of the Canadian union (after he was granted amnesty in 1844 he had returned to Lower Canada) were well known. Youthful intellectuals belonging to the Institut canadien, a literary and debating society in Montreal, or who wrote for the newspaper *L'Avenir*, took up the annexationist cause. They declared that they preferred "Brother Jonathan," with his egalitarian principles, to John Bull, with his haughty and aristocratic airs. A naive but sincere Louis-Antoine Dessaulles, Papineau's nephew, expressed his ardent desire that French Canada imitate Louisiana in order to obtain the advantages both of a separate state and of American prosperity and democracy. Des-saulles, journalist Jean-Baptiste-Eric Dorion (appropriately nicknamed the *"enfant terrible,"*) and their friends, however, constituted but a tiny group. Their movement had no popular base, and other elites in French Canada vociferously condemned annexation. George-Etienne Cartier echoed con-servative sentiment when he warned that American democracy signified that "the dominant power was the will of the crowd, of the masses." The Roman Catholic clergy, for its part, feared that annexation would put an end to the liberty that it enjoyed under Britain.

English-speaking annexationism, though noisy, made little headway in Canada West. Newspapers frequently published statements of citizens lauding the benefits of the relationship with Britain. John Strachan, now Anglican Bishop of Toronto, roundly denounced annexation as opposed to "the plainest and most solemn declarations of the revealed will of God," for it signified union with republicans who sanctioned slavery. Opponents of annexation published their own manifestos in the press.

264

In July 1849 Tories frustrated by the Reform government and by sup-posed French "domination" gathered at Kingston to launch the British-American League. Future Prime Minister John A. Macdonald apparently played an active behind-the-scenes role in its organization, but the Toronto *Globe*, edited by George Brown, Macdonald's great political opponent, reported that he "said little in the convention and indeed he never says much anywhere except in barrooms ... ." Patriotic delegates overwhelm-ingly rejected a resolution favourable to annexation. One delegate declared passionately, "It was never intended by Providence that the American, or Gallic, eagles should ever build their nests in the branches of the British oak, or soar over her prostrate lion."

A later convention, held in Toronto in November, voiced support for a union of the British North American colonies, that many delegates viewed as a means of escaping from French domination. Macdonald judged this scheme "premature and impractical for the moment."

With the revival of prosperity in the early 1850s, annexationist sentiment receded rapidly. Although union with the United States had been much discussed, it had little popular support. Also, the Americans' unrespon-siveness to annexationist sentiment hastened the movement's decline.

New Political Alliances

While English-speaking Conservatives attempted to find a new basis for unified action, the reform coalition also struggled to keep together. By 1850, with responsible government a reality, the Reform movement began to splinter, with tensions developing between moderates and radicals on issues such as political reform, railway policy, financial affairs and church–

state relations. The radical Reformers, whose stronghold was the area west of Toronto, denounced Montreal business interests, actively promoted agrarian democracy, and announced that they were seeking out "only men who are Clear Grit," grit being an American slang phrase implying firmness of character.[3] Under journalist George Brown's leadership, the Clear Grits became militant champions of "rep by pop," or representation according to population, the implication being that Canada West, with its larger and rapidly increasing population, deserved a greater number of seats than Francophone Canada East and therefore a preponderant influence over government policy.

At the same time, with Louis-Joseph Papineau's political revival, the French-Canadian *Rouges* made their appearance in the Assembly in 1848. They gained ground in the elections of 1851 and 1854, especially in the Montreal region. These radical reformers inherited the traditions of the *Parti patriote*. They tended to be somewhat anticlerical, republican, strongly nationalistic, and highly critical of the close links between government and business, notably the railways. Thus, in addition to its usual adversaries on the right, the governing coalition faced mounting pressures from the left, particularly after the retirement of Baldwin and La Fontaine in 1851. After initial attempts to attract Clear Grit support, it sought the support of the right, appealing for the endorsement of the Conservatives and of Hincks' moderate Reformers. By the mid-1850s, the so-called Liberal–Conservative alliance emerged, soon to be led jointly by Macdonald and Cartier.

265

A Capital is Chosen

In the 1850s, politics appeared largely divorced from the concerns of common people. The question of the choice of a capital for the united province symbolized this futility. Indeed, between 1841 and 1859, the Legislative Assembly voted no fewer than 218 times on this seemingly straightforward matter. Political, ethnic, and geographical rivalries transformed the issue into one of the most divisive confronting the union. The British government chose the small town of Kingston as the first capital in 1841, because it judged both Toronto and Montreal difficult to defend in the event of American attack; moreover, Toronto was too far west. Quebec, surrounded by French-speaking citizens, was not acceptable either. But according to Lord Sydenham, a capital somewhere in Upper Canada would be good for French members because it "would instil English ideas into their minds, [and] destroy the immediate influence upon their actions of the host of little lawyers, notaries and doctors."

Many liberal-minded members soon found Kingston to have too many supporters of Orangism and Toryism. The politicians, therefore, moved

to Montreal. But in 1849, the burning of the Parliament there again necessitated a move, and the seat of government migrated to Toronto. After
stormy debate, legislators agreed that, following two years on the humid
shores of Lake Ontario, the capital would sojourn for four years in Quebec
City and then move back to Toronto. Citizens of both cities were reluctant
to see the capital depart, but Protestant or Catholic, English or French,
the members of this so-called "log-rolling compact" preferred relinquish-
ing the seat temporarily to seeing it settle on a permanent basis in some
other city.

Eventually, the Assembly appealed to Queen Victoria to choose a capital.
After receiving memorials from all appropriate Canadian towns, and some
less appropriate, the British government selected Bytown, recently rebaptized Ottawa. Quebeckers were dismayed. The Toronto *Globe* was outraged by this choice of a city in which five-eighths of the population was
Roman Catholic and half were of French origin. After more bickering,
266   the Assembly finally deferred to the queen's decision and Ottawa began
functioning as the capital of the Canadas in 1865.

Politics and Business

Economic progress and, especially after 1845, railway development, most
engaged the attention of the legislators. Railways required extensive government financial assistance through tax concessions, guarantees, bonds,
the assumption of bad debts and outright grants when private capital
subscribed was insufficient, as it always was (see chapter 15).

At the time, some politicians were closely linked to business enterprises
and tended to confound personal and state interests. Sir Allan MacNab,
co-prime minister in the MacNab-Morin and MacNab-Taché administra-
tions from 1854 to 1856, was one. He affirmed candidly, after consuming
"one or two bottles of good port," that "all my politics are railroads."
The great reformer, Francis Hincks, an unabashed defender of railway
schemes, provides another example. His conduct was studied by a parliamentary committee, which found no evidence of corruption, although the
former premier had obviously been in situations of conflicting interest.
Alexander T. Galt of Sherbrooke, named minister of finance in the Cartier-
Macdonald ministry in 1858, was also a very pragmatic businessman. He
was a leading force behind, a large shareholder in, and eventually president
of the St. Lawrence and Atlantic Railway that linked Montreal to Portland,
Maine, by way of Sherbrooke. The Grand Trunk absorbed the line shortly
after its completion in 1853. Galt also sat on the board of directors of the
Grand Trunk and, in politics, sought to expand Montreal's influence
westward.

George-Etienne Cartier, too, actively concerned himself with Montreal business and served as director of a host of banking, insurance, transportation and mining companies. Railways, though, were his main activity. Over the course of many years, he held positions as cabinet minister, chairman of the Legislative Assembly's Railway Committee, and solicitor for the Grand Trunk Railway. Cartier guided the Grand Trunk's charter through the Assembly in 1854 and was prouder of that than of any other action in his life. Hugh Allan, a banker, shipping magnate, and railway promoter, made large contributions to Cartier's election campaigns. In return for the donations he received railway charters, favourable legislation, and the repeal of laws he disliked.

Politics and business were thus closely entwined. Hugh Allan's lawyer for example, later testified before the Railway Committee: "On every one of these subjects—steamships, railways, canals—the Government had a policy which was favourable to his [Allan's] views, and in my opinion three times the sum would have been well spent had it been necessary to keep a government in power which had ... the improvement of the country so deeply at heart as this Government appears to." Cartier, who reportedly said that Irish voters could be bought for a "barrel of flour apiece and some salt fish thrown in for the leaders," was obviously able to make good use of Hugh Allan's money.

267

The politicians themselves usually had fierce verbal battles in committee and on the floor of the Assembly concerning any business-related decisions that the government made. Representatives from Quebec City, for example, like Commissioner of Crown Lands Joseph Cauchon and Mayor Hector Langevin, protested vehemently that their pet project, the North Shore Railway to Quebec, was sabotaged by the Grand Trunk and its Montreal political allies Cartier and Galt (who had no intention of allowing trade to be diverted downstream).

"Rep by Pop"

As time passed, dissatisfaction with the legislative union grew, particularly in Canada West. Some representatives of both sections advocated the double majority vote. This implied that government ministers from each section of the colony needed the support of the majority of their section's members and, as a corollary, that controversial legislation could not be imposed upon one section of the colony by a majority comprised largely of members from the other. Yet governments frequently had a difficult time building a simple majority, let alone finding majority support in both Canadas. In the 1840s, many measures were indeed "imposed" upon the eastern section of the colony by majorities from the west. After 1850, the shoe was often on the other foot as large numbers of *Bleus* helped adopt laws such as the Scott Act of 1863, which gave added privileges to Canada

West's Roman Catholic schools, that were approved by only a minority of members from the upper section (see chapter 15). The double majority principle was simply unworkable. Only separation of the two sections, albeit within a federal system, could permit development according to each section's special needs and interests.

In the early 1850s, Canada West's population surpassed that of Canada East. The Clear Grits now took up as their campaign slogan "rep by pop." By 1857 it was the foremost plank in the Reform platform. Most inhabitants of Canada East responded with a resounding "no," however. Union had instituted equality of representation in 1841; both languages had official status; governments were headed by co-premiers, one from each of the Canadas; and each section of the province had its own attorney general and solicitor general, its own educational legislation, and its own deputy superintendent of education. Even the old pre-union names—Upper and Lower Canada—remained in common use. Some semblance of equality, indeed a crude sort of federalism, had been achieved in spite of the original intentions of the architects of union. Representation by population, it was feared, would only destroy this.

268

Towards Confederation

At the Reform party's November 1859 convention in Toronto, George Brown began to promote the idea, already advocated by the *Rouges* of Canada East, of transforming the legislative union into a highly decentralized federative union of the two Canadas. The Conservatives, however, who governed only because of their large block of French support from Canada East, refused. Moreover, they countered with suggestions for a wider British North American union. Galt entered the ministry only after extracting from the Conservatives a promise to work towards Confederation, but initially the idea aroused only perfunctory interest. The Montreal *Gazette* believed that the proposal had possibilities and suggested forming a new English-speaking province that would join portions of eastern Upper Canada with Montreal and the Eastern Townships. Then the French-speaking East could "stand still as long as it likes" and the West could "rush frantically forward," while the centre enjoyed "that gradual, sure, true progress which is the best indication of material prosperity."

The Reformers were understandably suspicious of any Conservative proposal. After all, they had just witnessed Macdonald's political manoeuvres of 1858 that had permitted him to regain power only a few hours after it had been lost to a Brown–Dorion Reform–*Rouge* coalition, aptly termed the "Short Administration."

Confederation projects were discussed throughout the early 1860s. Many

Upper Canadians were angry at having to pay for the expenditures voted by majorities built on eastern support. At last, a century after the Conquest, as George Brown said in the Canadian Legislature, the representatives of the British population might aspire to justice without having to wait while "the representatives of the French population [sit here] discussing in the French tongue whether we shall have it." At the same time, Lower Canadians protested as the newspaper *L'Ordre* put it, that without Lower Canadian help to pay Upper Canadian debts, Upper Canada today would be "nothing more or less than a forest put up for auction by British capitalists to repay their investments."

The deteriorating external situation seemed to instil a sense of urgency in resolving the political deadlock. Across the border, the Civil War raged and Britain's relations with the soon-to-be-victorious North were strained. Canadians began to fear that the Americans might decide to seek revenge on the British by attacking Canada. In addition, trade relations, which had been greatly stimulated by the Treaty of Reciprocity of 1854 as well as by the North's needs during the Civil War, continued to be endangered.

269

The deadlock that virtually paralyzed the union government provided the necessary push for change. In May 1862, the Cartier-Macdonald ministry resigned when, in the face of *Bleu* defections over the issue of conscription, its Militia Bill was defeated by the Legislature, much to the chagrin of the British government and "Little Englanders," who wished to shift more of the burden of Canadian defence away from British taxpayers. John A. Macdonald, the minister responsible for militia affairs, was unavailable during most of the debate. A Liberal administration under John Sandfield Macdonald and Louis-Victor Sicotte, a moderate liberal or "*Mauve*," took office, but the following year it failed to survive a vote of confidence and went to the people.

The 1863 elections saw the Liberals strengthened in Canada West, while in the East, the *Bleus* at least avoided a rout. The Liberal camp, however, was weakened by internal division, and in 1864 Sandfield Macdonald gave up the hopeless task of governing. The Etienne-Pascal Taché–John A. Macdonald regime that replaced it was defeated in June 1864, after barely a few weeks in office. Now that opposing forces were almost evenly balanced, Canada had clearly become ungovernable.

Any evaluation of the rather brief union period must be qualified. Certainly there was progress in many areas. The coming of responsible government represented a significant milestone in the movement toward democracy and autonomy. For the French, in particular, the dire prophecies of assimilation, made at the birth of union, did not materialize, though ethnic and religious prejudice remained rampant throughout the era. Chronic political instability sealed the fate of the union. By 1864, Canada was thus once again in the throes of constitutional change.

NOTES

[1] Mason Wade, *The French Canadians, 1760–1967*, vol. I (Toronto, 1968), 220.
[2] Maurice Séguin, *L'idée d'indépendance au Québec, genèse et historique* (Trois-Rivières, 1971), 36.
[3] John Robert Colombo, "Grit," *The Canadian Encyclopedia*, vol. 2 (Edmonton, 1985), p. 775. Grit is fine sand or gravel, which is often valued for its abrasive quality. The Clear Grits characterized themselves as, "all sand and no dirt, clear grit all the way through."

Related Readings

R. Douglas Francis and Donald B. Smith, *Readings in Canadian History: Pre-Confederation*; 2d ed. (Toronto, 1986) contains two important articles on this topic; see Jacques Monet, "The 1840s," pp. 287–305; and Maurice Séguin, "A Disaster," pp. 306–13.

270

BIBLIOGRAPHY

The union years are examined in J. M. S. Careless, *The Union of the Canadas: the Growth of Canadian Institutions, 1841–1857* (Toronto, 1967) and in W. L. Morton, *The Critical Years: The Union of British North America, 1857–1873* (Toronto, 1964). Maurice Séguin defends his thesis in *L'idée d'indépendance au Québec: genèse et historique* (Trois-Rivières, 1968). Paul G. Cornell, in *The Alignment of Political Groups in Canada, 1841–1867* (Toronto, 1962), treats the rather complex development of party groupings. R. C. Brown, ed., *Upper Canadian Politics in the 1850s* (Toronto, 1967) contains several helpful articles, while J. M. S. Careless, ed., *The Pre-Confederation Premiers: Ontario Government Leaders, 1841–67* (Toronto, 1980), constitutes a valuable addition to political history of the period.

Several other works also elaborate on the political developments of the period. On responsible government see George Metcalf's essay, "Draper Conservatism and Responsible Government in the Canadas, 1836–1847," *Canadian Historical Review*, 42 (1961): 300–324. A useful article on the annexation movement in Upper Canada is Gerald A. Hallowell's "The Reaction of the Upper Canadian Tories to the Adversity of 1849: Annexation and the British American League," *Ontario History*, 62 (1970): 41–56. Annexationist sentiment in French Canada is described in Jean-Paul Bernard, *Les rouges: libéralisme, nationalisme et anticléricalisme au milieu du* xixe siècle (Montréal, 1971) pp. 61–73. The conflict over the choice of a capital is recounted in David R. Knight, *A Capital for Canada: Conflict and Compromise in the 19th Century* (Chicago, 1977).

British policy towards Canada is discussed in William Ormsby, *The*

Emergence of the Federal Concept in Canada, 1839–1845 (Toronto, 1969), in Peter Burroughs, *British Attitudes towards Canada* (Toronto, 1971), and in Phillip Buckner, *The Transition to Responsible Government: British Policy in British North America* (Wesport, Conn., 1985). On French Canada in particular, see Jacques Monet's *The Last Cannon Shot: A Study of French Canadian Nationalism, 1837–1850* (Toronto, 1969). It should also be noted that many of the public figures of this age—including La Fontaine, Baldwin, Hincks, Cartier, and Morin—have been studied in the currently available volumes of the *Dictionary of Canadian Biography*.

For the Indian policy of the Union period, see John S. Milloy, "The Early Indian Acts: Developmental Strategy and Constitutional Change," in *As Long as the Sun Shines and Water Flows: A Reader in Canadian Native Studies* edited by Ian A. L. Getty and Antoine S. Lussier (Vancouver, 1983); and J. E. Hodgetts' chapter, "Indian Affairs: The White Man's Albatross," in *Pioneer Public Service, an administrative history of the United Canadas, 1841–1867* (Toronto, 1955), pp. 205–25.

271

CHAPTER FIFTEEN

Union of the Canadas: Economic and Social Developments, 1840–64

272   Great economic and social transformation accompanied political change in the two Canadas in the mid-nineteenth century. In the late 1840s Britain adopted free trade, an event that led, with the signing of a reciprocity treaty with the United States in 1854, to a new north–south orientation to the Canadas' trade. The United Canadas also in the 1850s obtained a railway system that greatly transformed the agricultural, commercial, and urban character of the province. Large-scale immigration to Canada West and considerable emigration from Canada East altered social and cultural life at mid-century. Education, especially in Canada West, became a much-debated social issue.

Commercial Empire of the St. Lawrence

Canadian historian Donald Creighton developed the Laurentian interpretation of Canadian history; that is, whoever controlled the St. Lawrence could dominate the economic life of the continent.[1] The American Revolution and the Treaty of 1783 created an artificial political boundary along the St. Lawrence and the Great Lakes, dividing the continent into two political units. But the political boundary did not immediately become a commercial one. Until the 1860s the merchants of Montreal vied with those of New York for dominance of the commercial trade of the interior of North America.

In the early 1840s the merchants of Montreal continued to compete successfully against their American counterparts, thanks to the highly favourable mercantile system of trade that the British North American colonies had with Britain. The British desired two staples that were readily available in the United Canadas: timber and wheat. Square-hewed timber, made from Canadian white and red pine, continued to be in demand for the masts of sailing ships. In addition, sawed lumber for construction found a lucrative market in Britain in the 1840s. Wood thus became British North America's most valuable export commodity, making up nearly two-thirds of the value of all the colonies' exports to Britain in the 1840s. But the lumber industry was a vulnerable and volatile one, subject to fluctuating demand in Britain, low tariffs after 1842, and overproduction—all of which caused many businesses to go bankrupt during the 1840s and 1850s.

Within the United Canadas a second commodity—wheat, in the form of either coarse grain or ground flour—rivalled timber. Canada West was the greatest producer of wheat in British North America. After 1840 a combination of good weather and increased acreage due to rapid settlement of the rich farmland of Canada West greatly increased yields. The average farmer's export of wheat doubled from 45 bushels in the 1840s to 80 in the 1850s, and went as high as 135 bushels in the 1860s. Improved transportation on the St. Lawrence–Great Lakes with the completion of the *273* canal system lowered transport costs and reduced insurance rates, all helped to increase Canadian exports. The fact that Britain lowered duties on colonial wheat in 1842, and again in the fall of 1843, also raised exports; this made Canada West one of the chief suppliers of wheat to feed the growing urban population of industrial Britain.

TRANSPORTATION

The export of bulky staples like wheat and timber required a sophisticated transportation system. Roads were needed to get wheat to urban centres for local marketing or export. In the 1840s a series of roads, some of which were little more than dirt paths, crisscrossed the United Canadas. More important for transportation was the canal system linking Lake Erie with Montreal and the Atlantic Ocean. During the 1840s the government of the Canadas widened and deepened existing canals such as the Welland and the Lachine. It built new canals between Montreal and Prescott, where rapids and shallows had always impeded shipping, and at Beauharnois, Cornwall, and Williamsburg. In 1848 a chain of first-class canals enabled the St. Lawrence–Great Lakes to rival the Erie–Hudson River route and to compete with New York as the major exporting and importing centre for the North American continent.

New York, however, had considerable advantages. It was a larger and, unlike Montreal, a year-round ice-free port. Also, in 1845–46 the American government passed the Drawback Acts, which allowed Canadian exports and imports to pass in bond through American waterways duty free, thus making it profitable for Canada West farmers and timber merchants to ship via the United States. Finally, New York had the advantage of being linked to the growing American Midwest by an extensive railway system.

Advent of British Free Trade and Repercussions for the United Canadas

In 1846 the British government under Prime Minister Robert Peel made an important decision that had far-reaching implications for the British North American colonies: it adopted free trade measures (for the political repercussions of this decision see chapter 14). Pressure on the British government to end the old colonial mercantile system came chiefly from factory owners who wanted to reduce tariffs, thus enabling Britain to compete in a world market. They also sought the repeal of the Corn Laws, British protective tariffs on grain, arguing that repeal of the laws would mean cheaper food for the working class, and hence employers could lower wages.

274

Liberal economists such as Richard Cobden disproved traditional mercantile theories by pointing out the costs, economically and militarily, of keeping colonies. They argued persuasively in favour of *laissez-faire* economics and free trade as benefitting all Britons. Historian J.M.S. Careless has summarized their argument: "When the whole world was its domain for markets and supplies, what reason was there to guide and husband overseas possessions that cost much more to maintain than they could ever return?"[2]

These free-trade lobbyists formed the Anti-Corn Law League, which convinced the Peel government to repeal the Corn Laws in 1846. Other free-trade measures included the lowering of the timber preference in 1842, when the duty on foreign imports was cut in half, from fifty-five shillings to thirty shillings a load. Further reductions followed in 1845, 1846, 1848, and 1851. Then in 1849 Britain ended the Navigation Laws, which had restricted the ports to which British ships could sail and the markets in which they could sell their produce. Britain wanted to purchase raw materials at the lowest possible price and to sell manufactured goods wherever it desired. The United States, in turn, obtained access to the Canadian–British trade and to all the Great Lakes trade.

Britain's move to free trade initially had a catastrophic impact on the Canadas. The economic and political life of the British North American colonists rested on their relationship to England. They had lived in a protected trading system, with a privileged access to British markets. Now it appeared as though they had been set adrift by an indifferent mother country. They reacted with resentment, especially the Montreal merchants who, with the arrival of free trade, saw the demise of their dream of the commercial empire of the St. Lawrence. The current world depression added to the city's problems as bankruptcies spread. A movement to eliminate the problem by gaining access to the large American market began to take shape. Annexation manifestos circulated throughout the Canadas (see chapter 14).

From Transatlantic to Transcontinental Trade

With the advent of British free trade the Canadas neither collapsed nor joined the United States. Commerce revived as British North Americans adjusted to meet the new challenges and to set new economic priorities. This process of adjustment first involved increased trade with the United States and, second, a new emphasis on railways as the major means of transportation. These two goals were complementary. Just as the waterways had been the best means of facilitating east–west trade across the continent and ultimately with Britain, railways best linked the Canadas with the United States for the north–south trade.

275

This transition came swiftly and dramatically. By 1850 the world depression was lifting and prosperity returning through increased trade. Whereas industrialism in Britain had led indirectly to a *decrease* in trade for the British North American colonies, industrialism in the United States led directly to an *increase* in markets for the Canadian staple products—timber and wheat. The rapidly growing cities of the eastern seaboard and of the American Midwest needed lumber, the universal building material at the time, to construct houses and commercial buildings.

The era of the 1850s inaugurated what one historian, A.R.M. Lower, has described as "the North American assault on the Canadian forest."[3] Demand for Canadian lumber increased, and American lumber firms and sawmill owners established themselves in Canadian forest areas, especially the Ottawa valley.

Equally, Canadian timber found a rising market in the United Canadas with its growing immigrant population. Pioneer settlers were as much consumers as producers. Saw and planing mills, sash and shingle factories, and cabinet-making firms served this market. Britain also increased its demand for Canadian lumber in the prosperous years of the 1850s; despite the move to free trade, it remained the most lucrative market for Canadian timber until into the 1860s.

Canadian wheat did equally well during the prosperous 1850s. A wheat boom developed during the Crimean War of 1854–56, when Britain excluded Russian grain from its ports. Americans also purchased quantities of Canadian wheat to feed their growing urban population. Exports of Canadian wheat and flour via the St. Lawrence more than doubled to nearly ten million bushels by 1856—a figure not surpassed until the next decade. Furthermore, prices tripled in the same period. As a result, agriculture surpassed timber as the major staple of Canadian—indeed of all British North American—trade in the 1850s.

Farmers in Canada West benefitted the most from this increased demand for wheat. Good prices along with high yields provided them with capital to increase their acreage and to diversify their farming. In addition to wheat, they exported wool, meat, eggs, butter, and cheese, especially to the United States.

Their compatriots in Canada East did not fare as well. Contrary to Canada West, where new fertile land remained available until the mid-1850s, a shortage of good agricultural land along with problems of climate and a lower fertility led to serious farm problems. Farmers in Canada East produced little wheat for export, although they did export such other grains as oats and barley, along with dairy products in limited quantities.

276

Reciprocity with the United States

To secure this lucrative trade with the United States, the government of the Canadas wanted a reciprocal trade agreement. Negotiations continued for eight years due to strong American protectionist sentiment. When the Americans finally became receptive to the idea in the early 1850s, Canadians were less enthusiastic, because they were then enjoying active trade with the Americans without an agreement. But, as J.M.S. Careless notes: "The emerging economic pattern of the early fifties indicated that if Canada could do without reciprocity, she could do much better with it."[4] The British government endorsed the idea, too, seeing closer economic ties between these two countries as a means of easing tensions and reducing Canadian dependence on the mother country.

Before agreement could be reached, however, two contentious issues needed to be settled. One, internal to the United States, was the slavery issue, because it affected the entry of new territories into the union. The divisions between the slave South and the free North affected all aspects of American development at the time, including economic relations with the British North American colonies. By the early 1850s a delicate balance had been achieved, and both sides feared that the incorporation of new states would offset this balance in favour of the other side. Northern senators favoured free trade because they believed it was a prelude to annexation, which in turn would lead to a preponderance of free states in the union. Southern senators opposed it for the same reason, until Lord Elgin, who went to Washington in May 1854 to persuade American senators to endorse free trade, convinced them that a prosperous Canada through free trade would be more likely to *want* independence from, rather than to favour annexation to, the United States.

The other issue in dispute concerned Maritime fisheries. Britain and the United States had different interpretations of the territorial waters from which American fishermen were excluded under the Convention of 1818. New England fishermen claimed a right to fish in waters three miles (five kilometres) out from shore and following the shoreline. Maritime fishermen claimed a boundary three miles from headland to headland, thus leaving most of the bays and inlets as exclusive British territory. Neither side wanted an armed conflict, and Britain was willing to use the fisheries issue as a negotiating tool for free trade of colonial natural products in the United States.

THE RECIPROCITY TREATY

The Reciprocity Treaty of 1854, approved by the American Congress and ratified by the colonial legislatures, allowed for free trade of major natural products, such as timber, grain, coal, livestock, and fish, between the British North American colonies and the United States, mutually free navigation on the American-controlled Lake Michigan and the Canadian-controlled St. Lawrence, and joint access to all coastal fisheries north of the 36th parallel. The agreement ran for a ten-year period commencing in 1855 and was subject to renewal or termination

For Canadians, this reciprocity agreement bolstered the era of prosperity already underway. After 1854 Canadians had one foot in the British market and the other in the American market. They moved closer to their future role as a member of the North Atlantic triangle, a reciprocal trade relationship between Britain, the United States, and Canada.

The Railroad Era

Closer economic ties with the United States coincided with the railway building era in the Canadas. Suddenly canal-building seemed old-fashioned. Increased Canadian-American trade provided the incentive, rationale, and prosperity for railway building; in turn, the railways provided the means for greater continental economic integration.

Railroad building proceeded at a rapid pace in the 1850s. At the beginning of the decade, there were only 105 km of track in all British North America; by the end of the decade, there were 2880 km in the Canadas alone. Such expansion came as a result of the combination of popular interest, public and private financial support, and private promotion.

Governments eagerly courted railways. Railways required large expenditures of public funds and brought governments to the brink of bankruptcy, but they were believed to be worth the price. Since Canadians arrived late in the competition for railways (compared to Britain and the United States) and the country was as yet hardly industrialized, most of the capital for railway building had to come from outside the country, usually first from Britain and then from the United States.

As the governments in British North America had insufficient credit ratings to borrow vast sums abroad, they inevitably became involved in railway financing. But unlike canal building, in which the government often took control through public ownership, private corporations built railways with extensive government financial assistance. This partnership between government and private business built railways, but at the same time it led to waste, duplication of services, an excessive drain on the public treasury, and, most of all, to corruption through bribery of politicians for railway contracts (see chapter 14).

Two parliamentary acts introduced the government of the Canadas into railway financing. The first was the Guarantee Act. In April 1849, Francis Hincks, the father of railway financing in the Canadas, put forward a bill that would allow the government to guarantee the interest, at a rate not more than 6 percent, on half the bonds of any railway more than 120 km in length, provided that half of the railway had already been built. The act made it considerably easier for railway companies to secure capital, but it also encouraged overexpansion; companies built more track than they would have without such assistance. Under the Guarantee Act the Canadian government extended approximately $33 million to railways. In most cases, the assistance amounted to an outright subsidy, since the private companies eventually repaid little of the money.

With the second bill, the Municipal Act, government became involved in railway financing to an even greater extent. This act empowered municipalities to lend money to railway companies for construction within their boundaries. Unfortunately, however, most municipalities lacked the large amounts of revenue needed to invest and did not have a sufficient credit rating to borrow abroad. So in 1852 Hincks devised the Municipal Loan Fund Act, by which the municipalities could pool their credit and grant the Canadian government the right to float the necessary loans on their behalf. Once the money was acquired, the government then lent it to the municipalities, who in turn invested it in the railways. Before being discontinued in 1859, the fund added $15 000 000 (£3 million) to the provincial debt.

Private companies built four key railway lines in the United Canadas in the 1850s. Begun in 1850 and completed in 1853, the St. Lawrence and Atlantic line between Montreal and Portland, Maine, gave Montreal a year-round ice-free port on the Atlantic. This rail link once more made Montreal competitive with New York in continental trade. The second line, the Great Western Railway, completed in 1855, went from Niagara Falls via Hamilton and London to Windsor. In the east, the line joined with the New York network of railways, while in the west it connected with the Michigan Central. Ultimately, it was intended to capture the trade of the American Midwest by offering a quick route from Chicago through to New York via the Canadas. Presided over by Sir Allan MacNab and backed by British and American capital, this 575 km railway made a profit from the start. The third major line, the Northern Railway, went from Toronto on Lake Ontario to Collingwood on Georgian Bay, a distance of roughly 160 km. The Northern serviced the rich farmland north of Toronto, opened up the forested area of the Georgian Bay and Muskoka regions, and provided access to the upper lakes. The fourth and most ambitious railway scheme of the decade was the Grand Trunk.

THE GRAND TRUNK RAILWAY

Chartered by Parliament in 1853, the Grand Trunk, when completed, was to extend from Windsor, Canada West, to Halifax, Nova Scotia, thus linking the interior of British North America with an ice-free Atlantic port. When plans to build the Maritime section failed to materialize, the company purchased the St. Lawrence and Atlantic running between Montreal and ice-free Portland, Maine. The scheme proved costly, though, because the St. Lawrence and Atlantic track needed major repairs. Equally expensive was the Grand Trunk directorate's decision to build a competing line through the heart of Canada West from Toronto to Sarnia, rather than join up with the Great Western. As a result, both railways ran through the same major urban centres, often parallel to each other.

In 1859, the final year of construction, the Grand Trunk completed the Victoria Bridge, one of the great engineering feats of the century. This 2700 m bridge spanned the St. Lawrence from the north shore to the island of Montreal, thus providing rail connections between Sarnia, Canada West, and Portland, Maine.

When completed, the Grand Trunk Railway at 1760 km was the longest railroad in the world. This distinction came at great cost to the Canadian public. From the beginning, the company ran into financial trouble. Difficulty on construction plus strong competition and inflationary labour costs made the railway too costly an undertaking for London bankers Thomas Baring and George Glyn, the railway's British investors. The railway company had to come to the provincial government for relief. The government felt obligated to bail it out, especially since six of the railway company's twelve directors belonged to the Canadian cabinet.

In the end, the Canadian government's debt exceeded $60 million, with a large part of it from the Grand Trunk Railway. To make matters worse, this trunk line, designed to tap American trade for the Canadas, had a 1.65 m track gauge—wider than that used in the United States. That meant

280

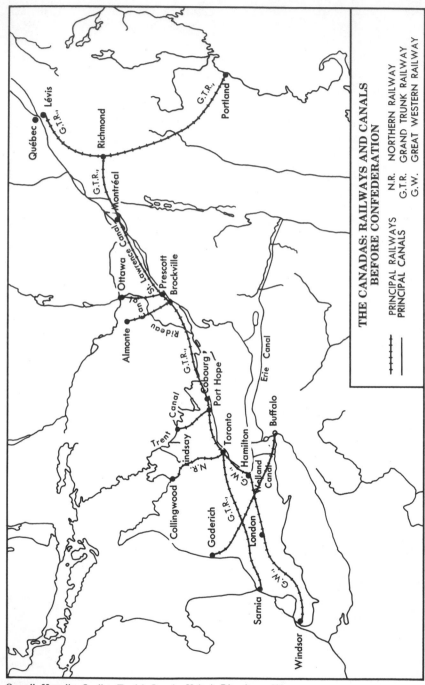

THE CANADAS: RAILWAYS AND CANALS
BEFORE CONFEDERATION

PRINCIPAL RAILWAYS	N.R.	NORTHERN RAILWAY
PRINCIPAL CANALS	G.T.R.	GRAND TRUNK RAILWAY
	G.W.	GREAT WESTERN RAILWAY

Cornell, Hamelin, Ouellet, Trudel, Canada. *Unity in Diversity*, p. 239.

American goods shipped via the Grand Trunk had to be reloaded at the border, and the railway lost most of the competition that it was built to capture! Throughout the pre-Confederation era, it never made a cent.

Urban and Commercial Development in the Canadas

The railways spurred commercial development. They required thousands of workers to lay the track and then to maintain it. New railway-related industries sprang up across the province—engine foundries, car shops, rolling mills, and metalwork shops—and all needed skilled and unskilled workers. By 1860 Canadian railways had 6600 people on their combined payrolls.

Along with canal and shipbuilding, railroads encouraged the development of a host of other secondary industries: flour mills, saw mills, tanneries, boot and shoe factories, textile shops, breweries, distilleries, wagon and carriage manufacturers. Shipbuilders in Montreal and Quebec City built many of the steamboats that plied the St. Lawrence and Great Lakes after 1809, using timber from the Ottawa valley. Ironworks were established in Hamilton because of the city's easy access to the American coal fields in Pennsylvania. Significant developments in the manufacturing of agricultural implements occurred, especially at Newcastle in Canada West, where Daniel and Hart Massey produced a combined rake, reaper, and mowing machine in 1855; it was the beginning of a lucrative Canadian business.

281

This industrial growth led to the creation of a host of towns, mainly along the rail lines, to service the prosperous agricultural hinterland. In Canada West the number of towns doubled to more than eighty between 1850 and 1870. Each provided a market centre for local produce and an import centre for manufactured goods. Fewer towns developed in the countryside of Canada East. Since limited agricultural land and poor climate in the 1850s held back urban growth in the region, French Canadians tended to emigrate to New England or to the American Midwest.

Eventually, a hierarchy of towns and cities developed, with larger urban centres servicing the smaller towns and villages within their radius of influence. London became the major centre in southwestern Canada West. Its population tripled from five thousand in 1850 to fifteen thousand in 1856. The port of Hamilton dominated the hinterland to the west and south, extending its influence into the Niagara Peninsula. Both these urban centres, London and Hamilton, became supply depots but also manufacturing centres and, in the case of Hamilton, an early industrial city.

RIVALRY OF TORONTO AND MONTREAL

Toronto became the metropolitan centre of Canada West, servicing a wealthy rural hinterland roughly extending east to Durham County, north to Barrie on Lake Simcoe, and west to Peel County. Toronto had the advantage of good harbour facilities on Lake Ontario, and as the railway hub of Canada West, it had excellent rail service to various regions of the province. Import trade was its leading commerce, rising more than fivefold in value, from $1 200 000 in 1849 to more than $6 600 000 in 1856. Its export trade continued to be based on grain and wood to external markets, especially in the United States but also in Britain.

A new urban mercantile elite appeared in Toronto in the 1850s. Its members founded the Toronto Board of Trade as a means of strengthening the city's hold on commerce. In 1852 the Toronto Stock Exchange opened, and in 1856 the Bank of Montreal inaugurated its Toronto office. By the end of the decade the city had become the undisputable regional business centre of Canada West.

282

Toronto, however, could not replace Montreal as the largest city in British North America and the dominant metropolitan centre of the United Canadas. As one of the oldest centres in British North America, Montreal had an initial advantage that increased during the booming years of the mercantile system of trade. After a temporary setback in the late 1840s, the city surfaced again as a prosperous centre in the 1850s. Its important location on the St. Lawrence continued to benefit the city, especially since canal improvements in the 1840s still made it cheaper and more efficient to ship goods by water than by rail.

Even in the competition for rail traffic, Montreal fared well once the Grand Trunk Railway was completed. The Portland, Maine branch provided the city with an ice-free port on the Atlantic and provided access to the agricultural hinterland of Canada West and, to an extent, the American Midwest. Equally, Montreal served as an important import centre for the growing population of Canada West, rivalling Toronto for this lucrative market. Montreal also benefitted from the Reciprocity Treaty of 1854, which helped it to become a major export centre of Canadian timber and wheat for American markets.

Service industries in Montreal grew in conjunction with increased trade. Footwear manufacturers, furriers, wood products manufacturers, distilleries, breweries, tobacco factories, brickyards, and sugar refineries opened their doors. Metal-based industries, such as the Victoria Iron Works (the largest industry with 120 workers), also developed.

Social Developments in the United Canadas

Canadian society in the mid-nineteenth century was in a state of transition. Annually, 25 000–40 000 immigrants entered the province, especially into the western section. In 1851 Canada West for the first time surpassed the population of Canada East. Overall, the Canadas' population went from 1 100 000 in 1841 to almost 2 000 000 in 1851. A large number of new immigrants came from Ireland, part of the famine migration resulting from the failure of the potato crop.

Traditionally, historians have described these Irish as mainly impoverished Catholics from southern Ireland who lacked farming experience and money; they ended up in ghettos in the cities and towns, especially in Canada East. Recent research by historian Donald Akenson reveals, however, that by far the largest percentage (more than 75 percent) of Irish immigrants farmed on isolated homesteads in rural areas. Furthermore, more than two-thirds were Protestant.

More American Blacks came to the United Canadas. The passage of the Fugitive Slave Act in the United States in 1850 meant that thousands of presumably free Blacks living in the northern states were liable to be captured and sent back into bondage. Canadian abolitionists organized the Canadian Anti-Slavery Society in 1851 to help these refugees escape. The largest number crossed at Detroit and settled near the border. Most went home after the passage of the Emancipation Act of 1863, having found temporary refuge, but no more tolerance than they had experienced in the United States.

MIGRANT MOBILITY

Within the province itself, people moved frequently. In a case study of rural Peel County, just west of Toronto, social historian David Gagan has shown that prior to 1840, the county had ample cheap land and a relatively self-sufficient population living off its own land and livestock. Two decades later, it had become a major wheat exporting region. Young people moved away from the now-overpopulated country areas, either to newer farming areas within the province, to the growing towns and cities of Canada West, or to other areas, such as the American Midwest. Those who stayed in Peel tended to be better off, with larger farms, a higher standard of living, and better-educated children than those who left. In general, people who did not move tended to be more prosperous than the transient in nineteenth-century North America.

Transiency also characterized the urban centres of Canada West. In a quantitative study of Hamilton, social historian Michael Katz notes that the city's population increased in five years (1846–50) by 150 percent, and that individuals within this rapidly growing city moved frequently. More than one-third of those listed in the 1851 census could not be located for the 1861 census. This mobility was true of all social groups, from lower to upper class; people of all groups and all ages sought to improve their lot in life. And within the various occupational categories, the stable populations again tended to be more prosperous than those on the move.

URBAN SOCIAL STRUCTURE

Within the city of Hamilton, as in the other towns and cities of Canada West, a fairly rigid social structure existed, with a small elite dominating the social and political life of the community. As well, a growing commercial middle class consisting of merchants, shopkeepers, and artisans had a prominent place. In Toronto, a wealthy elite of entrepreneurs such as William McMaster, an Irish wholesale merchant, banker, and philanthropist (McMaster University is named after him) and William Gooderham, a distiller, businessman, and banker; and in Hamilton, Charles and Edward Gurney, American-born stove manufacturers, dominated the commercial life of their cities, making their influence felt even in the small neighbouring towns that depended on imported and manufactured goods from their companies.

Equally evident in the towns and cities was a rising professional class of clergymen, lawyers, doctors, and teachers. Below them stood the large class of wage labourers, made up mostly of immigrants. This urban proletariat suffered from poor housing, inadequate sanitation conditions, and seasonal unemployment. Most relied on their own ingenuity to survive, as virtually no help came from government. The prevailing ethos held that success came to those who worked hard; frustration and failure could only be the result of waste and a lack of individual initiative. Canada West thus remained a society modelled on the agrarian values of hardy "yeoman farmers" and robust, self-reliant pioneers.

The church reinforced that attitude in its parishioners. Religion played an important role in Upper Canadian society. Most Canadians attended church. The Church of England was the declared church of 22 percent of the population in 1840. The Presbyterians at 20 percent and the Methodists at 17 percent (several schisms within the Methodist Church had caused them to lose their position as the most numerous denomination in Canada West) were the next largest denominations. The Baptists, Quakers, Lutherans, and Congregationalists together had 6 percent. The Roman Catholic population stood at 14 percent in 1841, most of it made up of Irish-Catholic immigrants.

In Canada East people migrated as well, many to the United States. With a decline in agriculture and a sluggish timber trade (the two mainstays of the Quebec economy), hard economic times overtook the French Canadians in the 1840s and 1850s. Existing land was depleted, new agricultural land was scarce, seigneuries were subdivided to the point where the habitants could no longer support their families, and unemployment was high in the urban centres. This crisis, along with continued high birth rates, a declining death rate, and increased British immigration, forced many French Canadians to move.

Some chose to settle in the Eastern Townships, where limited good agricultural land still existed, but most went to work in the New England factories. Others went to farm the virgin land of the American Midwest. As the Quebec historian Fernand Ouellet has noted: " ... between 1840 and 1850 French-Canadian emigration to the United States acquired a magnitude hitherto unknown."[5] An estimated thirty thousand emigrants left during the decade.

The move of French Canadians to the cities and to the United States alarmed the Quebec clergy, who feared a loss of spiritual influence over their parishioners. After 1844 the Roman Catholic church became actively involved in the colonization movement designed to settle the northern areas of Quebec and, more importantly, to preserve the attributes of traditional family and religious life. "Let us take possession of the soil, it is the best means of preserving our nationality" became the rallying cry of the agrarian nationalism of the 1840s and 1850s. Yet for many French Canadians, the appeal went unheeded. They wanted to escape agriculture, and left for better economic conditions in "les Etats."

URBAN DEVELOPMENT IN QUEBEC

Some signs existed of increased urban growth in Canada East, but urban concentration took place only in a few centres. Even a long-established town like Trois-Rivières had a population of only three thousand in the 1840s, while Sorel and Hull were virtually villages. The educated professional middle class of doctors, lawyers, and teachers constituted the elites in these communities. Sherbrooke was becoming the commercial centre for the predominantly English-speaking area of the Eastern Townships, but at mid-century it was still a village with a population of less than one thousand.

Only two urban centres could claim the title "city" in Canada East in the 1850s. The oldest of the two was Quebec, the centre of the timber trade. The majority of its commercial elite were English-speaking families associated with that trade in some respect. Many of the city's numerous

National Gallery of Canada.

286

William Raphael, a German-born Jewish artist, emigrated to Montreal in 1857.
A decade later, he captured the activity of Montreal's waterfront in this painting.

labourers, who inhabited the lower part (*basse-ville*) of the city, also worked
in the timber industry. Here in overcrowded and dirty conditions French
Canadian and Irish workers intermingled. In contrast, the upper town,
made up predominantly of the English, was considered "one of the cleanest
cities in the world." In the northern section around St. John Street (rue
St. Jean) lived merchants, retail traders, artisans, and numerous tavern-
keepers, while in the southern part resided officers and government officials.

Montreal was the largest and most socially advanced city in British North
America. As factories were built in the 1840s and 1850s on the shores of
the Lachine Canal in the west and closer to the centre of town, along the
St. Lawrence in the neighbourhoods of Sainte-Marie and Hochelaga, the
population grew rapidly. Employment prospects attracted workers from
the countryside who might otherwise have emigrated to the United States;
these French Canadians, along with the Irish immigrants, provided cheap
labour for the new industries.

The eastern end of the city, particularly the districts of Sainte-Anne
and Sainte-Marie, was overwhelmingly working class and predominantly
French Canadian. The west end was decidedly bourgeois and British. The
English-Canadian commercial entrepreneurs had begun to move "up the
mountain" to build luxurious residences on Mount Royal. The Quebec
historian, Paul-André Linteau, argues that "social divisions became so
visible in Montreal's industrial sector that the city earned the fitting description: 'City of wealth and death.' "[6]

A WORKING-CLASS CONSCIOUSNESS

A working-class consciousness began to develop in the Canadas by mid-century. A few, generally skilled, workers joined together in the 1830s to form local trade unions or self-help organizations such as the Ship Labourers' Benevolent Society. With a definite skill to offer employers, they enjoyed far more job security than the labourers. Occasionally, when conditions became desperate, skilled and unskilled workers united to stage strikes. Labourers on the Lachine Canal in 1843 and those on the Welland Canal in 1844–45 went on strike to demand better working conditions and proper wages in what was clearly a draconian working environment. Railway workers engaged in bitter strikes that at times ended in rioting and the destruction of property. In 1849 during the protests over free trade, shoemakers in Montreal ravaged a shoe factory and destroyed the sewing machines, in the tradition of the British Luddites, who opposed the mechanization of industry.

287

These expressions of working-class dissatisfaction were countered by the police or military personnel hired by employers or directed by government officials. They acted swiftly; the Rebellions of 1837–38 had shown the danger of letting unrest go unchecked.

Another impact of a rising proletariat, especially in Canada East, was the abandonment of children of poorer families to the Grey Nuns' Foundling Hospital. An estimated twelve thousand children became wards of the church between 1840 and 1870. The majority died at a young age as a result of their weakened condition upon arrival and the lack of pasteurized milk.

PROHIBITION MOVEMENT

The rise of an urban working class also had an impact on the prohibition movement throughout British North America. By the 1850s there was a noticeable shift in emphasis from temperance—abstinence through self-discipline—to prohibition—use of the power of the state to control, and hopefully eliminate, alcohol. Social historian, Graeme Decarie, suggests that this shift in Canada West came about from a perceived threat to traditional Protestant middle-class values from the growing working class (often made up of non-Protestants, such as Irish Catholics). Prohibition was a means for middle-class Protestants to reassert their position of power and prominence. Furthermore, many rural inhabitants saw alcoholism as a predominantly urban phenomenon, another example of urban moral decay. "To them," Decarie notes, "a vote for prohibition was a vote for rural virtue and against urban decadence."[7]

288

Archives Nationale du Quebec.

Sexual escapades and charges of embezzlement ended the priesthood of Charles Chiniquy, Lower Canada's greatest temperance speaker in the 1840s. After his excommunication in 1856, he became a Protestant and waged a war of slander against the Roman Catholic Church until his death in 1899.

Quebec's great "apostle of temperance" was Charles Chiniquy, a lively and eccentric Roman Catholic priest. He founded the Société de Tempérance in 1840 and by 1844 persuaded thousands to take the pledge of abstinence. "Everywhere his zeal goes, intemperance flies," the newspaper *Le Canadien* reported. His "zeal" took him to Kamouraska, Longueuil, and Montreal. (Later involved in a scandal he was sent to Kankakee, a region in Illinois about eighty kilometres south of Chicago. After his subsequent expulsion from the Church, he married and converted to Protestantism).

Education and Culture in the United Canadas

In the mid-nineteenth century, education became a critical issue. Schools grew at a rapid rate to keep pace with the growing population, and the question of separate schools soon became a controversial one.

A move to non-sectarian education in Canada West took place in the 1840s and 1850s. State-supported schools under the sponsorship of the churches still existed, but they were on the defensive. In 1841 the government of the Canadas passed an Education Act extending the common schools throughout the western half of the united province. The act created the office of Superintendent of Education to oversee educational matters and established local boards of education with powers to tax inhabitants in each district to build and maintain a school. Opposition to the bill arose among those who argued for separate denominational schools to insure that religion was an integral part of education. The government gave in to this pressure to introduce a separate school clause and to elect trustees responsible for establishing and maintaining separate common schools. These separate schools received funding in proportion to the number of children in attendance.

At the heart of the separate school controversy lay the question of the role of education. Roman Catholic leaders believed that education should have a religious component and that religious instruction should be in keeping with the teachings and beliefs of the Roman Catholic church. Catholic bishops argued that the common schools were non-religious or, at best, Protestant in orientation. They opposed teaching Catholic children from the Protestant Bible; only separate schools, they felt, could insure a proper Catholic and moral education. Furthermore, such church leaders as Rev. Armand Charbonnel, Bishop of Toronto, argued for the right of Catholic parents to direct the education of their own children.

Opponents of separate schools, such as Egerton Ryerson, the Methodist minister who served as superintendent of education for Canada West (Ontario) from 1844 to 1876, and George Brown, the influential political reformer and editor of the Toronto *Globe*, argued that education should be free, publicly funded, and non-sectarian. They believed that separate schools perpetuated sectarianism—an unhealthy development in education—and undermined the common school system. Brown further argued that separate schools would allow the church to undermine the educational system and give the Bishop of Rome undue influence in national affairs. The debate raged in the religiously intolerant atmosphere of the 1850s, hindering any acceptable compromise.

Separate and common schools proliferated in the 1850s and 1860s. By the School Act of 1853, a full-scale Catholic separate school system came into effect. The system had its own separate school board, with tax support coming from parents, who were exempt from paying common school taxes. A share of the provincial grant also paid expenses. Another school bill in

1855 allowed ten resident Roman Catholic freeholders the right to set up a separate school by electing three trustees and notifying the municipal authorities of their action. The number of separate schools grew from 41 in 1855 to 161 by 1867.

The final pre-Confederation education act, that of 1863, allowed separate schools to receive a share of both the provincial and municipal grants. Separate schools were also extended into rural areas. In return for these concessions, separate schools, like their common school counterparts, submitted to provincial inspection, centralized control of curriculum and textbooks, and government control of all teacher training.

This was the system in effect when Canada West entered Confederation as the province of Ontario in 1867. It was also the system referred to in section 93 of the British North America (BNA) Act, which stated that nothing in any law relating to denominational schools "shall prejudicially affect any right or privilege ... which any class of persons have by law in the province at the Union."

Common schools also came under greater centralized control as a result of Superintendent of Education Egerton Ryerson's efforts. In his Common School Act of 1846, he established a board of education (later the Council of Public Instruction) responsible for assisting the chief superintendent in establishing provincial standards, founded a normal school to train teachers, and held locally elected school boards responsible for operating the schools in their sections. Here lay the basis for the modern Ontario school system.

In Canada West a similar process of secularism occurred in higher education. Under the direction of Ryerson, in 1849 the government changed the Anglican-affiliated King's College into the non-sectarian University of Toronto. Once King's was transformed into the "godless" University of Toronto, Strachan in 1851 founded the Anglican Trinity University. (At the turn of the century, Trinity, the Methodist Victoria University, and St. Michael's, a Roman Catholic college founded in 1852, all became affiliates of the University of Toronto.)

EDUCATION IN QUEBEC

Canada East or Quebec had Roman Catholic and Protestant schools, but the majority of schools were Catholic. The Lower Canadian School Act of 1846 provided for the two state-aided school systems. Within each, the curé or minister had the right to veto the selection of teachers and textbooks, thus leaving only the task of financing the schools to the provincial authorities. Most teachers belonged to religious orders.

Not until 1851 did the Legislature pass an act to establish a normal school to educate teachers, and then it took six years before it became operational. In 1859 the Council of Public Instruction was established. Consisting of fourteen members (ten Catholic and four Protestant) plus the superintendent of education, it was responsible for assisting the superintendent in making regulations for the normal school, for the organization and administration of common schools, and for the grading of schools and teachers.

At the university level, McGill University, chartered in 1821, became an influential institution. It admitted both English and French Canadians (although instruction was in English only) for advanced education in law, medicine, and the arts. Under the guidance of its able principal, William Dawson, appointed in 1855, McGill later acquired a distinguished reputation, especially in scientific research and medicine. In 1852 the Université Laval was established, having developed out of the Séminaire de Québec founded by Bishop Laval in 1663. Steeped in the French Catholic tradition, the first French-Canadian university soon came to hold a position of respect in Canada East, with offerings in theology, civil law, medicine, and the arts.

291

CULTURE IN THE CANADAS

With the growth of towns and cities the United Canadas witnessed the transformation of Canadian society. This maturity was reflected in cultural developments. In Canada East, François-Xavier Garneau wrote a monumental history of French Canada. Good quality newspapers existed, such as Montreal's *La Minerve* and Quebec City's *Le Canadien*. French-Canadian journalists and public figures gave well-attended lectures (many at Montreal's *Institut canadien*) on popular topics of the day—education, national traits, and *la position de la femme*. In 1843 Ludger Duvernay, the editor of *La Minerve*, organized the Société Saint Jean Baptiste de Montréal. Many prominent French Canadians joined this patriotic organization, established to help, and to promote the interests of, French Canada. In the larger centres of Montreal and Quebec, drama, art, and music flourished.

There also appeared the beginnings of an English-Canadian culture. William Kirby described the migration of Loyalists to Niagara in his poem *The U.E.*, while Charles Sangster captured the majestic beauty of the Canadian landscape in *The St. Lawrence and the Saguenay*. Amateur historians, such as John Richardson (*The War of 1812*) and Robert Christie (*History of the Late Province of Lower Canada*), extolled the virtues of the early pioneers of the provinces. From 1847 to 1851, George Copway, an Ojibwa Indian from Rice Lake in Canada West, published four books in the United States, including the first autobiography by a Canadian Indian, and the first history of the Ojibwa Indians. In 1855 John McMullen, a journalist, produced the first history of English Canada, *The History of Canada from First Discovery to the Present Time*. While lacking Garneau's drive and flair, McMullen did have a justification for his history: "to infuse a spirit of Canadian nationality into the people generally—to mould the native born citizen, the Scotch, the English and the Irish emigrant into a compact whole." Newspapers, among them Toronto's *Globe* and the *Leader*, helped cultivate this national feeling.

Between 1840 and 1864 the United Canadas underwent considerable economic and social change. Canadians adjusted to the end of the mercantile system of trade, to the advent of the railway age, and to rapidly changing social conditions in both rural and urban life. This was an age of transition from a British-oriented to an American-oriented economy and from a pioneer to a commercial society. The shift took decades to complete, but it began in the period 1840–60.

292

NOTES

[1] See Donald Creighton, *The Commercial Empire of the St. Lawrence* (Toronto, 1937).
[2] J.M.S. Careless, *The Union of the Canadas: The Growth of Canadian Institutions, 1841–1857* (Toronto, 1967), p. 111.
[3] See A.R.M. Lower, *The North American Assault on the Canadian Forest* (Toronto, 1938).
[4] Careless, *Union of the Canadas*, p. 136.
[5] Fernand Ouellet, *Economic and Social History of Quebec, 1760–1850* (Toronto, 1980), p. 481.
[6] Paul-André Linteau, "Montreal—City of Pride," *Horizon Canada*, number 4 (1984): 88.
[7] Graeme Decarie, "Prohibition in Canada", Canadian Museum of Civilization's *Canada's Visual History Series*, vol. 29, p. 3.

Related Readings

R. Douglas Francis and Donald B. Smith, *Readings in Canadian History: Pre-Confederation*, 2d ed. (Toronto, 1986) contains the following articles related to this topic: Jean Burnet "Occupational Differences and the Class Structure," pp. 257–69; Peter A. Russell, "Upper Canada, A Poor Man's Country? Some Statistical Evidence," pp. 269–85; John McCallum, "Urban and Commercial Development until 1850," pp. 365–83, and "Transportation," pp. 392–98; and T.C. Keefer, "Philosophy of Railroads," pp. 383–92.

BIBLIOGRAPHY

J.M.S. Careless provides an excellent survey in *The Union of the Canadas: The Growth of Canadian Institutions, 1841–1857* (Toronto, 1967). For Canada East (Quebec), also consult the final chapters in Fernand Ouellet's *Economic and Social History of Quebec, 1760–1850* (Toronto, 1980). Donald Creighton develops the Laurentian thesis in *The Commercial Empire of the St. Lawrence, 1760–1850* (Toronto, 1937). Economic questions are addressed in Michael Bliss, *Northern Enterprise, Five Centuries of Canadian Business* (Toronto, 1987); W.L. Marr and D.G. Patterson, *Canada: An Economic History* (Toronto, 1980); W.T. Easterbrook and H.G.J. Aitken, *Canadian Economic History* (Toronto, 1963); G.N. Tucker, *The Canadian Commercial Revolution 1845–1851* (Toronto, 1934; reprinted 1964); and D.C. Master, *The Reciprocity Treaty of 1854* (Toronto, 1963).

On agricultural developments in the Canadas, see John McCallum, *Unequal Beginnings: Agriculture and Economic Development in Quebec and Ontario Until 1870* (Toronto, 1980); for Canada East, see R.L. Jones, "Agriculture in the St. Lawrence Valley, 1815–1850," in *Approaches to Canadian Economic History*, edited by W.T. Easterbrook and M. Watkins (Toronto, 1967), pp. 110–26; for Canada West, see R.L. Jones, *History of Agriculture in Ontario, 1613–1880* (Toronto, 1977), and D. McCalla, "The Canadian Grain Trade in the 1840s: The Buchanan Case" and "The Wheat Staple and Upper Canadian Development," in the *Canadian Historical Association Report*, 1974, pp. 95–114 and that of 1978, p. 34–46, respectively. On the timber trade, see A.R.M. Lower, *Great Britain's Woodyard: British America and the Timber Trade 1763–1867* (Montreal, 1973). On railway building in the 1850s, see G.P. de T. Glazebrook, *A History of Transportation in Canada*, vol. 1 (Toronto, 1964); for an appreciation of the excitement of railway building, see T.C. Keefer's *The Philosophy of Railroads* (1849), reprinted with an introduction by H.V. Nelles (Toronto, 1972).

Urban and commercial development in Canada West is discussed by Jacob Spelt, *Urban Development in South-Central Ontario* (Toronto, 1972; first published 1955); and Douglas McCalla, *The Upper Canada Trade 1834–1872: A Study of the Buchanan's Business* (Toronto, 1979). For Canada East, see G. Tulchinsky, *The River Barons: Montreal Businessmen and the Growth of Industry and Transportation, 1837–1853* (Montreal, 1977); and J.I. Cooper, "The Social Structure of Montreal in the 1850s," *Canadian Historical Association Report*, 1956, pp. 63–73.

The chapters "Quebec in the Century After the Conquest," pp. 65–109; and "Ontario," pp. 110–68, in R.C. Harris and J. Warkentin, *Canada Before Confederation* (Toronto, 1974) provide an overview of social developments in the United Canadas. Donald H. Akenson's *The Irish in Ontario: A Study in Rural History* (Montreal, 1984) is a revisionist study. Two good quantitative studies to consult are David Gagan, *Hopeful Travellers: Families, Land and Social Change in Mid-Victorian Peel County, Canada West* (Toronto, 1981) and Michael Katz, *The People of Hamilton, Canada West: Family and Class in a Mid-Nineteenth Century City* (Cambridge, 1976). On French-Canadian migration, see J. Little, "The Parish and the French-Canadian Migrants to Compton County, Quebec, 1851–1891," *Histoire*

Sociale/Social History, 11 (1978): 134–43; and on immigration and cholera, G. Bilson, *A Darkened House: Cholera in the Nineteenth Century* (Toronto, 1980). Micheline Dumont *et al.*, *Quebec Women. A History* (Toronto 1987), reviews the lives of women in Lower Canada in the mid-nineteenth century.

On the history of the working class in the United Canadas, consult M.S. Cross, ed., *The Workingman in the Nineteenth Century* (Toronto, 1974); and S. Langdon's pamphlet *The Emergence of the Working-Class Movement, 1845–1875* (Toronto, 1975). On strikes, see H.C. Pentland, "The Lachine Strike of 1843," *Canadian Historical Review*, 29 (1948): 255–77; and Ruth Bleasdale, "Class Conflict on the Canals of Upper Canada in the 1840s," *Labour/Le Travailleur*, 7 (1981): 9–39, and reprinted in M.S. Cross and G.S. Kealey, eds., *Pre-Industrial Canada 1760–1849: Readings in Canadian Social History*, vol. 2 (Toronto, 1982).

Educational questions are treated in J.D. Wilson, R.M. Stamp, and L.-P. Audet, *Canadian Education: A History* (Toronto, 1970), pp. 167–89 and 214–40. For Canada West, see as well Franklin A. Walker, *Catholic Education and Politics in Upper Canada*, vol. 1 (Toronto, 1976; first published 1955), and for Canada East, Claude Galarneau, *Les collèges classiques au Canada français* (Montreál, 1978). On religion, see John S. Moir, *The Church in the British Era: From the British Conquest to Confederation* (Toronto, 1972).

Many portraits of the leading individuals in the Canadas between 1840 and 1864 appear in the *Dictionary of Canadian Biography*.

CHAPTER SIXTEEN

The Maritime Colonies, 1785–1864

After the American Revolution and the arrival of the Loyalists, four sep-   *295*
arate British Maritime colonies emerged: Nova Scotia, New Brunswick,
Prince Edward Island, and Cape Breton, the latter being separated from
the peninsula of Nova Scotia in 1784. Economically, the Maritime provinces depended on the fisheries and farming, but the full development of
the land-based resources began in the early nineteenth century. Although
Nova Scotia (to which Cape Breton was reattached in 1820) kept largely
to fishing and to trade, New Brunswick started to cut its extensive pine
forests. On Saint John's Island (renamed in 1798 Prince Edward Island
after Prince Edward, Duke of Kent, the future father of Queen Victoria)
agriculture became the mainstay of the colonial economy. The Maritimes
prospered when agriculture, the lumber industry, shipbuilding, and trade
with the West Indies expanded. By the mid-nineteenth century coal mining
had also developed in importance.

Politically, the Maritime colonies advanced from representative to responsible government in the eighty-year period from 1785 to 1864. By the
1850s Nova Scotia, New Brunswick, and Prince Edward Island had reached
political maturity. They enjoyed responsible government and had healthy
economies based on agriculture, fish, and forest products. Settled communities with churches and schools had been established. Although much
progress had been made in politics and in the economy, the Maritimes
remained an area of distinct regions and of independent ethnic groups.

Economic Developments, 1785–1815

For more than a century, trade linked New England with Britain and the
West Indies. New England sold fish, lumber, and foodstuffs to the West

Indies, which supplied molasses to New England and sugar to Britain. The mother country in turn provided New England with manufactured goods. Britain originally intended the Maritime colonies to take over New England's functions after the United States gained independence. This new trade relationship would bind the remaining colonies in the North Atlantic and the Caribbean to England. To help create such a system, Britain closed its West Indian ports to American ships.

TRADE WITH THE WEST INDIES

The Maritime colonies at this stage, however, lacked the resources and the manpower needed to supply the British West Indies. They could provide only a very small amount of the islands' needs in fish and lumber. They could not meet at all the demand for foodstuffs. Nova Scotia and New Brunswick even had to import American farm products. The Maritimes' expensive labour, its inadequate transportation system, and its landgranting system which encouraged a general dispersal of the population, all contributed to the slow development of agriculture. Moreover, with cheap imported food from the United States, little incentive existed to begin full-time farming.

Direct trade between Nova Scotia and the West Indies actually decreased in the 1790s, when Britain met the planters' demands for cheap foodstuffs by allowing American shipping access to the West Indies. Maritime merchants now found it more profitable to sell their fish in New England for export to the West Indies in American ships rather than to export directly from Nova Scotia in British vessels.

THE BEGINNINGS OF REAL ECONOMIC GROWTH

Real economic growth in the Maritimes only began with the outbreak of war with the French in 1793 and particularly with the rise of Napoleon in the late 1790s. The British government then spent lavishly on fortifications in Halifax, constructing public and military buildings. As a result, Halifax became the strongest fortress outside of Europe.

Shortly after the beginning of the Napoleonic wars a flourishing timber industry developed in British North America (see chapter 13). Industrializing Britain required a safe supply of masts and spars for the Royal Navy, and it needed building timber. The imperial government's heavy tariff preferences to British American timber stimulated New Brunswick's lumber boom. Each winter, armies of lumberjacks cut the trees and then in the spring floated them down the St. John, St. Croix, and Miramichi rivers on huge rafts. Heavily forested New Brunswick was well situated for the trade, since it was closer than Canada to Britain. By 1825 New Brunswick supplied 40 percent of Britain's huge timber requirements.

Inadvertently, the United States also promoted the prosperity of the Maritimes. After France and Britain had imposed mutual blockades on each other in 1806, President Thomas Jefferson in December 1807 prohibited all commerce out of American ports, in retaliation against both countries' restrictions on neutral trade. The policy backfired, however, for by closing American ports the American president ruined New England's trade and forced it to be conducted through illegal channels, because Britain depended on American foodstuffs as much as the United States required British manufactured goods. An active smuggling trade developed, with cargoes being transferred at sea or carried overland across the British-American frontier. In defiance of their government, American ship captains sailed into British ports, making the Maritime provinces in 1808 into a great clearinghouse for international trade. The Maritime provinces purchased and re-exported American produce and goods as if they were their own; in turn, they sold British manufactured goods to the Americans.

297

This economic activity continued during and after the outbreak of war in 1812 between Britain and the United States. The long-standing trade between the fish-exporting houses of Halifax and the British West Indies expanded in the early nineteenth century, at the time of the American embargo acts. Britain encouraged this by paying bounties on fish exported from Nova Scotia and New Brunswick to the West Indies. Convoy protection was provided, for after the British defeated the French navy at Trafalgar in 1805 there was no more danger of a French naval invasion of Britain and the admiralty could spare ships for convoy duty. The shipping of American flour, beef, and dry goods to the West Indies via the Maritime provinces began.

Ironically it was the continuance of strict American prohibitions against British trade that made Maritime harbours and towns among the busiest and most prosperous on the Atlantic seaboard. Nova Scotia's and New Brunswick's merchants and sea captains began to acquire the skill, experience, and self-confidence to allow them to challenge New England's supremacy in West Indian markets.

With only slight inconvenience, the War of 1812 actually improved the highly favourable terms of trade enjoyed by New Brunswick and Nova Scotia. Throughout the war New England participated with great reluctance. The legislatures of the New England states openly condemned the war that had ruined their commerce. So much trade continued that the Halifax paper, the *Acadian Recorder*, wrote on May 14, 1814: "Happy state of Nova Scotia! amongst all this tumult we have lived in peace and security; invaded only by a numerous host of American doubloons and dollars, which have swept away the contents of our stores and shops like a torrent... ."

298

Provincial Archives of New Brunswick.

Breaking a log jam in New Brunswick's Miramichi region, 1890. New Brunswick was British North America's greatest "timber colony."

Political History, 1785–1815

Although many economic changes came in the Maritime colonies in the thirty-year period after the American Revolution, there were but two periods of political upheaval. The first was in New Brunswick, over the methods of raising and spending public monies, and the second centred on the same issue in Nova Scotia. In 1795 the opposition in the New Brunswick assembly was focussed on James Glenie, a Scottish lumberman, who had challenged the governor's financial controls over the assembly. Governor Thomas Carleton, a younger brother of the more famous Sir Guy, believed that the opposition sought New Brunswick's independence and a revival of the principles of the American Revolution. For four years he resisted the assembly's demands for greater control over money bills and government ground to a halt. Finally Glenie's coalition broke down, but only after Carleton made great concessions. As historian W.G. Godfrey has written: "New Brunswick was witnessing the emergence of the as- *299* sembly's 'political hegemony' as power passed to the elective branch of government".[1] While Carleton officially served as the governor of New Brunswick until 1817, he left the province forever in 1803, and lived thereafter in England.

In contrast to New Brunswick the authoritarian structure and operation of the Nova Scotia government stayed largely intact. At first, a constitutional contest took place between the Loyalists and the English-speaking settlers who had arrived before the Revolution, but a wise distribution of patronage to both groups by Governor John Wentworth in the early 1790s cooled passions. Early in 1803, however, the firebrand Cottnam Tonge (pronounced "tongue") did lead a revolt in the Nova Scotia assembly. Tonge became the champion of the townspeople and the farmers then working towards responsible government. Their opponents consisted of the governor, his officials, and the great Halifax merchants.

Although initially unsuccessful (Tonge himself left the colony in 1808), the Nova Scotia Assembly in the late 1840s did eventually obtain control over the spending of public funds raised by its own vote.

Prince Edward Island in these years still suffered the effects of its land-ownership system (see chapter 8). In 1769 the island's proprietors had convinced the British government to establish a separate administration complete with a governor, council, and assembly. The tenants gained control of the assembly, but they could obtain no redress from the proprietors, many of whom were absentee owners and failed to meet their colonizing obligations or to keep up the payment of their quitrents (payments to the landlord for the use of the land).

In the early nineteenth century a popular political movement emerged, one associated with the word *escheat* which, to the tenants, meant the confiscation of all the lands of proprietors who failed to uphold their original agreements with the Crown. To a certain extent members of the local elite waged the battle for self-interested reasons. They sought to displace the absentee landlords, as the island's rulers. Well-protected by powerful groups in London the proprietors in the early nineteenth century successfully fended off the protests of the tenant-controlled assembly.

Economic Prosperity, 1815-64

The Maritimes prospered for a half century after the War of 1812. As a result of the war, the Americans lost access to Maritime in-shore fisheries.

The peace treaty of 1783 had granted American citizens fishing privileges in the in-shore waters of the British North American colonies. However, at the Treaty of Ghent, which ended the War of 1812, the British had argued that the Americans had abrogated this right by declaring war. Under the Convention of 1818 American fishermen lost the privilege of landing and drying their fish in the three Maritime colonies, retaining it only on the unsettled shores in Newfoundland. American vessels could now only enter Maritime harbours to obtain water, purchase wood, or repair damages.

For a time the Maritimers also succeeded in improving their trade ties with the West Indies. After the war when the Americans requested free access to the markets of the British West Indies, Nova Scotia and New Brunswick protested that these privileges rightly belonged only to loyal British colonies. Britain initially agreed, passing several measures to favour the shipping of goods between St. John and Halifax and the West Indies, but in the face of subsequent American retaliatory measures it backed down; the British West Indies also had complained about the higher cost of shipping American imports by the roundabout Maritime route. Finally, in 1830, Britain removed the restrictions on American trade to the islands but left duties on certain essential commodities. This arrangement allowed Nova Scotia and New Brunswick to import American produce duty free and then re-export it to the West Indies as their own. Colonial ships thus maintained much of their share of the trade.

AGRICULTURE

Improved trade relations with the West Indies strengthened the Maritime economy, but one sector remained weak—agriculture. While farming flourished in Nova Scotia's Annapolis valley, and New Brunswick's St. John River valley it did not prosper as well in other sectors of the two provinces. Nova Scotia and New Brunswick as a whole continued to depend on American foodstuffs to feed their populations and to re-export goods to the West Indies. Commercial farming remained very limited, with only Prince Edward Island, the "Garden of the Gulf," exporting large amounts of farm produce. Lack of good roads, a scattered population, and absence of protection against American imports account for the limited agricultural exports. Farming, though, remained the livelihood of more Maritimers than either logging or fishing, and a large number of lumbermen and fishermen worked on a part-time basis in agriculture to support their families.

An increase in immigration after 1815 added to the size of the local market and encouraged greater agricultural production. New Brunswick had roughly 75 000 inhabitants in 1824 and almost 200 000 by 1851. In the same period in Nova Scotia, the population rose from approximately 100 000 to 275 000. Prince Edward Island's population increased from 23 000 in 1827 to 72 000 in 1855. It became the most densely inhabited colony in British North America.

301

Population of the Maritimes

Two groups took advantage of low fares on the returning timber ships to settle in Nova Scotia and New Brunswick—the Scots and the Irish.

THE SCOTS

Even though the journey from Scotland was perilous (on one ship that left in 1827, 20 percent of those aboard died), still the Gaelic-speaking Highlanders came, usually in groups or clans.

The promise of forty hectares of free land led thousands of landless Scots to immigrate to Nova Scotia. About forty thousand Scots came to Nova Scotia in 1815–38, in particular to Cape Breton Island. On Cape Breton they became fishermen and boat builders. Others, who had been enticed to immigrate by the promise of forty hectares of free land, went into the interior to farm. Although the magnificent hills and seacoast of Cape Breton reminded them of home, the Scots were ill prepared for clearing virgin forest and had many difficulties in beginning their farms.

THE IRISH

If Scottish immigrants were more numerous than Irish in Nova Scotia, Irish immigrants outnumbered the Scots in New Brunswick. The deteriorating Irish economy and the island's overpopulation forced many Roman Catholic and Protestant Irish to move. The potato blight in the 1840s led to widespread starvation and drove nearly two million people out of Ireland.

Of the tens of thousands of Irish who boarded the timber ships headed for British North America, thousands died en route from cholera and typhoid. Still, 8000 came to New Brunswick in 1842, 9000 in 1846, and 17 000 in 1847. Only in 1848 did the numbers fall below 4000. Many of these poverty-stricken Irish congregated in the ports and lumber camps of eastern New Brunswick. A large number who had the passage money continued on to the United States. The main areas of Irish settlement in New Brunswick before 1850 were the upper St. John valley, the Bay of Fundy, and the south shore of Chaleur Bay.

302

THE BLACKS

Another group of newcomers arrived in two waves. The first post-Loyalist Blacks were the Maroons, a tribe of runaway slaves from Jamaica who had fought off all attempts to re-enslave them. With a successful slave revolt then underway in neighbouring Haiti the British grew anxious and arranged in 1796 to ship the Maroons off to Nova Scotia. But the bitter winters and the unpalatable food made Nova Scotia unbearable to them. At their own request, the British transported the Maroons and a number of the Loyalist Blacks to Sierra Leone in West Africa.

The second wave came at the end of the War of 1812. These "refugee Blacks," 3000–4000 strong, escaped from Chesapeake plantations during the British raids on Washington and Baltimore and asked to be taken to freedom. Unfortunately, they arrived when abundant, cheap white labour made it very difficult for them to find work, and they had to face discrimination and prejudice in Nova Scotia and New Brunswick. Historian W.A. Spray has written of the nearly 400 Blacks who reached St. John, New Brunswick: "It is quite clear that the black refugees were treated differently than white settlers. The policy in New Brunswick at this time was to give free grants of at least 100 acres to white settlers ... Yet the black refugees were to get only 50 acres, they were to pay for the surveys, and they were to receive licenses of occupation for three years."[2] The black holders of these documents had no security of possession as the government could simply refuse to reissue the licences.

THE ACADIANS

Just before the arrival of Scots, Irish, and Blacks, many Acadians returned from exile. The Acadians clung tenaciously to the Roman Catholic church as the one institution that took an interest in their well-being. The church established elementary schools and, in 1864, the French-language Collège Saint-Joseph at Memramcook, New Brunswick. The Collège (which a century later became the nucleus of today's Université de Moncton) furnished the Acadian population with an educated professional elite from which the community drew many of its future political leaders and its sense of Acadian identity.

In the mid-nineteenth century the Acadians began to feel a new pride in their past. Undoubtedly influenced by Henry Wadsworth Longfellow's *Evangeline*, a number of Acadians became ever more convinced that they belonged to a distinct people. In the late nineteenth century the Acadian community in northeastern New Brunswick assimilated, through intermarriage with many Irish, Scots, and English. These individuals' modern-day descendants have names like McGraw, Finn, McLaughlin, Ferguson, and Kerry, but their mother tongue is French and they consider themselves Acadian. French-Canadian immigrants from Quebec, who arrived in the late nineteenth century, were also assimilated into these Acadian communities.

303

THE AMERINDIANS

Amid the Scots, Irish, Blacks, Acadians, and descendants of the old American and Loyalist settlers, the Maritimers with the longest residency in the area had the greatest difficulty in adjusting to the changing conditions. Unlike the Indians in Upper Canada after the Proclamation of 1763, the Maritime Indians did not sign treaties with the British government by which they surrendered their lands to the Crown. In New Brunswick, for example, the newly established government simply assumed that the Crown already owned all the land. The provincial government set aside reserves for the Micmacs and the Malecites, but these lands were subject to severe encroachment. The lack of a proper description and survey of the reserve lands encouraged squatters to move into the areas that the Micmac had not settled and cultivated. Similarly, Nova Scotia established reserves upon which the Indians could settle and begin farming, but, as in New Brunswick, white squatters encroached on them.

By the 1860s the approximately 1000 Micmacs and 500 Malecites in New Brunswick had a land base of about 24 000 ha. In Nova Scotia the 1400 to 1800 Micmacs had only 8000 ha. But perhaps the Indians who faced the most difficult conditions of all were the several hundred Micmacs in Prince Edward Island who, until 1870, had just a few campsites as reserve land. In that year an English-based organization, the Aborigines' Protection Society, arranged to buy for them Lennox Island, a small island off Prince Edward Island.

Timber Industry and Shipbuilding

The exploitation of Maritime forests continued unabated after the War of 1812. Local entrepreneurs, many of them farmers and small merchants, began operations in settled or semi-settled areas of the Maritimes. The timber trade also brought into the colonies a new group of British traders and contractors interested in quick profits.

In his 1825 *History of New Brunswick*, Peter Fisher noted the heavy cost of the indiscriminate cutting down of the forests during the previous twenty years:

> The persons principally engaged in shipping the timber have been strangers who had taken no interest in the welfare of the country; but have merely occupied a spot to make what they could in the shortest possible time ... Instead of seeing towns built, farms improved and the country cleared and stocked with the reasonable returns of so great a trade, the forests are stripped and nothing left in prospect, but the gloomy apprehension when the timber is gone, of sinking into insignificance and poverty.

Initially, timber companies simply went on Crown land and cut trees, even though the trees belonged to the Crown. But from the 1820s on, the colonial government asserted themselves against the timber barons. It sold timber licences and taxed output.

Forest revenues thus became vital to New Brunswick's economy. Already by 1826 three-quarters of the province's export revenues came from wood products—square timber, lumber, and ships. In mid-century one New Brunswick resident noted that the timber trade "has brought foreign produce and foreign capital into the province, and has been the chief source of the money by which its roads, bridges and public buildings have been completed; its rivers and harbours made accessible; its natural resources discovered and made available; its provincial institutions kept up and its functionaries paid."

National Archives of Canada / C10103.

Lumbering and ship-building went together. Dorchester, New Brunswick, was one of a hundred shipbuilding villages on the Maritime coast.

305

THE RISE OF SHIPBUILDING

The timber industry gave rise to shipbuilding. Square timber, a bulky commodity, had to be shipped in relatively large vessels, and as Britain could not meet the need in wartime, the Maritime shipbuilding industry expanded. The Maritimes soon supplied many of the new wooden ships being used to ferry timber to Britain. Shipbuilding became the first major manufacturing industry in the Maritime region employing, at the large yards, a hundred or so workers at one time.

From the 1820s onward, the Nova Scotia and New Brunswick fleets grew continuously. Maritime timber merchants found they could keep transportation costs low if they owned their own vessels. When prices for vessels rose, they made additional profits by selling the ship as well as its timber cargo. Other Maritime businessmen saw money to be made in owning ships involved in lucrative coastal trading, particularly the West Indian trade.

By 1850 the region had gained a reputation as one of the leading maritime areas of the world. Maritimers built broad-beamed vessels designed to maximize carrying capacity, not speed. They increased sail capacity and improved ships' hulls. They extended the average life of Nova Scotia and New Brunswick vessels from a mere nine years in the 1820s to fifteen by the end of the century. Shipbuilders also constructed the vessels cheaply; an iron steamer in Britain cost four or five times as much in the 1860s as did a Maritime wooden vessel.

In New Brunswick the major shipowners included many timber exporters, whereas in Nova Scotia the majority were fish exporters, West Indies traders, and import–export merchants. Sir Samuel Cunard, the most famous of the Nova Scotia shipowners, had interests in the West Indies trade, a tea business, a bank, and the sale of imported goods. In 1840 he initiated the first regular steamship service across the Atlantic. Cunard was one of the first Nova Scotians to build a business empire.

Many shipowners in Prince Edward Island sailed and then sold their vessels in Britain. In the 1850s a number of the shipowners entered into new businesses, Thomas Killam of Yarmouth illustrating the trend. This small shipowner and West Indies trader of the 1830s had, before his death in 1868, expanded his operations to include a ship-outfitting business, a marine insurance company, a telegraph company, a gas lighting company, and a bank. He shifted capital from one industry to another, taking earnings from shipping and re-investing in industry. Enos Collins of Halifax had diversified his shipping interests after the War of 1812. When the old sea captain died in 1871 at the age of ninety-seven he left behind an estate of six million dollars.

Thousands of men and hundreds of women worked in the Maritime shipyards or in shops making materials for the ships. The sailors were young men, most often in their twenties or early thirties. For most, seafaring was a short-term activity—a means of supplementing the family income or a job when work was scarce on land.

It was demanding. No trade unions existed on board ship, where the jobs were arduous and often unsafe; the food was poor, and the working hours long. Desertion was one means of protection, and one-quarter of the crew usually deserted during a voyage. Until the sailing industry declined in the late 1870s, the numerous sailors in the ports of eastern Canada lived in what were called "sailortowns."

BANKING

The financial needs of the merchants (the term "businessman" only came into use in the last half of the nineteenth century) involved in the timber industry and shipbuilding led to the rise of banks (see chapter 15). In Britain commercial banks developed in the eighteenth century, and in the 1790s scores opened in the United States. The banks dealt in foreign-exchange transactions, made loans, and circulated bank notes, on the understanding that the paper notes could always be redeemed, on demand, in real coin. Depending on the risk the bankers were prepared to take, the banks could generally keep two to three times as many notes in circulation as they had gold or silver coins to redeem them. (The issuing of notes, instead of the distribution of coins, allowed the banks to double or triple the amount of interest it collected.) 307

The first bank in Nova Scotia, the Halifax Banking Company (fore-runner of the Imperial Bank of Commerce) began trading in money in 1825. A group of merchants founded the Bank of Nova Scotia in 1832, and by 1840 it had branches in Windsor, Annapolis Royal, Pictou, Yarmouth, and Liverpool. New Brunswick's first bank, the Bank of New Brunswick, was founded in St. John in 1820; the second, the Commercial Bank, in 1834.

Urban Centres

St. John, Halifax, and the much smaller Charlottetown became the dominant centres of the Maritimes, with lines of trade reaching into the outlying regions. With a population larger than Halifax's, St. John was the third-largest city in British North America in the mid-nineteenth century (after Montreal and Quebec) and the largest on its Atlantic seaboard. In the 1850s it controlled the timber trade of the St. John River valley and was the natural market for the farmers and fishermen on both sides of the Bay of Fundy. Nearly half of the industrial output of New Brunswick was produced in and around St. John. The great merchants of St. John, however, delayed investments in manufacturing iron and steel, concentrating instead on the traditional timber industries—shipbuilding, construction, and saw-milling. This held back the development of a viable industrial base in New Brunswick by two decades, when the metal ship replaced the wooden sailing ship in the late nineteenth century.

In the 1850s Halifax also sought to become the commercial metropolis of the Maritimes. Although it had a large, secure, ice-free harbour and was situated very close to the major North Atlantic shipping lanes, Nova Scotia's capital had no economic hinterland. Unlike Montreal and St. John, it lacked a major waterway comparable to the St. Lawrence or the St. John River, which extended more than 700 km into the interior. Halifax did, however, succeed in dominating the commerce of Prince Edward Island, Cape Breton Island, and the Miramichi country of eastern New Brunswick, but it lost the Bay of Fundy to St. John. Reliant on imperial spending for much of its prosperity, Halifax also benefitted from the Caribbean trade and its role as the banking, judicial, and intellectual centre of Nova Scotia. It produced two of the wealthiest individuals in British North America: Enos Collins and Sir Samuel Cunard.

In both St. John and Halifax there were charitable organizations to help penniless immigrants as well as the resident urban proletariat. In winter the poor faced cold, hunger, illness, and unemployment—or under-employment—until spring returned. The seasonal nature of North Atlantic shipping meant that labourers, mill hands, seamen, carpenters, and other building trades workers lost their jobs in the autumn. The voluntary charitable organizations run by churches and ethnic groups in Halifax and St. John had very limited means. Fortunately, towards the end of the period under study, the colonial governments had begun a modest entry into the charitable field with the establishment of orphanages.

The Maritimes and Reciprocity

When Britain adopted free trade in the 1840s many Maritimers came to favour the idea of reciprocity, or the free admission into British North America and the United States of each other's natural resources. For New Brunswick, reciprocity was the key to gaining entry for its timber into the American market of twenty-three million people.

Relations beween New Brunswick and the United States were greatly improved since the settlement of a border controversy between New Brunswick and Maine in 1842. The Treaty of Paris in 1783 had set the boundary to run north from the St. Croix River to an undetermined height of land. In 1839, New Brunswick and Maine lumbermen almost caused a border war over which group had the right to cut in the no-man's land at the

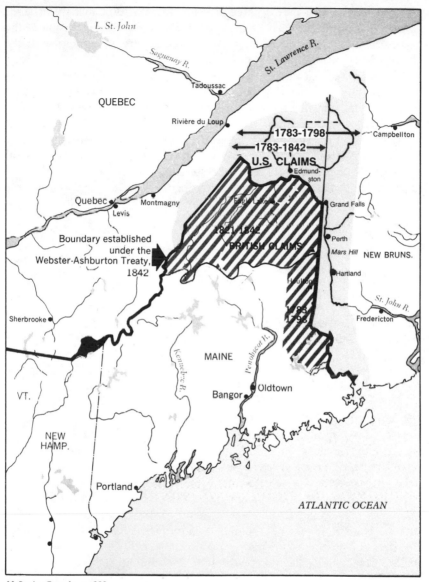

McInnis, *Canada*, p. 283.

mouth of the Aroostook River (see page 146), which was part of the disputed territory. Three years later Daniel Webster, the American secretary of state, and Alexander Baring, Lord Ashburton, the British envoy, resolved the controversy. The Webster-Ashburton Treaty of 1842 established the present-day New Brunswick–Maine boundary.

Reciprocity proposals also met with a favourable response in Nova Scotia (with its fish) and Prince Edward Island (with its farm produce). The

Americans, for their part, wanted access to the Maritime inshore fisheries from which they had been legally excluded in 1818. The inclusion of the fisheries led the United States to sign a reciprocity agreement with the British North American colonies in 1854.

The treaty led to the desired increased trade with the United States. The Maritime colonies now bought one-quarter to one-half of their total imports from the Americans. New Brunswick shipped increased amounts of lumber, Prince Edward Island more foodstuffs, and Nova Scotia a slightly greater amount of fish. Certainly, the years of the reciprocity treaty proved prosperous, but not solely on account of the treaty. The great demand for the Maritimes' natural resources, brought about by the outbreak of the American Civil War, also helped. From 1860 to 1865 wartime prices for the Maritimes' fish, timber, and foodstuffs doubled.

310

RAILWAYS

Railway construction in Nova Scotia and New Brunswick in the 1850s and 1860s also promoted the economic boom. From 1853 to 1866 New Brunswick built 350 km of railway. During the same period, Nova Scotia constructed 235 km at a cost of about $7.5 million. Maritime promoters dreamed of continental expansion, of one day linking the ice-free Maritime ports with the St. Lawrence valley and with the grain-producing American Midwest.

Merchants in Halifax and St. John had visions of their respective cities serving as the focal point from which European commerce could be channelled into the continent and from which American and Canadian exports could be sent abroad. Yet railways were expensive to build and operate (see chapter 15). A single kilometre of track could cost as much as a sizeable sailing vessel. To make money, the owners needed densely populated areas to provide local revenue and the shortest possible direct routes; neither Halifax nor even St. John had such hinterlands. Their land routes to the interior were too distant, in contrast with Boston's, New York's, or Montreal's, and they passed through thinly populated territory.

Political Change, 1815–64

In the mid-nineteenth century the Maritime colonies reached both their economic and political maturity. Britain's cutting of the last bonds of her old commercial empire in the late 1840s and early 1850s removed the rationale for close political control over the colonies' internal affairs. Throughout the 1830s and 1840s the conviction had grown that government should be taken from the hands of the privileged and delivered into the hands of the people. In Nova Scotia the middle class began openly to oppose the small ruling clique, or to use the Upper Canadian phrase, the "family compact," in Halifax.

The Maritime assemblies in the early nineteenth century were small and elected by a limited provincial franchise. In 1836 in Prince Edward Island women were barred by statute from voting, and in New Brunswick in 1843; only in Nova Scotia in the 1840s could women meeting the property qualification exercise the franchise, until 1851 when all women were disenfranchised.

Politics revolved around local personalities and interest groups. Standing as individuals, elected members represented local concerns in the assembly, vigilantly seeing that their constituencies obtained their fair share of the provincial revenues. Yet, in Nova Scotia at least, by the early 1840s two political groups, the Reformers and the Conservatives, had taken shape, both co-ordinating their activities in the legislature.

311

THE REFORM MOVEMENT IN NOVA SCOTIA

In Nova Scotia the nucleus of the Reform party first developed in the mid-1830s under the leadership of Joseph Howe, a journalist then in his early thirties. As a young man Joseph had little formal schooling, but he read widely on his own. Having purchased the *Novascotian*, a Halifax paper, he quickly made it the most influential newspaper in the province. During each session of the assembly he personally reported on the debates. Howe's perceived enemy became the Council of Twelve, or the governor's executive council (or cabinet) which still conducted its meetings behind closed doors. An interrelated merchant oligarchy, largely from Halifax, controlled the council and through it the political life of the province. Elected to the Nova Scotian assembly in 1836, the young newspaper editor led attacks against this privileged group, calling for an elected council and the assembly's control over Crown revenues.

The assemblies elected in 1836 and 1840 favoured reform, Howe being one of its most influential advocates. In the election of 1847, the Reformers fought on the issue of responsible government, and finally won a majority. On February 2, 1848, the Colonial Office agreed that henceforth the Executive Council, or "cabinet" of the lieutenant governor, must collectively resign if they lost the assembly's confidence. Nova Scotia became the first British North American colony to achieve responsible government, and Howe boasted that the Reformers had achieved it peacefully without "a blow struck or a pane of glass broken." Yet, he should have added that the rebellions in the Canadas had themselves done much to convince

Britain to concede responsible government in British North America (see chapter 14).

THE REFORM MOVEMENT IN NEW BRUNSWICK

In New Brunswick the political situation differed somewhat. Of all the British North American colonies, this province had always been among the easiest to rule. A relatively homogenous group of Loyalists and their descendants had controlled the colony until the 1830s. Moreover, as Anglicans initially constituted a near majority of the population, the position of the Church of England as the established church caused less resentment than elsewhere. The New Brunswick assembly in 1837 had even secured control of the revenues of Crown lands, including timberland revenues, in return for the provision of a civil list guaranteeing the salaries of officers of government.

From 1837 on two men, Charles Fisher and Lemuel Allan Wilmot, were the backbone of the New Brunswick reform movement, working mainly for responsible government. They made great advances. In practice, the colonial office—even before the official granting of responsible government in New Brunswick in 1848—made the Executive Council in the province responsible to the elected representatives in the assembly.

Responsible government, though, had its unattractive side. Patronage now passed into the reformers' hands, giving the assembly the benefit of making appointments to public office. Lemuel Allan Wilmot was one of the reformers who took full advantage of the opportunity to benefit himself. C.M. Wallace, his biographer, has noted: "His pursuit of office, first on the Executive Council, then on the bench, and finally as lieutenant governor might well be classed as rapacious."[3]

REFORM IN PRINCE EDWARD ISLAND

The winning of responsible government became an important issue in Prince Edward Island in the 1840s. Initially, the Colonial Office opposed granting internal self-government to such a small colony but eventually conceded. The Reformers on the island insisted on full equality with the mainland colonies. When they won the general election in 1850, they demanded cabinet government, which the Colonial Office granted in 1851. Immediately, the population hoped that the constitutional change would lead to a settlement of the neo-feudal land tenure system. Two-thirds of the island's inhabitants in the 1830s still lived on land owned by absentee owners, few of whom were descendants of the original grantees of 1767—

most having purchased their lands on speculation. Samuel Cunard, the Halifax merchant, controlled an estate of 85 000 hectares (an area more than twice as large as all the Indian reserve lands in the Maritimes).

The Colonial Office, however, refused to consider escheat and upheld the rights of private property. The island's Executive and Legislative councils, both controlled by a small group of the leading families in Charlottetown, also protected the proprietors. To challenge this position, the assembly set up an investigative commission to study the problem. It recommended in 1860 that tenants be allowed to purchase their land and that owners obtain a fair valuation of their property.

Cultural Developments

The cultural life of Maritimers was enriched in the nineteenth century. Throughout the colonies church choirs flourished. In the urban centres the large Anglican and Roman Catholic churches often had organs, and skilled musicians. Music societies existed in the cities, among the earliest in British North America were the New Union Singing Society of Halifax (1809) and the Philharmonic Society of St. John (1824).

313

Throughout the nineteenth century theatre could be seen in Maritime cities. Performing at first in makeshift theatres in taverns and other public buildings the Halifax garrison put on plays, and in 1789 opened the New Grand Theatre. For the opening the officers and men produced Shakespeare's *Merchant of Venice*. Charlottetown constructed its first theatre in 1800, and by 1809 St. John had its own Drury Lane Theatre. Professional companies from the United States and Britain, and leading actors from both countries, visited in the mid-nineteenth century.

The Maritimes produced one major North American literary figure in the mid-nineteenth century, Thomas Chandler Haliburton. From 1823 to 1860 the Nova Scotian judge wrote many works in provincial history, and political pamphlets, but it is for his fiction that he is best remembered. Haliburton's classic, *The Clockmaker; or, the Sayings and Doings of Samuel Slick, of Slickville*, first appeared in 1836, and was followed by two more series of the humorous stories about the Yankee clock peddler who crossed the province selling his poorly-produced clocks to easily fooled Nova Scotians. As many as seventy editions of *The Clockmaker* have since appeared. Haliburton was the first British North American writer to obtain an international reputation in literature.

Religion and Education in the Maritimes, 1785–1864

Religion was a major source of discord in the Maritimes. To introduce what they considered the correct religious principles, Nova Scotia's leaders appealed in 1787 to the Right Reverend Charles Inglis, former rector of Trinity Church in New York City, to become the colony's first bishop, with jurisdiction as well over Canada, New Brunswick, and Newfoundland. Inglis saw his task as one of securing the Anglican church's predominance in the Maritimes. Bishop Inglis succeeded in founding an Anglican college, King's College, at Windsor in 1788; but otherwise he failed in his attempt to make the Church of England a dominant force in Maritime society.

THE DENOMINATIONS

314

The Anglicans quickly lost ground to the Baptists, which was the most active of the Protestant faiths. With their close-knit organizations and high degree of church discipline, the Baptists filled the religious void left in the rural areas of the Maritimes after Henry Alline's death in 1784. The Baptists became the largest Protestant denomination in New Brunswick. Next to the Baptists came the Methodists, who had succeeded by the 1820s in building up an influential following, including converts from the professional classes, taken largely from among the ranks of the evangelical Anglicans. Presbyterians came into their own with the large Scottish immigration to the Maritimes and became scattered throughout the Maritime colonies. Catholics could draw on the support of sizeable numbers of Scots, Irish, Acadians, and Micmacs throughout Nova Scotia, and particularly in northern and eastern New Brunswick. In the 1860s almost one-half the population of Prince Edward Island was Roman Catholic. Lutheranism was strong in Nova Scotia's Lunenburg county. Small Quaker and Jewish communities existed as well.

EDUCATION

As in the Canadas (see chapter 15) religious conflicts entered into the field of education. As late as 1825 only one-quarter of Nova Scotia's school-aged children outside of Halifax attended school, and subsequently the provincial government intervened. The colonial legislatures in the other two Maritime colonies also made provision for public schools to complement the church-run or separate schools.

Maritime Roman Catholics sought state financial support for their church-run schools. The Anglicans, Baptists, Methodists, and Presbyterians, however, generally favoured publicly funded, state primary schools. Fearful of the electoral consequences among Protestant voters none of the colonial governments gave separate schools formal legislative approval. Without legal status, financial aid to denominational schools was not guaranteed in any of the three colonies in the 1860s, on the eve of Confederation.

Higher education remained largely the churches' responsibility. King's College at Windsor excluded four-fifths of all possible candidates for degrees in arts because of their insistence upon an oath supporting the doctrines of the Church of England. Therefore, Governor Dalhousie, a Presbyterian, founded the college in 1818 that still bears his name, to provide education for students of all religious denominations. But each denomination wanted its own college.

In the early nineteenth century the Presbyterians built Pictou Academy, while the Baptists established Horton Academy at Wolfville, Nova Scotia in 1828 (ten years later it became Acadia College). Roman Catholics built by mid-century St. Mary's College in Halifax. In 1853 Scottish Roman Catholics in eastern Nova Scotia opened Arichat Seminary, which moved to Antigonish in 1855, becoming St. Francis Xavier University. Just across the border, Methodists established Wesleyan Academy at Sackville, New Brunswick—the forerunner of Mount Allison. The Anglicans founded King's College at Fredericton in 1830, which became the non-sectarian University of New Brunswick in 1859.

315

By the mid-nineteenth century the three Maritime colonies had come of age economically and politically. Eight out of every nine people in the region had been born there. But the inhabitants were far from homogeneous. Religious, ethnic, and provincial divisions remained, particularly among the groups pushed to the margins of Maritime Society, like the Micmacs and Blacks, and to a lesser extent the Acadians. Regional loyalties also were strong. Many Maritimers were skeptical of the possibilities of Maritime union when politicians first seriously discussed the idea in the early 1860s. The idea of Union with the Canadas seemed even more remote.

NOTES

[1] W.G. Godfrey, "Thomas Carleton," *Dictionary of Canadian Biography*, vol. 5:1801–1820 (Toronto, 1983), p. 160.

[2] W.A. Spray, "The Settlement of the Black Refugees in New Brunswick 1815–1836", in vol. 1; *The Acadiensis Reader, Atlantic Canada Before Confederation*, edited by P.A. Buckner and David Frank (Fredericton, 1985), pp. 152–53.

[3] C.M. Wallace, "Lemuel Allan Wilmot," *Dictionary of Canadian Biography*, vol. 10:1871–1880 (Toronto, 1972), p. 710.

Related Readings

R. Douglas Francis and Donald B. Smith, *Readings in Canadian History: Pre-Confederation Canada*, 2d ed. (Toronto, 1986), has two articles on this topic: David Sutherland's "Halifax Merchants and the Pursuit of Development, 1783–1850," pp. 400–13; and T.W. Acheson, "The Great Merchant and Economic Development in St. John 1820–1850," pp. 413–35.

BIBLIOGRAPHY

The basic study of Maritime history in these years remains W.S. MacNutt, *The Atlantic Provinces: The Emergence of Colonial Society, 1712–1857* (Toronto, 1965); for New Brunswick, see also his *New Brunswick: A History, 1784–1867* (Toronto, 1963). A.H. Clark reviews Prince Edward Island's story in *Three Centuries and the Island* (Toronto, 1959). For a short history of Cape Breton as a separate colony, see Robert J. Morgan, "Cape Breton by Itself," *Horizon Canada*, number 9 (1987):2390–95. Two useful overviews are William Menzies Whitelaw, "The Atlantic Provinces and their Neighbors," in his study *The Maritimes and Canada Before Confederation* (Toronto, 1966; first published 1934), pp. 9–37; and John Warkentin, "The Atlantic Region," in *Canada Before Confederation*, edited by R. Cole Harris and John Warkentin (Toronto, 1974), pp. 169–231. Michael Bliss reviews economic developments in *Northern Enterprise: Five Centuries of Canadian Business* (Toronto, 1987).

Economic and social questions receive attention in the following: S.A. Saunders, "The Maritime Provinces and the Reciprocity Treaty," in *Historical Essays on the Atlantic Provinces*, edited by George A. Rawlyk (Toronto, 1967), pp. 161–78; Eric W. Sager and Lewis R. Fischer, *Shipping and Shipbuilding in Atlantic Canada, 1820–1914*, Canadian Historical Association Booklet (Ottawa: 1986); Eric W. Sager, "Every Inch a Sailor," *Horizon Canada*, number 90 (1987):2150–55. *Atlantic Canada Before Confederation*, vol. 1: *The Acadiensis Reader*, edited by P.A. Buckner and David Frank (Fredericton, 1985), contains Judith Fingard's essay, "The Relief of the Unemployed Poor in Saint John, Halifax, and St. John's, 1815–1860," pp. 190–211. Fingard's "The Winter's Tale: The Seasonal Contours of Pre-industrial Poverty in British North America," appeared in the Canadian Historical Association's *Historical Papers*, 1974, pp. 65–94. Her *Jack in Port: Sailortowns of Eastern Canada* (Toronto, 1982) describes the life of merchant sailors in St. John and Halifax. William B. Hamilton reviews the educational history of the three Maritime colonies in *Canadian Education: A History*, edited by J. Donald Wilson, Robert M. Stamp, and Louis-Philippe Audet (Scarborough, Ont., 1970), pp. 86–

125. An entertaining popular account of Halifax is Thomas H. Raddall's *Halifax: Warden of the North,* rev. ed. (Toronto, 1971). T.W. Acheson's *Saint John: The Making of a Colonial Urban Community* (Toronto, 1985), is an in-depth study of New Brunswick's largest city.

Maritime political developments are examined in Phillip A. Buckner, *The Transition to Responsible Government: British Policy in British North America, 1815–1850* (Westport, Conn., 1985). W.G. Godfrey reviews Thomas Carleton's career as governor of New Brunswick in the *Dictionary of Canadian Biography,* vol. 5:1801–1820 (Toronto, 1983), pp. 155–63. A short sketch of Joseph Howe appears in the *Dictionary of Canadian Biography,* vol. 10:1871–1880 (Toronto, 1972), pp. 362–70, by Murray Beck, who has also written the two-volume study *Joseph Howe* (Kingston, 1982). Carmen Miller reviews the 1860s in "The Restoration of Greater Nova Scotia," in *Canada and the Burden of Unity,* edited by David Jay Bercuson (Toronto, 1977), pp. 44–59. Important portraits of Maritime political, economic, and cultural leaders appear in the volumes of the *Dictionary of Canadian Biography* devoted to the nineteenth century.

317

For an introduction to cultural developments in the Maritimes in the nineteenth century see the following two short articles in *The Canadian Encyclopedia* (Edmonton, 1985): Helmut Kallman, "Music History," vol. 2, pp. 1183–87; and L.W. Conolly, "English-Language Theatre," vol. 3, pp. 1805–07. Fred Cogswell has written an interesting biography of Thomas Chandler Haliburton in the *Dictionary of Canadian Biography,* vol. 9:1861–1870 (Toronto, 1976), pp. 348–57.

A useful study for reviewing the history of the native peoples of the Maritimes is L.F.S. Upton, *Micmacs and Colonists: Indian–White Relations in the Maritimes, 1713–1867* (Vancouver, 1979). G.F.G. Stanley, "The Flowering of the Acadian Renaissance," in *Eastern and Western Perspectives,* edited by David Jay Bercuson and Phillip A. Buckner (Toronto, 1981), pp. 19–46, outlines the Acadians' experience. Charles Dunn's classic *Highland Settler: A Portrait of the Scottish Gael in Nova Scotia* (Toronto, 1953), and D. Campbell and R.A. MacLean, *Beyond the Atlantic Roar: A Study of the Nova Scotia Scots* (Toronto, 1974) deal with the Scots in Nova Scotia. For a discussion of the Blacks in the Maritimes, consult Robin W. Winks, *The Blacks in Canada: A History* (New Haven, 1971); and see W.A. Spray's "The Settlement of the Black Refugees in New Brunswick 1815–1836," in vol. 1: *The Acadiensis Reader, Atlantic Canada Before Confederation,* pp. 148–64.

For maps of the Maritimes in the late eighteenth and nineteenth centuries see Donald Lemon's *Theatre of Empire* (St. John, 1987).

CHAPTER SEVENTEEN

Newfoundland to the 1860s

318   In the sixteenth century the fleets of four nations—England, France, Spain, and Portugal—sailed to the Newfoundland banks and shared its deep, land-locked eastern harbours. The ships came to one of the world's greatest fishing grounds for the codfish, called "the beef of the sea," and a staple food of Roman Catholic Europe.

England, and then France, tried to colonize the Avalon Peninsula of Newfoundland in the seventeenth century. This attempt led the Beothuk, the local Indians, to withdraw from the area, and within two centuries they were gone completely. The tribe could not adjust to permanent European settlement, like the Micmacs in the Maritimes. By avoiding the newcomers and by staying in the interior, the Beothuk lost access to the valuable food supplies off the coast. They became greatly weakened by starvation and by tuberculosis—inadvertently introduced by the Europeans.

After a half-century of Anglo-French conflict, France ceded Newfoundland to England by the Treaty of Utrecht in 1713. Powerful English merchants, mostly from Devon and Dorset in the West Country, sought exclusive fishing rights to the fishing grounds and successfully persuaded British monarchs and parliaments in the late seventeenth century to discourage additional permanent settlement on the island. In the eighteenth century the merchants' opposition ended, and the British government passively sanctioned settlement. Early in the next century the island had a permanent population of more than forty thousand people. Their livelihood depended on exporting fish and on trade with Britain, the Mediterranean, the West Indies, and, to a more limited extent, with the rest of British North America.

By the mid-nineteenth century the spirit of political reform that swept through the other British North American colonies surfaced in Newfoundland and led to intense and bitter disputes. On the eve of Confederation Newfoundland was in many respects like the other British North American colonies and yet in other ways, quite different.

Growth of the International Fishery

The success of the early Newfoundland cod fishery initially depended on the harvesting of salt left by the evaporation of sea water. This salt was better than the mineral variety for curing fish because it was more uniform in quality. France, Spain, and Portugal produced an abundance of "solar salt," but England, not as blessed with sunshine, did not. This hurt England in the age of the "green fishery," the term sailors used to describe a method of catching the fish by immediately salting them and then transporting them back to Europe for drying. To compensate for their lack of solar salt, the English developed "dry fishing"—drying their lightly salted fish on platforms before returning home.

England profited greatly by the decline of Spanish and Portuguese naval strength after the defeat of the Spanish Armada in 1588. It gained a market for its dried cod in southern Europe, including Spain. The English sold the firmest and whitest cod in the Mediterranean. They classified slightly damaged fish as second grade and also shipped it to overseas buyers. They packed the poorest grade fish in casks and sold them to slave owners in the West Indies.

319

English fishing expeditions to Newfoundland became an annual event. From December to February the English fishermen cleaned, overhauled, and completely fitted their ships. Then in March they left from the great English ports in southwestern England—Plymouth, Poole, and Dartmouth, with sufficient provisions and stores for eight months. Estimates of the number of English ships involved around 1600 vary from 250 to 400, and the number of men from six thousand to ten thousand. These expeditions made good England's claim to the Avalon Peninsula on Newfoundland's eastern coast, the location of the best English fishing and processing sites.

The English introduced methods of fishing they had first practised on the coast of Iceland. They fished from open boats or from barrels suspended over the ship's side. Before the fishing began, they scrambled for the most convenient "room" or stretch of beach on which to build a timber stage (a small wharf with a roof over it) for landing and "flakes" for drying the cod. A large fishing room was called a "plantation," and its owner, if he lived permanently on it, a "planter." Most of the ships carried a crew of twenty, of whom a dozen fished while the rest cured the fish ashore. The fishing day was an arduous one. The men fished until 4:00 P.M. and then about 6:00 P.M. the first boat reached the staging to unload the catch. The method of curing introduced from Iceland involved splitting, lightly salting and drying the cod which produced an excellent "stock" fish that did not spoil during the long voyages to the tropics.

On the high seas, many dangers awaited—fog, floating ice, and pirates. During the early seventeenth century the "Barbary Rovers" (North African Moslems who travelled the coasts of Europe) allied themselves to France

French Shore, 1713-1783

French Shore, 1783-1904

STRAIT OF BELLE ISLE

L'Anse aux Meadows (Vikings, c. 1000 A.D.)

Point Riche

GULF OF
SAINT LAWRENCE

Great Northern Peninsula

White Bay

Cape St. John

Exploits River

BONAVISTA
BAY

Cape Bonavista

Trinity

TRINITY BAY

Cape Ray

Conception Bay

Cupids

St. John's

Ferryland

PLACENTIA
BAY

Plaisance

MIQUELON

St. Mary's
Bay

Avalon Peninsula

Trepassey

CAPE

BRETON

ISLAND

ST. PIERRE

EARLY NEWFOUNDLAND

Adapted from Cornell, Hamelin, Ouellet, Trudel, *Canada, Unity in Diversity*, p. 111.

and extended their operations to the approaches to the English Channel. There they waited for the unarmed ships from Newfoundland to return. They sold into slavery any seamen who were not needed to work on the pirate ships. The town of Poole in Dorset, which sent out twenty ships annually to Newfoundland, lost twenty ships to the pirates —or one-quarter of their fleet—over a four-year period. Only after an Anglo-Dutch mission bombarded the pirates' North African headquarters in the late seventeenth century did the danger to English shipping diminish.

Early Settlement in Newfoundland

England was anxious to secure a permanent foothold in Newfoundland, believing that whoever controlled settlement would hold the fisheries. Newfoundland came second only to Virginia in British attempts to colonize North America. Between 1610 and 1661 private individuals made seven different attempts to establish settlements on the island.

In 1610 a group of London and Bristol merchants formed the London

321

National Archives of Canada / C3686.

The picture above, from an engraving on a map of North America prepared by Herman Moll, Geographer, and published within the period 1712-1714, shows the methods of drying cod. This engraving tells a complete story, the key to which reads as follows:
A View of a Stage & also of ye manner of Fishing for, Curing & Drying Cod at NEW FOUND LAND. A. The Habit of ye Fishermen. B. The Line. C. The manner of Fishing. D. The Dressers of ye Fish. E. The Trough into which they throw ye Cod when Dressed. F. Salt Boxes. G. The manner of Carrying ye Cod. H. The Cleansing ye Cod. I. A Press to extract ye Oyl from ye Cod's Livers. K. Casks to receive ye Water and Blood that comes from ye Livers. L. Another Cask to receive ye Oyl. M. The manner of Drying ye Cod.

and Bristol Company. That same year they sent a governor, John Guy, and forty men to establish Newfoundland's first colony at Cupids on Conception Bay. The London and Bristol Company believed its men would have an advantage over the visiting fishermen by being there when the annual visitors arrived. But the plan did not work out. The colonists did not have a significant advantage—the visiting fishermen caught fish that was just as good. Moreover, the settlers had to charge as high or higher prices for their fish to cover the colony's expenses. Finally, the settlement could not sustain itself. Settlers could not grow grain and their cattle died from lack of fodder. The failure to discover mineral resources and to begin a commercial trade in furs with the resident Beothuk Indians equally doomed the colony.

Another drawback to colonization was the weather. Lord Baltimore, for example, founded Ferryland, south of St. John's, in 1621. But after wintering on the island in 1628–29 he wrote of his wife and family: "I have sent them home after much sufferance in this wofull country, where with one intolerable wynter were we almost undone. It is not to be expressed with my pen what wee have endured." Lord Baltimore re-directed his colonizing efforts to Virginia, where just after his death in 1632 his son received a charter to what became known as Maryland. Some of the Newfoundland settlers, however, remained behind after the colony disintegrated and became part of the continuing permanent population of Ferryland.

In spite of several unsuccessful colonization attempts, the permanent non-native population of the island slowly grew. By 1650 an estimated 500 English-speaking residents, including 350 women and children, lived in about forty settlements scattered along on the eastern coast, between Cape Bonavista and Trepassey. The population rose to an estimated 2000 by 1680 and consisted of two groups: the first included descendants of settlers brought out by colonizers like John Guy and Lord Baltimore; the second was made up "bye-boatmen" from England's West Country, who came out as passengers on the fishing ships and returned in the autumn. They worked for the settlers or merchants who owned the bye-boats, the small fishing boats left in Newfoundland harbours for use in the spring. As time went on, many of these skilled fishermen remained in Newfoundland during the winter and frequently stayed for several years. Some became permanent settlers.

Without any organized government on the island the settlers and the bye-boatmen often faced difficult times. They had to earn their living during the short season of cod fishing in the summer, for there was no employment in the winter. When the fishing fleet departed in September or early October it left the isolated communities on their own until the following spring. If food ran out, they starved. If illness occurred, no medical people could be called. No births, marriages, or burials could be legally registered, since no clergymen lived on the island between 1650 and 1702. The island had no law officers or courts because it had no official status as a colony.

The English government faced a difficult problem in the late seventeenth century. First, it wanted to prevent settlement on the island as it would weaken the West Country ship fishery. The Royal Navy relied on the annual fishing voyages to train seamen and to maintain ships, and the British government feared that a Newfoundland resident fishery would put an end to the English migratory fishery, as had been the case in New England. Yet without the settlers and the bye-boatmen on the island, France might seize Newfoundland. According to historian Frederick W. Rowe, three-quarters of the island's 10 000-km-long coastline, "was already, in effect, almost wholly under the control of the world's most powerful country. How long would it be before France would be occupying the entire Island of Newfoundland?"[1] England resolved this dilemma in

323

Royal Ontario Museum, Toronto.

"A Fishing Station" by Gerard Edema (c. 1652-c. 1700), a harbour in Placentia Bay about 1690.

1699 by allowing permanent settlement on the island but without government. The Act to Encourage Trade to Newfoundland, or Newfoundland Act, the first English statute governing the island, was the constitution of Newfoundland for the next 125 years, until it became a British colony in 1824.

The Anglo-French Struggle for Newfoundland

While England began settlements on Newfoundland's east coast (the eastern Avalon Peninsula), the French claimed Newfoundland's south shore. In 1662 the French fortified Plaisance (Placentia), about 100 km across the Avalon Peninsula from St. John's. The deep, ice-free harbour offered an excellent refuge for French ships. To build up settlement the French government for a few years provided free passage and support for one year to settlers migrating to Plaisance. As in New France, however, large-scale French assistance ceased in the early 1670s. The colony grew very slowly thereafter and its population probably never exceeded nine hundred—a number far smaller than the English colony.

324

Conflict between the English and French settlements seemed inevitable. War broke out in 1689, and seven years later Pierre Le Moyne d'Iberville, New France's greatest soldier, laid waste thirty-six English settlements on the island which led to the killing of two hundred people and to the taking of seven hundred prisoners. The English retaliated when an expedition in 1697 recaptured all the settlements. From that point on, the English presence was secure, thanks largely to its superior naval power. But the devastation caused by the French did much to slow down the development of the permanent English settlements.

By the Treaty of Utrecht, England gained control of the entire island. The French ceded Plaisance and its claim to Newfoundland but retained the right to dry cod on the shore between Cape Bonavista and Point Riche (in the northeastern bays and around Newfoundland's Great Northern Peninsula, to a point located about one-quarter down the west coast); this area included approximately one-third of Newfoundland's coastline.

By the second Treaty of Paris in 1783 Cape Ray, on the island's southwestern tip, was substituted for Point Riche and the eastern boundary moved from Cape Bonavista to Cape St. John (see page 320). The French shore now encompassed the entire west coast, the Great Northern Peninsula, and White Bay. British or Newfoundland fishermen were not allowed to interrupt the French fishery in that area and the French disputed their right to settle there. The question of the French shore troubled Anglo-French relations for nearly two centuries, until England purchased French landing rights in 1904.

Although the French settlement at Plaisance became British, the French still held New France and the great fort of Louisbourg on Cape Breton Island. On account of France's naval strength, Newfoundland was in danger of a French naval attack until the 1760s. In 1762 the French actually took St. John's, although the English re-captured the town the following year. The first Treaty of Paris in 1763 had reaffirmed France's Newfoundland landing rights, and to compensate for the loss of French fishing bases in Cape Breton, Britain ceded the islands of St. Pierre and Miquelon off Newfoundland to France, "to serve as a shelter to the French fisherman." Two centuries later, the definition of the French fishing zone in the waters around St. Pierre and Miquelon remains a contentious issue in Franco-Canadian relations.

Law and Order in Eighteenth-Century Newfoundland

325

As early as the seventeenth century competition for favourable harbours reached such a high level that the fishing fleets, by necessity, evolved a crude system of administration. They worked out the "fishing admiral system," a rough-and-ready means of keeping some kind of order in the harbours. To the first ship in the respective port, regardless of nationality, went the right to take the best fishing room or beach. The first ship's captain became the "fishing admiral," who enjoyed the customary right to maintain law and order in each harbour. Much of the admiral's authority, however, rested on his strength. If he had a sizeable and well-armed vessel and a large crew, then his will could be enforced.

In 1634 the English government had confirmed the admiral system in the Western Charter, the first regulation issued on the Newfoundland fishery. The Newfoundland Act of 1699 again affirmed the rights and the authority of the fishing admirals. The system had several serious defects, however. First, the admirals only stayed for three or four months in the spring and summer, and for the rest of the year no one had authority to maintain law and order. Second, even when present, the admirals had no way of enforcing their rulings, and as settlement grew, the problems they had to resolve grew more complex. Third, the admirals received no payment for presiding over the courts and, since they had come primarily to fish, had little interest in enforcing the law.

Conditions on the island degenerated rapidly under the fishing admiral system. In the long period between the departure of the ships in the late summer and their return the next year, those guilty of murder, rape, and robbery had ample opportunity to escape. Historian Keith Matthews has offered two explanations for England's delay in establishing a proper legal system. One is that the establishment of law and other services on the island would only have encouraged further permanent settlement, an object the government sought to discourage. The other is that the placement of law enforcement officers in many different parts of the island would have required enormous expenditures by the British government.[2]

In 1729 the British government finally made a modest improvement in the system. The commander of the annual naval convoy to Newfoundland became the island's governor and commander-in-chief, but he lived on a ship and remained in Newfoundland only during the the summer fishing season. Whenever the governor deemed a local regulation desirable he could issue a proclamation and his word became law. As governor he had also the right to appoint justices of the peace from the most respected local residents as magistrates. While the fishing admirals—until the late eighteenth century—retained their authority under the Newfoundland Act of 1699 to rule in the summers on the fisheries and on related matters, the magistrates developed increasing jurisdiction, both in terms of the cases they could hear, and at what time of year.

326

The Beothuk

Newfoundland's original inhabitants, the Beothuk Indians, suffered greatly from the presence of the newcomers. The Beothuk first encountered European fishermen in the sixteenth century. On account of their use of ochre on their bodies, clothing, and utensils, the early Europeans called them "Red Indians"—an expression still used in Britain to describe the American Indians. The word Beothuk means "people," and it is the term that the aboriginal Newfoundlanders applied to themselves.

Unlike the Micmac in the Maritimes, who accommodated themselves to living near the French, the Beothuk habitually withdrew from the Europeans. With the increasing number of European fishermen on the Newfoundland coast it became difficult in the mid-seventeenth century for the Indians to obtain access to their seaside summer campsites and food resources, particularly those on the eastern and southern coast. Starvation became a major problem.

The pressure on the Beothuk became progressively more intense. Early in the 1700s a salmon fishery developed near the mouths of the rivers of northeast Newfoundland. Settlers also began to trap fur-bearing animals in the interior. The rapid growth of the spring seal hunt, which was best operated from the northeast coast, also speeded up the expansion of settlement to the area. The British settlers became seal hunters in the spring, salmon catchers in the summer, and trappers in the winter, thus depriving the Beothuk of their traditional sources of food and clothing.

When the Beothuk encountered the Europeans on the northeastern coast, violence often broke out. The settlers harrassed them, chasing them in their canoes and raiding their camps. George Cartwright, a prominent merchant in Labrador, issued a warning to the Colonial Office in 1784:

Instead of a friendly intercourse with these Indians, our people dispossessed them from beaches and salmon rivers and it is now well known, that the poor Indians are put to the greatest difficulties to procure a scanty subsistance. If some effectual measures will not be taken, that unhappy race of mortals will soon be extirpated, to the disgrace of our Government, our country and our religion.

The Beothuk retaliated. According to contemporary reports and oral traditions, the Beothuk killed about a dozen settlers and wounded nearly as many more between 1750 and 1790. The settlers took their own revenge, killing and wounding Indians in their canoes and destroying their wigwams. The fact that the Indians had no firearms weakened their ability to defend themselves against the settlers.

Justice went undone. Neighbours and employers were reluctant to become involved in the prosecution of the British criminals, especially since it could mean missing out on the summer's fishing and having to pay for the return expenses from St. John's. The culprits remained at large, unpunished. Even when murder trials were held at St. John's in the mid-eighteenth century, the court made few convictions.

Several concerned naval officers and settlers in the late eighteenth and early nineteenth centuries worried about the Beothuk's fate. A number of attempts to reach the Beothuk failed, but one in 1811 succeeded. After trekking for twelve days up the Exploits River (see page 320) in heavy snow and sub-zero temperatures, Captain David Buchan and his party of twenty-seven made contact with a band of about forty Beothuks. The Indians, though, remained suspicious and killed the two seamen left with them as hostages.

Attempts made to locate the Indians the following summer failed. Many of the Beothuks apparently died, most likely from starvation and tuberculosis. From evidence accumulated by anthropologist Ingeborg Marshall, a few Beothuks joined the Micmac in the southern part of the island, either voluntarily or as the result of kidnapping.[3]

In 1823 three starving Beothuk women surrendered to a British settler. Both the mother and one of her two daughters died shortly afterward of tuberculosis. The second daughter, Shanadithit, called Nancy, who was between sixteen and twenty years old, survived for six years. She lived at first as a servant in the household of a justice of the peace and spent the last year of her life in St. John's informing William Cormack, a Newfoundland champion of the Beothuk, about her people's culture, history, and language. Shanadithit died in 1829, as the St. John's *Royal Gazette* reported on June 16: "She died of consumption, a disease which seems to have been remarkably prevalent among her tribe, and which has unfortunately been fatal to all who have fallen into the hands of the settlers." Apart from two or three of her people who may have lived with the

Newfoundland Micmac, no other members of her tribe are known to have survived.

Newfoundland Becomes a British Colony

At the end of the eighteenth century the population of Newfoundland grew rapidly. The number of permanent residents rose from approximately 2300 in 1720 to about 20 000 by 1800, and to about 40 000 in 1815. The environmental impact of the increased coastal population was striking. As the settlers built dwellings and warehouses and used increasing amounts of firewood, the forests rapidly disappeared. According to geographer Grant Head, the coastal forests were replaced by a "clutter of stages, flakes, boats, ships, warehouses, dwellings, vegetable patches, wandering cattle, and snaking trails."[4]

328

Much of the population growth came from natural increase but also from a large influx of immigrants, chiefly Irish. The first potato famines in the 1720s and 1730s led thousands of Irish to seek refuge across the Atlantic, and Newfoundland was the first place in the New World to receive large numbers of Irish immigrants. By the 1750s Irish Catholics probably constituted half of the Avalon Peninsula's total population, and by the 1830s they numbered half of the entire island's population.

The Irish immigrants brought with them little love for England, which had repeatedly invaded Ireland, seized their lands, and then proscribed their religion. The Irish came with respect and strong loyalty to their priests, but found that Roman Catholic priests were not allowed on the island. Not until 1784 did the governor allow religious freedom.

Mistrusting the English (as the English settlers mistrusted the Irish), the two communities segregated themselves geographically from each other. Irish Roman Catholics populated almost all the southern shore and St. Mary's and Placentia bays. Even in the larger towns like St. John's, most English and Irish settlers lived in separate neighbourhoods. When the Roman Catholic Irish moved away from the Avalon Peninsula they kept to themselves and settled in harbours not occupied by English Protestants.

As the population expanded the economy became more diversified and the shore cod fishery was no longer the only industry. The development of salmon fishing, sealing, and the fur trade led to an expansion to the northern bays on the island. Settlers occupied hundreds of coves, harbours, and islands chosen on account of their proximity to the fishing grounds. The Avalon Peninsula's scattered pockets of fertile land were put under cultivation.

THE RISE OF ST. JOHN'S

By the late eighteenth century St. John's came into its own as the dominant urban centre on the island. The settlement had become the island's capital in 1729, when the British naval convoy commander became the governor. The convoy's main rendezvous was St. John's harbour. A number of the settlers in St. John's had left the fishery and opened up taverns and stores to cater to the needs of the thousands of fishermen who came annually. Already the administrative capital of the island, St. John's became the business centre in the late eighteenth century. An English garrison was also located in the town.

At first glance, St. John's, located at the extreme eastern tip of the island, does not seem an obvious choice to become the island's great commercial centre. Yet it lay in the heart of the most densely populated area—the Avalon Peninsula, which is larger than Prince Edward Island. The peninsula itself was fortunately located, lying almost equidistant between the chief ports of New and Old England; in historian William Menzies Whitelaw's words, it was "the natural stepping stone between the old world and the new."[5] In addition, the peninsula stood immediately west of the North Atlantic's best fishing grounds—the Grand Banks.

329

St. John's importance increased further in the late eighteenth and early nineteenth centuries. The governor had made his headquarters there. The establishment of the Newfoundland Supreme Court in 1792 and of customs and naval offices further raised the town's standing. After the American Revolution merchants involved in the Canada and West Indies trade established themselves in St. John's. The town's merchants and shipowners financed the fishing trade, marketed dry cod, and distributed foodstuffs and manufactured goods to the outports. The merchants at St. John's had a commanding position over the island's affairs, with the merchants in the outports indebted to them. Newfoundlanders originated a new word, the "fishocracy," to describe the powerful St. John's merchants involved in the export of cod and the supplying of smaller merchants and fishermen in the outports.

As St. John's wealth grew the town established newspapers, health services, and schools. It thus became the only community on the island with an educated and moderately wealthy middle class. The capital, though, did not escape its past, or its continuing livelihood. George Warburton, an Irish soldier and writer, visited St. John's in the mid-1840s on a tour of British North America. In his book, *Hochelaga; or, England in the New World* (1846) he provides a delightful sketch of St. John's, Newfoundland—the "fishiest" capital in the world:

> In trying to describe St. John's there is some difficulty in applying to it an adjective sufficiently distinctive and appropriate. We find other cities coupled with epithets which at once give their predom-

inant characteristic: London the richest, Paris the gayest, St. Petersburg the coldest. In one respect the chief town of Newfoundland has, I believe, no rival: we may therefore call it the fishiest of modern capitals. Round a great part of the harbour are sheds, acres in extent, roofed with cod split in half, laid on like slates, drying in the sun, or rather the air, for there is not much of the former to depend upon. Those ships, bearing nearly every flag in the world, are laden with cod; those stout weatherly boats crowding up to the wharves have just now returned from fishing for cod; those few scant fields of cultivation, with lean crops coaxed out of the barren soil, are manured with cod; those grim, snug-looking wooden houses, their handsome furniture, the piano and the musical skill of the young lady who plays it, the satin gown of the mother, the gold chain of the father, are all paid for in cod; the breezes from the shore, soft and warm on this bright August day, are rich not with the odours of a thousand flowers but of a thousand cod. Earth, sea and air are alike pervaded with this wonderful fish . . .

330

THE OUTPORTS

Life was often much harsher in the outports than in St. John's. Jacob Mountain, a young Anglican priest, discovered as much during his seven years of missionary work on Newfoundland's south coast. There is no such thing, he wrote in his posthumously published *Some Accounts of a Sowing Time on the Rugged Shores of Newfoundland* (1857), as a typical Newfoundland fishing village:

In one place you will find them clean, tidy, thriving; houses neatly and substantially built, and a certain air of sobriety and self-respect about the people; the children a picture of delight, with their beautiful eyes, well-formed faces, soft flaxen hair. In another close by, the very reverse of all this; houses, or rather hovels of studs, the crevices gaping wide or filled with moss, the roof covered with rinds of trees and sods, the entrance constructed by heaps of dirt, often nothing that deserved the name of door, the aperture so low that one must stoop to enter, the interior without any furniture but a low table and rough stool, scarcely raised three inches from the ground, the children wretchedly ragged and dirty, crouching round, or creeping into the smoky wood fire, an oil sail and a few more studs forming the only partition between the kitchen and sleeping-room, if such terms can be applied to such miserable dens.

Mountain died in 1856 after a protracted bout of fever "caught in his constant visiting in infected houses." The missionary, a grandson of Jacob Mountain, the first Anglican Bishop of Quebec, was only thirty-eight.

Scattered along ten thousand kilometres of coast, the population of almost all of Newfoundland's distant and remote coves and harbours grew up without the benefit of clergy or schoolteachers. One result of this isolation was a rich and varied language. Numerous words survive today in Newfoundland that are only found—if anywhere else at all—in dialects in the British Isles. Residents of various Newfoundland areas can still be distinguished from one another by their accents, which all hark back to western England or Ireland.

RELIGION AND EDUCATION

Organized religion came to the island in the eighteenth century. The Anglicans began their work in 1703 with the appointment of the Reverend John Jackson as the first missionary in Newfoundland for the Society for the Propagation of the Gospel in Foreign Parts (SPG). During the century two or three Anglican clergymen were stationed on the island. The Roman Catholic church at this same time was not legally allowed on the island, although secretly Roman Catholic priests probably had arrived and were working in Newfoundland before freedom of worship was granted in 1784. After this date Protestant groups (Methodists and Congregationalists) also organized churches on the island. On the Labrador coast the Moravian missionaries began their work among the Inuit in 1771.

No school is known to have existed in Newfoundland until the eighteenth century, when the SPG established a few schools for the poor and underprivileged. Later the Wesleyan Methodists and other groups did. Most children, however, had no schooling and reached adulthood illiterate. The availability of education improved with the foundation of the Newfoundland School Society in 1823. The Society, which was closely identified with the Church of England, operated forty schools at its peak in the decades to follow.

In the larger towns, particularly St. John's, the upper classes had private tutors, private schools, and in a few cases sent their children off to be educated in England, since "respectable classes" did not want their children to attend the SPG or Methodist schools with the "lower orders." A very rigid class structure existed in the capital.

The Migratory Fishery Becomes Resident

Both the American and the French Revolutions and the subsequent Napoleonic Wars had a profound impact on Newfoundland's trade patterns.

With the departure of New England from the empire in 1783 and Britain's subsequent exclusion of Americans from the empire's carrying trade, Newfoundland became the major supplier of fish to the British West Indies. Fishery production expanded, creating new jobs and, in turn, causing emigration from Newfoundland to New England to decline sharply. Newfoundland became an integral part of the triangular trade linking it with Britain and the West Indies. A growing fleet of ships now operated from Newfoundland ports. As American-built ships could no longer be owned by British subjects, the island began to construct its own.

The outbreak of the last and the longest of the wars with France, the Napoleonic Wars (1793–1814), also contributed to the new prosperity on the island. The price of dried fish reached extremely high levels during the later years of the war because the French had to abandon their Newfoundland fishery; France simply could not protect its fishing fleet in wartime when the country needed to mobilize fully all of its naval resources to fight England.

During more than two decades of war with France, Newfoundland's fishery underwent a complete transformation. The three-centuries-old migratory West Country–Newfoundland fishery came to an end. Just as the French no longer came to fish off the "French Shore," the English vessels also stayed at home. Fears of press-gangs in England forcefully seizing sailors for service in the Royal Navy also convinced many of the bye-boatmen to remain on the island. The resident population and fishery grew. By 1815 residents owned almost the complete fishing fleet and produced the entire yield of saltfish, whereas immediately before the Napoleonic Wars the English migratory fishery produced more than half the total English–Newfoundland catch.

During these years of prosperity, ship owners, settlers, and St. John's entrepreneurs invested heavily in the fishery, creating a resident Newfoundland fleet. They began sending ships to less crowded parts of the coast, to the northern part of the island, and on to Labrador. Each June, thousands of Newfoundland fishermen sailed for Labrador to catch cod. Those who fished out of fixed locations with a "room" on shore became known as the "stationers" (or "squatters" or "roomers"); those who lived aboard their schooners and followed the fish were the "floaters" (or "green fish catchers"); those who chose to settle permanently on the Labrador coast became "the livyeres" (most likely a corruption of "live here"). As the Labrador fishery expanded, Britain decided to re-attach Labrador to Newfoundland, taking it from the control of Quebec in 1809.

THE RISE OF THE SEAL FISHERY

Seamen also went into Labrador waters and off Newfoundland's northern coasts to harvest the seal herds on the ice floes. Mammals and fish provided the bulk of the world's industrial oil in the early nineteenth century, and young seals had an excellent fat for fine-quality oil. Their skins could also be sold in England. The industry grew rapidly. Between 1831 and 1833 the seal fishery averaged between 30 and 40 percent of Newfoundland's total exports. Output reached more than six hundred thousand seals in 1831 alone, and by the 1850s, thirteen thousand men were annually employed. In the 1860s, however, a decline due to overharvesting set in.

The lack of written records makes it difficult to re-create a feeling of the independence and outlook of these hardy Newfoundlanders on the Labrador coast. Their spirit, though, echoes forth in one of their favourite nineteenth-century chanteys (and one still popular in Newfoundland today), "Jack was every inch a sailor":

'Twas twenty-five or thirty years since Jack first saw the light.
He came into this world of woe one dark and stormy night.
He was born on board his father's ship as she was lying to.
'Bout twenty-five or thirty miles southeast of Bacalieu.
Chorus
Jack was every inch a sailor, five and twenty years a whaler,
Jack was every inch a sailor, he was born upon the bright blue sea.
When Jack grew up to be a man, he went to the Labrador.
He fished in Indian Harbour, where his father fished before.
On his returning in the fog, he met a heavy gale,
And Jack was swept into the sea and swallowed by a whale.
Repeat Chorus
The whale went straight for Baffin's Bay, about ninety knots an hour,
And every time he'd blow a spray he'd send it in a shower.
"O, now," says Jack unto himself, "I must see what he's about."
He caught the whale all by the tail and turned him inside out.
Repeat Chorus[6]

Political Changes in the Nineteenth Century

Until 1832 Newfoundland's government differed completely from that of any other British North American colony. There was no official encouragement of settlement and no legislature. On the island the naval governor still had near-dictatorial powers.

In the early nineteenth century St. John's new mercantile and professional elite led the struggle for social and political reform. Cut off from

334

Provincial Archives of Newfoundland and Labrador.

Sealers "copying" the floes, c. 1920. "Copying" in Newfoundland and Labrador means leaping from floe to floe.

regular communication with the capital, the distant outports remained removed from the discussion, which really only preoccupied the Avalon Peninsula. The campaign for self-government was thus led by a group of first-generation arrivals anxious for political power, who knew little about the island except what happened in St. John's.

A Scottish physician, William Carson, who had come to St. John's in 1808, led the reform movement. In his first tract, written three years after his arrival, he argued against the system of naval governors and called for constitutional reform. The first advance came in 1817, when Newfoundland officially became more than a summer fishery; the Colonial Office decided that the governor should remain all year on the island and not just for two or three months in the summer. Parliament listened further to the Newfoundland reformers and in 1824 established Newfoundland as a true colony. It repealed the old fishing laws, an action which, among other things, allowed residents to hold clear title to land. In addition, in 1832 Parliament made provision for a Newfoundland legislature with elec- *335* tive and appointed chambers. Almost all of the male residents of the island gained the franchise.

Political reform regrettably increased internal dissension between Protestants and Roman Catholics (now almost evenly divided in number), between English and Irish, between radicals and conservatives, between merchants and fishermen, and between St. John's and the outports. In 1842 Britain suspended Newfoundland's constitution in order to end the political deadlock. The Colonial Office then formed a new amalgamated legislature, formed of eleven elected members and ten Crown appointees. This reduced the reformers to a small minority, at least until the two-chamber system was restored in 1848.

With Carson's death in 1843 the reform movement lost much of its momentum, but it revived in 1850 with a platform of obtaining responsible government. Carson's successors, such as John Kent, a fiery reform politician, demanded that the island obtain cabinet or responsible government. This goal was achieved in 1855, finally ending direct British rule. The first premier, the Reform or Liberal Leader Philip Francis Little, a Roman Catholic, tried to bridge the divisions between the two religious communities by appointing two Protestants to his cabinet, a goal which a conservative successor, Frederick Carter, a Protestant, also pursued and effectively achieved in the 1860s.

On the eve of the discussions for British North American federation, Newfoundland looked eastward, not westward towards the mainland. Newfoundland was a North Atlantic country, with patterns of trade and settlement linking it to Europe, the West Indies, and the United States. The development of the western part of the island, which contained the land most suitable for agriculture, would have served as a bridge to Canada.

Until 1904, however, the French held on to their treaty rights to dry fish on the western coastline.

On account of geography and its own distinctive history, Newfoundland stood very much apart from the Canadas and even from the three Maritime colonies. As the historian William Menzies Whitelaw wrote of Newfoundland in the mid-nineteenth century: "In many ways it was an integral part of British North America, but in others it remained as remote as Bermuda had been from the thirteen colonies."[7]

NOTES

[1] Frederick W. Rowe, *A History of Newfoundland and Labrador* (Toronto, 1980), p. 109.
[2] See Keith Matthews's comments on the growth of law in Newfoundland in *Lectures on the History of Newfoundland, 1500–1830* (St. John's, 1973), pp. 131–50.
[3] Ingeborg Marshall, personal communication, May 22, 1987.
[4] C. Grant Head, *Eighteenth Century Newfoundland: A Geographer's Perspective* (Toronto, 1976), p. 245.
[5] William Menzies Whitelaw, *The Maritimes and Canada before Confederation* (Toronto, 1966; first published 1934), p. 29.
[6] Shannon Ryan, "Jack Was Every Inch a Sailor," in "The Seal and Labrador Cod Fisheries of Newfoundland," in Canadian Museum of Civilization's *Canada's Visual History Series*, vol. 26, p. 16.
[7] Whitelaw, *Maritimes*, p. 28.

Related Readings

For a short survey of early Newfoundland history, see Keith Matthews's "The Nature and the Framework of Newfoundland History," in R. Douglas Francis and Donald B. Smith, eds., *Readings in Canadian History: Pre-Confederation*; 2d ed. (Toronto, 1986), pp. 75–82.

BIBLIOGRAPHY

Frederick W. Rowe's *A History of Newfoundland and Labrador* (Toronto, 1980) is at the present time the most complete study of Newfoundland's history. Peter Neary and Patrick O'Flaherty provide a short introduction to the island's history in their popular work, *Part of the Main: An Illustrated History of Newfoundland and Labrador* (St. John's 1983). G.O. Rothney has written a short survey in the Canadian Historical Association booklet series, *Newfoundland: A History* (Ottawa, 1964). For a brief historical overview Shannon Ryan's essay, "The Fishing Station," *Horizon Canada*, number 8 (1985): 169–75, is useful, as is his article, "The Seal and Labrador Cod Fisheries of Newfoundland," in the Canadian Museum of Civilization's *Canada's Visual History Series*, vol. 26, pp. 1–8. Another useful review is Patrick O'Flaherty, *The Rock Observed: Studies in the Literature of Newfoundland* (Toronto, 1979).

Studies on the history of Newfoundland in the pre-nineteenth century period include Gillian T. Cell, *English Enterprise in Newfoundland, 1577–1660* (Toronto, 1969); and Keith Matthews, *Lectures on the History of Newfoundland: 1500–1830* (St. John's, 1977). Several essays on early Newfoundland appear in G.M. Story, ed., *Early European Settlement and Exploitation in Atlantic Canada: Selected Papers* (St. John's, 1982). For the eighteenth century, see C. Grant Head, *Eighteenth Century Newfoundland: A Geographer's Perspective* (Toronto, 1976). Several sections of W.S. MacNutt's *The Atlantic Provinces: The Emergence of a Colonial Society, 1712–1857* (Toronto, 1965), refer to Newfoundland, as do portions of William Menzies Whitelaw's, *The Maritimes and Canada before Confederation* (Toronto, 1966; first published in 1934).

The mid-nineteenth century political history of the island is reviewed by Keith Matthews, "The Class of '32: St. John's Reformers on the Eve of Representative Government," in *Atlantic Canada Before Confederation*, vol. 1: *The Acadiensis Reader*, edited by P.A. Buckner and David Frank (Fredericton, 1985), pp. 212–26; and Gertrude E. Gunn in *The Political History of Newfoundland, 1832–1864* (Toronto, 1966). P.B. Waite has written a sketch of John Kent, the reform politician, in the *Dictionary of Canadian Biography*, vol. 10: 1871–1880 (Toronto, 1972), pp. 398–401. Other important biographies of prominent Newfoundlanders appear in this invaluable biographical series.

337

An entertaining collection is R.G. Moyles' "Complaints is many and various, but the odd Divil likes it." *Nineteenth Century Views of Newfoundland* (Toronto, 1975). James Hiller and Peter Neary have edited a collection of articles, *Newfoundland in the Nineteenth and Twentieth Centuries: Essays in Interpretation* (Toronto, 1980). Shannon Ryan reviews nineteenth-century economic developments in "Fishery to Colony: A Newfoundland Watershed, 1793–1815," in *Atlantic Canada Before Confederation*, vol. 1, pp. 130–48, and in "Seals Spelled Survival," *Horizon Canada*, number 27 (1985): 638–43. A short introduction to Newfoundland dialects appears in Phillip W. Rogers, "The Dictionary of Newfoundland English," *Queen's Quarterly*, 91 (1984): 832–37.

A substantial literature exists on Newfoundland's Indian population. Book-length treatments include James P. Howley's *The Beothucks or Red Indians: The Aboriginal Inhabitants of Newfoundland* (Toronto, 1974; first published in 1915); and Frederick W. Rowe, *Extinction: The Beothuks of Newfoundland* (Toronto, 1977). Valuable articles include L.F.S. Upton, "The Extermination of the Beothucks of Newfoundland," *Canadian Historical Review*, 58 (1977): 133–53; Ingeborg Marshall, "Disease as a Factor in the Demise of the Beothuck Indians," *Culture*, 1 (1981): 71–77, and her "The Beothuk," *Horizon Canada*, number 14 (1985): 326–31; and Francoy Raynauld, "Les pêcheurs et les colons anglais n'ont pas exterminé les Beothuks de Terre-Neuve," *Recherches amérindiennes au Québec*, 14 (1984): 45–59. Ralph Pastore reviews the history of the Micmac in Newfoundland in "Indian Summer: Newfoundland Micmacs in the Nineteenth Century," *Canadian Ethnology Society*, Papers from the Fourth Annual Congress, 1977 (Ottawa, 1978), pp. 167–78.

338

CHAPTER EIGHTEEN

The Northwest to the 1860s

The Blackfoot Indians occupied the rich buffalo ranges of southern Alberta and northern Montana in the mid-eighteenth century. The horse, brought to Mexico by the Spanish, reached them about 1730, at the same time Cree middlemen brought them guns. Apart from possibly one or two "northern white men," as they later termed the English, the only Europeans they encountered on the northern plains in the 1740s and 1750s were French traders from Canada, whom they called "real white men." 339

After the fall of New France in 1760 hundreds of Europeans entered the interior from the north, the east, and the south. The best furs came from the Northwest, and independent fur traders from Montreal came to buy them. In the early 1780s these Scotch and American fur traders formed the North West Company to challenge the Hudson's Bay Company, already more than a century old. Thirty years of competition between the two companies ended with their merger in 1821. Even after the Métis broke the Hudson's Bay Company monopoly in the Red River in 1849, the company remained the leading commercial power in the Northwest.

The establishment of a Red River settlement by Lord Selkirk in the early nineteenth century helped change the Europeans' perceptions of the country. Two expeditions in the late 1850s also contributed. Once the Hind and Palliser scientific exploring expeditions in the Northwest reported on the agricultural potential in the Red River, tens of thousands of landless British North Americans sought to settle there. No longer did British North Americans look upon the Northwest as a vast fur preserve with a harsh climate.

The French and the English in the Interior

The French came west in search of a short route to China. Since Verrazzano's voyage in 1524 the French had believed in the existence of a gulf

Glenbow-Alberta Institute.

"Indian Greeting White Man." "Real White Man" is still what the Blackfoot Indians of Alberta call the French, probably because the French were the first Europeans to make contact with them. The painting is by Frederic Remington, the famous American illustrator.

like Hudson Bay or the Gulf of Mexico, one which intruded deeply into the continent from the Pacific (see chapter 3). Jean Nicollet de Belleborne, the first explorer charged with the mission of finding the "inland sea," left Quebec in 1634, taking with him a colourful flowered Chinese robe so as to be properly attired when he encountered the officials of the Chinese emperor. When René-Robert Cavelier de La Salle travelled inland in 1669 in search of China, his neighbours gave the name "La Chine" (China) to his land grant on the south bank of Montreal Island, in recognition of his ambition of reaching the Orient by way of "La Mer de l'Ouest" (the Western Sea). Half a century later the French still hoped that somewhere between the 40th and 50th parallels of latitude they would find a navigable strait joining the Western Sea to the Pacific.

THE FRENCH SEARCH FOR THE "WESTERN SEA"

In 1717 the French Crown supported attempts to discover this sea but did not provide financing. Profits from fur-trade posts west of Lake Superior went to cover the exploration costs. Finally, in 1730 Lieutenant Pierre Gaultier de Varennes et de La Vérendrye, commander of the fur

Trudel, *Introduction to New France*, p. 83.

The "Western Sea"—the "Mer de l'Ouest." A report made in 1752 to the Académie des Sciences in Paris still includes it.

341

trading post of Kaministiquia (present-day Thunder Bay), offered to establish a post on Lake Winnipeg. From this base he agreed to conduct explorations for the Western Sea, at no expense to the Crown.

La Vérendrye and his sons carefully chose locations for their fur-trade posts that allowed for a progressive advance inland. From his supply base at Kaministiquia, La Vérendrye travelled westward in the 1730s, building posts on the Lake of the Woods and around Lakes Winnipeg and Winnipegosis. The Chevalier de La Corne, a successor, later founded a fort further west near the forks of the north and south branches of the Saskatchewan River in 1753, and some evidence exists that two years earlier a small French expedition had reached the Rockies.[1] The French never found "La Mer de l'Ouest," but they did locate the key to the interior—

the Saskatchewan River, whose twin branches flow through the central plain in a huge, wavering Y.

THE HUDSON'S BAY COMPANY'S INLAND EXPEDITIONS

The English had established trading posts in the late seventeenth century at the mouths of rivers emptying into Hudson Bay. From their forts on the bay the English carried on a profitable trade with Cree and Assiniboine middlemen who brought furs to them. After a series of armed clashes on the bay, France recognized English possession of the coastline of Hudson and James Bays in the Treaty of Utrecht in 1713.

The English sponsored only two inland expeditions southwest of York Factory, their major post on Hudson Bay. In 1690–91 they sent Henry Kelsey, a young employee known to the Hudson's Bay Company's committee in London as "a very active lad, delighting much in Indians' company, being never more pleased than when he is travelling amongst them," to explore the interior. He travelled with a Cree band and reached the prairies, probably in present-day east–central Saskatchewan. But upon his return the company decided not to establish costly forts in the interior, since it already enjoyed a great advantage over the French because of the shorter bay route. As long as the Crees and Assiniboine brought good furs to them, the English stayed on Hudson Bay.

More than half a century after Kelsey's journey, however, the English felt the effect of French competition from the La Vérendryes and their successors. In 1754 they sent another employee, Anthony Henday, to convince the Indians to give up their trade at the French posts and to come down to the bay. In his journal, which is far more precise than Kelsey's, he identified the specific tribes in the interior and provided notes on their way of life. In present-day central Alberta Henday met the "Archithinues," or Blackfoot; these were actually three tribes (the Blackfoot proper, the Bloods, and the Peigans), who called themselves the "Prairie People." The young trader became the first Englishman to describe the buffalo hunt, for which the Indians used bows, arrows, and lances while on horseback.

Impact of the Gun and the Horse

Guns and horses wrought great changes in the life of the native peoples in the Northwest. The European musket became one of the most sought-after trade items by the Woodland Crees and Assiniboines. The guns did have disadvantages: loading powder and shot was awkward; the gun barrels were always prone to explosion; the guns broke easily in the cold and

342

required maintenance by European gunsmiths; and the Indians in the interior could not obtain ammunition easily, since the traders did not stock large supplies. Despite these limitations, the gun had enormous advantages in warfare. Its bullets went a longer distance than arrows and with greater killing power. Rawhide shields and armour offered no protection against a musket ball. Equally, the gun's loud report gave a psychological advantage over one's enemies.

TRIBAL MIGRATIONS

As the Woods Cree penetrated northward into the Chipewyan's hunting grounds, the Assiniboine invaded those of the Dakota Sioux to the west of the Great Lakes. Ample supplies of arms and ammunition enabled both of the invading tribes to push back their enemies. In the north the Chipewyan, an important Dene-speaking tribe, were able to turn back the Woods Cree only when the Hudson's Bay Company opened Fort Prince of Wales at present-day Churchill in the early eighteenth century, allowing them to obtain guns and ammunition at the new post.

343

In the early eighteenth century the Chipewyan tribe also began to move into the woodlands immediately north of the Woods Cree. Directly supplied by the English at Churchill, the Chipewyan sold European goods to interior tribes. Like the Crees, they became the traders' middlemen. In addition, the European gun gave them an advantage in their struggle with the Inuit to the north and the Crees to the southwest. In 1770–72 Samuel Hearne, a Hudson's Bay Company explorer, made an epic journey with a group of Chipewyans across the barren lands from Churchill to the Arctic Ocean. His account, *A Journey from Prince of Wales's Fort, in Hudson's Bay, to the Northern Ocean,* is still regarded as one of the classics of North American travel and provides an eyewitness account of eighteenth-century Chipewyan life. To the west, the Crees' expansion continued along the North Saskatchewan River for nearly another century.

As the Woods Crees migrated farther west, they entered the plains and into Blackfoot country. Their intrusion ended the period of initially friendly relations between themselves and the "Prairie People." The Cree soon established control over a wide area north of the North Saskatchewan River.

THE ARRIVAL OF THE HORSE

The horse had an even greater impact on the Plains Indians than did the gun. Until the introduction of the repeating rifle in the 1860s, the Plains

344

AT THE PORTAGE.

Hudson's Bay Company's Employés on their annual Expedition.

National Archives of Canada / C3610.

Hudson Bay Company's employees with their stock and canoes, from *Picturesque Canada* (1882).

Indians preferred to use the sinew-backed bow with metal-tipped arrows for the buffalo hunt. This bow was more reliable, more accurate, and—unlike a gun—its noise did not prematurely stampede a buffalo herd. In contrast to the gun, the horse caused a cultural revolution on the Plains and became the standard of wealth. Some rich tribesmen owned herds of 70–100 horses. By giving away horses, or even by lending them, one could rise in prestige. Horses were borrowed for use in hunting and on war parties, with the borrower returning one-half of the game killed or of the captured goods. Poorer Indians with only one or two horses were forced to walk when the tribe migrated. The horse thus contributed to the development of a class structure among the Blackfoot, with rich, middle-echelon, and poor families separated from each other almost solely on the basis of the number of horses owned.

The introduction of the horse had other effects. It intensified intertribal warfare. Face-to-face combat on horseback with a bow and arrow, lance, war club, or knife—or a European gun—led to a great increase in casualties. The horse also enabled the Woodland Assiniboines and many of the Woodland Crees to hunt buffalo on the Plains, thus freeing them from their dependence on European guns and trade goods.

345

The Fur Trade After the Fall of New France

After the fall of New France in 1760 the Hudson's Bay Company hoped that it could now enjoy a trade monopoly in the Northwest. Yet the company soon faced new rivals: aggressive Scotch and American traders operating out of Montreal (see chapter 10). In the early 1770s they employed large numbers of voyageurs and sent large shipments of goods to the West. In the early 1780s the Montreal traders combined their capital and established a large organization to look after long-distance trade. They formed the North West Company, which soon expanded beyond the limits of the French fur trade to the Peace, Mackenzie, and Columbia rivers.

THE NORTH WEST COMPANY

On these expeditions the company employed Métis and Indian canoemen, because only they knew the fur country, the inland routes, and the native peoples. These hardy people crossed half a continent. Henry Youle Hind, the leader of the Canadian Northwest expedition in 1857, calculated that the voyageurs in his party made one stroke a second with their paddles, or sixty a minute. Since they paddled twelve hours a day, he added, each man made 3600 strokes per hour, or 43 200 a day.[2] They also carried loads of eighty kilograms on their backs over rocky portage trails.

The company underwent great expansion in the 1780s and 1790s. Fur trader Peter Pond lead the way for the Montreal merchants in the Athabasca and Peace River country in 1778. Later fur trader Alexander Mackenzie journeyed down the Mackenzie River in 1789 and reached the Pacific in 1793.

The North West Company then opened up the Mackenzie Basin and later the Columbia River, yet the cost of sending of supplies greatly curbed the company's profits. Its great handicap was its long supply line, which stretched from Montreal to Fort Chipewyan on Lake Athabasca (in present-day northern Alberta). The Nor'Wester organization, though, continued to grow and incorporated the xy Company, formed in the late 1790s by independent Montreal fur traders, in 1804.

Rivalry with the North West Company forced the Hudson's Bay Company to go further inland to obtain the best furs. This, in turn, led to the elimination of the Cree and Assiniboine middlemen, as both the Nor'Westers and the Hudson's Bay Company established direct contact with the hunting bands. Many of the Woods Assiniboine and the Woods Cree bands moved out onto the Plains permanently and became provisioners, supplying the two trading companies with dried buffalo meat and grease. The demands of both companies were enormous: a voyageur would consume nearly a kilogram of pemmican or dried buffalo meat a day—the equivalent of approximately three kilograms of fresh meat.

Despite its opponent's great size, the Hudson's Bay Company had the advantage of a shorter, hence less expensive, transportation route, Hudson Bay being much closer to the inland posts than Montreal was. The smaller company could take trade goods to the Athabasca country at one-half the cost. The Hudson's Bay Company's cumbersome York boats could also be used on the North Saskatchewan to carry much greater amounts of trade goods in, and furs out, than the Nor'Westers' canoes.

346

Rise of The Métis

French fur traders were well established in the Upper Great Lakes by the 1690s (see chapter 9). As they intermarried with the Indian women, a distinct group of "mixed bloods" or French Métis appeared. Their culture was a unique blending of the Indians' traditional ways and European customs. The Métis population increased at a more rapid rate than the Indians because the Métis had acquired from their French fathers a greater natural immunity to European diseases and the number of mixed marriages grew steadily. After a generation or two, Métis settlements extended from

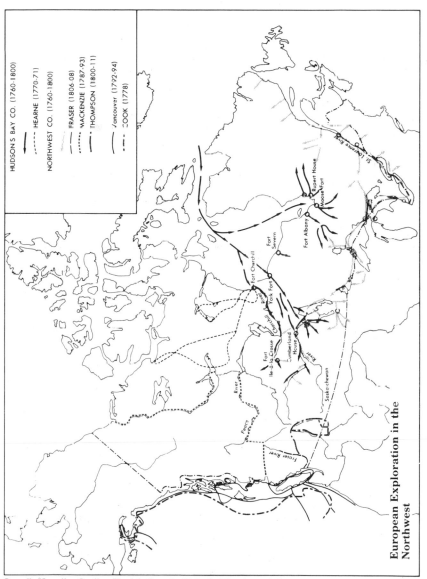

European Exploration in the Northwest

Cornell, Hamelin, Ouellet, Trudel, *Canada, Unity in Diversity*, p. 162.

the Upper Great Lakes west to the Red River and south through the plains to the Arkansas River.

The French and the Métis voyageurs travelled throughout present-day western Canada and the United States. They introduced a number of French words to describe the new terrain: "coulee" (from *coulée*) for a deep gulch or ravine; "butte," for a flat-topped hill; and the word "prairie," from *pré*, or meadow. The French also left a permanent record of their presence in the pronunciation of place names such as in the suppressed terminal "s" of Arkansas and Illinois.

THE MÉTIS AT THE RED RIVER

In the early nineteenth century encampments of the French and their mixed-blood descendants developed at the junction of the Red and the Assiniboine rivers (at present-day Winnipeg). Many voyageurs took Indian wives, and as their mixed-blood descendants intermarried, they furthered the growth of the "New Nation" of the Métis. Such Métis family names as Breland, Vandal, Desjarlais, Cardinal, Delorme, Dumont, Beaulieu, and Deschamps became well known.

Like the mixed bloods on the Upper Great Lakes, the Métis built homes of squared logs covered with bark roofs. From their European husbands the women learned to make a baking-powder biscuit called bannock, which is still a staple food in Métis communities. Although they did farm a little, growing peas and potatoes in small gardens behind their cabins, in the early nineteenth century, the Métis lived essentially off the buffalo hunt.

They also adapted European technology to prairie life. In the early nineteenth century they introduced the small wagons used by the French Canadians in Quebec. These "Red River carts," built entirely of wood and tied together with leather, were easy to repair. Although the carts were extremely efficient, the constant rubbing of wood on wood made a terrible noise (one observer described it as if a thousand fingernails were being drawn across a thousand panes of glass at the same time) and they gave off clouds of dust that could be seen several kilometres away. To cross a river one simply took off the wheels, some of which were two metres in diameter, strapped them underneath the cart, and used the vehicle as a raft. The Red River cart allowed the Métis to easily hunt the buffalo. An ox-drawn cart could carry a load of four hundred kilograms more than thirty kilometres in a day. Several carts might be tied together in a caravan, and a driver could handle five oxen and carts. Soon the Red River cart trails running across the prairies rivalled the rivers as transportation routes.

The Métis' blending of French and Indian worlds was also expressed in the development of a new language—French Cree, or, as the Métis called it, "Michif." John C. Crawford, a linguist, has described the language: "The extraordinary characteristic of Michif is the manner in which French and Cree components combine; the noun phrase is a French domain; verb structure is clearly and thoroughly Cree, and syntax is Cree with French and probably English influence."[3] An entirely different tongue evolved among the Ojibwa close to the Scottish settlement in the Red River—Bungi, which combined Ojibwa and Gaelic.[4]

By the late eighteenth and early nineteenth centuries most servants of the North West and Hudson's Bay companies had taken native wives. Besides companionship there were economic as well as emotional benefits of such marriages: a union with the daughter of leading hunters or chiefs brought to her new husband the trade of his new father-in-law, as well as that of his relations. Moreover, in order to survive, the fur traders needed someone to make pemmican, to fish, to gather berries, and to make moccasins and snowshoes. Some traders and voyageurs took several wives. Through the native women the men became acquainted with the customs and languages of the tribes, and the women acted for their husbands as guides and interpreters.

349

In the early 1800s marriage between whites and natives was so common that the North West Company was sheltering approximately one thousand women and Métis children at its posts. The Métis were not yet considered a distinct community, but they were on the verge of such recognition. By establishing an agricultural colony in the Red River in 1811, the Hudson's Bay Company inadvertently contributed to the Métis' rising consciousness as the "New Nation" of the Plains. In 1815–16 the Nor'Westers directly encouraged the Métis to regard themselves as a new nationality.

The Selkirk Colony and the Fur Trade Wars

In 1811, Lord Douglas, the Fifth Earl of Selkirk, established an agricultural colony for evicted Scottish tenant farmers at the forks of the Red and the Assiniboine rivers. He had already settled eight hundred displaced Highlanders on land previously purchased on Prince Edward Island and begun a less successful settlement at Baldoon on Lake St. Clair in Upper Canada. After his family purchased control of the Hudson's Bay Company, Selkirk was able to obtain from the company an enormous land grant of three hundred thousand square kilometres in the Red River Valley—an area five times the size of Scotland—that was named Assiniboia. The North West Company protested, however, because the founding of an agricultural colony in the heart of the Red River threatened the provisioning of their own interior posts.

ESTABLISHMENT OF SELKIRK'S RED RIVER COLONY

The advance party of 18 Selkirk settlers reached the Red River from Hudson Bay in late August 1811, and another 120 joined them in late October. Miles Macdonell, Selkirk's choice as governor, established them near the junction of the Red and the Assiniboine rivers (now downtown Winnipeg).

The idealistic but impractical Lord Selkirk had sent them off without ploughs, and they had only hoes and spades to use for cultivation. Their one line of communication stretched back more than a thousand kilometres to a tiny fort on Hudson Bay, visited once a year by ships from Britain. To survive that winter the newly-arrived colonists had to camp near the Hudson's Bay Company post at Pembina, about 125 km to the south. As for their crops the following year, only the potatoes planted the previous autumn yielded well. The settlers were forced to spend another rugged Red River winter at Pembina in log huts. Only the generous assistance of the local Métis and North West Company traders allowed the Selkirk settlers to survive those first two years. Then the aggressive Macdonell foolishly antagonized his benefactors, who were already upset by the presence of the newcomers.

Macdonell's "pemmican proclamation" of early January 1814 placed an embargo on the export of pemmican from the Red River. The proclamation confirmed the Nor'Westers' suspicions that the Hudson's Bay Company had indeed planted the Red River colony to ruin them. The North West Company retaliated first by approaching the Selkirk settlers and offering them free transport to new homes and better land in Upper Canada. Two-thirds of the two hundred settlers accepted the offer in 1815. After arresting Miles Macdonell and forcing the remaining settlers to withdraw, the Nor'Westers burned the settlement. Selkirk, meanwhile, sent more settlers to reoccupy the colony, and a new governor, Robert Semple, replaced Macdonell.

RISE OF A MÉTIS CONSCIOUSNESS

The North West Company also encouraged the Métis to think of themselves, through their Indian mothers, as the real owners of the Red River. The Nor'Westers selected young Cuthbert Grant, then in his early twenties, and three other mixed bloods as captains of the Métis. Grant, the son of a Scottish Nor'Wester and a Cree mother, became the leader of an organized movement to drive out the Selkirk colony. Named Captain General of the Métis by the North West Company in 1816, he gathered his forces in the Qu'Appelle Valley and then advanced towards the Red River colony.

On a battlefield called Seven Oaks, Grant and his men met Governor Robert Semple, who had with him about twenty-five colonists. During a short, tense confrontation, firing broke out. Semple and twenty of his men lost their lives in the Battle of Seven Oaks, but only one of Grant's men was killed.

The Métis victory sealed the Métis' unity, giving them a sense of nationhood. They now began to think of themselves as a new nation, the *Bois Brûlés*, (a French expression meaning "charred wood" or "burnt wood," referring to the brownish skin colour of the Métis), and the true owners of the Red River. Before the night of June 19, 1816 was over, the conflict had been made into a song by the Métis bard Pierre Falcon. That song became the Métis' national anthem.

Exasperated by the continuing violence between the Hudson's Bay and the North West companies, the British government urged a compromise solution. The death of Lord Selkirk in 1820 facilitated the task, and the following year the two companies were united. Immediately the consolidated company gave up its long canoe routes connecting the interior posts with Montreal in favour of its York boats from Hudson Bay. Under the direction of George Simpson, governor of the vast Northern Department (bounded by Hudson Bay, the Arctic and Pacific oceans, and the Missouri Valley), other changes followed. "The Little Emperor," as his employees nicknamed the red-haired Scot, brought peace and financial order to the new Hudson's Bay Company for the next forty years, until his death in 1860. He did this by introducing strict conservation measures in areas that had been overtrapped, laying off hundreds of redundant employees, keeping salaries down, and closing unnecessary posts.

351

The Red River in the Mid-Nineteenth Century

After 1817 and the re-establishment of Hudson's Bay Company's control in the Red River, the colonists' real challenges were environmental ones. Grasshoppers destroyed the crops in 1818–19, and the great flood of 1826 completely levelled the settlement. Whenever the Red River overflowed its banks the water spread quickly over huge areas, because the valley itself is flat. In 1826, in just one day, the flood waters rose nearly three metres, transforming the settlement into a lake. Houses were swept towards Lake Winnipeg. For shelter the survivors dug cellars in the plain, roofed them with sod, and lived underground through the winter. Floods would strike the Red River colony twice again during the century, in 1852 and 1882.

THE "COUNTRY-BORN"

The Red River was a stable and prosperous community of six thousand inhabitants by the 1840s, and was more or less evenly split between English- and French-speaking settlers. Large numbers of fur traders retired there, bringing with them Indian and Métis wives and, in the 1820s and 1830s, their mixed-blood children. Names of English-speaking Métis, the so-called "Country-Born," who had come to the Red River from Hudson Bay include: Bird, Bunn, Cook, Flett, Isbister, Pruden, Sinclair, Sutherland. Many of their European ancestors were from Scotland and the Orkney Islands to the north.

The Hudson's Bay Company tried at first to enforce a policy of strict segregation between natives and Europeans, but the policy quickly broke down. Rarely, though, did the mixed-race families stay within the walls of the posts, since the company would not support them. The British fathers' opportunity to provide for their mixed-blood children came with the establishment of the Selkirk colony. Hundreds of Country-Born moved to the Red River in the 1820s and 1830s, after the two companies united. There their children were introduced to farming and became members of the Anglican church. (The Rev. John West, the first Anglican minister in the colony, arrived in 1820.) A few obtained lower-ranked positions in the Hudson's Bay Company, which had a bias towards employing Europeans in clerical-managerial posts. Although racial bonds united them with the French-speaking Métis, the Country-Born and the Métis did not mix a great deal. Religion, language, and their place of residence in the Red River divided them.

352

THE FRENCH-SPEAKING MÉTIS

The French-speaking Métis created a cohesive community focussed, in particular, on their Roman Catholic faith. The arrival of the first French-speaking missionaries in the Red River settlement in 1818, and then the first sisters, the Grey Nuns, in the 1840s, strengthened the Métis' Christian faith as well as their knowledge of the language and culture of their French-Canadian ancestors. The Métis also obtained a sense of community from their participation in their expanding buffalo hunt.

In the 1840s the Métis went on two annual hunts from the Red River— in June and in September or October. These expeditions included more than a thousand people. The Métis first elected ten captains by vote at a general council, one of whom they named chief of the hunt or governor. Each captain had ten "soldiers" under his command who helped the governor of the hunt maintain order and enforce regulations. Immediately after the election of the officers, regulations were drawn up which the crier repeated to all those in the hunt. Such rules as "no person or party to run buffalo before the general order" show the discipline of the hunt. Discipline was necessary to prevent the premature stampede of the herds and to repulse raids by the Sioux.

THE SAYER TRIAL, 1849

The test case of the Métis' power in the Red River came during the trial of Pierre-Guillaume Sayer, a Métis trader arrested in 1849 on a charge of illegally trafficking in furs. The Hudson's Bay Company insisted that it had a monopoly of selling goods to the colonists and trading with the Indians and that Sayer had broken it. The Métis, who had not yet left on the spring hunt, organized an informal self-defence committee. Outside the courthouse gathered 200–300 Métis. After hearing the evidence presented, the court found him guilty as charged. The judge, however, pronounced Sayer guilty but imposed no sentence. It would have been difficult to do so, because the Métis hunters constituted the most powerful military force in the colony. When Sayer emerged from the courthouse a free man the Métis knew that they had broken the Hudson's Bay Company monopoly. "*Vive la liberté, le commerce est libre* (Long live liberty, trade is free)," they shouted.

353

THE BATTLE OF GRAND COTEAU, 1851

The second test of the Métis' power came in present-day North Dakota in 1851. As the Métis moved farther to the southwest to buffalo hunt they came into conflict with the Sioux. The Métis-Sioux wars intensified in the 1840s and came to a head in 1851, at the battle of Grand Coteau (big hillock), southeast of present-day Minot, North Dakota. During the confrontation, in which the Métis hid behind a circular barricade made with their carts, packs, and saddles, at least twenty of the Sioux Indians died but only one Métis. Grand Coteau demonstrated the Métis' growing military supremacy in the area surrounding the Red River.

THE END OF THE RED RIVER'S ISOLATION

The community's isolation ended in the 1850s. The Métis now made frequent overland trips to St. Paul to sell furs and to acquire supplies.

From 1851 to 1869 the number of Red River carts making the journey rose from 100 to 2500. Mail service to the Red River came through St. Paul after 1853, rather than by the slower and more cumbersome mail route through York Factory on Hudson Bay. A railway reached St. Paul in 1855, and within a year the Hudson's Bay Company used it to bring in supplies. The establishment of a regular steamboat connection with St. Paul and to the Red River in 1859 made the ties with Minnesota (population nearly 200 000 by 1860) all the more binding. Indeed, only the depression of 1857, the American Civil War in 1861–65, and the outbreak of war between the Americans and the Sioux in 1862–64 checked Minnesota's desire to annex the Red River country.

The river settlement changed rapidly in the 1860s. Louis Goulet, a Métis who grew up in the Red River valley during the decade, left a colourful account of the region and the Red River Métis immediately before union with Canada. He later told an interviewer that with the

354

disappearance of the buffalo from the Red River country, farming became much more important: "Everything had been improved, from transportation to food on the table. Craftsmanship was considerably improved, thanks to superior tools that could now be bought in almost any ordinary general store and at prices most people could afford." Most houses had floors and were partitioned into rooms. From St. Paul and other settlements in the United States the Métis brought glass panes for use in windows. Cart wheels now had to be iron or steel. The spinning wheel and the weaving loom were also welcome additions in many Métis homes. Perhaps the only negative aspect of life in the late 1860s, in Louis Goulet's opinion, was the arrival of newcomers, whom he informed his interviewer "were eagerly sowing racial and religious conflict. The latest arrivals were looking to be masters of everything, everywhere." These were the several hundred Canadians who came west in the late 1860s.

Many Métis moved farther west in the 1860s in search of the larger buffalo herds. They established settlements at the forks of the Saskatchewan, in the North Saskatchewan River valley, in the Cypress Hills area of present-day southwestern Saskatchewan, and at Lac Ste. Anne, about eighty kilometres west of Fort Edmonton. Lac Ste. Anne was the largest Métis settlement west of the Red River until St. Albert (about fifteen kilometres west of Edmonton) was founded in 1862.

In 1871 approximately 2000–4000 mixed-bloods lived along the North Saskatchewan River between Red River and the Rockies, and about 11 000 at the junction of the Red and Assiniboine rivers. The Métis' and Country-Borns' population of 13 000 to 15 000 exceeded that of any of the Plains tribes. In 1863 Captain John Palliser, who had led the British-sponsored Palliser Expedition, estimated that the Plains Cree north of the United States border numbered about 11 500; the Assiniboines, 1000; (4000 more lived south of the border); and the Blackfoot Confederacy, 8000.

The Plains Indians in the Mid-Nineteenth Century

While the Métis and Country-Born population doubled in the Red River every fifteen to twenty years, the Plains Indians seriously declined in number in the mid-nineteenth century. In 1837–38 smallpox ravaged the Canadian Plains tribes. Their culture contributed inadvertently to the diffusion of the new diseases because they lived in close-knit family groups in very small living areas, as much for warmth as for friendship. Nor had the Indians any idea of how these new diseases were transmitted. As one Peigan told David Thompson: "We had no belief that one Man could give it to another, any more than a wounded Man could give his wound to another."

The idea of a quarantine being foreign to them, they insisted on visiting the sick to help and, in doing so, unknowingly spread the illness. The Assiniboine's population declined by two-thirds, as did that of the Blackfoot. Thanks to the efforts of the Hudson's Bay Company traders, however, many of the Cree around the company's posts were spared.

355

The spread of the epidemic was checked by a smallpox vaccine discovered in Europe around 1800. The Hudson's Bay Company, seeing the Indians fleeing northward, began the first extensive vaccination program among the western Canadian Indians. The vaccinated population constituted an effective barrier, and the highly contagious disease spread no farther north than the Hudson's Bay Company posts on the northern fringes of the Plains. On account of the vaccine the Cree became the most numerous Indian group on the Canadian Plains. After the epidemic had run its course the Crees could more readily move farther onto the Plains, since the strength of the Blackfoot had been so reduced.

Other infectious killer diseases were also rampant, for the Plains Indians had no immunity to the so-called "childhood diseases" of the Europeans. In 1864–65 a winter outbreak of scarlet fever carried away more than a thousand Blackfoot. An epidemic of measles hit the Cree. Influenza and whooping cough also took their toll. Smallpox carried away more than thirty-five hundred Indians and Métis on the Canadian Plains in 1870, since at this time little vaccine was on hand. A new disease—tuberculosis—arrived in the 1860s, brought by refugee Sioux from the United States and Red River Métis moving westward (both groups had already been exposed to the virus through contact with European carriers).

ARRIVAL OF THE WHISKEY TRADERS

In the mid-1860s the Blackfoot Confederacy in addition to disease, experienced another assault—that of American whiskey traders. In the 1850s and the early 1860s the Blackfoot had traded with both the Hudson's Bay Company and the American Fur Company. At Fort Edmonton and Rocky Mountain House they exchanged pemmican and horses (as well as the few beaver furs they trapped) for British trade goods; they traded bulky buffalo hides and robes (which were difficult for the Hudson's Bay Company to transport profitably in their York boats) for American goods at Fort Benton in Montana. The American Fur Company bought all it could, shipping the furs down the Missouri by steamer to St. Louis.

But in 1864 the American Fur Company suddenly collapsed, and the buffer zone between the two long-established companies became open ground. Shortly after the conclusion of the American Civil War in 1865, American whiskey traders, many of them Civil War veterans, entered southern Alberta to make their fortunes. Their arrival led to great social disruption among groups with little acquaintance with alcohol and no social controls for it.

356

Canadians and the Northwest

In the 1860s, Canadians coveted the Northwest. Good agricultural land was scarce in both Canada East and Canada West, and the western lands were most inviting. In the early 1860s both the Canadian and British expeditions published their findings on their explorations west from Lake Superior to the Rocky Mountains. Of the two, the British-sponsored expedition led by John Palliser is the best known. The Irish explorer was sent by both the Royal Geographical Society and the imperial government to report on the potential for agriculture, the mineral resources, and the possibilities for settlement. For two years, from 1857 to 1859, he and the scientists in his party conducted their investigations. Similarly, the Canadians dispatched in 1857 a scientific expedition headed by Henry Youle Hind, a professor of geology and chemistry at Trinity University in Toronto. He led two expeditions into the Red River, the Assiniboine, and the Saskatchewan River valleys in 1857 and 1858.

Both expeditions returned expressing great enthusiasm for the Northwest. They reported the magnificent possibilities for European agriculture, particularly in the "fertile belt" of the Red River and the well-watered North Saskatchewan River valley, with European-style agriculture being practised in only a thirty-six-square-kilometre area. Since all the available land in Canada had been claimed, the Canadians wanted to expand to the Prairies before the United States did.

The fur trade attracted Europeans to the Northwest, first the French and then the British. The Europeans' intermarriage with the Indians led to the creation of a new people, the Métis. By the mid-1860s this group had expanded in number to approximately 15 000, at the very moment that the Plains Indian population had declined to about 25 000. In terms of resisting any possible Canadian advance westward these small numbers would be a distinct disadvantage, for the Canadians numbered roughly three million. Already, many in the Union of the Canadas wanted to expand westward to the Northwest, and then eventually to the Pacific Ocean.

NOTES

[1] W.J. Eccles, the noted historian of New France, believes they reached the Rockies, and speculates that they built a small fort near the present-day site of Rocky Mountain House. See "La Mer de l'Ouest: Outpost of the Empire," in his *Essays on New France* (Toronto, 1987), pp. 105–106.
[2] Henry Youle Hind, *Narrative of the Canadian Red River Exploring Expedition of 1857 and of the Assiniboine and Saskatchewan Exploring Expedition of 1858*, 2 vols. (Edmonton, 1971; first published 1860), 1: 45.
[3] John C. Crawford, "What is Michif?: Language in the Métis tradition," in *The New Peoples: Being and Becoming Métis in North America*, edited by Jacqueline Peterson and Jennifer S.H. Brown (Winnipeg, 1985), p. 233.
[4] Diane Payment, "Review of *The New Peoples: Being and Becoming Métis in North America*," *The Beaver* 66, no. 6 (1986–87): 61.

357

Related Readings

Two useful essays on this topic appear in R. Douglas Francis and Donald B. Smith, *Readings in Canadian History: Pre-Confederation*, 2d ed. (Toronto, 1986): Arthur J. Ray, "Fur Trade History as an Aspect of Native History," pp. 162–73; and Sylvia Van Kirk, " 'Women in Between': Indian Women in Fur Trade Society in Western Canada," pp. 174–89.

BIBLIOGRAPHY

The literature on the Northwest is voluminous. For the archaeological background, see Olive P. Dickason's "A Historical Reconstruction for the Northwestern Plains," *Prairie Forum*, 5 (1980): 19–37, reprinted in *The Prairie West: Historical Readings*, edited by R. Douglas Francis and Howard Palmer (Edmonton, 1985), pp. 39–57. Gerald Friesen's *The Canadian Prairies: A History* (Toronto, 1984) provides an excellent overview of the entire period.

For information on the Indians in the eighteenth and nineteenth centuries, consult Arthur Ray, *Indians in the Fur Trade* (Toronto, 1974). John Ewers' history, *The Blackfeet* (Norman, 1958), also is essential. The impact of the horse and the gun on Blackfoot culture is reviewed by Oscar Lewis in *The Effects of White Contact Upon Blackfoot Culture: With Special Reference to the Role of the Fur Trade* (Seattle, 1942). Hugh Dempsey's biographies of three Plains Indian chiefs offer a vivid portrait of Blackfoot, Blood, and Cree life in the nineteenth century: see *Crowfoot* (Edmonton, 1972), *Red Crow* (Saskatoon, 1980), and *Big Bear* (Vancouver, 1984). A fascinating eye-witness account of the Chipewyan is Samuel Hearne's famous *A Journey from Prince of Wales' Fort, in Hudson's Bay, to the Northern Ocean* published in 1795—see the edition edited by Richard Glover (Toronto, 1958). For information on the health of the Plains Indians, see G. Graham-Cumming, "Health of the Original Canadians, 1867–1967," *Medical Services Journal of Canada* 23, no. 2 (1967): 115–66.

E.E. Rich provides an overview of the fur trade in western Canada in *The Fur Trade and the North West to 1857* (Toronto, 1967). Glyndwr Williams has written a short survey, "Highlights of the First 200 Years of the Hudson's Bay Company," *The Beaver*, outfit 301 (Autumn 1970): 4–63. The French experience on the western plains during the French regime is reviewed by W.J. Eccles in "La Mer de l'Ouest: Outpost of Empire," in *Essays in New France* (Toronto, 1987), pp. 96–109. For short sketches of the most important European fur traders, see the essays on Kelsey, La Vérendrye, Henday, Hearne, Thompson, and others in the multi-volume *Dictionary of Canadian Biography* (Toronto, 1966–).

The Métis are the subject of numerous studies. One popular work is D. Bruce Sealey and Antoine S. Lussier, *The Metis: Canada's Forgotten People* (Winnipeg, 1975). George Woodcock has recently translated into English Marcel Giraud's classic *Le Métis Canadien* (Paris, 1945); see *The Métis in the Canadian West*, 2 vols. (Edmonton, 1986). Jacqueline Peterson and Jennifer S.H. Brown have edited *The New People: Being and Becoming Métis in North America* (Winnipeg, 1985). Jennifer S.H. Brown's short essay, "Métis," in *The Canadian Encyclopedia* (Edmonton, 1985), vol. 2, pp. 1124–1227, provides a very good introduction to the subject. Guillaume Charette's *Vanishing Spaces: Memoirs of a Prairie Métis* (Winnipeg, 1980) contains the memoirs of Louis Goulet, who was born in the Red River valley in 1859. D.N. Sprague reviews Red River Métis history in his introduction to *The Genealogy of the First Métis Nation: The Development and Dispersal of the Red River Settlement 1820–1900*, compiled by D.N. Sprague and R.P. Frye (Winnipeg, 1983), pp. 11–28. Novelist Hugh MacLennan has written a delightful sketch of the Red River in his *Seven Rivers of Canada* (Toronto, 1977, first published in 1961), pp. 103–22.

The subject of native women and the fur trade is told by Jennifer S.H. Brown in *Stranger in Blood: Fur Trade Company Families in Indian Country* (Vancouver, 1980); and by Sylvia Van Kirk in *"Many Tender Ties": Women in Fur Trade Society in Western Canada* (Winnipeg, 1980).

CHAPTER NINETEEN

The Pacific Coast to the 1860s

The northwestern coast of North America remained unexplored by Europeans until the 1770s. The Indian population of present-day British Columbia lived alone along the major salmon rivers, at scattered village sites along the ocean, and near the important trade routes inland from the coast along the Fraser, Bella Coola, Skeena, and Nass rivers. Native groups claimed almost all the areas along the coastline, yet they lost control of the land within a century after European contact.

Initially, Spain, Russia, Britain, and the United States competed for the control of the North Pacific coast. Eventually, however, the sector between Russian Alaska and Spanish California was disputed by only Britain and the United States, which in 1818 agreed to joint occupancy of the area. In 1846 the two countries consented to extend the international border along the 49th parallel from the prairies to the Pacific and to include Vancouver Island in Britain's jurisdiction.

Immigrants first settled at the southern tip of Vancouver Island in the 1840s and then at the mouth of the Fraser River during the Gold Rush of 1858. In the 1860s these immigrants claimed ownership of the entire coast and interior of British Columbia.

The Northwest Coast Indians

The Indians had been living along the Pacific Coast for thousands of years. One of the oldest archaeological sites in the Fraser River Canyon dates back at least 8500 years. The Indians probably arrived in successive waves, for five native linguistic families live today on the British Columbia coast. Hemmed in by towering mountains, the narrow coastline supported the highest concentration of population in what is now Canada. For these maritime people salmon was the main food resource, and red cedar was used for the construction of their plank houses, canoes, containers, carved masks, and their most famous objects of all—totem poles.

NOTIONS OF PROPERTY

In several respects the Northwest Coast Indians' notion of property was like that of the Europeans. The primary unit of their society was a large group of kinsmen or a lineage—a group of people who shared a common ancestor in the real or mythological past. One or several kin groups might occupy the same winter village, and these villages in turn constituted independent units within the larger tribe. Local kin groups claimed ownership of the fishing stations, berry patches, cedar groves, and stretches of beach. When they left their permanent winter villages for the salmon fisheries they went to their own recognized stretches of the salmon rivers. When the Europeans came, the chiefs or leaders of the kin groups made them pay for the wood and even the fresh water they used.

THE POTLATCH AND SOCIAL STRUCTURE

Both European and Indian societies had a hierarchical social structure. Among the local Indian kin groups an elaborate stratification existed. At the bottom stood the slaves, acquired in war or by purchase, and then above them, in a very careful ranking, everyone else. The anthropologist Philip Drucker confirms that "each society consisted not of two or more social classes, but of a complex series of statuses graded relatively, one for each individual of the group."[1] The ranking existed for functions such as the potlatch, which involved a distribution of gifts according to each person's position.

European society had no direct equivalent for the potlatch. Anthropologist Wilson Duff has described it as "a large gathering to which important people were invited in order to witness some event, such as a young person assuming a new name or the completion of a new house and erection of a totem pole. On such an occasion the host would display his wealth and present gifts to his guests. The more he gave away, the more prestige he acquired."[2] Honour came in giving, not in receiving. In the late nineteenth century European missionaries succeeded in outlawing the potlatch ceremonies. They regarded them as immoral squandering of wealth and a barrier to converting Indians to Christianity.

While similar in some respects, the Europeans and the Northwest Coast

Indians differed in others. Each local Indian kin group, for example, had identifiable privileges indicating their common origins. One lineage of the Nimpkish, a village group among the Kwakiutl, believed themselves descended from a giant halibut and a thunderbird that transformed themselves into men. This lineage had the right to display the thunderbird and the halibut as crests on their houses, dance blankets, and on painted screens. Today, the Nimpkish can point out the rock where the thunderbird first landed.[3] The kin group also had the right to specific perogatives in their intricate ceremonial system, such as the right to certain names, songs, and dances.

ARRIVAL OF THE EUROPEANS

Two centuries ago the Northwest Coast Indians were mystified by the white strangers' arrival. Well into the early twentieth century, the Squamish Indians of the Capilano reserve at Vancouver had an oral tradition of the first time their ancestors encountered the newcomers a century and a half earlier. As Chief Mathias told the story, the warriors hesitated for a long time about boarding the floating island with cobwebs hanging from the sticks growing on it, until with great misgivings, the bravest climbed the rope ladder onto the deck. The pale-faced captain who looked like a corpse advanced with outstretched hand. Never having heard of the handshake, the chief thought they were being challenged to an Indian finger wrestling match. He therefore waved away the man with whom the captain was trying to shake hands and called for the Squamish strong-man to accept the challenge. Seeing he was misunderstood, the captain shrugged and approached the chief with outstretched hand. The chief then said to the strong-man: "He doesn't want you. He thinks you are not strong enough." With that, the chief refused to consider the captain's "challenge." The strangers' gifts also greatly puzzled Mathias' ancestors. They gave the Indians what they believed to be snow in a sack (flour) and buttons (coins).[4]

THE ARRIVAL OF THE SPANISH

Spain reached the Pacific before any other European power. Nevertheless, it took the Spanish two and a half centuries to advance northward from Mexico. In effect, their expansion ended after the conquest of Mexico and Central and South America—huge territories with great populations. Apostolos Valerianos, a Greek pilot who spent forty years in the Spanish

361

service in the Americas, better known by his Spanish name of Juan de Fuca, supposedly discovered in 1590 a vast gulf or wide inlet between the 47th and 48th latitudes that led into a broader sea with many islands. Fuca believed this strait to be the western outlet of the fabled Straits of Anian, a body of water which could provide a convenient, practical sea passage between Europe and Asia. But Spain took so little interest in the expedition they had sponsored that they failed to preserve any authentic record of it, and only Fuca's later statement that he made the voyage survives.

Crippled by depressions, epidemics, and defeats on European battlefields, Spain lost its pioneering spirit. Rival European empires had seized Spanish islands in the West Indies, but luckily for Spain, its European rivals seldom ventured to the Pacific until the Russians arrived in the eighteenth century.

362

RUSSIAN ACTIVITY IN THE NORTH PACIFIC

The first documented Russian voyage to Alaska was that of Vitus Bering, a Danish navigator in the Russian service. In 1728 he completed the epic land journey from European Russia. He built a ship and sailed along the eastern coast of Siberia until he found the strait that now bears his name. On another voyage in 1741 he reached North America and explored an area in present-day southeastern Alaska. His return, however, proved disastrous: the sixty-year-old mariner died of scurvy after being shipwrecked on an island off the Siberian coast. This ill-fated voyage first established Russia's claim to the Alaskan Panhandle.

Bering's last voyage led to Russian economic expansion in the Pacific. The survivors from Bering's ship brought with them to the mainland a cargo of nine hundred sea-otter pelts. In Chinese markets these brought high prices, since the Chinese upper classes prized the furs for their warmth and their glossy beauty. The highly profitable sea-otter trade thus began and within a half-century led to an international rivalry among Russia, Spain, and later Britain and the United States.

Rumours of Russian activity prompted Spain to advance northward to protect Mexico. In 1767 the Spanish developed a major port at San Blas on the western coastline of Mexico and established settlements in California at San Diego, Monterey, and San Francisco. They also sponsored expeditions to investigate Russian advances along the northern coast and to take formal possession of the area for Spain. Juan Perez sailed from San Blas in late January 1774 to Alaska, but bad weather caused him to turn back in Alaskan waters just north of the Queen Charlotte Islands. Perez met 150 Haida Indians off the Queen Charlottes, the first recorded meeting between Europeans and British Columbian Indians. In a second expedition in 1775, the Spaniards learned that the Russians had not yet established posts along the Alaskan Panhandle.

THE ARRIVAL OF THE BRITISH

In place of the Russians, the British became the Spaniards' greatest threat in the late 1770s. Captain James Cook, already renowned for his discoveries in Australasia and Antarctica, visited the North Pacific Coast on his third expedition to the Pacific. As a young man the distinguished naval officer had been present at the French surrender of Louisbourg in 1758 and had helped to guide the English armada to Quebec in 1759.

In the spring of 1778 Cook's two vessels, *Discovery* and *Resolution*, arrived at Nootka Sound, sighted by Perez four years earlier. Here Cook spent a month re-fitting his ships. Since no other European power knew of the Spaniards' previous visit, Cook (who was murdered in January 1779 by natives in Hawaii) received credit as Nootka's discoverer, and the British claim to the North Pacific coast received international recognition.

363

To strengthen their claim to the North Pacific the Spanish in 1789 established a colony at Nootka Sound and maintained a garrison there of 200–250 men for six years, with only a brief absence during the winter of 1789–90. The Nootka Sound Controversy, as it became known, brought Spain and Britain to the brink of war. Spain argued that it had the exclusive right to trade and to control the coast, while Britain claimed that navigation was open to any nation. But in 1795 Spain agreed to share the northern ports and resources because it badly needed British assistance in its current war against France. Thus ended Spain's attempts to exert a Spanish presence north of California. Today, about one hundred geographical names, such as those of Valdes and of the Galiano Islands, remain to remind us of the early Spanish expeditions.

The Maritime and Inland Fur Trade

The publication in 1784 of the official account of James Cook's third voyage became a turning point in the international contest for the Northwest Coast. Captain James King, who had taken command shortly after the death of Cook, recounted in *A Voyage to the Pacific Ocean* (1784) how sea-otter pelts obtained in trade on the Northwest Coast had brought as much as $120 each at Canton, China. Other mariners now saw their opportunity to make their fortunes. The first was the sea captain James Hanna, who sailed in a British vessel appropriately named *Sea Otter*. Several British and American ships followed. In 1784 the Russians had established a base at Three Saints Harbour on Kodiak Island in the Gulf of Alaska. North of the present-day Alaskan boundary the Russians soon encountered intense British and American competition for sea-otter pelts.

The withdrawal of Spain in the mid-1790s left the Northwest Coast open to three contenders: Russia, England, and the newly independent United States. The Russian traders, however, laboured under several major handicaps. In contrast to both the Americans and the English, they possessed fewer and poorer trade goods and inferior trading vessels. The Russian advance slowed down in the Alaskan Panhandle, where they faced strong competition from British and American traders and from the Tlingit Indians, who acted as middlemen, trading European goods to the interior bands in the present-day Yukon and northwestern British Columbia.

Britain strengthened its claim to the Northwest Coast with the dispatch of a three-year expedition under George Vancouver, a naval officer who had served with Cook's expedition to the Northwest Coast. From 1792 to 1794 Vancouver methodically and painstakingly charted the intricate coastline from Oregon to Alaska. This thorough survey proved that Juan de Fuca Strait was not the entrance to the great inland sea that Fuca had reported. Vancouver later wrote in *Voyage of Discovery to the North Pacific Ocean*: "I trust the precision with which the survey ... has been carried into effect, will remove every doubt, and set aside every opinion of a *northwest passage*, or any water communication navigable for shipping, existing between the north pacific, and the interior of the American continent, within the limits of our researches."

Before leaving the Northwest Coast the navigator named the huge island now known as Vancouver Island, Quadra's and Vancouver's Island (sharing the honour with his friend, Juan Francisco de la Bodega y Quadra, the Spanish Commander at Nootka Sound). Later it became known simply as Vancouver's Island, and finally as Vancouver Island.

The outbreak of war between Britain and France in 1793, which lasted until 1815, curtailed British voyages to the Northwest Coast. As Britain withdrew seamen from its merchant ships for service in the Royal Navy, American entrepreneurs captured their trade in the North Pacific. From the mid-1790s onwards, American traders dominated the coastal trade until the mid-1820s, by which time the sea otter was virtually extinct due to over-hunting.

THE INDIANS AND THE MARITIME FUR TRADERS

The Indians welcomed the Maritime fur traders and their iron trading goods. They particularly wanted the metals out of which the European tools were made in order to construct their own. The Spanish, in fact, discovered that the Indians coveted iron so much that they even took off the metal strapping on the sides of the ship. Not even the rudder chains were safe. The Indians horrified the friars when they tore down a large cross to take out the nails that held it together.

In addition to iron goods the Indians bought cloth, clothing, and blankets. They also developed a liking for rum, smoking tobacco, and molasses. The Indians paid careful attention to the quality of goods they purchased and refused iron that contained flaws or was too brittle. The natives wanted muskets as well.

Often the Indians that the traders met were middlemen who had their own mark-up. Although the linguistic diversity of the Pacific Coast exceeded that of Europe, the Indian middlemen knew the Chinook jargon or trade language spoken all along the coast and the inland districts. Indians on the coast traded European goods to interior groups at 200–300 percent mark-ups. The coastal Indians initially exercised considerable control over the early European fur trade, preventing the Europeans' contact with inland groups. The entry around 1810 of the fur traders in the interior, however, took away much of the Indian middleman's trade.

The fur trade enriched the coastal Indians' culture. The tools they made from the abundant supply of iron allowed them to produce better and more refined ceremonial headdresses, costumes, and masks for feasts and ceremonials. In addition to the new tools, new colours became available through the traders. Although the Indian carvers favoured the traditional colours, weavers began to supplement the original pigments—red and yellow ochres, black and blue-green copper oxide—with the whole spectrum of European trade colours. Wood carving expanded. During these years the totem poles, which displayed individual family's genealogies, underwent much elaboration and were built to greater heights.

365

THE INLAND FUR TRADE

After European navigators had reached the Northwest Coast from the sea, European fur traders arrived by land. Anxious to find a short supply line to the Pacific, the North West Company searched for a new route westward from Lake Athabasca to the Pacific. The Nor'Wester Alexander Mackenzie, the first European to canoe the northern river that now bears his name and reach the Arctic Ocean, completed the first overland crossing of the continent in 1793 by travelling down the Fraser River, then over to the Bella Coola River, and down to the Pacific. The arduous route proved useless for transporting furs, but the journey made the twenty-four-year-old Mackenzie's reputation as one of the most fearless and daring trader-explorers.

Two other Nor'Westers tried to find a commercial route to the Pacific. Simon Fraser, who had first opened up fur-trading posts in the interior of present-day British Columbia, travelled in 1808 with a small party down the treacherous river named for him. He succeeded, but the route was unnavigable. Finally, in 1811 the third Nor'Wester, David Thompson, succeeded where the other two had failed. He located the Columbia River, the last link in the highway of navigable waterways stretching across North America (see page 347).

Unfortunately, Thompson reached the mouth of the Columbia only to find the Americans already established there. After the successful overland journey of Lewis and Clark in 1804–05 the United States had become interested in the lands adjacent to the Columbia River. A sea expedition sent by John Jacob Astor's Pacific Fur Company had arrived in late March 1811, several months before Thompson. On the basis of their having founded Fort Astoria, the Americans claimed the Oregon country.

366

JOINT OCCUPATION OF OREGON TERRITORY

As a temporary compromise, Britain and America agreed in 1818 to occupy the district jointly and to decide its fate later. The agreement left commerce open to both British and American traders between latitudes 40° and 54°40′ (from the northern boundary of California to the southern limits of Alaska).

With the merger of the North West Company and the Hudson's Bay Company in 1821, the new Hudson's Bay Company under the management of Sir George Simpson began to exploit the rich fur resources of the Northwest Coast. Having obtained a twenty-one-year lease from the British Crown to the trade in the "Indian Territory" (the lands between the Rocky Mountains and the Pacific), George Simpson located a Pacific depot at Fort Vancouver, 150 km up the Columbia River. Other forts followed. The three most important were Fort Langley near the mouth of the Fraser River, built in 1827; Fort Simpson on the boundary of the Russian territory to the north, in 1831; and Fort Victoria on the southern tip of Vancouver Island, in 1843. The Hudson's Bay Company's energetic commercial activities thus established a strong British presence on the Pacific coast.

American interest in the Columbia country mounted in the early 1840s. American adventurers began arriving in the 1830s and by 1843 numbered about one thousand. Over the next three years another five thousand settlers arrived in the Columbia River valley. Thanks to the Hudson's Bay Company's network of posts, inland trails, and shipping routes, however, Britain dominated north of the Columbia River. Nevertheless, the American President James Polk, who came into office in 1845 with an electoral

Boundary Settlement of 1818

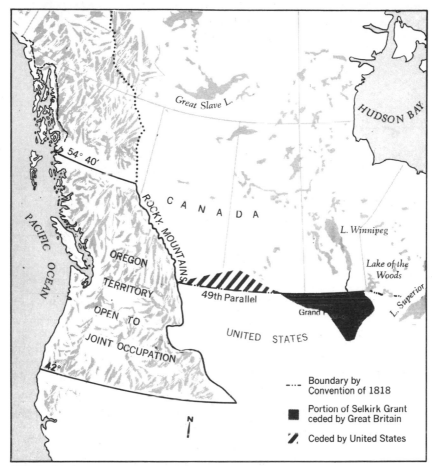

McInnis, *Canada*, p. 223.

promise of "54' 40 or fight," demanded all of "Oregon," right up to the Alaskan Panhandle.

Fortunately for Britain's claim, however, the Americans began a war with Mexico in 1846 and Polk did not want a war on two fronts. An obliging Britain also retracted its claim to all the land north of the Columbia River. The Anglo-American treaty signed in June 1846 extended the 49th parallel (which became the international border across the Plains in 1818) from the Rockies to the Pacific and left all of Vancouver Island in British hands.

Anxious to counter the threat of American squatter settlement in its remaining Pacific territory, the British government asked the Hudson's Bay Company to colonize, as well as to manage, Vancouver Island. The company accepted. A royal grant of 1849 stipulated that the company had to develop the island, make lands available to settlers at reasonable prices, and also safeguard the rights of the Indians. By the end of 1849 Fort Victoria served as the company's western headquarters, its shipping depot, and its provisioning centre, as well as the capital of the colony of Vancouver Island. The Colonial Office extended the governor of Vancouver Island's jurisdiction to the Queen Charlotte Islands in 1852.

On the Eve of the Gold Rushes

In the mid-1850s there were approximately one thousand whites living in British Columbia. The discovery of coal at Nanaimo on the east coast of Vancouver Island had led to the founding of a small permanent European settlement there. Until the Fraser River gold rush, however, in 1858 the colony really continued as a fur-trading region with its centre at Fort Victoria. The existence of virtually free land in Oregon and Washington attracted potential settlers there and not to Vancouver Island, where land had to be purchased. At the time perhaps as many as two hundred Europeans lived in the various fur-trading posts on the mainland. On Vancouver Island and the mainland the Indians outnumbered the whites by roughly fifty to one.

Although the Northwest Coast native peoples perhaps lived better materially after European contact, they also began to die in large numbers. The absence of accurate statistics makes it difficult to provide even rough estimates of the casualties, but diseases such as measles, mumps, and, especially, small pox and tuberculosis took their toll, as they did elsewhere in the Americas upon European contact (see chapters 1, 4, 11, 17, 18). Anthropologist Wilson Duff estimates that the smallpox epidemic that started in Victoria in 1862 killed about one-third of the native people within two years.[5] Some historians argue that no real evidence exists that the losses were indeed this high, but they do not deny the actual occurrence of this epidemic and its catastrophic impact on native society.

JAMES DOUGLAS AS GOVERNOR OF VANCOUVER ISLAND

James Douglas became governor of the Colony of Vancouver Island in 1851, to replace Richard Blanchard, the first governor, who resigned one year after arriving in Fort Victoria. A "Scotch West Indian", Douglas was born in British Guiana, South America, the son of "a free coloured woman" and a Scottish merchant. Sent to Scotland for his schooling at the age of twelve, James later left school and joined the North West Company as an apprentice four years later. After the union of the two rival companies he entered northern "Oregon," or New Caledonia, as the company called it. There in 1828, he married Amelia Connolly, the Métis daughter of fur trader William Connolly and his Cree Indian wife. In 1830 the company transferred James to Fort Vancouver, and nine years later the industrious and capable employee became chief factor. With his promotion to Victoria in 1849, he became the senior company officer west of the mountains.

JAMES DOUGLAS'S INDIAN POLICY

While governor Douglas applied many of the lessons he had learned in the fur trade, he did not intervene in quarrels among the Indians, but he did punish individual Indians who attacked Europeans. On occasion he used the Royal Navy's gunboats to settle disputes between Europeans and Indians. Shortly before he became governor, Douglas wrote that in all his dealings with Indians he had "invariably acted on the principle that it is inexpedient and unjust to hold *tribes* responsible for the acts of *individuals*." The governor meted out stern discipline selectively, not indiscriminately, to those that warranted it. Unlike many of the early settlers on the island, Douglas tried to understand Indian society. Above all, he did not want the open warfare that had broken out between the American settlers and the Indians in Washington to spill over the border.

369

Anxious to avoid conflict between the Indians and the settlers, Douglas purchased the Indians' land before settlement occurred. In the 1850s he made fourteen treaties with groups on Vancouver Island. The governor allowed the Indians to select the land they wanted and instructed the surveyors to meet the Indians' wishes:

> To include in each reserve the permanent Village sites, the fishing stations, and Burial grounds, cultivated land and all the favorite resorts of the Tribes, and in short to include every piece of ground to which they had acquired an equitable title through continuous occupation, tillage, or other investment of their labour.

In hindsight, Douglas was not terribly generous. Although the island is half the size of New Brunswick, the Douglas treaties provided only an average of some four hectares of reserve land per Indian family (the Canadian standard on the Plains in the 1870s was 246). But he at least acknowledged Indian ownership over their lands.

Some of the white settlers complained that although the governor might handle Indians well, he could not handle them properly. They protested that Douglas had not carried out his obligation to settle the island, that he ruled autocratically, and that he relied too heavily on the company's officials for advice. Most of all, they objected to his setting the price of land at £1 for two-fifths of a hectare (the minimum holding being eight hectares) and that free grants of eighty to one hundred and twenty hectares were not made, whereas neighbouring Washington territory provided land without charge.

When settlement on Vancouver Island spread in the late 1850s, Douglas continued to make determined efforts to purchase the Indians' land and to set aside reserves in the areas the settlers were moving into. Want of funds, however, made the process much more difficult. In 1858 the governor left the Hudson's Bay Company and no longer had access to the company's storehouses. Moreover, the Indians wanted larger payments for their lands, as they had come to realize its true value to the newcomers. The Vancouver Island House of Assembly, established in 1856, looked to Britain to loan it money for Indian land payments. The Colonial Office refused and replied that the fund should be raised locally. As the colonial legislature considered itself unable to buy out Indian title on Vancouver Island, they gave the Indians no compensation for their lands after 1859. The government of Vancouver Island (and later British Columbia) set aside Indian reserves without extinguishing the Indians' title to the land.

Gold Rushes

Repercussions from the discovery of gold on the lower Fraser River in 1858 worried James Douglas. When word of the new mining field reached California in the spring of 1858, the rush northward began. In the last two weeks of May, ten thousand men started up the Fraser by canoe, sailboat, and raft; another fifteen thousand came by the end of the year. Many new businesses or branches of American firms, financed by San Francisco capital, were established in Victoria.

The entry of thousands of Americans on the mainland threatened British sovereignty and raised the danger of an Indian war. As he was the senior British official in the neighbourhood of the Fraser River, the governor of Vancouver Island claimed the mainland and its minerals for the Crown. He drew up mining regulations, licenced miners, and hired constables. The Colonial Office praised Douglas for having taken the initiative, even though, strictly speaking, he lacked legal authority on the mainland. The British government then established a second colony on the mainland, separate from that of Vancouver Island. Queen Victoria named it British Columbia.

James Douglas became British Columbia's first governor while still serving as governor of Vancouver Island (which in 1859 also came under the direct control of the Colonial Office after the royal grant to the Hudson's

Bay Company was terminated). Colonel Richard Clement Moody, the first lieutenant governor of British Columbia, placed the site of the colony's new capital near the mouth of the Fraser River. Queen Victoria christened it New Westminster.

James Douglas, together with Matthew Baillie Begbie, British Columbia's first chief justice, immediately worked to establish a uniform judicial system for the colony. Douglas and Begbie worked well together. Historian Margaret Ormsby has given us this portrait of Begbie: "A Cambridge graduate of considerable intellectual attainment, a man with a natural *hauteur*, an accomplished teller of anecdotes, and something of a musician, Begbie had the distinction of mind and manner so much admired by Douglas."[6]

Judge Begbie's circuit court tours established a frontier version of British law in the scattered mining camps. His and Douglas' efforts to establish a strong, centralized administration helped to ensure that the colony remained British.

371

In 1860 four thousand gold miners (the majority from California and Oregon, the rest from eastern Canada, Britain, Europe, and even China) proceeded further eastward, pushing into the Thompson, Lillooet, and then the southern Cariboo regions. By 1861, with big strikes at Richfield, at Barkerville, and at Lightning on Williams Creek, the Cariboo had become the major mining field.

The gold resources in the interior could not be exploited without a road link to the coast. Using public funds, James Douglas built the 650 km Cariboo Road, that was completed in 1863.

JAMES DOUGLAS'S ACCOMPLISHMENTS

Douglas remained in office as both governor of British Columbia and Vancouver Island until 1864. The settlers had long complained about the veteran fur trader's autocratic ways and his "despotism," but in their haste to condemn the governor they overlooked his accomplishments—the establishment of the basic industries of coal mining, lumbering, fishing, and farming. On the mainland, he had also confronted the Americans and firmly established British institutions there. By building the Cariboo Road he solved the problem of inland communication.

The governor's Indian policy constituted perhaps his greatest achievement. Thanks largely to him, Vancouver Island and British Columbia avoided the fierce wars between Indians and settlers in the United States. The real test came in the Fraser River valley and the Cariboo country during the Gold Rush days in the late 1850s and early 1860s. Apart from an attack in 1864 by Chilcotin Indians on a road building crew who had

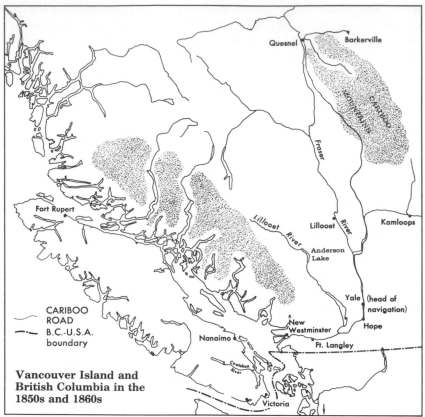

Cornell, Hamelin, Ouellet, Trudel, *Canada, Unity in Diversity*, p. 313.

entered their territory uninvited, no major acts of Indian armed resistance occurred. When he died in Victoria on August 2, 1877, James Douglas was already known as "The Father of British Columbia."[7]

British Columbia in the Mid-1860s

British Columbia experienced a post-gold-rush slump in the mid-1860s. Gold production fell and people left the colony. It was rich in many natural resources, but high transportation costs ruled out their large-scale exploitation. High American tariffs also reduced British Columbia's and Vancouver Island's trade with the United States, although Vancouver Island did sell some coal to San Francisco. Beginnings also had been made in lumber and fishing as export industries, but mining was still the most important industry, despite its decline. Some farming had begun, with specialization in wheat in the upper Fraser region, and with dairy and market gardening underway on the island.

In the late 1860s, 12 000 non-Indians lived in British Columbia and on Vancouver Island, more than half of them in the southwestern corner of the island. About 1000–2000 lived in the lower Fraser valley, with the remainder along the routes to the gold fields or at fur-trading posts. Since most Americans had by now left, at least three-quarters were British or Canadians and of these, males predominated. More than 1000 Chinese from California remained to work finds in the Cariboo.

Apart from doing some backpacking and some work at the diggings, the Indians, who were the largest ethnic group in the two colonies, had obtained little economic benefit from the gold rush. Since no land-ownership treaties had been made, they had received no compensation for the expropriation of their lands. The miners simply intruded on their village sites, fishing stations, and cultivated areas. The increased number of non-Indians also led to the outbreak of disease, such as the smallpox epidemic of 1862 that claimed the lives of many Indians living both along the coast and the interior.

373

CHRISTIAN MISSIONARIES AND THE INDIANS

Some of the Indians who survived the epidemics converted to Christianity. The missionaries began out-reach work to the Indians immediately before the great epidemic of 1862–64; this catastrophe no doubt shook the Indians' faith in their old religion's power to protect them. The missionaries tried to make the Indians into good Christian Europeans. This attempt was revealed in the early church architecture. Historian Robin Fisher writes that "in the main, the churches expressed the missionaries' overall intent to replace that which was Indian with that which was European."[8]

James Douglas encouraged and assisted the missionaries as much as possible. William Duncan began his work at Fort Simpson in 1857 and then at neighbouring Metlakatla, where he built a model mission. Other Anglican missionaries followed. Methodists from Canada West also came, men like Thomas Crosby, who worked on Vancouver Island and along the northern coastline. In the late 1850s the Oblate Fathers established Roman Catholic missions along the south coast and in the Okanagan and the Fraser valleys.

For the next two or three generations, many British Columbia Indians lived in Christian mission villages where the Protestant and Roman Catholic missionaries regulated every aspect of their lives. In their zeal the missionaries even banned totem poles. In 1900 the annual report of the De-

374

Provincial Archives of British Columbia (33784).

A Haida village on the Queen Charlotte Islands, July 1878.

partment of Indian Affairs noted that roughly eighty percent of British Columbia's Indians were reported to be Christians.

At the same time, the disruption to Indian culture can be overstated. Anthropologist Rolf Knight points out that many Indians near the settlements adjusted to the new economic conditions.[9] Independent of both mission and government direction, some Indians began to tend potato gardens in the 1850s, and in the decades to follow, they commenced mixed farming. As early as the mid-1850s independent Indian loggers delivered logs to sawmills. Many of the Hudson's Bay Company supply ships and several private trading schooners employed Indians as seamen throughout the nineteenth century. They worked as hunters and crewmen on European sealing ships and, on occasion, wintered in Japan. Indian-owned schooners began to appear in the 1870s, some of which were constructed by the Indians themselves. From the 1870s on, Indians entered the commercial fishing and canning industry. Thus under difficult circumstances, many Indians adjusted to the new conditions.

UNION OF THE TWO COLONIES

Major economic problems faced the two colonies of British Columbia and Vancouver Island in the mid-1860s. With the end of the gold rush, the economy was depressed and the two governments were nearly bankrupt. Anxious to save money, Britain promoted union of the two colonies, which would allow substantial reductions in administrative costs. In 1866 the colonies joined together and New Westminister became the capital. (A vigorous lobby, however, led by John Sebastian Helmcken, James Douglas' son-in-law, convinced the governor to move the capital to Victoria in 1868.) But despite the political consolidation of the two colonies the depression continued. In 1867 a new issue arose: the American purchase of Alaska. This put in doubt the independence of British Columbia. As Dr. Helmcken noted in his diary, the Americans "boasted they had sandwiched British Columbia and could eat her up at any time!"

In 1867 the new united colony of British Columbia, but one year old, was the youngest of all of Britain's North American colonies. Apart from a handful of European fur traders none of the approximately 8000 Europeans in the colony had lived for more than twenty-five years on Britain's North Pacific coast. Thanks to the Hudson's Bay Company, Britain had retained this huge territory against Russian, and particularly against American, advances. But what now would be the province's fate? *375*

As the Canadas, New Brunswick, and Nova Scotia completed their final arrangements for their union, white British Columbians started to debate the options open to them—interestingly at no point did they consult the 25 000 Indians in the province, but proceeded as if the original inhabitants did not exist. The options were three: England, the United States, or Canada. Emotionally, most favoured the province's continuation as a British colony. Those seeking to increase British Columbia's trade with its most important trading partner, though, endorsed annexation to the United States. Finally, many British Columbians who had been born in the Canadas and the Maritimes wanted union with Canada, as did those who saw Confederation as the best means of protecting British institutions on the North Pacific, and of developing British Columbia's resources.

NOTES

[1] Philip Drucker, "Rank, Wealth, and Kinship in Northwest Coast Society," in *Indians of the North Pacific Coast*, edited by Tom McFeat (Toronto, 1966), p. 137.

[2] Wilson Duff, *The Indian History of British Columbia*, vol. 1: *The Impact of the White Man* (Victoria, 1964), p. 58.

[3] Peter L. Macnair, *The Legacy: Continuing Traditions of Canadian Northwest Coast Indian Art* (Victoria, 1980), p. 21.

[4] Chief Mathias Capilano quoted in "Strangers Appear on English Bay," *Romance of Vancouver*, compiled by Native Sons of British Columbia (Vancouver, 1926), p. 5.

[5] Duff, *History*, p. 43.

[6] Margaret Ormsby, *British Columbia: A History* (Vancouver, 1958), p. 171.

[7] Margaret Ormsby, "James Douglas," *Dictionary of Canadian Biography*, vol. 10: 1871–1880 (Toronto, 1972), p. 248.

[8] Robin Fisher, "Missions to the Indians of British Columbia," in *British Columbia: Historical Readings*, edited by W. Peter Ward and Robert A.J. McDonald (Vancouver, 1981), p. 123.

[9] Rolf Knight, *Indians at Work: An Informal History of Native Indian Labour in British Columbia, 1858–1930* (Vancouver, 1978), pp. 7–27.

> ### Related Readings
>
> Two articles in R. Douglas Francis and Donald B. Smith, eds. *Readings in Canadian History: Pre-Confederation*, 2d ed. (Toronto 1986), are useful for this topic: L.F.S. Upton's "Contact and Conflict on the Atlantic and Pacific Coasts of Canada," pp. 438–48; and Barry M. Gough, "The Character of the British Columbia Frontier," pp. 448–58.

BIBLIOGRAPHY

376

The best overview of the history of the two Pacific colonies remains Margaret Ormsby's *British Columbia: A History* (Toronto, 1958); however, the author's omission of a discussion of the native peoples is a serious shortcoming. A geographical overview is provided in R. Cole Harris, "British Columbia," in *Canada Before Confederation*, edited by R. Cole Harris and John Warkentin (Toronto, 1974), pp. 289–311. Barry Gough provides an analytical review of the early history of the province in "The Character of the British Columbia Frontier," an article mentioned in the "Related Readings" for this chapter.

Good reviews of British Columbia's Indian past appear in Wilson Duff, *The Indian History of British Columbia*, vol. 1: *The Impact of the White Man* (Victoria, 1965); Robin Fisher, *Contact and Conflict: Indian-European Relations in British Columbia, 1774–1890* (Vancouver, 1977); Robin Fisher, "Missions to the Indians of British Columbia," in *British Columbia: Historical Readings*, edited by W. Peter Ward and Robert A.J. McDonald (Vancouver, 1981), pp. 113–26; and Rolf Knight, *Indians at Work: An Informal History of Native Indian Labour in British Columbia 1858–1930* (Vancouver, 1978). Chief Mathias Capilano presents a Squamish Indian version of the Europeans' arrival in "Strangers Appear on English Bay," in *Romance of Vancouver*, compiled by the Native Sons of British Columbia vol. 2 (1926), 2: 5–6. A beautifully illustrated introduction to Northwest Coast art is *The Legacy: Continuing Traditions of Canadian Northwest Coast Indian Art*, edited by Peter L. Macnair *et al.* (Victoria, 1980). Tom McFeat provides excerpts from important anthropological articles in his edited work, *Indians of the North Pacific Coast* (Toronto, 1966). A bibliographical guide has been compiled by Robert Steven Grumet, *Native Americans of the Northwest Coast* (Bloomington, Ind., 1979).

Warren L. Cook's *Flood Tide of Empire: Spain and the Pacific Northwest, 1543–1819* (New Haven, 1973), and three articles by Christon Archer, "The Transient Presence: A Re-appraisal of Spanish Attitudes Toward the Northwest Coast in the Eighteenth Century," *B.C. Studies*, no. 18

(1973): 3–32, "Spanish Exploration and Settlement of the Northwest Coast in the 18th Century," *Sound Heritage*, 7, no. 1 (1978): 33–53, and "Cannibalism in the Early History of the Northwest Coast: Enduring Myths and Neglected Realities," *Canadian Historical Review*, 61 (1980): 453–79, provide the background on Spanish activities. Alan Rayburn has recorded many of the North Pacific Spanish names in "Spanish Names Along Our West Coast," *Canadian Geographic*, 105, 3 (June–July 1985): 86–87.

For a review of Russian and American activities in the North Pacific, see James R. Gibson's "Bostonians and Muscovites on the Northwest Coast, 1788–1841," in *British Columbia: Historical Readings*, edited by Ward and McDonald, pp. 66–95; and, for the Russian presence, see Glynn Barratt, *Russia in Pacific Waters, 1715–1825* (Vancouver, 1981). Barry Gough has reviewed early British contact in *Distant Dominion: Britain and the Northwest Coast of North America, 1579–1809* (Vancouver, 1980); he has studied the later period in *Gunboat Frontier: British Maritime Authority and Northwest Coast Indians, 1846–90* (Vancouver, 1984). Vol. 4: 1771– 1800 of the *Dictionary of Canadian Biography* (Toronto, 1979) contains sketches of James Cook by Glyndwr Williams, pp. 162–67, and of George Vancouver by W. Kaye Lamb, pp. 743–48.

Other items can be cited for the nineteenth century. Margaret Ormsby concisely reviews the life of James Douglas in the *Dictionary of Canadian Biography*, vol. 10: 1871–1880 (Toronto, 1972), pp. 239–49. Of particular interest in *British Columbia and Confederation*, edited by W. George Shelton (Victoria, 1967), is Paul A. Phillips's essay, "Confederation and the Economy of British Columbia," pp. 43–60. *British Columbia: Historical Readings*, edited by Ward and McDonald, includes James E. Hendrickson's "The Constitutional Development of Colonial Vancouver Island and British Columbia," pp. 245–74. David R. Williams has written a biography of Mathew Baillie Begbie, "… *The Man for a New Country*" (Sidney, B.C., 1977). Dorothy Blakey Smith provides a sketch of J.S. Helmcken in her introduction to *The Reminiscences of Doctor John Sebastien Helmcken* (Vancouver, 1975).

377

CHAPTER TWENTY

The Road to Confederation

Proposals for British North American union had been considered before the 1860s, but the timing proved premature. As historian P.B. Waite aptly put it: "The Confederation movement followed Newton's first law of motion: all bodies continue in a state of rest or of uniform motion unless compelled by some force to change their state."[1] By the 1860s, however, those "forces" were suddenly present. The danger of an American attack after the American Civil War drew the British North American colonies together. At the same time, Britain also pressured them to unite to defend themselves. Simultaneously, internal problems in the colonies, such as public debt from extensive railway building and, in the case of the Canadas, political deadlock (and the desire to acquire the Northwest), convinced both Canadians and Maritimers of the necessity of union. These unique circumstances, rather than a spirit of nationalism, prepared the way for Confederation.

Impact of the American Civil War

Fear of an American takeover during the Civil War was perhaps the leading cause of Canadian confederation. As historian F.H. Underhill once wrote: "Somewhere on Parliament Hill in Ottawa ... there should be erected a monument to this American ogre who has so often performed the function of saving us from drift and indecision."[2]

Britain's proclamation of neutrality during the Civil War and its recognition of the South as a belligerent convinced many Unionists that it favoured the South. The British policy of allowing Confederate ships to be built and fitted out in British ports further antagonized the North. These armed cruisers, like the *Alabama*, the most famous of all, inflicted great damage on the North's merchant marine. The American government argued that because Britain knew the uses to which the South put these ships, it therefore was a contributor to the war and should pay for damages caused by this policy. One proposed payment included all of Canada as compensation.

Another incident heightened Anglo-American antagonism during the Civil War—the *Trent* affair. In November 1861 an American warship stopped the British steamer *Trent* and forcibly removed two Confederate agents on their way to England to secure assistance for the Southern cause. Tempers flared on both sides, with Britain threatening retaliation if these Confederate agents, seized in neutral waters, were not freed. Anxious to avoid war with Britain, President Abraham Lincoln released the prisoners on Christmas Day, 1861.

These hostilities inevitably affected the British North American colonies. Fear of an appending American attack led Britain to send the largest detachment of troops from Britain to America since the War of 1812: fourteen thousand soldiers. The resulting tension made Britain anxious to withdraw its expensive garrisons from North America once an honourable settlement could be reached, and London encouraged the colonies to shoulder the burden for their defence. 379

The colonies were certainly aware of the need to assume more responsibility for defence. They also realized the necessity for a railroad from an ice-free port on the Atlantic into the interior entirely through British North American territory—the fourteen thousand British troops sent to protect the Canadas had to travel overland through New Brunswick by sled in the middle of winter. A federation of the British North American colonies could lead to the construction of an intercolonial railway, and to the organization of a united colonial army.

THE ST. ALBAN'S RAID

The Trent affair, the raids of the *Alabama* and the other Confederate ships, and then the St. Alban's raid, increased Anglo-American tension. As the Union army began its victorious march south, the Confederacy in desperation planned to launch attacks on the North via Canada. At St. Alban's, Vermont, on October 19, 1864, twenty-six Confederate sympathizers terrorized the town, robbed three banks of $200 000, set several fires, wounded two men and killed another, and then fled to Canada. The government arrested them, but a Montreal magistrate, Charles Joseph Coursol, released them (and even returned the money to them) on a technicality raised during the lawsuit.

More than the raid itself, this act infuriated Americans and was the lead story in Vermont newspapers for weeks. The Canadian government quickly condemned Coursol's action, and in January 1865 passed a new Alien Act that provided for the deportation of aliens involved in acts against a friendly foreign state. Nevertheless, Canada once again became suspect in Northern eyes. General John A. Dix, commander of the American military district in the east, threatened Canada with retaliation if it refused to turn raiders over to American authorities immediately.

The Great Coalition

In this tense atmosphere Canadian politicians tried to solve the problem of political deadlock in their Assembly. Neither the conservatives nor the reformers could form a stable government. Between 1861 and 1864, for example, there were two elections and three changes of administration without either side being able to command a majority of seats. On June 14, 1864, the most recent government, the Macdonald–Taché coalition, went down to defeat. Macdonald requested dissolution, but rather than accept his request, Governor General Monck urged the Conservative leader to open negotiations with George Brown, leader of the Clear Grit reform party, with the possibility of forming a coalition. For two weeks, the two sides negotiated. On June 30, a jubilant House heard the announcement that Brown had agreed to enter a coalition cabinet, along with two others of his Reform party—Oliver Mowat and William McDougall—and to work for federation. This was the famous "Great Coalition of 1864."

Brown immediately made three demands in return for his support. First, he insisted that the coalition government work towards a federation of all the British North American colonies and, if this failed to materialize, then at least a federation of the two Canadas. Second, he demanded representation by population, or "rep by pop," as it became popularly known. The Clear Grits, who modelled themselves on American democratic practices and who were well aware of Canada West's greater population than Canada East, believed that representation in the Assembly or Lower House should be based on population distribution; after 1851, this meant that instead of an equality in the number of seats (see chapter 14), Canada West would have more than Canada East. Third, he called for the incorporation of the Northwest into Confederation.

For George Brown, eastward expansion and incorporation of the Maritimes into a federal union had to be accompanied by westward expansion to the Pacific. Brown had a strong interest in the Northwest. For nearly a decade his newspaper, the Toronto *Globe*, had kept Upper Canadians well informed on the Hudson's Bay Company's rule of the area. The *Globe* provided generous excerpts from the reports of the two scientific expeditions in the late 1850s—the British Palliser and the Canadian Hind expeditions. Brown's interest in the Northwest lay in its potential for the development of Canada West. On January 22, 1863, for example, Brown wrote a very revealing article, outlining his imperial dreams for the Canadas in the Northwest:

> If Canada acquires this territory it will rise in a few years from a position of a small and weak province to be the greatest colony any country has ever possessed, able to take its place among the empires of the earth. The wealth of 400 000 square miles of territory will flow through our waters and be gathered by our merchants, manufacturers and agriculturists. Our sons will occupy the chief places of this vast territory, we will form its institutions, supply its rulers, teach its schools, fill its stores, run its mills, navigate its streams.

Charlottetown Conference

At the same time that the Canadian politicians formed their Great Coalition, the Maritimes considered union among themselves. To some, a Maritime federation would allow for a greater regional vision and strength. Union could also help secure an intercolonial railway linking Halifax to the eastern terminus of the Grand Trunk Railway at Rivière-du-Loup. The Colonial Office strongly endorsed the idea, believing Maritime union would reduce the military and economic dependency of these colonies on Britain. Charles Tupper, the Premier in Nova Scotia, and Leonard Tilley, his counterpart in New Brunswick, concurred, as did premier John H. Gray of Prince Edward Island. Although all three governments had some reservations about the suggestion, they agreed to meet. No date or place, though, had been set for the conference when in July 1864, the members of the Great Coalition of the Canadas suddenly asked permission to attend such a conference and present a proposal for a wider British North American federal union. Their request accepted, the Canadian Cabinet spent July and August drawing up a plan for federation to be presented during a meeting to be held on Prince Edward Island.

The delegates met at Charlottetown on September 1, 1864. At the conference the Canadian delegation presented an impressive *tour de force*. John A. Macdonald and George-Etienne Cartier set out the arguments in favour of Confederation and the general terms of the Canadian proposal, particularly those aspects dealing with the division of powers between the central and provincial governments. Alexander Galt, the minister of finance in the Canadas, dealt with financial issues, while George Brown handled constitutional concerns. The main features of their proposal included: continued loyalty to the British Crown through membership in the British Empire; a strong central government within a federal union in which the provinces retained control over their own local affairs; and federal representation in the Lower House based on population and on regional

382

National Archives of Canada/C733.

A group of future Fathers of Confederation seen on the steps of the Prince Edward Island legislative building during the Charlottetown Conference of 1864. In the foreground are John A. Macdonald (seated) and to his right Georges Etienne Cartier.

representation in the Upper House. Within four days the Canadians had presented such a convincing case that the Maritime delegates were no longer interested in only Maritime union. Before the conference adjourned on September 7, the delegates agreed to meet again on October 10 at Quebec City to work out the final details of Confederation.

Quebec Conference

Within one month the Canadian cabinet translated the broad general principles of Charlottetown into specific resolutions and presented them at Quebec in the form of seventy-two resolutions. For the next two weeks the Maritime and Canadian delegates refined and altered the resolutions, finally reaching agreement on the terms of what, with only a few minor alterations, became the British North America Act. The danger of an American attack, British encouragement of the scheme, and a desire for the Northwest, all combined to maintain the momentum of Charlottetown. The Fathers of Confederation, representing diverse and separate British North American colonies, caught the spirit of the moment and hastened to conclude what they regarded as the most important event in the history of British North America.

383

As in Charlottetown, the delegates at Quebec agreed in principle on federation, but they strongly disagreed over whether the union should have a highly centralized structure or whether it should include an equitable division of powers between the central and provincial governments. Macdonald favoured a legislative union, arguing that the Civil War in the United States could be attributed to overly powerful state governments. The Maritime governors and the Colonial Office in Britain agreed with Macdonald. The Maritime delegates, however, feared a loss of their identity in a legislative union and opposed such a measure. Through their spokesman, George-Etienne Cartier, the French Canadians also insisted that the provincial governments retain control over their own religious, linguistic, and cultural rights.

The delegates finally reached a compromise by granting the central government residuary powers (powers not specifically assigned to the provinces), and by including under the powers of the federal government such general and vague phrases as "to make laws for the peace, order and good government of Canada." The federal government also gained the power of disallowance—the right to reject provincial laws of which it did not approve.

DEBATE OVER THE SEVENTY-TWO RESOLUTIONS

The delegates confirmed their agreement at Charlottetown to have a two-chamber system. The lower house would be based on representation by population, and the upper house on regional representation. But they disagreed strongly on the number of representatives from each region in the Senate. This issue almost destroyed the conference. The issue became contentious because the smaller Maritime provinces saw the Senate as a means of strengthening their regional representation to offset their numerical weakness in the lower house. They therefore objected to being considered one unit, and opposed the proportion of Senate seats allotted to them (twenty-four), which was the same number given to Ontario and to Quebec. Debate also followed over the means of choosing senators. Only after the delegates had discussed and eliminated a number of proposals did they agree on appointment for life by the central government.

384   After considerable discussion, the delegates accepted the financial proposals put forward by A.T. Galt. He had suggested that the new federal government assume the public debts—up to a maximum amount—of all the provinces that joined; any province with less than its maximum debt would receive five percent interest on the difference. In addition, the federal government would finance the Intercolonial Railway (under an agreement written directly into the constitution) as well as be responsible for funding those general powers assigned to it.

Galt also argued that the central government, with its heavy financial obligations, should receive the main sources of revenue; that it should collect such indirect taxes as customs and excise duties which provided one of the main sources of revenue at the time; and that it should be able as well to raise money by any other mode of taxation. To compensate the provinces for the cost of education, roads, and other local obligations, he proposed that the federal government pay annual subsidies based on eighty cents per head of their population. The provinces could raise additional revenue by direct taxation or by selling their natural resources (public lands, minerals, and waterpower), which remained in provincial hands.

Responses to the Confederation Proposals

When the Quebec Conference ended, the delegates returned to their respective provinces to secure approval for the resolutions. The Fathers of Confederation had originally considered submitting the draft constitution for popular approval but later decided to follow the British procedure of ratification by the provincial legislatures. They did this out of fear of the rejection of Confederation if it were put to a popular vote. Thus union was the work of a small but influential political elite.

In the Canadas there was less resistance to Confederation than in the Maritimes, although significant opposition existed when debate began on February 3, 1865. George Brown and his Reformers initially expressed concern about a wider union with the Maritimes, favouring instead a revised union of the Canadas as being more advantageous to Upper Canadians; Canada West's Reform leader also believed the Intercolonial Railway would be another expensive publicly funded railway like the Grand Trunk. Still Brown was willing to overlook both these reservations if federation were to be based on "rep by pop" and if it included the Northwest. Otherwise, Upper Canadian leaders tended to favour confederation, realizing that they had the most to gain from the union.

DEBATE OVER CONFEDERATION IN CANADA EAST

385

The *Rouges* under the leadership of Antoine-Aimé Dorion had serious reservations. Canada East's Reform leader argued: "It is not at all a confederation that is proposed to us, but quite simply a Legislative Union disguised under the name of a confederation. How could one accept as a federation a scheme ... that provided for disallowance of local legislation?"

Furthermore, he pointed out that in the proposed House of Commons the English-Canadian representation from Canada West and the Maritimes greatly outnumbered the French-Canadian. Dorion also pointed out that union of the British North American colonies would heighten, rather than diminish, tension with the United States, as the increased armed might of British North America would pose a greater threat. Finally, this nineteenth-century liberal denounced the Fathers of Confederation for refusing to allow the people to make their views known, either through a plebiscite or an election. In a prophetic statement Dorion summarized his misgivings:

> I greatly fear that the day when this Confederation is adopted will
> be a dark day for Lower Canada ... I consider it one of the worst
> measures which could be submitted to us and if it happens that it
> is adopted, without the sanctions of the people of the province, the
> country will have more than one occasion to regret it.

George-Etienne Cartier countered Dorion's criticism with the argument that in the new federal union, French Canadians would retain control in the province of all matters relating to language, civil law, religion, and education. On the question of English-Canadian dominance, he pointed out that the "new nationality" would be a "political nationality" only and not a "cultural nationality" that would require French Canadians to submerge their cultural differences in a common pan-Canadian nationalism. He also reminded his French-Canadian compatriots of the importance of the British connection to offset the threat of American annexation and the resulting loss of identity. (Cartier had an almost morbid fear of the Americans and an equally strong dislike of republicanism.)

Finally, the practical politician Cartier presented confederation to French Canadians as their best hope for cultural survival in a world of limited possibilities. The existing union, crippled by deadlock, could not go on; for French Canadians, union with the United States would be the worst possible fate. Only a larger federation of British North American colonies, Cartier concluded, offered French Canadians possibilities beyond their own provincial boundaries, at the same time as it protected their affairs within their own province. Cartier's close association with the Grand Trunk Railway as one of the company's directors, and his desire to play a larger role as a statesman on a national stage, made him an enthusiastic advocate of union.

Cartier faced a difficult struggle promoting confederation in Quebec and therefore enlisted the support of the clergy, despite his personal concerns about mixing politics and religion. But he could not count on unreserved support. Ignace Bourget of Montreal, the most powerful bishop, feared for the future of the church in a new political union with other English-speaking colonies with large Protestant populations. He kept silent about his misgivings, however, since the other Quebec bishops were more favourably disposed, at least in principle. For the church to have opposed Confederation would have put them in the camp of their arch-enemies— the *Rouges*, who were strongly anti-clerical.

The Confederation debates in the Canadas lasted just over a month, from February 3 to March 11, 1865. In a final vote, 19 favoured and 33 opposed Confederation. In the breakdown of votes in the two sections, 54 of the 62 members from Canada West favoured the proposal, as did 37 out of the 62 members in Canada East. Of the 48 French-Canadian members present, 27 voted for and 21 against. Overall, Confederation won overwhelmingly, but among French Canadians the victory proved very narrow, indicating serious reservations on their part.

386

NEW BRUNSWICK INITIALLY REJECTS CONFEDERATION

The struggle for Confederation in the Maritimes became as intense as it was among French Canadians in Canada East. In New Brunswick, Leonard Tilley, a St. John druggist who had been premier of the province since 1857 and who had represented it at both the Charlottetown and Quebec conferences, learned on his return how vehemently the provincial opposition resisted Confederation. A.J. Smith, the opposition leader, argued that union with the Canadas offered few—if any—benefits to New Brunswick. There was no guarantee that the Intercolonial Railway would be constructed nor that if it were built, where it would run and which area of the province (the north shore or the southern St. John valley) would benefit from it. One member of the Assembly asked derisively: "Mr. Tilley will you stop your puffing and blowing and tell us which way the Railway is going?"

The opposition pointed out that New Brunswick's economic trade pattern, especially since the Reciprocity Treaty of 1854, had a north–south rather than east–west orientation. Commercial interests in the province had no economic ties with the Canadas. Furthermore, union with Canada could lead to a flooding of the New Brunswick market by Canadian imports. In addition, New Brunswickers would be forced to assume a portion of the heavy Canadian debt from canal and railway building. Smith also argued that Confederation would diminish New Brunswick's political power by giving the province representation of only 15 MPs in a House of 194 members.

387

The Roman Catholic clergy in the province opposed Confederation as well, believing that a Canada dominated by Protestant extremists like George Brown would attack Roman Catholic schools and the church itself.

These arguments against Confederation found an effective forum in the election campaign in early 1865, fought chiefly on the issue of Confederation. New Brunswickers responded clearly and decisively—the Tilley pro-Confederation government lost heavily.

OPPOSITION IN NOVA SCOTIA

In Nova Scotia, Charles Tupper faced a challenge equal to Tilley's in New Brunswick. Opposition to the Quebec resolutions and to Confederation transcended party lines and centred on Joseph Howe, now no longer a member of the Assembly but still the most powerful political figure in Nova Scotia. As the Father of Responsible Government, the "voice of Nova Scotia" saw Confederation as restricting the colony's potential by reducing it to a backwater province in an insignificant North American nation. If it accepted Confederation, Nova Scotia would lose its identity and cease to be an important colony in a great empire. Howe presented his position in a series of letters he entitled "The Botheration Letters." In Howe's opinion the province looked eastward to the Atlantic Ocean and Britain, rather than westward to the continent and the Canadas. As Howe vividly expressed it: "Take a Nova Scotian to Ottawa, away above tide-water, freeze him up for five months, where he cannot view the Atlantic, smell salt water, or see the sail of a ship, and the man will pine and die."

Like Antoine Dorion, Howe objected to Confederation becoming law without consulting the electorate. In the winter of 1865–66 the veteran politician went to England to present his case to the colonial secretary and the British Parliament. Dissent in the province against Tupper's School Act of 1864, that placed the cost of education on the localities themselves not on the provincial government, aided Howe in his anti-Confederation campaign. Knowing full well that he could not win an election on the Confederation and schools issues, Tupper pressured the other British American colonial leaders to conclude their union before he had to face another election in 1867.

REJECTION OF CONFEDERATION IN PRINCE EDWARD ISLAND

In Prince Edward Island, the situation went from bad to worse. At the Charlottetown and Quebec conferences, the island representatives had driven the hardest bargain, pressing for better terms on representation in the Senate and the House of Commons and for better economic terms. The final agreement gained their consent, the last delegate to agree being Edward Whelan, the Irish-Catholic editor of the Liberal *Examiner*, who was converted to the idea of Confederation at the Quebec Conference, having been inspired to see beyond the small island of Prince Edward Island to a greater transcontinental nation.

This solidarity and inspiration, however, had disappeared once the delegates returned home. Disagreement broke out across party lines, as personal feuds and in-party fighting erupted. Within the governing Conservative party, chaos occurred after Premier Gray resigned in mid-December 1864 over his own party's opposition to Confederation. He was replaced by an anti-Confederate, J.C. Pope, the provincial secretary. Ironically, the new premier's own brother, W.H. Pope, the provincial secretary, supported Confederation.

The real opposition, however, came from the islanders themselves. Prosperous and content, many Prince Edward Islanders wanted nothing to do with Confederation. On December 30, 1864, the Charlottetown *Islander* wrote: "the majority of people appear to be wholly averse to Confederation ... We have done our duty. We have urged Confederation—the people have delared against it."

Islanders opposed Confederation for two reasons. One was the age-long issue of absentee landlordism. From the mid-eighteenth century onwards, the island had been controlled by absentee British landlords, much to the resentment of the local population. In 1860 a British commission appointed to investigate the question issued a report favourable to the islanders, only to have it rejected by the proprietors and by the Colonial Office. Thus, when the Colonial Office pressured Prince Edward Islanders to adopt Confederation, they resisted. Also, many islanders saw Confederation as simply replacing one set of distant landlords in Britain with another in Ottawa. Second, islanders believed that Confederation would give them very little. Union would mean higher taxes to support the enormous Intercolonial Railway project and higher tariffs to create interprovincial trade— neither of which would greatly benefit Prince Edward Island. They also disliked the proposed form of representation in the Senate and House of Commons, which would give them little, if any, power in distant Ottawa.

DEBATE OVER CONFEDERATION IN NEWFOUNDLAND

In Newfoundland, Confederation failed from apathy not opposition. Newfoundland had not participated in the Charlottetown Conference, but it had sent two representatives to the Quebec Conference. These representatives—Ambrose Shea, a liberal Catholic, and F.B.T. Carter, a conservative Protestant—had endorsed Confederation at Quebec. But they returned to a colony that was initially mildly interested and then soon indifferent. The initial enthusiasm came as a result of Newfoundland's destitute conditions. Fishing, the chief industry, was in decline throughout the 1860s. Agriculture and the timber trade, while distant seconds to fishing as commercial activities, were also experiencing hard times. Newfoundlanders hoped that Confederation might solve their economic ills, but for them (much more so than for the three Maritime colonies) Canada seemed so far away; the island looked eastward to Britain, not westward to Canada. Apathy then set in.

The politicians never overcame the Newfoundlanders' indifference to Canada. Premier Hugh Hoyles, who had also been premier at the time of the Quebec Conference, favoured Confederation, as did most members from both parties in the Legislature and the Assembly, but few people outside government circles endorsed the idea. In April 1865 Hoyles retired, to be replaced by F.B.T. Carter. He allied with his political opponent, Ambrose Shea, to form a coalition government to persuade Newfoundland to join Confederation. They even had the enthusiastic support of the pro-Confederation governor, Anthony Musgrave. But even this impressive political coalition could not stir interest in the subject. R.J. Pinsent, a representative of the Legislative Council, spoke for many Newfoundlanders when he noted: "There is little community of interest between Newfoundland and the Canadas. This is not a Continental Colony."

External Pressures

By the end of 1865 the idea of Confederation appeared to have little support among the British North American colonies, except in Canada West. All four of the Atlantic colonies opposed it. Two developments, though, helped to alter the situation: British intervention and the American threat.

Anxious to rid herself of the expense of defending British North America and seeking to ease the tensions with the United States, Britain now intervened directly to bring about a colonial federation. When a Canadian delegation arrived in London in the autumn of 1865, it was warmly received; a counter-delegation from Nova Scotia under Joseph Howe received a cool reception. The British government replaced the governor of Nova Scotia with a new appointee, one more sympathetic to Confederation; it ordered New Brunswick Governor Arthur Gordon to intervene in his province's politics to insure the success of Confederation; and through the initiative of Edward Watkins, a member of the directorate of the Grand Trunk Railway, the British government also agreed to guarantee the loan interest for the Intercolonial Railway, giving the Maritime provinces an additional incentive to unite with the Canadas.

While Britain applied pressure directly, the United States supplied it indirectly. When the Civil War ended in 1865, extremists now suggested that the Northern army be used to annex Canada. Moreover, influential American politicians in the Midwest—Senators Alexander Ramsey of Minnesota and Zachariah Chandler of Michigan—advocated annexation of the British Northwest. Other American politicians, such as Congressman Nathaniel Banks, Senator Charles Sumner, and even the secretary of state in Ulysses S. Grant's administration, Hamilton Fish, wanted all the British territory in North America.

At the same time, the American government moved to terminate the Reciprocity Treaty of 1854 (see chapter 15). The treaty had come under pressure from American protectionist interests as early as 1862. American annexationists believed that the treaty's abrogation would lead the British colonies to welcome union with the United States, that the colonies would find it impossible to survive economically without American trade. In December 1865 Congress passed a motion to end the Reciprocity Treaty, with the law to come into effect in March 1866. Ironically, rather than forcing the British colonies into the arms of the United States as expected, the abrogation of reciprocity instead encouraged the colonies to form a new commerical union among themselves.

FENIAN RAIDS

A more direct American threat also furthered the cause of Canadian Confederation. The Fenians, fanatical republican Irishmen, formed a brotherhood in 1859 in the United States for the independence of Ireland. They devised a grandiose scheme to capture the British North American colonies and use them as ransom to negotiate with the British government for the liberation of Ireland. Their marching song was an explicit expression of their goals:

> We are the Fenian Brotherhood,
> skilled in the art of war,
> And we're going to fight for Ireland,
> the land that we adore,
> Many battles we have won, along with
> the boys in blue,
> And we'll go and capture Canada for
> we've nothing else to do.

391

The Fenians fully expected the sympathy and support of their Irish-Catholic brothers in the British colonies to the north.

The Fenians posed little threat until the end of the American Civil War. In the summer of 1865 the Union army released thousands of Irish-American soldiers, who were trained, idle, and receptive to mobilizing in defence of their native country. Furthermore, the Fenians met with little resistance and even muted support from an American government that sympathized with their anti-British sentiments. Many American politicians also feared alienating American Irish-Catholic voters.

The Fenian threat tended to be more psychological than physical, with the actual military activities restricted to a few border skirmishes. But the Fenians made two concerted attacks that alarmed British North Americans. The first took place in New Brunswick. In April 1866 small bands of Fenians moved into the coastal towns of eastern Maine. New Brunswickers were alerted and volunteer soldiers called out to meet the challenge. This attack conveniently coincided with a hotly contested election on the issue of Confederation, and in the end the raid strengthened the Confederation cause in New Brunswick. The Fenians succeeded only in stealing the flag from a customs house before the New Brunswick militia and British regulars overwhelmed them, forcing them back across the border.

The second incident, at Fort Erie on the Niagara frontier, was more serious. On May 31, 1866, some fifteen hundred Fenians crossed the Niagara River into Canada West. For two days, sporadic fighting continued between the Fenian soldiers and the Canadian militia and British soldiers. The final battle took place at Ridgeway, near Fort Erie. On June 3 the

Fenians withdrew across the border. This was the last serious attack by the Fenians, although they continued to threaten Canada until 1870.

These Fenian raids contributed to the electoral victory for the pro-Confederationists in New Brunswick in 1866, and to increased support for union in Canada West.

Confederation Opposed and Accepted

In New Brunswick the anti-confederationist government of A.J. Smith that took office in 1865 ran into considerable difficulties shortly thereafter. Smith's government contained many conflicting interests and lacked internal unity.

392

The first blow came in the autumn of 1865, when R.D. Wilmot and T.W. Anglin, two of Smith's ablest cabinet ministers, resigned. Wilmot was converted to the support of Confederation during a visit to the Canadas in September 1865. Anglin left for another reason: he opposed his government's decision to assist a private company to build an important provincial railway (he wanted the New Brunswick government itself to construct it). A second blow came in November when the Smith government lost an important by-election in York County to Charles Fisher. The win in York was interpreted as a victory for the pro-Confederation forces, especially since the government of the Canadas had contributed handsomely to Fisher's campaign fund. Finally, Smith failed in his bid to persuade the American government to renew the Reciprocity Treaty of 1854. In addition to these setbacks, Smith had to fight Governor Arthur Gordon who, at the British government's insistence, encouraged New Brunswickers to support Confederation.

In exasperation, the Smith government resigned in April 1866. In the ensuing election, Leonard Tilley made a skilful presentation to the people of New Brunswick on what they could expect from Confederation: lower taxes, the Intercolonial Railway, a fair share in the running of the nation, and a market for their raw and manufactured materials. He and the pro-Confederates argued that union "will open up and colonize immense tracts of fertile lands ... lying unreclaimed and desolate. It will multiply the sources of industry and intensify the demand for labour. It will tend to keep our young men at home and allure those of other lands to our shores."

Both parties benefitted from external funds, with the anti-Confederates receiving money from Nova Scotia and probably the United States, and the pro-Confederates from the government of the Canadas. "Give us funds," a desperate Tilley cabled Macdonald. "It will require some $40 000 or $50 000 to do the work in all our counties." John A. Macdonald agreed, because he wanted to ensure that Confederation did not go down to defeat in New Brunswick simply for lack of money. Direct British intervention and threatened Fenian raids also assisted Tilley.

In the end, these various pressures, along with an ineffective campaign on Smith's part—he had lost his only viable alternative to Confederation (reciprocity with the United States)—resulted in a resounding victory for Tilley. The victory came as the delegates were meeting in London to finalize the Confederation agreement. Tilley had the New Brunswick legislature accept the proposal without reference to the voters.

THE LONDON CONFERENCE

In the autumn and winter of 1866 delegates from Nova Scotia, New Brunswick, and the United Canadas met in London to prepare the passage through the British Parliament of the British North America Act. At London, the Quebec resolutions served as the starting point for this last round of negotiations; they remained the final resolutions except for a few minor but significant changes. Instead of "federation," the union would be known as a "confederation." Subsidies to the provinces would be increased beyond the agreed eighty cents a head by a fixed grant from the federal government. The contentious issue of separate schools, which had been heatedly debated in the Legislature of the Canadas in the spring of 1865, was settled by applying the Quebec clause on education (which safeguarded the Protestant separate schools in Quebec) to all other provinces in the union, or to new provinces which had separate schools "by law" at the time they joined Confederation. Furthermore, religious minorities had the right of appeal to the federal government should their school systems be threatened by the actions of a provincial government.

Right up to the time of Confederation, opposition continued in Nova Scotia. While the delegates met in London to finalize the terms of Confederation, Joseph Howe contacted British officials to convince them to reject the union. He denounced the British and Canadian politicians who tried to force Confederation against the popular will. The British government refused to retract its support, however, and when the British North America bill was signed on March 29, 1867, Howe returned to Nova Scotia cured "of a good deal of loyal enthusiasm" and bitter against the Canadians. He was not alone. Many Nova Scotians saw Confederation as the end, not the beginning—or the beginning of the end—for Nova Scotia. The Halifax *Morning Chronicle*, for example, published a bitter epitaph.

Elsewhere, on July 1 Confederation was accepted—although not with enthusiasm in French Canada. The union became known as the Dominion of Canada. John A. Macdonald had preferred "Kingdom of Canada" to show a spirit of greater independence from Britain, but the British gov-

393

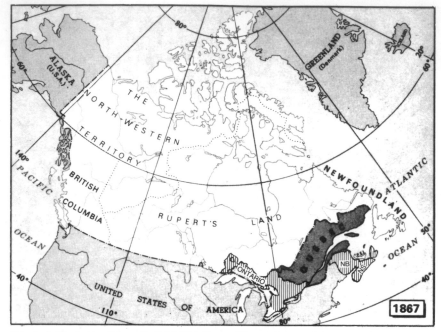

"Territorial Evolution of Canada", MCR 2306, Dept. of Energy, Mines and Resources, Ottawa, Ontario.

Nova Scotia, New Brunswick, and the Canadas joined to form the Dominion of Canada by the British North America Act of July 1, 1867.

ernment vetoed the idea. Leonard Tilley had chanced upon the alternative title of "Dominion" as well as an appropriate motto for the new nation, *A Mari Usque Ad Mare* (From Sea to Sea), while reading Psalms 72:

> Let his dominion also be from sea to sea, and from river unto the world's end
> And blessed be the name of his majesty forever.

A new nation in North America was born.

NOTES

[1] P.B. Waite, "Confederation," *The Canadian Encyclopedia*, vol. 1 (Edmonton, 1985), p. 399.
[2] F.H. Underhill, *The Image of Confederation* (Toronto, 1964), p.4.

Related Readings

R. Douglas Francis and Donald B. Smith, *Canadian History: Pre-Confederation*, 2d ed. (Toronto, 1986) includes several important articles on the subject of Confederation: J.M.S. Careless, "The Political Ideas of George Brown," pp. 343–49; Paul G. Cornell, "The Genesis of Ontario Politics in the Province of Canada, 1838–1871," pp. 349–63; D.G. Creighton, "The United States and Canadian Confederation," pp. 460–72; Jean-Charles Bonenfant, "The French Canadians and the Birth of Confederation," pp. 472–87; The Rowell–Sirois Report, "The Nature of Confederation," pp. 489–500; and George F.G. Stanley, "Act or Pact: Another Look at Confederation," pp. 501–23. The distribution of legislative powers in the British North America Act is reprinted on pp. 524–31.

BIBLIOGRAPHY

The three best general texts on Confederation are Donald Creighton, *The Road to Confederation: The Emergence of Canada, 1863–1867* (Toronto, 1964); W.L. Morton, *The Critical Years: The Union of British North America, 1857–1873* (Toronto, 1964); and P.B. Waite, *The Life and Times of Confederation, 1864–1867: Politics, Newspapers, and the Union of British North America* (Toronto, 1962). The Canadian Historical Association has issued a number of pamphlets on aspects of Confederation by leading scholars in their fields: J.M. Beck, *Joseph Howe: Anti-Confederate* (Ottawa, 1966); J.-C. Bonenfant, *The French Canadians and the Birth of Confederation* (Ottawa, 1966); P.G. Cornell, *The Great Coalition* (Ottawa, 1966); W.L. Morton, *The West and Confederation, 1857–1871* (Ottawa, 1962); P.B. Waite, *The Charlottetown Conference* (Ottawa, 1963); and W.M. Whitelaw, *The Quebec Conference* (Ottawa, 1966). Ramsay Cook has edited and written an introduction to *Confederation* (Toronto, 1967), a collection of interpretative essays on the subject. A good primary source is P.B. Waite, ed., *The Confederation Debates in the Province of Canada, 1865* (Toronto, 1963).

Confederation can also be studied through biographies of the protagonists; relevant biographies include D.G. Creighton, *John A. Macdonald*, vol. 1: *The Young Politician* (Toronto, 1952); J.M.S. Careless, *Brown of the Globe*, vol. 2: *Statesman of Confederation, 1860–1880* (Toronto, 1963); Brian Young, *George-Etienne Cartier: Montreal Bourgeois* (Kingston and Montreal, 1981); O.D. Skelton, *Life and Times of Sir Alexander Tilloch Galt*, rev. ed. (Toronto, 1966); and J.M. Beck, *Joseph Howe*, vol. 2: *The Briton Becomes Canadian, 1848–1873* (Kingston and Montreal, 1983).

On the Maritime provinces and Confederation in 1867, see Ken Pryke, *Nova Scotia and Confederation, 1864–1871* (Toronto, 1979); W.S. MacNutt, *New Brunswick: A History, 1784–1867* (Toronto, 1962); F.W.P. Bolger, *Prince Edward Island and Confederation, 1863–1873* (Charlottetown, 1964); H.B. Mayo, "Newfoundland and Confederation in the Eighteen-Sixties," *Canadian Historical Review*, 29 (1948): 125–42. On Quebec, see J.-C. Bonenfant, *La Naissance de la Confédération* (Montreal, 1969); and on Ontario, see D. Swainson, *Ontario and Confederation* (Ottawa, 1967).

On the American and British influence on Confederation, consult Robin Winks, *Canada and the United States: The Civil War Years* (Montreal, 1960); John A. Williams, "Canada and the Civil War," in *Heard Round the World: The Impact Abroad of the Civil War*, edited by H. Hyman (New York, 1969); and C.P. Stacey, *Canada and the British Army, 1841–1871*, rev. ed. (Toronto, 1963).

Index

397

399

401

403

406

407

To the owner of this book:

We are interested in your reaction to Francis/Jones/Smith, **Origins: Canadian History to Confederation**. With your comments and suggestions, we may improve this book in future editions.

1. What was your reason for using this book?

____ university course   ____ continuing education course
____ college course   ____ personal interest
                                        ____ other (specify)

2. Which school? _____

3. Approximately how much of the book did you use?
      ____ $\frac{1}{4}$ ____ $\frac{1}{2}$ ____ $\frac{3}{4}$ ____ all

4. What is the best aspect of the book?

5. Have you any suggestions for improvement?

6. Is there anything that should be added?

Fold here

. . . .

Business
Reply Mail
No Postage Stamp
Necessary if Mailed
in Canada

POSTAGE WILL BE PAID BY
SUSAN LILHOLT
Publisher
College Editorial Department
HOLT, RINEHART AND WINSTON
OF CANADA, LIMITED
55 HORNER AVENUE
TORONTO, ONTARIO
M8Z 9Z9

Tape shut